2000 MOVIES

THE
1950s

Robin Cross

Arlington House
New York

This 1989 edition is published by Arlington House,
distributed by Crown Publishers, Inc.,
225 Park Avenue South, New York, New York 10003.

Printed and Bound in the United States of America

Library of Congress Cataloging-in-Publication Data
Cross, Robin.
  2000 movies.

  Includes index.
  1. Motion pictures—History. I. Title.
  II. Title: Two thousand movies.
  PN1993.5.A1C786   1989   791.43′75 88-34279
  ISBN 0-517-67973-6
  h g f e d c b a

Author's Acknowledgment

The author would particularly like to thank Tise
Vahimagi and all the staff of the National Film Archive
for their tireless help, and their unfailing good humor,
in the preparation of this book.

Picture Acknowledgments

The majority of the stills in this book were supplied by
the Stills, Posters and Design Department of the British
Film Institute. Acknowledgments are due to the
following film companies: Allied Artists, Allied Film
Makers, American International Pictures, Anglo
Amalgamated, Archway, Armada, Associated British
Picture Corporation, Balboa, British Lion, Buena Vista,
Carmel, Castle, Clarke, Clover, Columbia Pictures,
Coronada, Criterion, Danzigers, Disney, Eagle Lion,
Ealing Studios, Eros, Exclusive, Fairbanks, Festival
Films, Film Locations, Film Makers, Futura,
Gainsborough, Golden State, Grand National Pictures,
Group 3, Hammer Films, Harefield, Holiday, Hollywood
Pictures, Indio, Lippert Pictures, Lopert/Korda, London
Films, Malibu, Metro Goldwyn Mayer, Mid-Century,
Mogador, Molton, Monarch, Monogram, Nacerima,
Nicholson/Arkoff, Oberler, Palo Alto, Paramount, Ponti-
di Laurentiis, Praesans, Premium, Producers-Actors,
RKO Radio Corporation, Rank Film Distributors, Regal,
Remus, Renown, Republic Pictures, Reynolds,
Romulus, Santa Rosa, Sunset, Toho, Twentieth Century-
Fox, Two Cities, Ventura, United Artists, Universal
Studios, Vogue, Warner Brothers, Wessex Films,
Warwick, Winchester, Woolner, Zigmor.

Author's Note

The dating of movies can be something of a problem,
and different reference books frequently offer different
dates for films. In order to remain consistent, we have
followed the system used in the British National Film
Archive's comprehensive Catalogue of Stills. In this
Catalogue the date for each film is the year during which
the film was copyrighted/registered/reviewed by the
appropriate censorship authorities and is in most cases
the year which appears on the copy of the film itself.
This will account for the apparent time lapse between
some dates for films and the year in which they received
Oscar nominations or Awards.

A small number of abbreviations have been used in the
captions.

ABPC	–	Associated British Picture Corporation
AIP	–	American International Pictures
Fox	–	Twentieth Century-Fox
MGM	–	Metro Goldwyn Mayer
UA	–	United Artists

CONTENTS

INTRODUCTION

In Billy Wilder's *Sunset Boulevard* (1950) the old Hollywood, in the form of Gloria Swanson's forgotten silent star Norma Desmond, comes into uncomprehending and fatal contact with the new Hollywood, represented by William Holden's would-be screenwriter Joe Gillis. Scratching in the dim recesses of his memory, Holden observes that Gloria used to be big in pictures. The reply is hissed back, 'I *am* big. It's the pictures that got small.'

In 1950 Hollywood's horizons were shrinking, its nerve failing and its very future shrouded in uncertainty. During the war cinemagoing had reached a peak. Virtually anything on celluloid was guaranteed an audience, and in the firmament the great fixed stars – Clark Gable, Bette Davis, Robert Taylor, Joan Crawford – glittered brightly. But by the end of the decade the studio empires on which their fortunes had been built were crumbling. In the 1940s the grip of the studios had been weakened by the greater artistic freedom conceded to powerful producer-directors like Alfred Hitchcock, William Wyler and King Vidor, and writer-directors like John Huston, Preston Sturges and Joseph L Mankiewicz. Following Olivia de Havilland's landmark legal victory over Warner Brothers in 1945, the studios could no longer discipline wilful stars with restrictive and punitive clauses in their contracts. A succession of labor disputes, including an eight-month union strike in 1945, prompted the House Un-American Activities Committee to launch an investigation of alleged Communist subversion in Hollywood. The onset of the Cold War brought with it a witch-hunt for Communists which spread its tentacles throughout the film capital. This set in motion a debilitating cycle of paranoid loyalty tests, fear and betrayal which was given a savage twist by the outbreak of the Korean War in June 1950.

By then the Hollywood majors had suffered another body blow. In 1949 the Supreme Court's 'consent' decree forced them to split their theater organizations from the production-distribution side of the business and to abandon such 'monopolistic' practices as block booking, which obliged exhibitors to take movies they did not want. The implementation of the consent decree was a long-drawn-out process, but by the end of the 1950s the old vertically integrated studio system – which had guaranteed the profitability of most films – had been dismantled.

Audiences were falling, costs were rising, and over the horizon a new and increasingly powerful competitor – television – rode into view. With its steady diet of domestic comedies, cop thrillers and Westerns,

television quickly killed off the B-movie industry, for so long the forcing ground for new talent and the pasture on which fading stars were put out to graze. Television threw a welcome lifeline to a number of second-rank stars, among them Dan Duryea, Ann Sothern, Gale Storm and Guy Madison, and provided regular work for competent journeymen directors like Joseph Kane, Lew Landers and Lesley Selander. A bigger name, Alfred Hitchcock, shrewdly realized the possibilities of television, and his TV series 'Alfred Hitchcock Presents' (1955-62) enhanced his reputation as a director-superstar and made his corpulent silhouette a familiar trademark. The most spectacular success on the small screen was achieved by Lucille Ball, whose 'I Love Lucy' show brought her a popularity and wealth she could hardly have dreamed of when in 1935 she signed with RKO as a $50 a week contract player. In 1957 her TV company, Desilu, acquired the bankrupt RKO studios. At the beginning of the decade, however, the Hollywood majors adopted a policy of no-surrender. Jack Warner decreed that no TV set was to be seen in a Warner Brothers movie. But an accommodation with the new medium was not long in coming and, ironically, Warners themselves were soon to develop a stable of TV programs.

At first Hollywood attempted to regain the ground lost to television by deploying spectacular technologies which could not be matched by the small screen. The pictures would have to become big again. The campaign to win back audiences began in 1952 with *Bwana Devil*, the first feature to be released in 3-D. *Bwana Devil* promised to 'put a lion in your lap', and the flavor of cheap gimmickry persisted throughout the process' short vogue. *The Charge at Feather River* (1953) put a gob of spit in the audience's lap. By 1954 3-D had fallen out of favor. Alfred Hitchcock, who had filmed *Dial M for Murder* (1954) in 3-D, observed that the process was 'a nine day wonder, and I arrived on the ninth day'.

On the tenth day audiences were introduced to CinemaScope, the wide screen process invented in France in the 1920s by Henri Chrétien. Fox patented CinemaScope and were the first in the field with *The Robe* (1953), a Biblical spectacular in which the stars addressed each other across the yawning spaces of the big screen and Richard Burton's hair turned a disconcerting shade of purple in the final reel. The epic was considered the most appropriate form for CinemaScope, and for the rest of the decade and well into the 1960s armored hordes lumbered from one side of the screen to the other in a series of hugely expensive exercises in negative dynamism. In other genres CinemaScope and its rivals were a mixed blessing, initially threatening to destroy the intimacy of the musical and slowing the pace of comedy to a crawl because of a reluctance to use rapid cutting on so wide a screen. The wide screen presented directors of Westerns with the chance to exploit landscape and panoramic vistas, although few troubled to explore these possibilities. Many films succeeded in spite of rather than because of CinemaScope, and it required a director of the stature of Nicholas Ray or Elia Kazan to turn the wide screen to truly cinematic advantage.

Hollywood opened up a second front on television with films which took an ostensibly daring approach to subjects previously thought risqué or taboo. The Western came down on the side of the Indians in Delmer Daves' *Broken Arrow* (1950) and established a pattern in which Hollywood's big male stars – Burt Lancaster, Robert Taylor, and even Elvis Presley – could play heroic redskins in conflict with duplicitous white men. However, in 1950 racial barriers were still too strong to allow James Stewart to ride off into the sunset with his Indian bride. One of them had to meet a symbolically unhappy end, and Hollywood convention was bound to spare Stewart.

In the late 1940s a number of commercially and critically successful films like *Gentleman's Agreement* (1947), *Pinky* (1949) and *Intruder in the Dust* (1949) had tackled racial problems. In spite of the ravages of McCarthyism, this liberal strain was carried over into the 1950s, tempered by the casting of personable Sidney Poitier as the object of racism in such films as *No Way Out* (1950), *Edge of the City* (1957), *Something of Value* (1957), and *The Defiant Ones* (1958). The long Production Code ban on the depiction of drug addiction was broken by Otto Preminger's *The Man With the Golden Arm* (1956), which was followed by Fred Zinnemann's *A Hatful of Rain* (1957) and André de Toth's underrated *Monkey on My Back* (1957). Sex, too, came in for franker treatment. Audiences could hear words like 'virgin' and 'seduce' in Preminger's *The Moon is Blue* (1953), which was released without a Production Code Seal of Approval. 'Contraception', 'rape' and the slightly more unfamiliar 'spermatogenesis' were bandied about in *Anatomy of a Murder* (1959). On a less cerebral level, they could ogle Sophia Loren in a clinging dress in *Boy on a Dolphin* (1957).

But no matter how big the screen, the theme or the leading lady's breasts, audiences still queued to see the stars. Many felt the chill of the harsh ecomomic winds blowing across the backlot. Cut adrift from their comfortable studio moorings, old-style stars like Robert Taylor drifted forlorn and rudderless, his handsome features freezing in a sullen middle-aged glare. Sheer guts and professionalism sustained Joan Crawford and Barbara Stanwyck. Crawford, stalking grimly into middle age, now seemed determined to play both the male and female leads in her films, but Nicholas Ray used her basilisk humorlesness with great skill in the baroque Western *Johnny Guitar* (1954). Stanwyck also profited from the Western revival to establish herself as a hard-boiled heavy in *Cattle Queen of Montana* (1954), *The Violent Men* (1954) and *Forty Guns* (1957).

A number of top stars were quick to take shrewd advantage of the fragmenting studio system. James Stewart signed an innovatory contract with Universal in which he took a percentage of his films' profits, a move soon followed by almost every star in the business. Others, including Burt Lancaster and Kirk Douglas, set up their own production companies, a reflection of the rapid growth of independents, who by 1958 were producing about 65 per cent of Hollywood's output.

If sustaining stars in the old-fashioned way was no longer practical, creating new ones was equally problematic. In the early 1950s Universal were still in the business of manufacturing stars in the tradition of a vanishing Hollywood. Their investment in a 'slave market' of young talent paid off handsomely in the persons of Tony Curtis and Rock Hudson, who served their apprenticeships in the last great spate of Hollywood adventure movies. Originally introduced as a kind of Bronx Ali Baba in *The Prince Who Was a Thief* (1950), Curtis matured into an assured dramatic actor in *Sweet Smell of Success* (1957) and a deft comedian in *Some Like It Hot* (1959). Hudson stoically endured a long run of formula actioners before Douglas Sirk allowed him to put his shirt back on and revealed the innately gentle character concealed beneath the muscular exterior, transforming him into the romantic sustaining figure of a series of masterly melodramas.

Nevertheless, what irked the moguls was the feeling of control slipping through their fingers. Marilyn Monroe became a star virtually in spite of 20th Century-Fox's attempts to mould her into a dumb bonde sex bomb. Columbia's Harry Cohn, the archetypal Hollywood thug, spent a fortune trying to build up Kim Novak as a replacement for the fading Rita Hayworth. Novak had been discovered touring the States advertising refrigerators as 'Miss Deepfreeze.' She never really thawed out under the studio lights, and therein lies much of her bashful charm. But the element of strain which clings to her work led critics to claim

– unfairly – that she couldn't act. Cohn was characteristically blunt when he told Garson Kanin: 'I broke my ass trying to make a star out of Kim Novak. So what happens? She turned out to be Kim Novak . . . She had talent . . . but she didn't have the one thing, that plain one thing that makes a star.'

One who did have that plain one thing, in superabundance, was Marlon Brando, who more than any other exemplified the new approach to screen acting adopted by graduates of the Actors' School in New York, founded in 1948 by Lee Strasberg and home of 'The Method.' Old-time stars like John Wayne had their own Method, which consisted principally of being themselves on screen, and were openly contemptuous of the new style. But Brando was followed by a small army of formidable actors, including Rod Steiger, Eli Wallach, Montgomery Clift, Joanne Woodward, Anthony Perkins, Karl Malden, Paul Newman, and James Dean.

Dean's death in 1956 coincided with the explosion of teen culture, in great measure the result of postwar consumerism and a phenomenon adroitly manipulated by a gang of middle-aged entrepreneurs – 'Colonel' Tom Parker, Albert Zugsmith, Alan Freed – a process brilliantly caricatured by Frank Tashlin in *The Girl Can't Help It* (1956). The icons borne aloft into the explosion of teenpix which followed Sam Katzman's *Rock Around the Clock* (1956) were those of Marlon Brando in *The Wild One* (1954) and James Dean in *Rebel Without a Cause* (1955).

The restructuring of Hollywood gave independent producers the chance to unleash a series of delirious Z-grade productions which recalled the 1940s heyday of Poverty Row outfits like PRC, which literally created movies out of thin air. Nature and the exploitation producer, abhor a vacuum, and this instant audience fodder – often torn from the latest tabloid headlines – was perfectly adapted to the burgeoning drive-in market.

These teenpix sat happily alongside, and frequently plundered elements from, a parallel stream of rock-bottom science fiction features which reflected the decade's fascination with Things From Outer Space. In the 1950s science fiction emerged as a fully fledged genre in its own right. The Cold War threatened a world so recently saved for democracy. The paranoia which lay under the bland surface of Eisenhower's America was channeled into the science fiction film, whose conflicting demands – the need both to alarm and reassure its audience simultaneously – captured perfectly the tensions of the age.

Hollywood was not only undergoing seismic changes at home but was also facing challenges from abroad. In the vanguard was Italy, whose film industry was virtually prostrate at the end of the war. Revival, which followed the impact made by the new-realist films of the late 1940s, led to a cinema boom. While film production fell steadily in Hollywood, from over 400 films in 1951 to 171 in 1959, Italian output leapt to an average of 140 movies a year, with film audiences reaching a peak of 819 million in 1955. Many of these films were broad comedies and melodramas aimed at the domestic market, but this explosion of activity threw up new stars and directors with worldwide reputations. Sophia Loren and Gina Lollobrigida were both presented as international cleavage celebrities long before their qualities as actresses were recognized. Rossano Brazzi became a Hollywood heartthrob and at the end of the decade Marcello Mastroianni emerged as a star in Federico Fellini's *La Dolce Vita* (1959). Fellini and his fellow directors Vittorio de Sica, Luchino Visconti and Michelangelo Antonioni achieved a remarkable pre-eminence for Italian film culture during the decade and banished for ever the tainted image of Italian cinema during the Mussolini dictatorship. These were years of almost manic enthusiasm in the Italian film industry during which producers like Carlo Ponti and Dino de Laurentiis moved easily from lurid cape-and-sword melodramas to Fellini classics like *Le Notti di Cabiria* (1956) and Hollywood co-productions like King Vidor's *War and Peace* (1956). Throughout the 1950s there was a direct Hollywood involvement in the Italian production of epic films, which could be shot at the famous Cinecittà studios for a fraction of the cost in America. When MGM remade *Ben-Hur,* they chose Cinecittà rather than Culver City.

Appearing as a handmaiden in Warner's Italian-shot *Helen of Troy* (1955) was French starlet Brigitte Bardot. Two years later she had metamorphosed into BB, sultry symbol of beckoning postwar affluence and a sophisticated sexual candor which Hollywood could never hope to match with top-heavy juggernauts Jayne Mansfield and Mamie Van Doren. At the time Bardot was virtually synonymous with French films, but within 18 months a 'New Wave' began to lap cinema's shores as a group of young critics – Claude Chabrol, Francois Truffaut and Jean-Luc Godard – turned from writing about films to directing them.

British cinema in the 1950s suffered from a failure of nerve similar to that which had infected Hollywood. The high hopes raised by a revitalized wartime cinema were not fulfilled. In the late 1940s J Arthur Rank, the most powerful figure in British films, had over-reached himself with an ill-advised foray into the American market and an over-ambitious expansion programme. By 1949 Rank was $16 million in debt. The accountants took over and economic retrenchment became the order of the day, a rescue operation given greater urgency by plummeting audiences and wholesale cinema closures. In the Rank empire films took a back seat to investment in photocopying machines, leisure activities and commercial television. The films it produced were associated with safe, pedestrian family entertainment. The Rank cinemas banned all X-certificate films, a policy which had a considerably inhibiting effect on the range of subjects which film-makers could tackle and stopped the career of Britain's very own blonde sex-bomb, Diana Dors, virtually dead in its tracks. Potentially exciting stars like Dirk Bogarde were shunted into formula war films and undemanding comedies.

The genre most closely associated with British cinema of the period is the war film. Like the Western, it had its own readily recognizable language and characters. When Michael Powell was setting up *The Battle of the River Plate* (1956) the only question 20th Century-Fox asked was, 'Is Jack Hawkins going to play the admiral?' Hawkins, whose tremblingly stiff upper lip is redolent of the war film of the 1950s, became a grizzled axiom of British cinema, a war-weary colonel or squadron leader around whom buzzed eager young subaltern types like Anthony Steel, John Gregson and Kenneth More.

The war film was a convenient vehicle for celebrating an ossified past while ignoring the problems of the present. Ealing Studios, which more than any other had captured the wartime solidarity of the 1940s, still clung to a fading vision of consensus in a Britain which was growing more affluent, greedy and divided. It declined into picturesque whimsy and closed in 1957. Its two finest films of the 1950s, Alexander Mackendrick's *The Man in the White Suit* (1951) and *The Ladykillers* (1955) are brilliantly barbed comedies satirizing the British diseases – class antagonism, reverence for stifling tradition and fear of innovation. It was not until the end of the decade that this displaced comment was channeled into dramas like *The Angry Silence* (1959), *Sapphire* (1959), *Blind Date* (1959) and *Room at the Top* (1959), harbingers of the renewed British cinema of the 1960s.

1950

Sensation of the year was Marlon Brando's screen debut in *The Men,* playing an embittered paraplegic ex-GI, the first in a string of roles in which he was cast as inarticulate and frequently violent characters. Hollywood's Old Guard remained unimpressed. Joan Crawford, the archetype of star glamor, claimed: 'I don't believe you want to go to the theater to see somebody you can see next door.' Another new arrival in Hollywood was Sidney Poitier, who co-starred with Richard Widmark in Joseph L Mankiewicz's *No Way Out,* one of the first major movies to deal directly with color prejudice. Equally striking was Jack Palance's debut as a plague-carrying criminal in Elia Kazan's *Panic in the Streets.* Marilyn Monroe made her first big impression in John Huston's *The Asphalt Jungle,* sprawling across a sofa in Louis Calhern's love nest and charging the screen with sexual static. In *All About Eve* she appeared briefly on George Sanders' arm, drawlingly introduced as a 'a graduate of the Copacabana School of Dramatic Art.'

All About Eve was the film of the year, winning the Academy Award for Best Picture. Its writer-director Joseph L Mankiewicz won Academy Awards on both counts; George Sanders won the Best Supporting Actor Oscar for his performance as the waspish theater critic Addison de Witt, a supreme example of velvet-lined caddishness, his feline voice-over providing a barbed commentary on the everyday lives of back-stabbing theater folk. The film also won the Best Costume Design Award for Edith Head and Charles LeMaire and, for good measure, the Best Sound Recording Award. But above all it was Bette Davis' stinging riposte to those critics who had written her off as a fading star. In Davis' pulsing eyes and angular mannerisms, notably when clutching a cigarette in her talons, there had always been a strong streak of vulgarity. Her performance as Margo Channing – the ageing theater star undermined by protégé Anne Baxter – was quintessential Davis, as cosy as a curdled cocktail, her corncrake voice dispensing measured venom in all directions, her lips glistening with greasepaint. Margo, like Davis, affects to despise 'cheap sentiment', yet her survival depends on it. Davis won the New York Critics Award, but the Best Actress Oscar went to Judy Holliday, who recreated her stage triumph as the 'dumb broad' Billie Dawn in George Cukor's *Born Yesterday,* triumphantly turning the tables on brutish Broderick Crawford.

Seldom if ever has the competition for the Best Actress Oscar been more fierce. Holliday also beat off Gloria Swanson, whose Norma Desmond in Billy Wilder's *Sunset Boulevard* is one of the cinema's most compelling grotesques, a mad silent movie queen haunting a decaying mansion where thousands of images of herself gather the dust of ages and the 'waxworks' from Hollywood history – Buster Keaton, H B Warner and Anna Q Nilsson – gather to play macabre hands of bridge. Time and the distorting lens of *Sunset Boulevard* have fixed Swanson in the image of Norma Desmond, dreaming of an impossible comeback. Billy Wilder's dissection of Hollywood's past was filled with references to Swanson: Norma, blood-dark nails clawing the air, caught in the flickering light cast by *Queen Kelly* (1927), whose director Erich von Stroheim, was cast in *Sunset Boulevard* as her butler and former husband and director; Norma's visit to Swanson's old stamping ground, Paramount, where the real Cecil B DeMille is directing *Samson and Delilah* (1949) and calls her 'young fellow', just as he had addressed Gloria in the dream time when they were making *Male and Female* (1919).

Jose Ferrer won the Best Actor Award for his performance in the title role of *Cyrano de Bergerac,* produced by Stanley Kramer, and the Best Supporting Actress Oscar went to Josephine Hull for her work in *Harvey.*

Among the oustanding movies of the year were Vincente Minnelli's *Father of the Bride,* with Spencer Tracy, Elizabeth Taylor and Joan Bennett; Nicholas Ray's *In a Lonely Place,* in which Humphrey Bogart and Gloria Grahame gave two of the finest performances of their careers; George Pal's *Destination Moon,* which won the year's Best Special Effects Oscar and marked the beginning of the decade's science fiction cycle; and *Winchester '73,* a classic Western directed by Anthony Mann and starring James Stewart which inaugurated a fruitful collaboration between the director and star.

Death took Al Jolson, Maurice Costello, matinée idol of the early silents, and showman Sid Grauman, outside whose celebrated Chinese Theater the stars had fixed their hand prints in the sidewalk cement. Sonja Henie left the marks of her skate blades, Joe E Brown the outline of his mouth, and Rin Tin Tin his paw marks. Rex Ingram, director of *The Four Horsemen of the Apocalypse* (1923) and mentor of the young Michael Powell, died in obscurity. Emil Jannings, immortalized as the stuffy schoolmaster bewitched, then broken and humiliated by Marlene Dietrich's incomparable nightclub slut Lola Lola in *The Blue Angel* (1930), died in Austria, having been blacklisted for his support of the Nazis. Character stars Walter Huston and Alan Hale also passed away, along with directors Christy Cabanne and John M Stahl.

Among the best British films of the year were the Boultings' *Seven Days to Noon; Gone to Earth,* a neglected masterpiece by Michael Powell; and *The Wooden Horse,* directed by Jack Lee, an early example of one of the staples of the decade, the prisoner-of-war camp drama. In Italy Federico Fellini co-directed his first feature, the enchanting *Luci del Varieta.* France produced two classics: Jean Cocteau's *Orphée,* in which Jean Marais entered the Underworld through a shimmering mercury mirror; and Max Ophuls' bitter-sweet *La Ronde.* Akira Kurosawa's *Rashomon* brought Japanese cinema to an international audience, and Luis Buñuel's *Los Olvidados* – filmed in Mexico – painted a searing portrait of society's lower depths.

ACTION

The Enforcer (UA) d.Bretaigne Windust: Roy Roberts, Humphrey Bogart, King Donovan. Bogart is hard-driving DA, cracking down on crime baron Everett Sloane in pacy police procedure drama

Breaking Point (Warner) d.Michael Curtiz: John Garfield, Wallace Ford, Victor Sen Yung. Efficient retread of *To Have and Have Not* (1944), with California setting, marked Garfield's last for the studio.

The Big Lift (Fox) d.George Seaton: Montgomery Clift, Paul Douglas. Location-shot account of the Berlin air lift of 1948 provides backdrop to Clift's romance with local girl Cornell Borchers

American Guerrilla in the Philippines (Fox) d.Fritz Lang: Micheline Presle. Tyrone Power stars as a naval officer fighting alongside the Filippino resistance in one of Lang's less happy efforts. Even great directors have to eat.

Captain Carey USA (Paramount) d.Mitchell Leisen: Francis Lederer, Alan Ladd. Former soldier Ladd buckles on his trenchcoat and returns to Italy in pursuit of an informer who betrayed a village to the Nazis. Theme song 'Mona Lisa' won an Oscar

Halls of Montezuma (Fox) d.Lewis Milestone: Richard Widmark, Jack Webb. 'Give 'em hell!' bellows Widmark as the Marines move in on a Japanese rocket-launching site. A long way from *All Quiet on the Western Front* (1930)

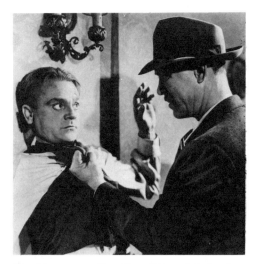

Kiss Tomorrow Goodbye (Warner) d. Gordon Douglas: James Cagney, Ward Bond. Cagney energetic as ever in role of two-timing hood, but this revival of the studio's gangster cycle lacks the style and vigor of the 1930s originals

I Was A Shoplifter (Universal) d. Charles Lamont: Tony Curtis, Andrea King. Mona Freeman is blackmailed into joining vixenish King's shoplifting gang. Rock Hudson turns up in a bit part.

Korea Patrol (Monarch) d.Max Nosseck: Richard Emery, Teri Duna. Crass little quickie in which a handful of US and South Korean soldiers hold off several divisions of Communists to blow a vital bridge

Between Midnight and Dawn (Columbia) d. Gordon Douglas: Edmond O'Brien, Mark Stevens. The hand of *The Naked City* (1948) hangs heavy over this routine tale of cops in pursuit of escaped crooks

Breakthrough (Warner) d.Lewis Seiler: David Bryan, John Agar. An infantry platoon fights its way through Normandy in unpretentious attempt to capture the flavor of war

Sound of Fury (UA) d.Cyril Endfield: Frank Lovejoy, Lloyd Bridges. Handsome psychopath Bridges inveigles unemployed Lovejoy into a two-man crime wave which ends with a gruesome lynching

The Fireball (Fox) d.Tay Garnett: Beverly Tyler, Mickey Rooney. Ferociously animated performance from Rooney as a cocky roller derby champ felled by polio. He also gets a vamping from Marilyn Monroe

South Sea Sinner (Universal) d.H Bruce Humberstone: Shelley Winters, Liberace. Overblown saloon bar chanteuse Shelley blows unaccountably hot over sullen Frank Lovejoy in ramshackle remake of *Seven Sinners* (1940)

The White Tower (RKO) d.Ted Tetzlaff: Lloyd Bridges, Alida Valli, Glenn Ford. The struggle to conquer a killer Alpine peak brings out the best, and the worst, in the usual mixed bunch of mountaineers

Radar Patrol vs Spy King (Republic) d.Fred C Brannon: Kirk Alyn, Jean Dean. Radar Defence Bureau Agent Alyn thwarts saboteurs' plans to destroy the US early warning system in so-so serial

Right Cross (MGM) d.John Sturges: Dick Powell, Ricardo Montalban, June Allyson. Capable reworking of Standard Movie Plot No.3 with sports columnist Powell and fighter Montalban tangling over Allyson

Undercover Girl (Universal) d.Joseph Pevney: Scott Brady, Alexis Smith. Characteristically brisk Pevney outing in which gutsy cop Smith poses as a dope dealer to bust open a narcotics ring

Chain Lightning (Warner) d. Stuart Heisler: Eleanor Parker, Humphrey Bogart. Hangdog Bogart sleepwalks through part of World War II flying ace chosen to test new jet, ensuring that the movie never leaves the runway

Mystery Submarine (Universal) d.Douglas Sirk: Marta Toren, Macdonald Carey. A renegade U-boat, stalking the seas since 1945 and now in the pay of an enemy power, is sent to the bottom by action-man Carey

ADVENTURE AND FANTASY

Kim (MGM) d.Victor Saville: Dean Stockwell, Errol Flynn. One of the high spots of Flynn's declining years as he plays Stockwell's mentor in colorful, zesty adaptation of Kipling romance of the British Raj

Fortunes of Captain Blood (Columbia) d.Gordon Douglas: Louis Hayward, Patricia Medina. Hayward reprises Flynn role of renegade surgeon Peter Blood, fighting to right injustice in cost-conscious version of the Sabatini swashbuckler

Hidden City (Monogram) d.Ford Beebe: Johnny Sheffield, Sue England. Porky jungle hero Sheffield stars as Bomba in rock-bottom series spun off from his better days with Johnny Weissmuller in the Tarzan films

Double Crossbones (Universal) d.Charles Barton: Helena Carter, Donald O'Connor. Breezy pirate spoof in which apprentice shopkeeper O'Connor masquerades as a famous buccaneer and meets Captain Kidd, Henry Morgan and Ann Bonney but fortunately not Abbott and Costello

Killer Shark (Monogram) d.Budd Boetticher: Roddy McDowall, Nacho Garudo, Laurette Luez. Roddy learns new values as skipper of a fishing vessel hunting fanged fiends of the deep. *Jaws* this is not

The Black Rose (Fox) d.Henry Hathaway: Jack Hawkins, Tyrone Power. Medieval odyssey takes Saxon nobleman Power to China, where he discovers the secrets of gunpowder and printed books. Superb color photography by Jack Cardiff

Cyrano de Bergerac (UA) d.Michael Gordon:
Lloyd Corrigan, Jose Ferrer. Oscar-winning
performance from Ferrer as Rostand's long-nosed
swordsman succumbing to hopeless romantic
yearnings for the lovely Mala Powers

Tarzan and the Slave Girl (RKO) d.Lee Sholem:
Vanessa Brown, Lex Barker. A mystery epidemic
raging among the 'Lionian' tribe, ruled by Hurd
Hatfield, sends them on a kidnapping rampage
which includes Jane

Captain Horatio Hornblower (Warner)
d.Raoul Walsh: Gregory Peck, Virginia Mayo.
Peck even stiffer than usual as C S Forester's
naval hero of the Napoleonic Wars, romancing
admiral's widow Mayo between studio-bound sea
battles

Buccaneer's Girl (Universal) d.Frederick de
Cordova: Yvonne de Carlo, Philip Friend.
Splendid celebration of every pirate cliché in the
book with excellent supporting cast, including
Andrea King, Elsa Lanchester, and Douglass
Dumbrille

The Prince Who Was a Thief (Universal)
d.Rudolph Maté: Tony Curtis. Bernie Schwartz,
the Jewish bad boy from the Bronx, is transformed
into an adventurer in medieval Tangier in
quintessential Arabian Nights hokum

King Solomon's Mines (MGM) d.Compton
Bennett: Richard Carlson, Hugo Haas, Stewart
Granger, Deborah Kerr. Handsome version of the
H Rider Haggard classic won deserved Oscar for
cinematography. Much footage later reused in
Watusi (1959) and other cut-rate jungle epics

Treasure Island (RKO) d.Byron Haskin: Robert
Newton, Bobby Driscoll. 'Aaaargh! Shiver me
timbers, Jim lad!' The eye-rolling old reprobate
turns in definitive performance as Long John
Silver supported by host of juicy character actors

Tripoli (Paramount) d.Will Price: John Payne,
Maureen O'Hara. US Marines battle Barbary
Corsairs in so-so actioner enlivened by excellent
performance from ever-dependable Howard da
Silva

The Flame and the Arrow (Warner) d.Jacques Tourneur: Robin Hughes, Norman Lloyd, Aline MacMahon, Burt Lancaster, Nick Cravat. Carefree Technicolor romp in which Tourneur turns Lancaster into a Tuscan Robin Hood ably served by Waldo Salt's zesty screenplay

Destination Moon (UA) d.Irving Pichel. First important SF film of the decade adopts steadfastly documentary approach to pioneering moonshot. It took 100 men two months to build the impressive moonscape

MELODRAMA

Gambling House (RKO) d.Ted Tetzlaff: William Bendix, Victor Mature. Big Vic is a foreign-born gambler who faces deportation when his status is revealed in a murder trial

Caged (Warner) d.John Cromwell: Eleanor Parker. Parker suffers mightily as a 19-year-old (yes, 19) imprisoned for a crime committed by her husband. Mountainous Hope Emerson is the chief heavy

Harriet Craig (Columbia) d.Vincent Sherman: Wendell Corey, Joan Crawford. Joan is all too well cast as the overbearing perfectionist obsessed with material things to the exclusion of people. Remake of *Craig's Wife* (1936)

The Man on the Eiffel Tower (A & T) d.Burgess Meredith: Wilfrid Hyde-White, Charles Laughton. Laughton plays Simenon's celebrated Inspector Maigret in tense psychological thriller filmed in Paris

No Man of Her Own (Paramount) d.Mitchell Leisen: John Lund, Lyle Bettger, Barbara Stanwyck. Heavy-handed adaptation of Cornell Woolrich tale in which Stanwyck assumes another woman's identity and then undergoes the agonies of blackmail

Destination Murder (RKO) d.Edward L Cahn: Stanley Clements, Albert Dekker. Amateur sleuth Joyce MacKenzie becomes involved with three men – Dekker, Clements, Hurd Hatfield – who had a hand in her father's murder

The Man Who Cheated Himself (Fox) d.Felix Feist: John Dall, Lee J Cobb, Alan Wells. Ingeniously contrived suspenser in which bent cop Cobb covers up a murder committed by his mistress but is brought to book by his brother and fellow-cop Dall

Dark City (Paramount) d.William Dieterle: Lizabeth Scott, Charlton Heston. Intriguingly cast against subsequent type, Heston makes his Hollywood debut as a war hero turned heel in moody thriller

The Capture (RKO) d.John Sturges: Lew Ayres, Teresa Wright. Tangled, pretentious Mexican-set melo in which oil man Ayres just can't seem to steer clear of murder

The Men (UA) d. Fred Zinnemann: Marlon Brando, Everett Sloane. Explosive debut by Brando as a morose paraplegic war victim coming to terms with his disability. Brando prepared for the role by living for a while with paraplegics

The Company She Keeps (RKO) d.John Cromwell: Fay Baker, Jane Greer. Noble parole officer Lizabeth Scott steps aside as newsman boyfriend Dennis O'Keefe falls for rebellious parolee Greer

A Life of Her Own (MGM) d.George Cukor: Barry Sullivan, Lana Turner. Lana discovers that heartbreak lies behind the glittering facade of life as a top model. Stand-out performance by Ann Dvorak as an ageing mannequin

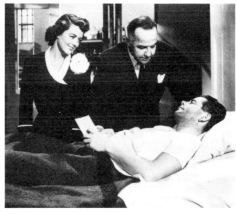

Convicted (Columbia) d. Henry Levin: Dorothy Malone, Broderick Crawford, Glenn Ford. Remake of Howard Hawks *Criminal Code* (1931) with Glenn fighting to prove his innocence helped by warden Crawford and daughter Malone

Crisis (MGM) d.Richard Brooks: Jose Ferrer, Cary Grant. Overheated drama in which brain surgeon Grant is forcibly held by brutal South American dictator Ferrer, who just happens to be in need of an operation

It's a Small World (Castle) d.William Castle: Anne Shotter, Paul Dale. Strange little B in which undersized Dale suffers several kinds of hell – including picking pockets dressed as a child – before he finds romance in a circus. Castle appears, Hitchcock-style, in a cameo role. Sympathetic and tasteless in turn

Deported (Universal) d.Robert Siodmak: Jeff Chandler, Marta Toren. Jeff is an Italian-born racketeer sent packing to the land of his fathers where he is redeemed, somewhat unconvincingly, by the aristocratic Ms Toren

In a Lonely Place (Columbia) d.Nicholas Ray: Gloria Grahame, Humphrey Bogart. One of Gloria's best performances as a starlet falling for self-destructive screenwriter Bogart, who's suspected of murder

All About Eve (Fox) d.Joseph L Mankiewicz: Gary Merrill, Anne Baxter, Bette Davis. Oscar-laden tale of back-stabbing theatre folk, with Davis reveling in the role of vulgar old ham Margo Channing, Baxter her scheming protegé and George Sanders scattering epigrams as feline critic Addison de Witt

The Miniver Story (MGM) d.H C Potter: Greer Garson, Cathy O'Donnell. Disappointing attempt to stir the nostalgic embers of the huge 1942 hit *Mrs Miniver,* set in postwar England. O'Donnell luminously beautiful

Edge of Doom (RKO) d.Mark Robson: Farley Granger. Goldwyn production in which mixed-up Granger murders a curmudgeonly old priest and is then befriended by a younger and more sympathetic man of the cloth (Dana Andrews)

The Asphalt Jungle (UA) d.John Huston: Sterling Hayden, Sam Jaffe, Louis Calhern. Looming bankruptcy plunges big-time lawyer Calhern into the machinations of a heist. Monroe languorously sexy as his dumb blonde mistress

Bright Victory (Universal) d.Mark Robson: Arthur Kennedy, Peggy Dow. Kennedy turns in moving performance as blind war veteran fighting back against his affliction with the help of the charming Dow. New York critics voted him best actor for 1951

The Damned Don't Cry (Warner) d. Vincent Sherman: Jacqueline de Wit, Joan Crawford. Basically the Crawford Plot No. 1 as Joan throws over life as a laborer's wife to become a gangster's moll

So Young So Bad (UA) d.Bernard Vorhaus: Anne Francis, Paul Henreid. Concerned psychiatrist Henreid wades in to sort out scandalous regime at a correctional school for girls

Born to be Bad (RKO) d.Nicholas Ray: Joan Fontaine, Mel Ferrer, Robert Ryan. Fontaine wildly miscast as adventuress hiding her ruthless streak under a deceptively innocent facade

The Glass Menagerie (Warner) d. Irving Rapper: Kirk Douglas, Jane Wyman. Kirk is the 'gentleman caller' and Wyman the crippled Laura in coarse-grained adaptation of Tennessee Williams play

Teresa (MGM) d.Fred Zinnemann: John Ericson, Pier Angeli. Touching story of World War II veteran Ericson bringing home an Italian bride, only to run into small town prejudice. Also Rod Steiger's debut as a psychiatrist

Sunset Boulevard (Paramount)d.Billy Wilder: Gloria Swanson, William Holden. Would-be screenwriter Joe Gillis (Holden) becomes reluctant gigolo to crazed old movie queen Norma Desmond (Swanson) but winds up face down and dead in her swimming pool

Walk Softly Stranger (RKO) d.Robert Stevenson. Joseph Cotten, Alida Valli. Smooth crook Cotten lies low in a small Ohio town, only to fall in love with crippled Valli. The last RKO movie to carry a Dore Schary credit

Three Secrets (Warner) d.Robert Wise: Leif Erickson, Eleanor Parker. Rescue attempt on infant survivor of an air crash is given twist by plight of three women who each believe she is his mother

Cause for Alarm (MGM) d.Tay Garnett: Barry Sullivan, Loretta Young. Luckless Loretta emotes furiously as she is framed for murder by maniacal husband Sullivan

Stage Fright (Warner) d.Alfred Hitchcock: Richard Todd, Jane Wyman. Hitchcock's mendacious flashback undermines rambling murder tale set in London theatre world. A gloriously bored Dietrich co-stars

The Secret Fury (RKO) d.Mel Ferrer: Philip Ober, Robert Ryan, Claudette Colbert. Bigamy, murder and a mental asylum straight out of *The Snake Pit* (1948) jostle for space in magnificently implausible farrago

The Prowler (UA) d. Joseph Losey: Evelyn Keyes, Van Heflin. Excellent low-budget *film noir*, by way of *Double Indemnity* (1944), in which scheming Keyes traps cop Heflin in a web of murder

No Way Out (Fox) d.Joseph L Mankiewicz: Sidney Poitier, Richard Widmark. Poitier's debut as a doctor menaced by racialist hoodlum Widmark, who sparks off race riots after his brother dies when being operated on by Poitier. Considered hard-hitting in its day

Under My Skin (Fox) d. Jean Negulesco: John Garfield, Micheline Presle. Has-been jockey Garfield's plans to double cross gambler Luther Adler have tragic consequences. Filmed most prettily in France

Panic in the Streets (Fox) d. Elia Kazan: Zero Mostel, Jack Palance. Blistering thriller, location-shot in New Orleans, in which medical officer Richard Widmark tracks down two gunmen infected with the plague

Pandora and the Flying Dutchman (Romulus) d.Albert Lewin: Ava Gardner. Ava is the ravishing centerpiece to this lush, ludicrous fable as she encounters mysterious yachtsman James Mason – a man with no future but a seemingly endless past

Outrage (RKO) d.Ida Lupino: Mala Powers, Jerry Paris. Powers suffers the trauma of rape in typically bold, and occasionally shrill, Lupino production

The Woman on Pier 13 (RKO) d. Robert Stevenson: Robert Ryan, Laraine Day. Shipping executive Ryan's radical past compromises his future in rabid Red-baiting tract. Aka *I Married a Communist*

Shakedown (Universal) d.Joseph Pevney: Howard Duff, Anne Vernon. Manipulative newspaper lensman Duff will stop at nothing, even blackmailing the Mob, to claw his way to fame and fortune. Splendidly wry ending

Our Very Own (RKO) d.David Miller: Ann Blyth, Farley Granger. Tearful Blyth discovers she is a foster child and sets out to find her real mother (Ann Dvorak) in smugly tedious problem picture

Storm Warning (Warner) d.Stuart Heisler: Steve Cochran, Ginger Rogers. Hand-me-down version of 'Streetcar Named Desire' in which New York model Rogers travels South and runs into the Ku Klux Klan, who memorably murder her younger sister Doris Day

Outside the Wall (Universal) d.Crane Wilbur: Richard Basehart. Released from a 15-year stretch in the pen, and determined to go straight, Basehart tumbles into the grasping arms of blonde floozie Marilyn Maxwell

Never Fear (Eagle Lion) d.Ida Lupino: Sally Forrest, Keefe Brasselle. Dancer Forrest is struck down by polio in another typically earnest Lupino production

My Forbidden Past (RKO) d.Robert Stevenson: Ava Gardner, Robert Mitchum. Period melo in which Gardner inherits a fortune and cold-bloodedly uses it to detach Mitchum from his wife

The Next Voice You Hear (MGM) d.William Wellman: James Whitmore, Nancy Davis. The Voice of God reaches Middle America via the radio causing an understandable stir. Nowadays, presumably, the Almighty would chose prime time television

Paid in Full (Paramount) d.William Dieterle: Lizabeth Scott, Diana Lynn. Turgid soaper in which Scott and Lynn display an unaccountable passion for bland Bob Cummings

No Sad Songs For Me (Columbia) d.Rudolph Maté: Wendell Corey, Margaret Sullavan, Natalie Wood. Sullavan's last, as a woman dying of cancer, saved from the maudlin by her graceful underplaying

One Way Street (Universal) d.Hugo Fregonese: Marta Toren, Jack Elam, James Mason. Crooked doctor Mason finds a well-upholstered bolt hole in Mexico, where his conscience begins to work overtime

Where the Sidewalk Ends (Fox) d.Otto Preminger: Dana Andrews. Psychopathic cop Andrews kills a man during an investigation, then tries to make it look like the work of hoodlums. But an innocent taxi driver is charged with the crime

The Underworld Story (UA) d.Cyril Endfield: Harry Shannon, Gale Storm, Dan Duryea. Has-been journalist Duryea finds a job in a small-town newspaper and then sets about tracking down the murderer of a newspaper magnate's daughter-in-law

The Scarf (UA) d.E A Dupont: Mercedes McCambridge, John Ireland. Ireland escapes from a criminal lunatic asylum convinced that he did not murder his fiancée. Could sinister psychiatrist Emlyn Williams hold the key to the mystery?

Whirlpool (Fox) d.Otto Preminger: Richard Conte, Gene Tierney. Vulnerable Tierney's shoplifting problem delivers her into the hands of homicidal hypnotist Jose Ferrer. Psychiatrist Richard Conte helps her expose the villain

Woman on the Run (Universal) d.Norman Foster: Robert Keith, Ann Sheridan. Efficient little thriller in which Sheridan searches San Francisco for husband Ross Elliott, who is the sole witness to a gangland killing

Where Danger Lives (RKO) d.John Farrow: Robert Mitchum, Faith Domergue. Sultry Domergue's debut as plausible psychopath who smothers husband Claude Rains to death and then tries the same trick on ol' sleepy eyes. She should have known better

COMEDY

Harvey (Universal) d. Henry Koster: Peggy Dow, Charles Drake, James Stewart. Screen version of the Pulitzer Prize-winning play with Stewart well cast as Elwood P Dowd, the gentle drunken fantasist whose constant companion is an invisible six-foot rabbit

A Woman of Distinction (Columbia) d.Edward Buzzell: Ray Milland, Rosalind Russell. Tired battle of the sexes frolic in which frosty college dean Russell is gradually unfrozen by smooth astronomer Milland

The Good Humor Man (Columbia) d. Lloyd Bacon: Jean Wallace, Jack Carson. Ice cream salesman Carson is caught up in a murder hunt, pursued by cops and criminals, has his hair set on fire, is frozen stiff and nearly drowns before being rescued by the Captain Marvel Club

The Milkman (Universal) d.Charles Barton: Jimmy Durante, Donald O'Connor. Simple-minded war veteran O'Connor crashes into the milk business, almost wrecking Durante's retirement plans and rounding up a blackmail gang

The Jackpot (Fox) d.Walter Lang: James Stewart, Barbara Hale, Natalie Wood. Stewart is the anguished Mr Average whose life is swamped by a torrent of prizes – including a Shetland pony and several tons of foodstuffs – won in a radio quiz program

The Fuller Brush Girl (Columbia) d.Lloyd Bacon: Lucille Ball, Eddie Albert. Ball wasted in frantic slapstick saga of saleslady mixed up with a bunch of thieves

Abbott and Costello in the Foreign Legion (Universal) d.Charles Lamont: Bud Abbott, Lou Costello. Bud and Lou stumble across the burning sands in desperate search of laughs but finding mostly mirages. Exotic support from Patricia Medina, Walter Slezak and Douglass Dumbrille

Born Yesterday (Columbia) d.George Cukor: Judy Holliday, Broderick Crawford, William Holden. No blonde was every more touchingly dumb than Holliday's Billie Dawn ordered by her ox-like 'protector' Crawford to pick up a little culture from college-boy reporter Holden

The Skipper Surprised His Wife (MGM) d.Elliott Nugent: Robert Walker. Seaman Walker decides to run his household like a ship in undemanding outing which also enlists Joan Leslie, Edward Arnold, Spring Byington and Jan Sterling

Fancy Pants (Paramount) d.George Marshall: Lucille Ball, Bob Hope. Lively remake of *Ruggles of Red Gap* (1935) with Hope in the Laughton role as butler accompanying nouveau riche spitfire Ball to the Wild West

Cheaper by the Dozen (Fox) d. Walter Lang: Bennie Bartlett, Jeanne Crain, Clifton Webb. Charming, episodic tale of turn-of-century family with 12 children. Webb is their exactingly quizzical father and Myrna Loy their gently sceptical mother

The Mating Season (Paramount) d.Mitchell Leisen: Gene Tierney, Miriam Hopkins. Spiky shaft at the American Dream in which John Lund marries socialite Tierney, and his plain-speaking mother Thelma Ritter is mistaken for a servant. Hopkins excellent as Tierney's snobbish mother

Mr 880 (Fox) d.Edmund Goulding: Burt Lancaster, Dorothy McGuire, Edmund Gwenn. Title refers to the FBI file on genial old counterfeiter Gwenn. Tracked down by agent Lancaster, he charms his way out of a long sentence. Apparently based on a real-life case

Three Husbands (UA) d.Irving Reis: Eve Arden, Ruth Warrick, Vanessa Brown. Diverting tale of three husbands' efforts to discover whether a deceased playboy has been canoodling with their wives

The Reformer and the Redhead (MGM) d.Norman Panama: June Allyson, Dick Powell. Would-be politician Dick gets a lion in his lap when he sets out to woo zookeeper's daughter Allyson

My Friend Irma Goes West (Paramount) d.Hal Walker: Jerry Lewis, Corinne Calvet, Dean Martin, John Lund. Klutzy Irma (Marie Wilson) joins Jerry and Dean as they set out for Hollywood

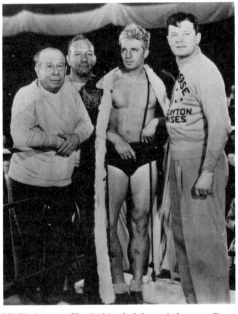

Mr Universe (Eagle Lion) d.Joseph Lerner: Bert Lahr, 'Slapsie' Maxie Rosenbloom, Vince Edwards , Jack Carson. Bodybuilder Edwards is catapulted into the wrestling game, where he has to contend with manager Carson trying to fix his big fight

Mother Didn't Tell Me (Fox) d.Claude Binyon: Dorothy McGuire, William Lundigan. Simple comedy of McGuire coping as busy doctor Lundigan's wife is sustained almost entirely by her abundant charm. Jessie Royce Landis in vigorous form as Lundigan's sniffy mother

Never a Dull Moment (RKO) d.George Marshall: Irene Dunne, Fred MacMurray, Andy Devine. Dunne plays a Manhattan sophisticate finding it hard going when she marries rodeo-cowboy MacMurray and settles for life on the ranch

Stella (Fox) d.Claude Binyon: Ann Sheridan, Victor Mature, Leif Erickson. Mature is an insurance investigator who falls for Sheridan, the only sane member of a crazy family who have a slight problem with the location of the corpse of a recently deceased and heavily insured uncle

Watch the Birdie (MGM) d.Jack Donohue: Arlene Dahl, Red Skelton. Photographer Skelton rescues rich, beautiful Dahl from the machinations of a crooked lawyer and also appears as his own father and grandfather

MUSICALS

The Daughter of Rosie O'Grady (Warner) d.David Butler: June Haver, Gordon MacRae. Glossy turn-of-the-century style filched from Fox as Haver falls for MacRae, who plays the great Tony Pastor, to the despair of her drunken father (James Barton)

I'll Get By (Fox) d.Richard Sale: Gloria de Haven, Harry James, June Haver. Limp remake of *Tin Pan Alley* (1940) with vocalist Haver romancing music publisher William Lundigan. Guest appearances by Jeanne Crain, Victor Mature, Dan Dailey

The Toast of New Orleans (MGM) d.Norman Taurog: David Niven, Mario Lanza, J Carrol Naish. Lanza is the warbling fisherman from the Louisiana bayou, taken in hand by suave manager Niven and taking the opera world by storm. Kathryn Grayson provides the love interest

Summer Stock (MGM) d.Charles Walters: Gene Kelly, Judy Garland. Judy's last for MGM is shameless variation on the old 'let's put on a show in the barn'. Kelly dances a memorable solo with a piece of newspaper and a squeaky floorboard

West Point Story (Warner) d.Roy Del Ruth: Virginia Mayo, James Cagney. Has-been producer Cagney makes a flag-waving comeback with a show at the military academy. Among the Jule Styne-Sammy Cahn numbers is 'The Military Polka'

Cinderella (RKO) d.Wilfred Jackson, Hamilton Luske, Clyde Geronimi. Superb realization of the Charles Perrault fairy tale in which engaging little mice Jacques and Gus-Gus make sure that Cinders gets to the ball

Mr Music (Paramount) d.Richard Haydn: Bing Crosby, Groucho Marx. Bing plays a songwriter who prefers golf to composing, sings 'Life is So Peculiar'. Well, when you're with Groucho . . .

Lullaby of Broadway (Warner) d.Roy Del Ruth: Doris Day, Billy de Wolfe. Musical comedy star Day blows into Broadway from London unaware that poor old Mum Gladys George has hit the skids. Billy, Anne Triola and S Z 'Cuddles' Sakall come to the rescue

Let's Dance (Paramount) d.Norman Z McLeod: Fred Astaire, Betty Hutton. Fred and Betty never really blend as wartime double act who resume their partnership, fall in love and save Betty's child from the clutches of nasty mother-in-law Lucille Watson

Two Weeks with Love (MGM) d.Roy Rowland: Jane Powell, Ricardo Montalban. Artful period piece finds pert Powell mooning over swarthy Ricardo while younger sister Debbie Reynolds makes a beeline for Carleton Carpenter

When You're Smiling (Columbia) d.Joseph Santley: Margo Woode, Jerome Courtland, Lola Albright. Frankie Laine, Billy Daniels, the Mills Brother and Kay Starr are guest stars in mild little romance between singing cowhand Courtland and secretary Albright

Wabash Avenue (Fox) d.Henry Koster: Betty Grable. Reprise of studio's *Coney Island* (1943), with Grable pursued by con-men Phil Silvers and Victor Mature, singing 'I Wish I could Shimmy Like My Sister Kate'

Young Man with a Horn (Warner) d.Michael Curtiz: Doris Day, Kirk Douglas. Kirk is the driven jazzman (based on Bix Beiderbecke and dubbed by Harry James) loved by long-suffering Day and given the runaround by rich bitch Lauren Bacall

Pagan Love Song (MGM) d.Robert Alton: Esther Williams. Coconut planter Howard Keel mistakes the lovely Williams for one of the natives in lush Tahiti-set romance. Don't eat that fish, Esther!

Tea for Two (Warner) d.David Butler: Doris Day, Gordon MacRae. Loose adaptation of the old stage hit 'No No Nanette' provides perfect showcase for Day's well-scrubbed, peaches-and-cream talent. Excellent choreography by LeRoy Prinz

Three Little Words (MGM) d.Richard Thorpe: Fred Astaire, Vera-Ellen. Snappy biopic of songwriters Kalmar (Astaire) and Ruby (Red Skelton). Debbie Reynolds delightful as Boop-Boop-a-Doop girl Helen Kane

Riding High (Paramount) d.Frank Capra: Bing Crosby, Percy Kilbride. Deft remake of Capra's own *Broadway Bill* (1934) with Bing as a horse trainer whose steed interferes with his love life

Annie Get Your Gun (MGM) d.George Sidney: J Carrol Naish, Betty Hutton. Betty in hyper-energetic form as sharp-shootin' Annie Oakley, Naish more sedate as Sitting Bull in faithful version of Irving Berlin's Broadway smash

My Blue Heaven (Fox) d.Henry Koster: Betty Grable, Dan Dailey. Betty and Dan are TV husband-and-wife team who adopt a child and then find they're about to have one of their own. Mitzi Gaynor's screen debut

WESTERNS

The Baron of Arizona (Lippert) d.Sam Fuller: Vincent Price. Masterpiece of pulp imagination in which land office clerk Price forges his way into dominion over a vast chunk of the Old West

Broken Arrow (Fox) d. Delmer Daves: James Stewart. Jeff Chandler is Cochise and Stewart a cavalry scout who lives with the Apache, marries one and prevents the outbreak of an Indian war. The film's sympathetic portrayal of Indian life was seen as daring at the time

Dakota Lil (Fox) d.Lesley Selander: John Emery, Marie Windsor. Firm-jawed Marie is twice as butch as co-stars George Montgomery, Rod Cameron in slight tale of Western counterfeiters

Sierra (Universal) d.Alfred E Green: Wanda Hendrix, Dean Jagger, Audie Murphy. Feisty little lawyer Hendrix clears Audie and his father Jagger of the crimes which forced them to take to the hills. Burl Ives engaging as a singing prospector

Branded (Paramount) d.Rudolph Maté: Mona Freeman, Charles Bickford, Alan Ladd. Atmospheric Western first for Maté with Ladd icily effective as the heel-hero pretending to be cattle baron Bickford's long-lost son

Dallas (Warner) d.Stuart Heisler: Gary Cooper, Ruth Roman. Cooper is a renegade Confederate colonel masquerading as a lawman to clean up Dallas and gain a pardon in resolutely old-fashioned big-budget Western

The Sundowners (Eagle Lion) d.George Templeton: Jack Elam, Robert Preston, Cathy Downs. Preston and Robert Sterling are brothers battling each other for domination of a ranch in rugged colorfully shot actioner

Two Flags West (Fox) d.Robert Wise: Linda Darnell, Joseph Cotten. Energetic Western, reminiscent of *Fort Apache* (1948), in which Cotten leads a group of Confederate prisoners against an Apache uprising sparked off by the inevitable Jeff Chandler

Surrender (Republic) d. Allan Dwan: John Carroll, Vera Ralston. Femme fatalle Vera plays hell with the men in a small border town but meets her come-uppance in the final reel

Frenchie (Universal) d.Louis King: Shelley Winters, John Russell, Elsa Lanchester. Winters is Frenchie Fontain, New Orleans gambling queen, who sets up business in Bottleneck with the aim of tracking down her father's killers

The Gunfighter (Fox) d.Henry King: Gregory Peck. Sombre, seminal Western in which weary, ageing gunfighter Peck cannot exorcise his past and falls to the guns of glory-seeking youngster Skip Homeier

Colt 45 (Warner) d.Edwin L Marin: Randolph Scott. Gun salesman Scott's long-barrelled Colt 45s are stolen by no-good Zachary Scott and used in a series of hold-ups

Copper Canyon (Paramount) d.John Farrow: Ray Milland, Hedy Lamarr, Macdonald Carey. Lamarr and Carey are hell-bent on inflaming old Civil War tensions to gain control of a copper mining empire

Wagonmaster (RKO) d.John Ford: Ben Johnson, Joanne Dru. Johnson gives dignified performance as a drifter guiding a band of Mormons on their trek West in optimistic, luminously beautiful fairy tale of search for the promised land. One of Ford's favorites

The Devil's Doorway (MGM) d.Anthony Mann: Paula Raymond, Robert Taylor. Taylor is an educated Indian, and Civil War hero, who uses his conventional military skills to save his tribe from massacre at the hands of landgrabbers. A bleak, thoughtful film with Taylor torn agonizedly between conflicting loyalties

Stars in My Crown (MGM) d.Jacques Tourneur: Joel McCrea. The story of a year in the life of a small Southern town which survives disease, the KKK and superstition thanks to their gunslinging man of the cloth McCrea

A Ticket to Tomahawk (Fox) d.Richard Sale. Chief Yowlachie, Anne Baxter, Rory Calhoun. Lively spoof Western in which stagecoach owner Calhoun resorts to desperate measures to stop the railroad winning a franchise in the Colorado territory. Monroe appears as a chorus girl

Rio Grande (Republic) d.John Ford: J Carrol Naish, John Wayne. Third in Ford's loose trilogy of his beloved 7th Cavalry, set in the aftermath of Civil War with Wayne pursuing Apache over the border

Winchester '73 (Universal) d.Anthony Mann: Shelley Winters, James Stewart. Classic revenge Western in which Stewart pursues the unique rifle he won in a shooting competition and the brother (Stephen McNally) who has murdered their father

Rocky Mountain (Warner) d.William Keighley: Errol Flynn. Confederate renegade Flynn tries to carve out a Californian outpost in his last Western, and contrives to go out in some style

High Lonesome (Eagle Lion) d.Alan LeMay: Lois Butler, John Barrymore Jr. Intriguing melodrama in which Barrymore is the dupe in the plans laid by Jack Elam and Dave Kashner to wipe out their enemies

Pals of the Golden West (Republic) d.William Witney: Pinky Lee, Roy Rogers. Roy's last series Western, in which he fights an outbreak of foot and mouth disease caused by cattle baron Roy Barcroft's infected beeves

Rawhide (Fox) d.Henry Hathaway: Hugh Marlowe, Tyrone Power. Taut thriller in which an outlaw gang lying in wait for a gold shipment terrorize unexpected arrivals Power and Susan Hayward

ROMANCE

When Willie Comes Marching Home (Fox) d.John Ford: William Demarest, Dan Dailey, Corinne Calvet. Eager beaver air gunner Dailey bales out over France and into the arms of Resistance heroine Calvet

The Admiral Was a Lady (UA) d.Albert Rogell: Hillary Brooke, Wanda Hendrix, Edmond O'Brien. Pert little Wanda is pursued by four work-shy suitors, including the immortal Rudy Vallee

To Please a Lady (MGM) d.Clarence Brown: Barbara Stanwyck, Clark Gable. Reporter Stanwyck falls into on again-off again affair with slightly less than chivalrous racing driver Gable

Four Days Leave (Praesans) d.Leopold Lindtberg: Simone Signoret, Cornel Wilde. Vacationing Wilde is vamped by Signoret, somewhat slimmer than in later years, in forgettable piece of fluff

September Affair (Paramount) d.William Dieterle: Joan Fontaine, Joseph Cotten. Married man Cotten and pianist Fontaine are mistakenly posted missing in an aeroplane crash, which gives them a chance to continue their affair. Effective classical music score

Three Guys Named Mike (MGM) d.Charles Walters: Van Johnson, Barry Sullivan, Jane Wyman, Howard Keel. Airline stewardess Wyman is the object of the relatively undemanding attentions of three of the studio's most eligible leading men

Please Believe Me (MGM) d.Norman Taurog: Robert Walker, Deborah Kerr, Peter Lawford. Kerr's cool sexiness provides pleasing counterpoint to the advances of assorted bachelors on seemingly endless ocean cruise

The Big Hangover (MGM) d.Norman Krasna: Van Johnson, Elizabeth Taylor. Boring attorney Johnson's allergy to alcohol provides mild complications in his pursuit of wealthy Ms Taylor, who at this stage in her career looks simply irresistible

AMERICANA

Father of the Bride (MGM) d.Vincente Minnelli: Spencer Tracy, Joan Bennett, Elizabeth Taylor. Artful confection paints witty picture of American life with Liz's upcoming marriage to Don Taylor providing aggravations for father Tracy

Bright Leaf (Warner) d.Michael Curtiz: Gary Cooper, Lauren Bacall. A simple tale of Southern tobacco barons who spend their time wrecking each other's lives, businesses, marriages. A little like South Fork, Texas. Patricia Neal overacts wildly as Cooper's vengeful wife

Father is a Bachelor (Columbia) d.Norman Foster: William Holden. Engaging hobo Holden takes five orphans under his wing and eventually finds a wife as well. Has something of the feel of *Rachel and the Stranger* (1947), but none of its style

It's a Big Country (MGM) d.Charles Vidor, Richard Thorpe, John Sturges, Don Hartman, Don Weis: Janet Leigh, S Z 'Cuddles' Sakall, Gene Kelly. Extremely uneven portmanteau film, narrated by Louis Calhern, designed to show just what a wonderful place the USA really is

Magnificent Yankee (MGM) d.John Sturges: Louis Calhern, Ann Harding. Sensitive biopic of the great American jurist Oliver Wendell Holmes, played with relish by Calhern, who is ably supported by Harding as his faithful wife

The Happy Years (MGM) d.William Wellman: Dean Stockwell, Leo G Carroll. The adventures of rebellious young Stockwell at a school for awkward children, adapted from Owen Johnson's 'Lawrenceville Stories' in the Saturday Evening Post. Carroll wryly authoritative as the housemaster, 'The Old Roman'

BRITISH AND FOREIGN

Your Witness (Coronada) d.Robert Montgomery: Robert Montgomery, Noel Hewlett. New York attorney Montgomery flies to England to clear a wartime buddy of a murder rap in slow-moving court-room drama

Waterfront (Rank) d.Michael Anderson: Richard Burton, Avis Scott. Noirish drama in which drunken seaman Robert Newton kills a shipmate in a brawl. Burton is the son he has never seen, Kathleen Harrison – in a rare straight role – the wife he deserted

Gone to Earth (London) d.Michael Powell: David Farrar, Jennifer Jones. Powell and Pressburger's characteristically quirky adaptation of Mary Webb period tale is a neglected masterpiece, pulsing with color and the pagan delights of the English countryside

So Long at the Fair (Gainsborough) d. Anthony Darnborough, Terence Fisher: Dirk Bogarde, Jean Simmons. Simmons' brother disappears in mysterious circumstances during 1889 Paris Exposition. Given Fisher's hand on the tiller, it can now be seen as a horror film in disguise

Morning Departure (Rank) d.Roy Baker: John Mills, Nigel Patrick. A submarine on a routine peacetime mission strikes a mine and sinks. Four men are left entombed in the sub. Officers remain firm-jawed, ratings either cowardly or breezily self-sacrificing in the manner of the period

Into the Blue (British Lion) d.Herbert Wilcox: Michael Wilding, Odile Versois. Stowaway Wilding involves yachts people Jack Hulbert and Constance Cummings in a bid to outwit an international gang of smugglers

Flesh and Blood (Harefield) d.Anthony Kimmins: Joan Greenwood, George Cole. Turgid family saga, beloved of the British cinema in the late '40s, in which poisoning, blackmail, suicide and general wantonness are the order of the day

The Magnet (Ealing) d.Charles Frend: William Fox, Stephen Murray. The magnet of the title is at the centre of an elaborate and whimsical plot which defies economical summary. More interesting, perhaps, is the fact that young William Fox grew up to be movie star James Fox

The Happiest Days of Your Life (British Lion) d.Frank Launder: Margaret Rutherford, Alastair Sim. Classic British comedy in which a bureaucratic blunder billets St Swithin's School for Girls on Nutbourne College for young gentlemen. Rutherford, Sim the harrassed head teachers

The Elusive Pimpernel (London) d.Michael Powell: Robert Griffiths, Cyril Cusack, David Niven. Powell and Pressburger's touch deserts them in remake of *The Scarlet Pimpernel* (1934), with Niven in the role of foppish aristocrat foiling agents of the French Terror

Chance of a Lifetime (British Lion) d.Bernard Miles: Kenneth More. Muddled, patronizing remake of Renoir's *Le Crime de Monsieur Lange* (1935) in which striking workers take over the running of their factory

My Daughter Joy (British Lion) d.Gregory Ratoff: Peggy Cummins, Edward G Robinson. Power-crazed financier Robinson tries to marry daughter off to a sultan's son in furtherance of mysterious Operation X. When he discovers she's not his daughter he goes mad

They Were Not Divided (Two Cities) d.Terence Young: Ralph Clanton, Edward Underdown. Competent account of an armored division during the last phase of World War II. Cast composed of actors who actually fought in the war, unlike some we could mention who choose to imagine they did

The Mudlark (Fox) d.Jean Negulesco: Irene Dunne, Andrew Ray. Dunne disappears under several layers of make-up to play Queen Victoria, befriending a scruffy urchin who strays into Windsor Castle

The Astonished Heart (Gainsborough) d.Terence Fisher: Margaret Leighton, Noel Coward. Silly triangle melo in which married psychiatrist Coward's affair with Leighton drives him to suicide. Celia Johnson his abjectly suffering wife

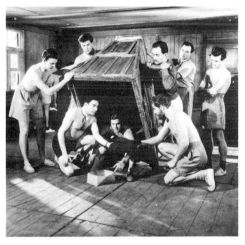

The Wooden Horse (Wessex) d.Jack Lee: David Tomlinson, Bill Travers, Leo Genn, Anthony Steel, Dan Cunningham, Peter Burton, Michael Goodliffe, Bryan Forbes. Stiff upper lip Brits use a vaulting horse as ingenious aid to escape bid from German POW camp

Odette (Rank) d.Herbert Wilcox: Trevor Howard, Anna Neagle. Workmanlike account of the wartime career of real-life French agent Odette Churchill. The stately Neagle remains suitably haggard throughout

Lili Marlene (Monarch) d.Arthur Crabtree: Richard Murdoch, Hugh McDermott. Lisa Daniely fills the title role as a female version of the infamous 'Lord Haw Haw', broadcasting bad news to the British during World War II

State Secret (London) d.Sidney Gilliat: Douglas Fairbanks, Glynis Johns. Pacy thriller pitches surgeon Fairbanks into Central European political intrigues in the state of Vosnia, for whose picturesque inhabitants director Gilliat created a complete language

The Blue Lamp (Ealing) d.Basil Dearden: Jack Warner, Dirk Bogarde. Bogarde adds a sensual streak, rare in British cinema of the period, to jittery young hoodlum whose robbery plans go badly awry

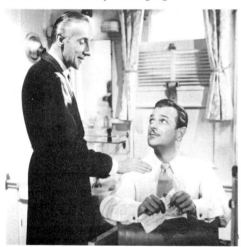

Trio (Gainsborough) d.Ken Annakin, Harold French: Wilfrid Hyde-White, Nigel Patrick. Three Somerset Maugham tales smoothly adapted for the screen. Patrick gives a beautifully judged performance as bumptious cruise liner passenger 'Mr Know-it-All'

Dance Hall (Ealing) d.Charles Crichton: James Carney, Diana Dors. Well-integrated portanteau film, revolving around the habitués of a local palais de danse. A fascinating compendium of social attitudes of the period

Seven Days to Noon (British Lion) d.John and Roy Boulting: Barry Jones. 'Dark, dark, dark amid the blaze of noon'. Deranged scientist Jones stalks the streets of a deserted London with nuclear device in his bag

Cage of Gold (Ealing) d.Basil Dearden: Jean Simmons, David Farrar. Simmons is courted and married by glamorous cad Farrar, who deserts her when he finds she is not as rich as he thought

The Woman in Question (Rank) d.Anthony Asquith: Susan Shaw, Dirk Bogarde, Jean Kent. Fortune teller Kent is found strangled. In police interviews the suspects see her in a variety of different lights

Double Confession (ABPC) d.Harry Reynolds: William Hartnell, Peter Lorre, Naunton Wayne. Murky melodrama piles up murders at a seaside resort. Policeman Wayne solves the mystery. Kathleen Harrison provides comic relief, Lorre just looks depressed

Happy Go Lovely (ABPC) d.H Bruce Humberstone: Vera-Ellen, David Lober. Vera-Ellen, David Niven and Cesar Romero sink without trace in feeble British stab at the kind of backstage musical which even Monogram could do standing on its head

Rashomon (Japan) d.Akira Kurosawa: Toshiro Mifune, Machiko Kyo. Huge international hit presents four versions of the same incident – a violent woodland encounter between a married couple and bandit Mifune

The Clouded Yellow (Rank) d.Ralph Thomas: Trevor Howard, Jean Simmons. Efficient, and at times atmospheric, 'double chase' thriller in the Hitchcock mould. Kenneth More delightful in small part as a breezily cynical Secret Service man

Tom Brown's Schooldays (Renown) d.Gordon Parry: John Howard Davies, John Forrest. Competent version of Thomas Hughes' tale of Victorian public school life, enlivened by ripe performances from Robert Newton and Hermione Baddeley. Forrest is the frightful cad Flashman

Bitter Springs (Ealing) d.Harry Watt: Charles Tingwell, Chips Rafferty, Gordon Jackson. Robust British 'Western' in which a pioneer family's land claim is resisted by the aborigines, who depend on the water the settlers need

The Naked Heart (British Lion) d.Marc Allégret: Jack Watling, Michele Morgan. Ex-nun Morgan returns to the Canadian wilds where she has a baleful effect on the local menfolk. A colossally incompetent film crammed with risible dialogue

Topaze (France) d. Marcel Pagnol: Fernandel. Remake of Louis Jouvet classic, from Pagnol's play, in which Fernandel plays a meek maths teacher who accidentally becomes the front man for a gang of crooks

La Marie du Port (France) d.Marcel Carné: Jean Gabin, Nicole Corcel. Realistic drama, based on a Simenon tale, in which middle-aged Gabin falls in love with younger sister of his mistress

La Ronde (France) d.Max Ophuls: Anton Walbrook, Simone Signoret. Walbrook is the elegantly ironic master of ceremonies in carousel of Schnitzler stories drenched in the melancholy of mittel-Europa

Orphée (France) d.Jean Cocteau: Jean Marais. Unforgettably, Marais enters the Underworld through the rippling surface of a mercury mirror. Cocteau's thrilling mixture of the fantastic and the mundane recalls the disturbingly surreal quality of Feuillade's silent serials

Le Journal d'un Curé de Campagne (France) d. Robert Bresson: Claude Laydu. Measured, austere account of the life and death of a young priest is suffused with the beauty of the French countryside

Luci del Varieta (Italy) d.Federico Fellini, Alberto Lattuada: Giulietta Masina, Peppino de Filippo. Fellini 's debut is a warmly observed comedy in which a fifth-rate variety company is undermined by the arrival of a pretty ingenue

Miracolo a Milano (Italy) d.Vittorio de Sica. Bitterly comic tirade against the treatment of displaced persons in which Toto the Good (Francisco Golisano) brings cheer to an impoverished village. Mixture of the everyday and the fantastic anticipates later Fellini

Los Olvidados (Mexico) d.Luis Buñuel: Estela Inda, Roberto Cobo. Buñuel's unblinking eye focuses on a Mexico City street gang, mixing passages of surreal beauty with images of chilling squalor

·1951·

Television continued to bite remorselessly into cinema's shrinking audience. There were now 15 million TV sets in America. The major studios forbade their contract players to appear on television and also refused to sell their film libraries to the menacing new medium. However, Universal, Paramount and Columbia announced plans to film TV material. Columbia's Harry Cohn, a legendary monster nicknamed 'White Fang' by Ben Hecht, was one of the first Hollywood moguls to grasp the opportunity offered by the TV market with Columbia Screen Gems. Virtually a caricature of the tyrannical movie tycoon, he nevertheless emerges as one of the few of that species – critically endangered by the 1950s – who understood his own business. One mogul whose touch had long since deserted him was MGM's Louis B Mayer, forced out in June by pressure from the East Coast money men.

Ironically, an MGM musical, *An American in Paris* directed by Vincente Minnelli and starring Gene Kelly and Leslie Caron (making her debut), won the year's Academy Award for Best Picture. It was Kelly's most ambitious musical, climaxing in an immensely complex 20-minute ballet, based on the work of the Impressionists, which took six months to rehearse, a month to shoot and cost over $450,000. *An American in Paris* also scooped Awards for Best Cinematography (Alfred Gilks, John Alton), Best Costume Design, Best Scoring and Best Screenplay (Alan Jay Lerner). Kelly won a special award as director and choreographer. George Stevens won the Best Director Award for *A Place in the Sun,* a film highly praised at the time but essentially a smoothly crafted woman's weepie full of dizzy close-ups. Humphrey Bogart was voted Best Actor for his performance as the stubble-caked, gin-swilling captain of *The African Queen*, gawkily romanced by spinster missionary Katharine Hepburn. Viven Leigh's haggard, touching Blanche Dubois in Elia Kazan's *A Streetcar Named Desire* won her the Best Actress Oscar. Kim Hunter and Karl Malden won the Best Supporting Actor and Actress Awards for their performances in *Steetcar*, both repeating the roles they had played on Broadway.

The year's biggest box-office hit was *David and Bathsheba,* a sublimely idiotic Biblical epic starring Gregory Peck and Susan Hayward. Among the outstanding movies of 1951 were Billy Wilder's *Ace in the Hole*, a blistering indictment of the public's eager complicity in the worst excesses of yellow journalism, with an overpowering central performance from Kirk Douglas as the has-been columnist Chuck Tatum making one last shot at the big time; Alfred Hitchcock's, *Strangers on a Train*, starring Robert Walker and Farley Granger, a chilling portrait of the psychopath hero; Robert Wise's *The Day the Earth Stood Still*, one of a growing number of science fiction features; and *Limelight*, Charlie Chaplin's last film in America and a sentimental return to the Victorian music hall and to the seedy South London back streets of his youth.

Newcomers included Lee Marvin and Charles Bronson, both well down the cast list in *You're in the Navy Now*; James Dean, fleetingly glimpsed as a twitchy soldier in Sam Fuller's *Fixed Bayonets*; and Aldo Ray in *Saturday's Hero*. Another new face, Anthony Dexter, was cast in the title role of *Valentino*, a botched biopic of the Great Lover, following which he was consigned to the outer limits of Z-movies.

Death took Warner Baxter, the mature, well-tailored leading man who successfully weathered the transition from silents to sound; Jack Holt iron-jawed action star; Maria Montez, queen of wartime dustbin epics, who succumbed to a heart attack on a crash weight-loss course of saline baths; Robert Walker, from respiratory failure after an overdose of barbiturates; Robert Flaherty, visionary pioneer of the documentary form; and B-movie veterans Edwin L Marin and Phil Rosen.

Doris Day, Dean Martin and Jerry Lewis achieved Top Ten stardom, joining John Wayne, Bing Crosby, Bob Hope, Gary Cooper, Spencer Tracy, Clark Gable, Randolph Scott and Abbott and Costello.

United Artists passed into new management after its surviving founders, Chaplin and Mary Pickford, sold out their interests. In a series of complex financial maneuvers Decca Records acquired 28 per cent of Universal for $3.8 million. By the spring of 1952 Decca owned a controlling interest in the studio.

The year saw the re-opening of hearings by the House Un-American Activities Committee. Under the virulent chairmanship of Senator John Wood from Georgia, the Committee went straight for the jugular. Among the Hollywood actors subpoenaed were Sterling Hayden, Will Geer, John Garfield, Gale Sondergaard, Jose Ferrer, Howard da Silva, Larry Parks and Karen Morley. All were asked for 'names'. Some recanted; others, including da Silva, director Abraham Polonsky and screenwriter Dalton Trumbo, remained defiant. This series of investigations, running parallel with Senator McCarthy's Communist witch hunt, resulted in the blacklisting of over 300 people whose views were in the slightest degree 'suspect.' Others were consigned to the limbo of the American Legion's 'grey list.'

In Britain, Ealing released two classic comedies: *The Lavender Hill Mob*, directed by Charles Crichton, a charming caper movie starring Alec Guinness and Stanley Holloway; and Alexander Mackendrick's *The Man in the White Suit*, also starring Guinness, a sly masterpiece whose sharpest ironies were reserved for the stagnation and fear of innovation which infected postwar Britain and which during the same period overwhelmed Ealing studios. In France, Jacques Tati's enchanting anarchist Monsiueur Hulot made his first appearance in *Les Vacances de Monsieur Hulot*, reducing a small seaside resort to chaos. In Italy Vittorio de Sica's harrowing *Umberto D* marked the end of the neo-realist cycle. Starlets like Sophia Loren and Gina Lollobrigida were waiting in the wings to capture a new international audience for Italian films.

ACTION

Thunder in the East (Paramount) d.Charles Vidor: Alan Ladd, Corinne Calvet. Ladd is his customary glacial self as a hardboiled gunrunner caught up in Indian political upheavals and finding a sliver of conscience in his trenchcoat pocket

Iron Man (Universal) d.Joseph Pevney: Jeff Chandler, Rock Hudson. Chandler plays an easygoing former miner who becomes a psychopath in the boxing ring. Buddy Hudson helps him fight the 'killer complex'

Calling Bulldog Drummond (MGM) d.Victor Saville: Robert Beatty, Margaret Leighton, Walter Pidgeon. 'Sapper's' clubland hero, in the middle-aged form of Pidgeon, is called out of retirement by Scotland Yard to fight the postwar crime wave in stolid British-shot thriller

The Fat Man (Universal) d.William Castle: J Scott Smart. Famous radio sleuth Smart makes his debut as corpulent gourmet Brad Runyan (no relation), sorting out a brace of murders and a $500,000 robbery. Rock Hudson plays a hood and Julie London his wife

Sirocco (Columbia) d.Curtis Bernhardt: Humphrey Bogart. Faint echoes of *Casablanca* (1942) are stirred by Bogart playing a cynical adventurer running guns in Damascus while keeping tongue firmly in cheek

Peking Express (Paramount) d.William Dieterle: Marvin Miller, Corinne Calvet, Joseph Cotten, Edmund Gwenn. Torpid remake of *Shanghai Express* (1932), with Calvet a pale shadow of Dietrich's sultry Shanghai Lily. Gwenn at his most maddeningly benevolent

The Hoodlum (Monarch) d.Max Nosseck: Lawrence Tierney. Part tailor-made for Tierney, who was always at his best playing barely controlled psychopaths. This time he's an embittered ex-con planning one last bank heist

I'll Get You for This (Romulus) d.Joseph M Newman: Coleen Grey, George Raft. Down among the B-men, Raft plays a gambler who turns detective when framed for a murder he didn't commit. Filmed in Italy

Flying Leathernecks (RKO) d.Nicholas Ray: John Wayne, William Harrigan, Robert Ryan. A case of leather from the neck upwards as martinet Wayne and relaxed Ryan clash over the best way to lick a fighter squadron into shape during the battle for Guadalcanal. Jay C Flippen diverting as an acquisitive sergeant

Fixed Bayonets (Fox) d.Sam Fuller: George Conrad, Bill Lundmark. Gritty Korean War drama in which sensitive corporal Richard Basehart takes command of a small group of infantrymen covering the rear as US forces withdraw through a snowy pass

Operation Pacific (Warner) d.George Waggner: John Wayne, Ward Bond. Wayne assumes command of the submarine Thunderfish when skipper Bond is wounded. Patricia Neal the woman who waits at home

The Desert Fox (Fox) d.Henry Hathaway: James Mason. Solidly mounted if over-romanticized portrait of a military legend. Understandably, perhaps, the complexities of Nazi politics and international events are smoothly glossed over

Sealed Cargo (RKO) d.Alfred Werker: Dana Andrews, Carla Balenda. Fearless fishing boat captain Andrews comes to the rescue of a seemingly innocent square-rigger which turns out to be the mother ship for a U-boat wolf pack

Captain Video (Columbia) d.Spencer Gordon Bennet: Judd Holdren. Jut-jawed Judd thwarts power-crazed Gene Roth's plans to take over the world in the only serial to be inspired by a TV series

ADVENTURE AND FANTASY

The Adventures of Captain Fabian (Republic) d.William Marshall: Errol Flynn, Micheline Presle. Flynn wrote the original screenplay for this soggy drama of a seadog saving the luscious Presle from a murder charge

Boots Malone (Columbia) d.William Dieterle: Johnny Stewart, William Holden. In his last for Columbia Holden revels in role of unscrupulous has-been jockey's agent bringing Stewart on for the big race. The seedier aspects of the racing game are skilfully etched in

Ten Tall Men (Columbia) d.Willis Goldbeck. Burt Lancaster, Mari Blanchard. Big Burt dallies with the statuesque Blanchard, a wonderfully busty 50s waxwork, in jaunty Foreign Legion send-up

Anne of the Indies (Fox) d.Jacques Tourneur: Jean Peters, Louis Jourdan. Peters looks divine in topboots as the scourge of the Spanish Main, psyching herself up for a climactic duel to the death with Blackbeard, juicily played by Thomas Gomez

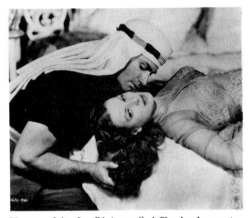

Flame of Araby (Universal) d.Charles Lamont: Jeff Chandler, Maureen O'Hara. Maureen's bosom heaves magnificently against a backdrop of burning Tunisian sand as desert hero Jeff sets out to snare the swiftest steed in Arabia

The Brave Bulls (Columbia) d.Robert Rossen: Mel Ferrer. Atmospheric, Mexico-shot account of the travails of twitchy bullfighter Ferrer. Based on a book by Tom Lea

Ivanhoe (MGM) d.Richard Thorpe: Robert Taylor, Elizabeth Taylor. Immensely handsome version of the Walter Scott epic is almost fatally compromised by a lame script. George Sanders purveys silky villainy throughout

Magic Carpet (Columbia) d.Lew Landers: Gregory Gay, Lucille Ball. Aberrational outing for the lovely Ball in atrocious Sam Katzman quickie co-starring the wooden John Agar as the Scarlet Falcon, rousing the people against treachorous, usurping uncle Raymond Burr

The Bullfighter and the Lady (Republic) d.Budd Boetticher: Gilbert Roland, Robert Stack. Boetticher recalls his own days as a tyro bullfighter with Stack playing an American whose attempts to become a matador result in tragedy

Mark of the Renegade (Universal) d.Hugo Fregonese: Gilbert Roland, Ricardo Montalban. Complicated tale of old California in which Ricardo's flashing blade and Cyd Charisse's flashing legs combine to provide a modicum of enjoyment

The Golden Horde (Universal) d.George Sherman: Marvin Miller, David Farrar. Gloriously hamfisted mishmash in which Ann Blyth is Princess Shalimar of Samarkand, threatened by Miller's uncouth, leering Genghis Khan. Farrar's Sir Guy gallops to the rescue

David and Bathsheba (Fox) d.Henry King: Susan Hayward, Gregory Peck. Peck puts his perfect profile to good use as the Lion of Judah, lusting after Hayward's Bathsheba and calling down the inevitable wrath of God. Stirring score by Alfred Newman

Jungle Manhunt (Columbia) d.Lew Landers: Rick Vallin, Sheila Ryan, Johnny Weissmuller. Sublimely idiotic Jungle Jim adventure in which Ryan and Weissmuller comb the rain forest for a sports star lost in a flying accident

Bird of Paradise (Fox) d.Delmer Daves: Debra Paget, Louis Jourdan. Stodgy remake of 1932 Dolores del Rio classic in which Polynesian princess Paget goes the same way, jumping into an erupting volcano to propitiate the grumpy island gods. What a waste

Valentino (Columbia) d.Lewis Allen: Patricia Medina, Anthony Dexter. Woeful biopic of the Great Lover leaves sullen Dexter looking like George Raft on a very bad day

The Strange Door (Universal) d.Joseph Pevney: Boris Karloff. Oddly resonant little programmer in which evil French nobleman Charles Laughton hams it up wildly in his dungeon-girt castle before meeting a watery doom

The Day the Earth Stood Still (Fox) d.Robert Wise: Lock Martin, Patricia Neal, Michael Rennie. Rennie is austere humanoid Klaatu arriving on Earth to warn us that we must live in peace or be destroyed. 'Gort! Klaatu barada nikto!'

The Man from Planet X (Mid-Century) d.Edgar G Ulmer: Margaret Field. Curiously affecting little cheapie from low-budget master Ulmer in which a wandering alien seeks help for his freezing planet only to meet incomprehension and hostility

Soldiers Three (MGM) d.Tay Garnett: Cyril Cusack, Robert Newton, Stewart Granger, David Niven. A gaudy remake of *Gunga Din* (1939) gives Newton ample opportunity to prove that he's the man who put the rum back into rumbustious

Flight to Mars (Monogram) d.Lesley Selander: Virginia Huston, Arthur Franz. Low-budget reply to *Destination Moon* (1950) which hijacked the latter's spacesuits and stranded a band of intrepid earthlings among the humanoid inhabitants of a back-lot Mars

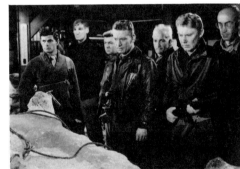

The Thing (RKO) d.Christian Nyby: Dewey Martin, Kenneth Tobey, Robert Cornthwaite. A scientific team find a giant spaceship and its terrifying inhabitant buried beneath the Polar ice cap. Remade in 1982

When Worlds Collide (Paramount) d.Rudolph Maté. Earth's very existence is threatened by the roving star Bellus. Mankind's only hope is to colonize Bellus' habitable satellite Zyra. Splendid special effects in a project originally considered by DeMille in the 1930s

MELODRAMA

Hollywood Story (Universal) d.William Castle:
Richard Conte, Julia Adams. Producer Conte
investigates an old tinsel town murder,
uncovering long-lost stars Francis X Bushman,
Betty Blythe, William Farnum and Helen Gibson

The House on Telegraph Hill (Fox) d.Robert
Wise: Richard Basehart, Valentina Cortese.
Moody thriller in which concentration camp
victim Cortese assumes a dead woman's identity
with fatal results for less than lovable husband
Basehart

Come Fill the Cup (Warner) d.Gordon Douglas:
James Cagney, Gig Young. Powerful, understated
performance by Cagney as a newsman fighting
the demon drink. Young's sad real-life death adds
poignancy to his role as a sozzled playboy

Elopement (Fox) d.Henry Koster: Clifton Webb,
Margalo Gilmore, Reginald Gardiner. Webb's
world is turned upside down when daughter Anne
Francis runs off to marry psychology tutor William
Lundigan. Eventually both sets of parents save
the marriage

I Was a Communist for the FBI (Warner)
d.Gordon Douglas: Frank Lovejoy. Glowering
Lovejoy plays real-life investigator Matt Cvetic,
finding Reds under every conceivable bed in
strident McCarthyite tract

Decision before Dawn (Fox) d.Anatole Litvak:
Oskar Werner, Hildegarde Neff. Outstanding
performance from Werner as the 'good German'
POW who agrees to act as a spy for the Americans
during the last months of the war. Features an
early appearance by Klaus Kinski

The Family Secret (Columbia) d.Henry Levin:
John Derek, Erin O'Brien Moore, Lee J Cobb.
Derek kills his best friend in a drunken brawl and
an attempt to cover it up leads to the arrest of an
innocent man. He dies during the trial but the
tormented Derek finally comes clean

Close to My Heart (Warner) d.William Keighley:
Fay Bainter, Gene Tierney, Ray Milland. Gene and
Ray discover that the child they want to adopt had
a murderer for a father, and set out to prove that
murder is not hereditary

Detective Story (Paramount) d.William Wyler:
Kirk Douglas. A case of one damned thing after
another at an NYC police precinct. Douglas is the
cop eaten up with cynicism, William Bendix his
amiable colleague, Joseph Wiseman an
hysterical thief and Lee Grant – making her debut
– a petrified shoplifter

Ace in the Hole (Paramount) d.Billy Wilder: Kirk Douglas, Richard Benedict. Grindingly heartless performance from Kirk as a washed-up journalist ruthlessly milking the story of a man trapped in an Albuquerque cave accident. Aka *The Big Carnival*

Another Man's Poison (Eros) d.Irving Rapper: Gary Merrill, Bette Davis. Davis slices the ham a trifle thick in role of writer who kills her escaped convict husband only to fall into the blackmailing clutches of Merrill. Shot in England

The Guy Who Came Back (Fox) d.Joseph M Newman: Paul Douglas, Linda Darnell, Joan Bennett. Ex-pro footballer Douglas is saved from sliding off the rails by wife Bennett and sympathetic 'other woman' Darnell

The Blue Veil (RKO) d.Curtis Bernhardt: Jane Wyman, Natalie Wood, Joan Blondell. Wyman is carried along on tidal wave of tears as a woman who loses husband and baby in World War I and devotes the rest of her life to the selfless service of others

The 13th Letter (Fox) d. Otto Preminger: Linda Darnell, Michael Rennie. Doctor Rennie arrives in a small Canadian town and becomes the object of a poison pen campaign conducted, as it turns out, by fellow medic Charles Boyer

He Ran All the Way (UA) d. John Berry: Shelley Winters, John Garfield. Garfield's last film, as hood on the run finding shelter with Winters' parents. But not for long

The Big Night (UA) d.Joseph Losey: Dorothy Comingore, John Barrymore Jr. Desperate to avenge the beating up of his father, mixed-up misunderstood teenager Barrymore lashes out in all directions against the adult world

I Can Get It for You Wholesale (Fox) d.Michael Gordon: Susan Hayward, George Sanders. Classic middle-period Hayward in which she sinks her teeth into role of an ambitious designer clawing her way to the top of the garment trade at the expense of partners Dan Dailey, Sam Jaffe

14 Hours (Fox) d.Henry Hathaway: Richard Basehart, Paul Douglas, Barbara Bel Geddes. Would-be suicide Basehart finds that standing on a ledge is a good way to make friends and influence people. Grace Kelly an upturned face in the crowd below

Strangers on a Train (Warner) d.Alfred Hitchcock: Farley Granger, Robert Walker. Remarkable performance from Walker as the playboy psychopath Bruno Anthony, casually swapping murders with Granger's morally inert tennis star Guy Haynes. The strong homosexual undertow makes this one of Hitchcock's most fascinating films

The Sellout (MGM) d. Richard Thorpe: Walter Pidgeon, John Hodiak. Small town newspaper editor Pidgeon bites off more than he can chew when he sets out to expose corrupt sheriff Thomas Gomez

M (Columbia) d.Joseph Losey: David Wayne. Low-budget remake of Lang's 1931 masterpiece is set in Los Angeles. Distinguished by its narrative economy and a fine performance from Wayne as the child killer hunted down by the underworld

Lightning Strikes Twice (Warner) d.King Vidor: Ruth Roman. Vacationing actress Roman falls in love with suspected wife killer Richard Todd. Don't worry, Mercedes McCambridge did it

The Tall Target (MGM) d.Anthony Mann: Adolphe Menjou, Dick Powell. Well-crafted, claustrophobic suspenser, set on a train, in which discredited detective Powell foils an attempt on Abraham Lincoln's life

On Dangerous Ground (RKO) d.Nicholas Ray: Ida Lupino, Robert Ryan. A brutalized cop (Ryan) investigates the murder of a schoolgirl and is regenerated by his relationship with the killer's blind sister (Lupino). Powerful if overly schematic

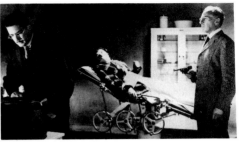

The Whip Hand (RKO) d. William Cameron Menzies: Edgar Barrier, Carla Balenda, Lewis Martin. Weird SF-tinged thriller in which newsman Elliott Reid stumbles on a Communist germ warfare establishment, presided over by an ex-Nazi scientist, in a remote American town. Stitched together from Menzies' earlier, unreleased project *The Man He Found,* which had Hitler hiding out in Minnesota

The Magic Face (Columbia) d.Frank Tuttle: Patricia Knight, Luther Adler. Deliriously bad melo in which Adler plays the Great Janus, an impressionist who escapes from a Nazi death camp, kills Hitler (who is apparently living with his wife!) and assumes the Führer's identity. William Shirer appears as himself and, for all we know, Hitler does as well

Two of a Kind (Columbia) d.Henry Levin: Edmond O'Brien, Terry Moore. Lizabeth Scott and Alexander Knox are a pair of swindlers out to cheat an elderly couple with the help of gambler O'Brien, who balks at murder

When in Rome (MGM) d.Clarence Brown: Van Johnson, Paul Douglas. Unlikely tale of con-man Douglas posing as a priest and then reforming under the prodding of real priest Van Johnson

The Unknown Man (MGM) d.Richard Thorpe: Walter Pidgeon, Ann Harding, Barry Sullivan. Lawyer Pidgeon discovers that a man he has cleared of murder is guilty. He embarks on an ingenious balancing of the scales of justice

Thunder on the Hill (Universal) d.Douglas Sirk: Ann Blyth, Claudette Colbert. A flood forces convicted murderess Blyth and her guards to take shelter in a convent, where Sister Claudette proves her innocence. Gladys Cooper splendid as the Mother Superior

Take Care of My Little Girl (Fox) d.Jean Negulesco: Jeffrey Hunter, Lenka Peterson, Jean Peters. A pointed attack on sorority houses starring Peters as the bright-eyed young thing who quickly becomes disillusioned by their snobbishness and studied philistinism

Saturday's Hero (Columbia) d.David Miller: Donna Reed, John Derek. Sullen Derek is college football star turned into cannon fodder by cynical entrepreneur Sidney Blackmer in angry attack on the commercialism of college sport

Something to Live For (Paramount) d.George Stevens: Ray Milland, Joan Fontaine. *Lost Weekend* (1945) in reverse as alcoholic actress Fontaine falls in love with Milland, the reformed lush from AA sent to help her

Under the Gun (Universal) d.Ted Tetzlaff: John McIntyre, Richard Conte, Audrey Totter. The high body count in this serviceable thriller includes its anti-hero Conte, playing a New York hoodlum discovering a cynical way to secure his release from a Southern prison

Scandal Sheet (Columbia) d.Phil Karlson: Donna Reed, John Derek. A Sam Fuller novel is the basis for this taut thriller in which a newspaper editor accidentally kills his ex-wife and then finds his star reporter delving into the story

Payment on Demand (RKO) d.Curtis Bernhardt: Barry Sullivan, Bette Davis. Bette pulls out all the stops in flashback-filled account of her divorce from Sullivan and the exquisite revenge she exacts on her wayward spouse

The People Against O'Hara (MGM) d.John Sturges: Louise Lorimer, Arthur Shields, Spencer Tracy. Lawyer Tracy can't stay off the booze, which costs him a case and forces a radical reappraisal of his life, etc, etc

Journey into Light (Fox)d.Stuart Heisler: Sterling Hayden, Ludwig Donath, Viveca Lindfors. The suicide of his alcoholic wife drives Hayden to Skid Row, at which low point he is saved by fellow cleric Donath and blind daughter Lindfors

The Man With a Cloak (MGM) d.Fletcher Markle: Barbara Stanwyck, Leslie Caron. Creaking period chiller, with twist ending, in which Stanwyck plays a Victorian Mrs Danvers, plotting to do away with wealthy Louis Calhern

The Racket (RKO) d.John Cromwell: Lizabeth Scott, Robert Mitchum. Robert Ryan is hypnotically repellent as high-voltage hood, slugging it out with incorruptible cop Mitchum. Scott the sultry torch singer in between

Kind Lady (MGM) d.John Sturges: Keenan Wynn, Ethel Barrymore, Angela Lansbury. Second screen version of creepy Hugh Walpole story in which con-man Maurice Evans takes the helpless Barrymore to the cleaners

Japanese War Bride (Fox) d.King Vidor: Marie Windsor, Shirley Yamaguchi, Don Taylor. Army veteran Taylor's marriage to Yamaguchi stirs strong family passions. Disapproving sister-in-law Windsor puts the pressure on with a poison pen letter

No Highway in the Sky (Fox) d.Henry Koster: James Stewart, Marlene Dietrich. Moderately suspenseful adaptation of Nevil Shute tale in which metal fatigue expert Stewart is convinced that the aircraft on which he is flying is about to break up. Marlene believes him

COMEDY

Double Dynamite (RKO) d.Irving Cummings: Groucho Marx, Jane Russell. Bank clerk Frank Sinatra's freak betting coup causes major complications. Groucho concentrates on ogling Russell's priceless assets in between the one-liners

His Kind of Woman (RKO) d. John Farrow: Robert Mitchum, Jane Russell. Tough-guy spoof brings Russell and Mitchum together in marvellously droll pairing. Gambler Mitchum is the fall guy in a plot to smuggle Mafia boss Raymond Burr back into the States. Vincent Price superb as a Hollywood ham

Excuse My Dust (MGM) d.Roy Rowland: Red Skelton, Sally Forrest. Pleasant musical comedy with Skelton cast as a fuddled automobile pioneer whose obsession tries the patience of sweetheart Forrest as he prepares for a big cross-country race

That's My Boy (Paramount) d.Hal Walker: Marion Marshall, Jerry Lewis. Former football star Eddie Mayehoff is determined to make schlemiel of a son Lewis follow in father's footsteps. So he hires Dean Martin as a coach

Abbott and Costello Meet the Invisible Man (Universal), d.Charles Lamont: Lou Costello, Bud Abbott, Arthur Franz. A & C are a pair of private dicks (in every sense of the word) coming to the aid of disappearing boxer Franz, who's being framed for murder

The Groom Wore Spurs (Universal) d.Richard Whorf: Ginger Rogers, Jack Carson. Sad waste of two troupers as attorney Ginger sets out to prove phoney cowpoke husband Carson is innocent of murder rap

Atoll K (France) d.Léo Joannon: Stan Laurel, Oliver Hardy. Infinitely melancholy final film for L & H, inheriting a uranium-rich island but managing only to look very old, weary and sad

Jack and the Beanstalk (Warner) d.Jean Yarbrough: Dorothy Ford, Lou Costello, Bud Abbott. Buddy Baer plays the giant in gaudy Super Cinecolor fairy tale played strictly for laughs

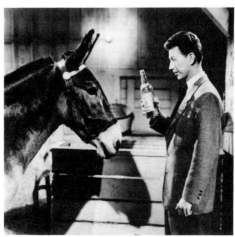

Francis Goes to the Races (Universal) d.Arthur Lubin: Donald O'Connor. The talking mule saves Piper Laurie's ranch from the bailiffs by predicting the winners at the Santa Anita race meeting. Funniest scene stolen from Billy Wilder's *The Emperor Waltz* (1947)

As Young as You Feel (Fox) d.Harmon Jones: Marilyn Monroe, Albert Dekker. Resentful at being retired at 65, spirited old gent Monty Woolley mounts a subversive campaign against his former employers. Now enjoy the picture of the wonderful Marilyn

Callaway Went Thataway (MGM) d.Norman Panama: Fred MacMurray, Howard Keel, Dorothy McGuire. Mild satire on the early success of TV Westerns. Keel copes well with double role of drunken sagebrush hero and lookalike hired to stand in for him

Bedtime for Bonzo (Universal) d.Frederick de Cordova: Ronald Reagan. Psychology professor Ronnie raises a chimp as a child in heredity experiment. Modest little comedy elevated to cult status by his subsequent political career. The chimp walks away with the acting honors

A Millionaire for Christy (Fox) d.George Marshall: Richard Carlson, Fred MacMurray, Eleanor Parker. Breezy throwback to classic screwball days in which genial rodeo entertainer MacMurray inherits a fortune and with it a complicated love life

Let's Make It Legal (Fox) d.Richard Sale: Macdonald Carey, Marilyn Monroe, Zachary Scott, Claudette Colbert. Claudette graduates to the glamorous grandmother category, ditching husband Carey and dithering over wealthy old flame Scott. Marilyn plays a wide-eyed manhunter

The Lemon Drop Kid (Paramount) d. Sidney Lanfield: Bob Hope, Marilyn Maxwell. Hope enjoys himself hugely as Damon Runyan's race track conman in hock to the Mob. First filmed in 1934 with Lee Tracy in the title role

Harem Girl (Columbia) d. Edward Bernds: Joan Davis. Super-klutz Joan mugs away gamely as she stands in for a Middle Eastern princess in tired Arabian Nights send-up

Room for One More (Warner) d.Norman Taurog: Betsy Drake, Cary Grant. Real-life husband and wife Grant and Drake play parents of five, two of whom are adopted. Well-turned if a trifle sentimental

People Will Talk (Fox) d.Joseph L Mankiewicz: Cary Grant, Jeanne Crain. Sophisticated, wordy comedy in which suavely unconventional doctor Grant saves pregnant Crain from suicide, marries her and comes under fire for his methods

Up Front (Universal) d.Alexander Hall: David Wayne, Tom Ewell. Bill Mauldin's wartime characters 'Joe' and 'Willie' are recreated in knockabout progress through Italy which misses the ironic flavor of the original cartoons

The Law and the Lady (MGM) d.Edward H Knopf: Greer Garson, Michael Wilding. Stylish but hollow resurrection of *The Last of Mrs Cheyney* (previously filmed in 1929, '37) with Greer playing the most chic of jewel thieves, gowned by Cecil Beaton no less

Darling, How Could You! (Paramount) d. Mitchell Leisen: John Lund, Mona Freeman, Joan Fontaine. Comedy based on J M Barrie's 'Alice Sit by the Fire' in which Freeman's hyperactive imagination leads to a series of near-catastrophic complications

Mr Belvedere Rings the Bell (Fox) d.Henry Koster: Clifton Webb, Joanne Dru. Once again Webb is the irresistible Lynn Belvedere, infiltrating an old people's home to prove that age is no barrier to having a good time

You're in the Navy Now (Fox) d.Henry Hathaway: Gary Cooper, Jack Webb. Absolute clinker casts Cooper as fumbling naval reserve officer placed in command of a temperamental experimental patrol vessel

Young Man With Ideas (MGM) d.Mitchell Leisen: Denise Darcel, Glenn Ford. Glenn virtually copyrighted this kind of role – an eager-beaver accident-prone lawyer moving with his family from Montana to California

My Favorite Spy (Paramount) d.Norman Z McLeod: Hedy Lamarr, Bob Hope. Bob thrashes around in the middle of an international intrigue, mistaken for a murdered spy. Lamarr looks elegantly out of place as his glamorous sidekick

MUSICALS

The Golden Girl (Fox) d.Lloyd Bacon: Mitzi Gaynor, Dennis Day. Effervescent Mitzi is Civil War entertainer Lotta Crabtree, defiantly singing 'Dixie' in New York's Niblo Gardens

An American in Paris (MGM) d.Vincente Minnelli: Gene Kelly, Leslie Caron. Slight tale of GI Kelly torn between shopgirl Caron and wealthy Nina Foch takes second place to its complex, brilliantly choreographed centrepiece, a 20-minute ballet based on the work of the Impressionists. Songs by George and Ira Gershwin

Here Comes the Groom (Paramount) d.Frank Capra: Bing Crosby. Laid-back reporter Bing acquires a couple of orphans and is given five days either to find a wife or give up the winsome little scraps. Usual artful Capra confection

Call Me Mister (Fox) d.Lloyd Bacon: Dan Dailey, Betty Grable. GI Dailey, based in Japan, goes AWOL to patch it up with estranged wife Grable, who's entertaining the troops. Loosely based on a 1946 Harold Rome Broadway revue

April in Paris (Warner) d.David Butler: Doris Day, Ray Bolger. Chorus girl Day is mistakenly given a ticket to a cultural junket in France, enjoys mild shipboard romance with diplomat Bolger

I'll See You in My Dreams (Warner) d.Michael Curtiz: Frank Lovejoy, Patrice Wymore, Danny Thomas. Deft showbiz biopic, with Danny Thomas playing Gus Kahn, provided the studio with a big box-office hit

Show Boat (MGM) d.George Sidney. Kathryn Grayson, Howard Keel. Third screen version of Edna Ferber's novel is given the plushest of MGM treatments. Ava Gardner outstanding as the mulatto Julie

On the Riviera (Fox) d.Walter Lang: Corinne Calvet, Danny Kaye. Remake of *Folies Bergère* (1934) and *That Night in Rio* (1941) in which Kaye revels in the double role of a celebrated financier and his nightclub entertainer lookalike

Texas Carnival (MGM) d.Charles Walters: Red Skelton, Ann Miller. Oddly damp squib from the normally capable team of Walters and Hermes Pan in which carnival bum Skelton is mistaken for a millionaire oil and cattle baron

Starlift (Warner) d.Roy Del Ruth: Doris Day, Ruth Roman. Korean War update of *Hollywood Canteen* (1944) strung around routine romance between starlet Janis Paige and Air Force corporal Ron Hagerthy

The Belle of New York (MGM) d.Charles Walters; Vera-Ellen, Fred Astaire. Debonair Fred is turn-of-the-century playboy leaving a string of brides at the altar until his spry progress is halted by starchy Salvation Army Girl Vera-Ellen. Stunning art direction by Cedric Gibbons

Royal Wedding (MGM) d.Stanley Donen: Fred Astaire. Donen's solo directorial debut despatches brother and sister act Astaire and Jane Powell to a London preparing for Princess Elizabeth's wedding. Watch out for Fred dancing on the ceiling and walls of his hotel room

Sunny Side of the Street (Columbia) d.Richard Quine: Terry Moore, Frankie Laine. Showcase for Laine and Billy Daniels as would-be singer Jerome Courtland tries to break into TV with the help of former sweetheart Audrey Long

Painting the Clouds with Sunshine (Warner) d. David Butler: Virginia Mayo, Tom Conway. Mayo, Lucille Norman and Virginia Gibson are three gold diggers on the make in Las Vegas. Comic relief from Wallace Ford and S Z 'Cuddles' Sakall

Meet Me After the Show (Fox) d.Richard Sale: Betty Grable. Jack Cole's lively production numbers pep up tale of Grable's on-off marriage with Macdonald Carey and her pursuit by singer Eddie Albert and beachcomber Rory Calhoun

Purple Heart Diary (Columbia) d.Richard Quine: Frances Langford, Judd Holdren. Langford, Ben Lessy and Tony Romano play themselves, bringing cheer to the troops in the wartorn Pacific during World War II

On Moonlight Bay (Warner) d.Roy Del Ruth: Doris Day, Gordon MacRae. Folksy adaptation of one of Booth Tarkington's Penrod stories in which girl-next-door Day marries boy-next-door MacRae

The Great Caruso (MGM) d.Richard Thorpe: Blanche Thebom, Mario Lanza. One of Mario's greatest hits, a breathtakingly cliché-clogged biopic of Enrico Caruso. Ann Blyth second billed as Dorothy Benjamin

WESTERNS

The Cimarron Kid (Universal) d.Budd Boetticher: Noah Beery Jr, Hugh O'Brian, Audie Murphy. Reluctant outlaw Audie rides with the Dalton gang before giving himself up and opting for the deferred pleasures of domesticity with Beverly Tyler

Distant Drums (Warner) d.Raoul Walsh: Gary Cooper, Richard Webb. Backwoodsman Cooper leads a punitive expedition against Florida gun runners and then fights his way back through Seminole country in western reworking of Walsh's *Objective Burma* (1945)

Best of the Badmen (RKO) d.William D Russell: Robert Ryan, Bruce Cabot, Walter Brennan. Confederate guerrilla Ryan is driven into outlawry by Robert Preston's omnipresent banking and railroad empire. His revenge includes stealing Preston's wife, Claire Trevor

Cattle Drive (Universal) d.Norman Panama: Joel McCrea, Dean Stockwell. Variation on the *Captains Courageous* (1937) theme in which prissy little rich boy Stockwell is stranded in the desert, hitches a lift home with McCrea's cattle drive and acquires all the rugged manly virtues on the way

Bugles in the Afternoon (Warner) d.Roy Rowland: Forrest Tucker, Ray Milland. Cavalry officer Milland is branded a coward but redeems himself with heroic conduct at the Battle of the Little Big Horn

Bend of the River (Universal) d.Anthony Mann: Arthur Kennedy, James Stewart. Former outlaw Stewart turns wagon train guide, clashing with old partner in crime Kennedy in majestically handled odyssey – full of symbolism – at the end of which Stewart purges his past and finds a new life

The Secret of Convict Lake (Fox) d.Michael Gordon: Gene Tierney, Glenn Ford. A group of escaped convicts, led by remorseful Ford, stumble on a settlement occupied by women whose menfolk are away on a silver strike

Oh, Susanna (Republic) d.Joseph Kane: Rod Cameron, Adrian Booth, Forrest Tucker. Cameron is captain Calhoun, cavalryman with a conscience, battling to keep prospectors out of the Sioux' sacred land in the Black Hills of Dakota

Across the Wide Missouri (MGM) d.William Wellman: Clark Gable. Lyrical, ravishingly shot and deeply felt parable of the destruction of the Colorado wilderness in the 1820s, as white settlers push inexorably westwards

Fort Defiance (Ventura) d.John Rawlins: Dane Clark. Civil War deserter Clark is pursued by vengeful former comrade Ben Johnson while the Navajo take to the warpath in pacy outing, strikingly photographed by Stanley Cortez

Westward the Women (MGM) d.William Wellman: Denise Darcel, Robert Taylor. Misogynist scout Taylor is hired to guide a wagon train of 150 women to their mail-order husbands in California. The women prove sturdy

Only the Valiant (Warner) d.Gordon Douglas: Gregory Peck. Tinny echoes of *Twelve O'Clock High* (1949) with Peck cast as an icy disciplinarian almost provoking a mutiny in his cavalry troop during a bloody bid to recapture a fort from the Apache

Tomahawk (Universal) d.George Sherman: Van Heflin, Yvonne de Carlo. Heflin is the buckskin-clad scout who fails to prevent the Sioux being massacred by the US Cavalry's new rapid-action, breech-loading rifles while wooing de Carlo in a manner best described as off-hand

Flaming Feather (Paramount) d.Ray Enright: Barbara Rush, Sterling Hayden. Sinewy Western finds rancher Hayden and cavalry officer Forrest Tucker on the track of outlaw Victor Jory and his band of renegade Indians

Lone Star (MGM) d.Vincent Sherman: Ava Gardner, Broderick Crawford, Clark Gable. Plodding account of the birth of the Lone Star State with Gable in expansive form as the cattle baron whose help Andrew Jackson enlists to stop Texas declaring itself an independent nation

Along the Great Divide (Warner) d.Raoul Walsh: Virginia Mayo, Kirk Douglas. Raw psychological Western – and Douglas' first – in which he plays a guilt-ridden Marshal escorting prisoner Walter Brennan through the desert on a journey which plunges him back into his past

Red Mountain (Paramount) d.William Dieterle: Alan Ladd, Lizabeth Scott. Is that a pistol in your pocket or is this just another formula Western? Ladd and Arthur Kennedy foil a plot by Quantrill (John Ireland) to build a personal empire in the West. Splendid climactic gunfight

Silver City (Paramount) d.Byron Haskin: Richard Arlen, Yvonne de Carlo. Mining engineer Edmond O'Brien romances de Carlo in rugged actioner punctuated by fist fights and explosions

The Wild North (MGM) d.Andrew Marton: Stewart Granger, Cyd Charisse. Standard Mountie fare with trapper Stewart accused of murder, Wendell Corey the stalwart out to get his man. The first film in Ansocolor, so now you know

Man in the Saddle (Producers-Actors) d.André de Toth: Joan Leslie, Alexander Knox, Ellen Drew, Randolph Scott. Laconically authoritative performance from Scott as he squares accounts with rival Knox. Plus some moody nighttime photography, and an extended fight between Scott and John Russell, one of the great heavies of the early 50s

The Red Badge of Courage (MGM) d.John Huston: Bill Mauldin, Audie Murphy. Much-mangled but nevertheless self-consciously arty adaptation of Stephen Crane's novella about a soldier (Murphy) caught up in a Civil War battle. Read the full story in Lillian Ross' book 'Picture'

Kangaroo (Fox) d.Lewis Milestone: Peter Lawford, Maureen O'Hara. Australian-set Western in which Lawford's plans to swindle Finlay Currie out of his ranch take a new turn when he meets daughter O'Hara

ROMANCE

I'll Never Forget You (Fox) d.Roy Baker: Tyrone Power, Ann Blyth, Beatrice Campbell. Remake of *Berkeley Square* (1933) in which atom scientist Power dreams himself back to 18th-century London, where his experiments earn him a spell in Bedlam

Limelight (UA) d.Charles Chaplin: Buster Keaton, Charles Chaplin. Self-indulgent but moving journey back to Chaplin's roots in turn-of-the-century London as a washed-up musical hall comic befriending a young dancer (Claire Bloom) crippled by hysterical paralysis

The Light Touch (MGM) d.Richard Brooks: Pier Angeli, Stewart Granger. Colorful European locations enliven this routine caper of art thief Granger and Italian girl-friend Angeli

Too Young to Kiss (MGM) d.Robert Z Leonard: Paula Corday, Van Johnson, June Allyson. June skilfully negotiates a potential morass of mawkishness as a pianist posing as a child prodigy to get a break, falling in love with Johnson

Her First Romance (Columbia) d.Seymour Friedman: Margaret O'Brien, Allen Martin, Mary Donahue. Sadly all child stars have to grow up, including O'Brien, MGM's miniature gold mine of the 1940s, who endures her first screen kiss in otherwise forgettable summer camp story

The African Queen (Romulus) d.John Huston: Humphrey Bogart, Katharine Hepburn. Bogart is the gin-soaked skipper of the rusting river-tub of the title, tetchily falling for Hepburn's prissy spinster as they battle the elements, a German gunboat and each other

Goodbye My Fancy (Warner) d.Vincent Sherman: Joan Crawford, Frank Lovejoy. Flimsy love triangle between Crawford, Lovejoy and Robert Young shrivels under the leading lady's basilisk glare

Rich, Young and Pretty (MGM) d.Norman Taurog: Danielle Darrieux, Wendell Corey. Frothy Paris-set musical in which Texan Jane Powell meets heartthrob Vic Damone and her mother, the lovely Darrieux, who wisely walked out on Corey years before

Katie Did It (Universal) d.Frederick de Cordova: Ann Blyth, Mark Stevens. Small-town girl Blyth's sudden fame as a billboard pin-up threatens her plans to marry artist Stevens

AMERICANA

A Place in the Sun (Paramount) d.George Stevens: Montgomery Clift, Elizabeth Taylor. Ambitious remake of Dreiser's *An American Tragedy* (1931) overbalances as it strives for effect. Clift excellent as the weakling fatally torn between factory slut Shelley Winters and rich bitch Taylor. Filled with swooning close-ups

I'd Climb the Highest Mountain (Fox) d.Henry King: William Lundigan, Susan Hayward. Charming period piece in which itinerant preacher Lundigan marries city girl Hayward and introduces her to the trials and tribulations of ministering to his Georgia flock

Jim Thorpe – All American (Warner) d.Michael Curtiz: Charles Bickford, Burt Lancaster. Burt well cast in the title role of workmanlike biopic of the great American Indian athlete who was stripped of his Olympic medals for playing pro baseball

Father's Little Dividend (MGM) d.Vincente Minnelli: Spencer Tracy, Elizabeth Taylor, Don Taylor. Inevitable sequel to *Father of the Bride* (1950) finds Tracy queasily contemplating grandfatherhood

A Streetcar Named Desire (Warner) d.Fred Zinnemann: Vivien Leigh, Marlon Brando. Immaculate adaptation of Tennessee Williams' play marred only by marginal tinkering. Leigh's haggard Blanche Dubois misses some of the character's pathos, Brando superb as Stanley Kowalski, a Caliban with sex appeal

Follow the Sun (Fox) d.Sidney Lanfield: Glenn Ford, Dennis O'Keefe. Golf afficionados will be amused by this fictionalized biopic of enigmatic golf champ Ben Hogan (Ford). Anne Baxter plays the ever-supportive wife indispensable in such undertakings

I Want You (RKO) d.Mark Robson: Farley Granger, Peggy Dow. Goldwyn product harking back to *Best Years of Our Lives* (1946), focuses on the emotional reactions of a small-town family to the outbreak of the Korean War

Anything Can Happen (Paramount) d.George Seaton: Kurt Kasznar, Jose Ferrer. Over-ripe performance from Ferrer as a Russian immigrant eager to adopt the American way of life while courting pert Kim Hunter

Death of a Salesman (Columbia) d.Laslo Benedek: Fredric March, Mildred Dunnock. Harrowing screen version of Arthur Miller's sombre allegory with March occasionally going over the top as the doomed Willy Loman. Cameron Mitchell, Kevin McCarthy his frightful sons

BRITISH AND FOREIGN

Mr Drake's Duck (Fairbanks) d.Val Guest: Yolande Donlan, Douglas Fairbanks Jr, Reginald Beckwith, Wilfrid Hyde-White. Honeymooners Fairbanks and Donlan discover a duck which lays radioactive explosive eggs in jaunty SF caper. *Million-Dollar Duck* (1971) is a virtual remake

Lady Godiva Rides Again (British Lion) d.Frank Launder: Diana Dors, Pauline Stroud. Pauline wins the Fascinating Soap Beauty Contest and a contract with a film studio's 'charm school' for young hopefuls

The Lavender Hill Mob (Ealing) d.Charles Crichton: Stanley Holloway, Alec Guinness, Alfie Bass, Sid James. Four no-hopers pull off an ingenious bullion robbery in classic Ealing daydream of the 'little man' outmaneuvering the big battalions of bureaucracy

The Browning Version (Rank) d.Anthony Asquith: Wilfrid Hyde-White, Michael Redgrave, Jean Kent, Nigel Patrick. Acutely observed performance from Redgrave as a desiccated, disillusioned schoolmaster in faithful adaptation of Terence Rattigan play

The Magic Box (Festival Films) d.John Boulting: Robert Donat, Laurence Olivier. Donat is film pioneer William Friese-Greene, Olivier his astounded constabular guinea pig in dull contribution from the Boultings to the Festival of Britain

Young Wives' Tale (ABPC) d.Henry Cass: Joan Greenwood, Derek Farr. Feline Greenwood and smooth Nigel Patrick are the Bohemian couple planting themselves on bourgeois chums Farr and Helen Cherry. Guy Middleton delightful as raffish friend with a finger in the black market

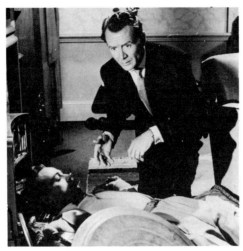

Mr Denning Drives North (British Lion) d.Anthony Kimmins: Herbert Lom, John Mills. Wealthy aircraft tycoon Mills accidentally kills the criminal his daughter foolishly intends to marry. As is always the way, an innocent man is placed in the murder frame

Laughter in Paradise (ABPC) d.Mario Zampi: Alastair Sim. A wealthy prankster leaves £50,000 each to four relations, but only if they meet some rather peculiar conditions laid down in the will

Appointment with Venus (Rank) d.Ralph Thomas: Glynis Johns, David Niven. Fanciful wartime adventure with Commando Niven liberating a prize cow (the one in the middle) from the Nazi-occupied Channel Islands

The Man in the White Suit (Ealing) d.Alexander Mackendrick: Howard Marion Crawford, Michael Gough, Alec Guinness, Cecil Parker, Ernest Thesiger. Brilliantly barbed social satire wrapped in story of maverick inventor Guinness' discovery of an indestructible, dirt-resistant textile

The Woman with No Name (ABPC) d.Ladislao Vajda: Edward Underdown, Phyllis Calvert. Portentious melodrama, complete with nightmare dream sequence in negative, in which amnesiac Calvert gropes her way back into the forgotten past

Hotel Sahara (Rank) d.Ken Annakin: Peter Ustinov, Yvonne de Carlo. Ustinov delightful as oleaginous North African hotelier in World War II, effortlessly accommodating successive Allied and Axis guests

Secret People (Ealing) d.Thorold Dickinson: Audrey Hepburn, Valentina Cortese. Overwrought thriller set in pre-war London and centring on the assassination of a Fascist dictator by a group of left-wing emigrés

Outcast of the Islands (British Lion) d.Carol Reed: Trevor Howard, George Coulouris. Howard goes agonizingly to the bad in confidently handled adaptation of Joseph Conrad's Far Eastern morality tale

Tales of Hoffman (British Lion) d.Michael Powell: Ludmilla Tcherina. Extravagant, color-drenched version of Offenbach's fantasy with magical art direction by Hein Heckroth

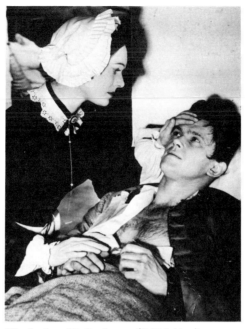

The Lady with the Lamp (British Lion) d.Herbert Wilcox: Anna Neagle, Nigel Stock. Stately performance from Neagle as Crimean heroine Florence Nightingale in historical waxworks show

Scrooge (UA) d.Brian Desmond Hurst: Alastair Sim. Dickens' 'A Christmas Carol' animated by Sim in commanding form as the miserable old miser who sees the light

His Excellency (Ealing) d.Robert Hamer: Cecil Parker, Eric Portman. Bluff trade union official Portman is appointed governor of a British colony, grapples with stuffy protocol and rebellious locals

The Gift Horse (Molton) d.Compton Bennett: Trevor Howard, Sonny Tufts. Howard is unpopular captain of ancient Lend-Lease destroyer who is brought closer to his crew by encounter with a U-boat. Film climaxes with the 'gift horse's' role in the St Nazaire raid

Circle of Danger (RKO) d.Jacques Tourneur: Naunton Wayne, Ray Milland. Sprightly Hitchcockian thriller in which Milland returns to England to smoke out his brother's killers. Wayne is a whimsical detective

Hunted (Rank) d.Charles Crichton: Dirk Bogarde, John Whiteley. Quirky thriller casts Bogarde as a murderer on the run with orphan Whiteley in tow. Much admired by French cinéastes

Der Verlorene (Germany) d.Peter Lorre: Peter Lorre. Remarkable attempt by Lorre to exorcise German guilt with bleak portrayal of an unhinged scientist adrift in a shattered postwar landscape

Les Jeux Interdits (France) d.René Clement: Brigitte Fossey, Georges Poujouly. Two children create a secret universe in the middle of war, providing potent metaphor for the folly of the outside world

Fanfan la Tulipe (France) d.Christian-Jacque: Gina Lollobrigida, Gérard Philipe. Plenty of dash from Philipe in enjoyable 18th-century swashbuckler, playing a country boy on the make in the army of Loius XV

Le Petit Monde de Don Camillo (France) d.Julien Duvivier: Fernandel. Big hit for the mournful clown as Giovanni Guareschi's village priest, battling Communist mayor Gino Cervi and enjoying cosy *tête à têtes* with God

Bellissima (Italy) d.Luchino Visconti: Anna Magnani. Flavorful comedy about a Roman mother hell bent on making her child a movie star

Les Vacances de Monsieur Hulot (France) d.Jacques Tati: Jacques Tati. Debut of Tati's endearing and alarming anarchist Hulot, innocently shattering the brittle order of small seaside resort

Umberto D (Italy) d.Vittorio de Sica: Carlo Battisti. Heartrending, if somewhat contrived, exercise in late neo-realism in which an old man struggles to sustain himself and his little dog on a meagre pension

Lo Sceicco Bianco (Italy) d.Federico Fellini: Brunella Bova, Alberto Sordi. Honeymooning Bova falls for Sordi's cartoon hero in Fellini's first solo film. Provided the inspiration for Gene Wilder's *The World's Greatest Lover* (1977)

Cecil B DeMille's *The Greatest Show on Earth* demonstrated that there was still a market for old-fashioned hokum. The year's biggest grosser at $12 million, it was also chosen as Best Picture by the Motion Picture Academy. The Best Actor Award was won by Gary Cooper for his performance in Fred Zinnemann's *High Noon*. Cooper's Sheriff Will Kane, troubled, decent and poignantly frail, could serve as a metaphor for the star in his declining years. Subsequently *High Noon*, with its theme of civic responsibility in a crisis and pessimistic view of the latent courage in non-heroic citizens, was seen as an allegory about McCarthyism, which is perhaps stretching allegory a little too far. Its more immediate impact was to revive Cooper's flagging career and underline the trend towards more 'adult' Westerns. Shirley Booth was voted Best Actress for her performance as the slatternly Lola Delaney in *Come Back Little Sheba*, co-starring Burt Lancaster as her barely reformed alcoholic husband. Anthony Quinn won the Best Supporting Actor Award as Marlon Brando's eldest brother in Elia Kazan's *Viva Zapata!* The Best Supporting Actress Oscar went to Gloria Grahame for her performance as a bitchy Southern belle in Vincente Minnelli's *The Bad and the Beautiful*.

Among the year's outstanding films were George Cukor's *Pat and Mike*, a delicious pairing of Katharine Hepburn and Spencer Tracy; Howard Hawks' *Monkey Business*, in which Cary Grant and Ginger Rogers found a second childhood and Marilyn Monroe played a stenographer whose assets were purely physical; and *Singing' in the Rain*, set in the early days of talkies and starring Gene Kelly at his most versatile, contriving another complex ballet, dancing with the superb Cyd Charisse and doing the simple thing perfectly with a lamp post, an umbrella and a shower of rain.

In September the wide-screen Cinerama process made its debut in New York with *This is Cinerama*, a two-hour travelogue featuring stereophonic sound from speakers positioned behind the screen and around the auditorium. Arch Oboler's *Bwana Devil*, an otherwise unremarkable safari adventure starring Robert Stack and Barbara Britton, introduced the Natural Vision 3-D process. Audiences ducked as everything but the kitchen sink hurtled towards them from the screen.

Remakes were in vogue, including *The Merry Widow*, *The Prisoner of Zenda* and *Scaramouche*, the last two starring British import Stewart Granger. Neither *Scaramouche* nor *The Prisoner of Zenda* captured the élan of the originals, but the latter featured a spectacularly protracted sword fight between Granger and suave heavy James Mason. Joan Crawford, released from her contract by Warner (for a fee of $200,000), turned producer with *Sudden Fear*, a taut thriller directed by David Miller in which she co-starred opposite Jack Palance. Richard Fleischer's *The Narrow Margin*, starring Marie Windsor and Charles McGraw, showed that there was still a kick in the B-movie. *Here Come the Nelsons* was an early example of a TV spin-off, with Rock Hudson in a supporting role. Jean Simmons made her Hollywood debut in *Androcles and the Lion*; other new faces included Tab Hunter, Anne Bancroft, Gene Barry, Chuck Connors, Carolyn Jones and Zsa Zsa Gabor.

RKO lurched from crisis to crisis. The first half of the year saw a bitter legal battle between Howard Hughes and Paul Jarrico, a screenwriter implicated as a Communist by McCarthy, who sued the studio for refusing to give him a credit on *The Las Vegas Story*. Hughes was also embroiled in a contract dispute with Jean Simmons, whose attorney Martin Gang filed his own suit against Hughes, RKO and a publicity firm, alleging that they had blackened his character during Simmons' court action. In September Hughes and corporate president Ned E Dupont sold their RKO stock to a Chicago-based syndicate, which was shown by *The Wall Street Journal* to have criminal connections. The new president, Ralph Stolin, was immediatly forced out and in November the new chairman, Arnold Grant, resigned. Simultaneously a minority stockholders' suit requested the appointment of a temporary receiver. RKO was now drifting in limbo, and the studio's losses over the year amounted to $10.2 million.

In Britain, Anthony Asquith's *The Importance of Being Earnest* provided an impeccable adaptation of Oscar Wilde, dominated by Edith Evans as the definitive Lady Bracknell. Less discerning tastes were catered for by *Cosh Boy*, a frenzied exposé of teenage 'razor gangs' in which a sexy young Joan Collins made a big impression. Ralph Richardson's performance as the driven aircraft designer in David Lean's *The Sound Barrier* won him the New York Critics' Award as the year's Best Actor.

A heartrending footnote to movie history was provided by Bela Lugosi, down on his luck and at the end of his tether, appearing as Dracula in a dire British Z-movie, *Mother Riley Meets the Vampire*, opposite music hall drag star Arthur Lucan. On 17 September Charles Chaplin, with his wife and four children, sailed from New York in the Queen Elizabeth for the British premiere of *Limelight*. The great liner had been at sea for only a few hours when the American Attorney-General James McGranery announced that he had ordered an inquiry as to whether Chaplin should be allowed to re-enter the United States. Two weeks later Chaplin was charged with being a member of the Communist Party and making statements which displayed a 'leering, sneering attitude' towards his adopted country. Chaplin had no intention of returning. In April 1953 he handed in his re-entry permit and settled in Switzerland. In Hollywood director Elia Kazan reversed an earlier stand and declared the names of fellow-Communists to the House Un-American Activities Committee. Shortly afterwards he signed a new contract (at a reduced salary) and his career continued to prosper. In New York, John Garfield – driven out of Hollywood by the blacklist – died of a heart attack.

ACTION

Battle Circus (MGM) d.Richard Brooks: Humphrey Bogart, June Allyson, Penny Sheehan. Routine Korean War drama finds medic Bogart laboring under double drawback of dire script and cloying performance from nurse Allyson

Red Ball Express (Universal) d.Bud Boetticher: Sidney Poitier, Jeff Chandler. Jeff battles the Germans and psycopathic top sergeant Alex Nicol in tribute to the US Army Transport Corps' role in the Normandy breakout

Lydia Bailey (Fox) d.Jean Negulesco: Anne Francis, Dale Robertson. US lawyer Robertson is caught up in 19th-century Haitian revolt against the French. Negulesco provides exotic background to the brisk action

Above and Beyond (MGM) d.Melvin Frank, Norman Panama: James Whitmore (left), Robert Taylor. Thoughtful account of Colonel Paul Tibbets (Taylor), the man chosen to drop the A-bomb on Hiroshima in August 1945

One Minute to Zero (RKO) d.Tay Garnett: Charles McGraw, Robert Mitchum. Case-hardened Colonel Mitchum bestirs himself to deal with swarming North Koreans and stubborn UN official Ann Blyth before sliding back into a coma

Lure of the Wilderness (Fox) d.Jean Negulesco: Walter Brennan, Jeffrey Hunter, Jean Peters. Remake of *Swamp Water* (1941), set in the Okefenokee, with Hunter fighting to clear Brennan of back-country frame-up

Atomic City (Paramount) d.Jerry Hopper: Michael Moore, Lydia Clarke, Gene Barry. Moderately suspenseful effort involving the kidnapping of the son of a Los Alamos scientist and an H-bomb ransom

Retreat, Hell! (Columbia) d.Joseph H Lewis: Frank Lovejoy, Richard Carlson. Above-average Korean War actioner, informed with Lewis' customary intelligence and bursts of cinematic flair

Big Jim McLain (Warner) d.Edward Ludwig: John Wayne, Veda Ann Borg. Commies beware! Two-fisted Red-hunter Wayne investigates subversive goings-on in Hawaii. Only worth it if you're a Borg fan

Diplomatic Courier (Fox) d.Henry Hathaway: Tyrone Power, Patricia Neal. Top State Department agent Power tumbles into Trieste-set thriller revolving around Soviet plans to invade Yugoslavia

The Sniper (Columbia) d.Edward Dmytryk: Arthur Franz. Tight little drama of unhinged marksman Franz going on the rampage. Good companion piece to *He Lived By Night* (1948) and *Targets* (1968)

My Six Convicts (Columbia) d.Hugo Fregonese: Henry Morgan, John Beal. Slick Stanley Kramer production mingles Big House drama with light relief as well-intentioned psychologist Beal tries to win trust of cons

The Narrow Margin (RKO) d.Richard Fleischer: Marie Windsor, Charles McGraw. Granite-jawed cop McGraw escorts gangster's widow to grand jury in tense train journey. One of the best Bs ever made, with Windsor in top form

Park Row (UA) d.Sam Fuller: Gene Evans. Fuller's tabloid skills animate raw drama of newspaper war in the 1880s. Ferocious opening shot remains justly famous

ADVENTURE AND FANTASY

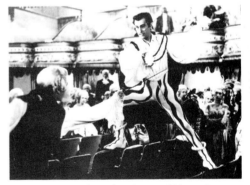

Blackbeard the Pirate (RKO) d.Raoul Walsh: Robert Newton, Keith Andes. Newton finally yaws wildly out of control as the pirate chief whose trade is 'sinkings, burnings, kidnap, murder . . . but larceny above all!'

Scaramouche (MGM) d.George Sidney: Stewart Granger. One of Granger's better performances as the duelling jester in vigorous adaptation of Rafael Sabatini warhorse first filmed in 1923

The Prisoner of Zenda (MGM) d.Richard Thorpe: Deborah Kerr, Stewart Granger. Glossy remake of the 1939 smash with Granger filling the Colman role as stand-in for the King of Ruritania, James Mason the smiling villain Rupert of Hentzau

Plymouth Adventure (MGM) d.Clarence Brown: Spencer Tracy. Tracy plays the cynical captain of the Mayflower, ferrying the Pilgrim Fathers across the Atlantic. Film stays resolutely becalmed in spite of excellent special effects

The Big Trees (Warner) d.Felix Feist: Kirk Douglas, Patrice Wymore. Logging saga in which Kirk's stonecracking grin flashes across Redwood country as he contemplates cheating homesteaders of their land. Similar to *Valley of the Giants* (1938)

Babes in Bagdad (UA) d.Edgar G Ulmer: Richard Ney, Paulette Goddard. Cut-rate harem adventure whose cast of has-beens also includes John Boles and Gypsy Rose Lee

Son of Ali Baba (Universal) d.Kurt Neumann: Tony Curtis, Piper Laurie. Tony's haircut is more appropriate to the Bronx than Bagdad in desert romp with Victor Jory in villainous form as the wicked Caliph

Les Miserables (Fox) d.Lewis Milestone: Michael Rennie, Robert Newton. Smooth, shallow version of the Victor Hugo classic with Newton as the obsessive Chief of Police Javert uncovering reformed criminal Rennie's hidden past

Against All Flags (Universal) d.George Sherman: Anthony Quinn, Errol Flynn, Henry Wilson, Maureen O'Hara. Flynn is 18th-century British naval officer who gets himself cashiered to infiltrate Quinn's pirate stronghold in Madagascar

The Story of Robin Hood (RKO) d.Ken Annakin: James Hayter, Richard Todd. High, wide and handsome retelling of medieval myth, full of ripe performances with Peter Finch outstanding as the hissable Sheriff of Nottingham

The Sea Devils (RKO) d.Raoul Walsh: Rock Hudson, Maxwell Reed. Napoleonic wars provide backcloth to romance between British spy Yvonne de Carlo and devil-may-care smuggler Rock. Reed snarls away superbly as the heavy

The Crimson Pirate (Warner) d.Robert Siodmak: Nick Cravat, Burt Lancaster, Eva Bartok, Noel Purcell. Athletic lampoon of all the adventure clichés as Burt plays both ends against the middle in an island revolution

Prince of Pirates (Columbia) d.Sidney Salkow: Barbara Rush, John Derek. Lively costumer finds Derek fighting his way through wars between France and Spain

World in His Arms (Universal) d.Raoul Walsh: Ann Blyth, Gregory Peck. Salt-caked, windswept actioner from Rex Beach novel, with schooner skipper Peck pursuing Blyth across the watery wastes off Alaska

Yankee Buccaneer (Universal) d.Frederick de Cordova: Jeff Chandler, Suzan Ball. Tight-lipped naval officer Jeff masquerades as a pirate to defeat a fleet plundering the Caribbean. Yes, it does sound a little familiar

The Snows of Kilimanjaro (Fox) d.Henry King: Susan Hayward, Gregory Peck. Hemingway hero Peck lies wounded on the foothills of an African mountain, searching his past for the meaning of life

Lady in the Iron Mask (Fox) d.Ralph Murphy: Louis Hayward, Steve Brodie, Judd Holdren, Alan Hale Jr. Dumas' musketeers rally round when Princess Anne (Patricia Medina) is kidnapped and her long-lost sister Louise put in her place in fiendish plot engineered by arch-heavy John Sutton

The Adventures of Robinson Crusoe (UA) d.Luis Buñuel: Dan O'Herlihy. Buñuel's version of Defoe's desert island classic is slyly subversive, with excellent performances from O'Herlihy and James Fernandez an Man Friday

Quo Vadis? (MGM) d.Mervyn LeRoy: Patricia Laffan, Peter Ustinov. Lumbering epic of ancient Rome with Ustinov a splendidly dotty Nero and statuesque Laffan his sultry consort, breathing heavily all over Praetorian Guard Robert Taylor

The Thief of Venice (Fox) d.John Brahm: Maria Montez. Lavish Italian-set spectacular in which Montez saves Venice from the clutches of Massimo Serato in her last screen appearance

Othello (Mogador) d.Orson Welles: Orson Welles, Suzanne Cloutier. The usual patchy production values and indifferent supporting cast mar another self-aggrandizing Welles film. Michael MacLiammoir marvellous as Iago

Androcles and the Lion (RKO) d.Chester Erskine: Elsa Lanchester, Alan Young. Uneasy Gabriel Pascal version of Shaw morality play, starring Young as the wimp whose impromptu surgery on a lion makes him a hero. Jean Simmons' Hollywood debut

The Master of Ballantrae (Warner) d.William Keighley: Errol Flynn, Roger Livesey. Freewheeling adaptation of Stevenson yarn, complete with 'happy ending', shows puffy-faced Flynn slowing down fast

The Black Castle (Universal) d.Nathan Juran: Richard Greene, Paula Corday. Amiable Greene braves wicked aristo Stephen McNally's torture chambers and alligator pit in search for missing friends. Boris Karloff, Lon Chaney in supporting cast

Zombies of the Stratosphere (Republic) d.Fred C Brannon: Judd Holdren (c). Star ranger Judd dons flying suit left over from *King of the Rocket Men* (1949), battles robot first seen in *Mysterious Dr Satan* (1940) to foil fiendish Martian plot. Leonard Nimoy appears as a zombie

Red Planet Mars (UA) d.Harry Horner: Peter Graves, Walter Sande, Andrea King. Heroically absurd SF thriller in which scientist Graves receives messages from Mars which turn out to be Word of God. The pathological anti-Communist plot too crazy to summarize

Tropic Zone (Paramount) d.Lewis R Foster: Rhonda Fleming, Argentina Brucetti, Ronald Reagan. Ronnie wades in to save a banana plantation from local desperadoes in South American-set programmer

The Twonky (Oboler) d.Arch Oboler: Hans Conried. Whimsical assault on television by radio producer Oboler in which a robot TV set threatens to take charge of professor Conried's life

The 5,000 Fingers of Dr T (Columbia) d.Roy Rowland: Tommy Rettig, Hans Conried. The fingers being those of 500 boys held prisoner by Conried's sinister music master Dr T in remarkable fantasy devised by Dr Seuss

Bwana Devil (UA) d.Arch Oboler: Robert Stack, Barbara Britton. Best thing about early 3-D safari adventure is the title and the publicity's promise to put 'a lion in your lap'

MELODRAMA

My Cousin Rachel (Fox) d.Henry Koster: Richard Burton, Olivia de Havilland. Daphne du Maurier mystery in which Burton falls for beautiful widow Olivia, even though she may be a poisoner

Flesh and Fury (Universal) d.Joseph Pevney: Tony Curtis, Jan Sterling, Tommy Farrell. Deaf-mute prizefighter Curtis is torn between praying mantis Sterling and nice young journalist Mona Freeman. Guess who gets him

Glory Alley (MGM) d.Raoul Walsh: Ralph Meeker, Leslie Caron. Flashback tale of fighter Meeker who decides to quit the ring before the biggest fight of his life. Features an appearance by Louis Armstrong

Phone Call from a Stranger (Fox) d.Jean Negulesco: Shelley Winters. Gary Merrill is the sole survivor of an air crash visiting the families of the victims in a journey of personal self-discovery

Face to Face (RKO) d.John Brahm, Bretaigne Windust: Michael Pate, James Mason. Back-to-back screen versions of Conrad's 'The Secret Sharer' (pictured here) and Stephen Crane's 'The Bride Comes to Yellow Sky', both handled with some flair

The Story of Three Loves (MGM) d.Vincente Minnelli: James Mason, Moira Shearer. Portmanteau film contains three bittersweet love stories told in flashback by passengers on an ocean liner

The Star (Fox) d.Stuart Heisler: Bette Davis. Washed-up movie goddess Davis has to sell off her belongings before finding a new life with Sterling Hayden in jaundiced view of Tinsel Town owing something to *Sunset Boulevard* (1950)

This Woman is Dangerous (Warner) d.Felix Feist: Joan Crawford, Dennis Morgan. Those glaring eyes burn away beneath the bandages as gangster's moll Joan finds true love with eye surgeon Morgan. Hypnotically awful

Sudden Fear (RKO) d.David Miller: Joan Crawford. Cracking Crawford vehicle as a wealthy playwright discovering plot to kill her hatched by sponging husband Jack Palance and floozie Gloria Grahame

Meet Danny Wilson (Universal) d.Joseph Pevney: Frank Sinatra, Shelley Winters. Singer Sinatra runs foul of the Mob in the bulky form of Raymond Burr, but still finds time to sing a string of standards

The Thief (UA) d.Russell Rouse: Rita Gam, Ray Milland. Milland cast as a heavily compromised nuclear physicist in spy thriller whose gimmick was the virtual absence of dialogue. However, this is no silent masterpiece

Paula (Columbia) d.Rudolph Maté: Tommy Rettig, Loretta Young. Sheer professionalism carries Young through tear-jerking role as hit and run driver who helps her small victim to regain his speech

Ruby Gentry (Fox) d.King Vidor: Jennifer Jones, Charlton Heston. Wrong side of the tracks girl Jones marries wealthy Karl Malden to spite snobbish lover Heston, with tragic results

The Turning Point (Paramount) d.William Dieterle: Edmond O'Brien, William Holden, Alexis Smith. Idealistic lawyer Holden and hardbitten newsman O'Brien join forces to bust open a bastion of organized crime

Force of Arms (Warner) d.Michael Curtiz: William Holden, Nancy Olson. War-scarred GI Holden falls for nurse Olson in update of Hemingway's 'A Farewell to Arms' to World War II. Stubbornly unmemorable

Kansas City Confidential (UA) d.Phil Karlson: John Payne. Hard-hitting actioner, always Karlson's forte, with ex-con Payne fighting to beat an armored car robbery frame-up

The Girl Who Had Everything (MGM) d.Richard Thorpe: William Powell, Elizabeth Taylor. Remake of 1931 Shearer/Gable vehicle *A Free Soul* in which Liz falls in love with the gangster client of her attorney father Powell

Angel Face (RKO) d.Otto Preminger: Robert Mitchum, Jean Simmons. Beautiful psychopath Simmons draws chauffeur Mitchum into a tangled web of paranoia and murder. A victory of style over content

The Devil Makes Three (MGM) d.Andrew Marton: Pier Angeli, Gene Kelly. Gene's brittle straight acting talents are overstretched in role of serviceman returning to postwar Munich and stumbling on a black market gang

Walk East on Beacon (Columbia) d.Alfred Werker: Virginia Gilmore, Karel Stepanek. Documentary-style thriller pitches the FBI against a spy ring with gritty location shooting in Boston

The Marrying Kind (Columbia) d.George Cukor: Aldo Ray, Judy Holliday. A young couple, teetering on the edge of divorce, recall their life together. The principals rise above the rather maudlin script

The Desperate Search (MGM) d.Joseph H Lewis: Keenan Wynn, Jane Greer. Characteristically crisp Lewis offering focuses on the efforts to find two children stranded in the Canadian wilderness after a plane crash

The Bad and the Beautiful (MGM) d.Vincente Minnelli: Kirk Douglas. Dyspeptic picture of Hollywood seen through the career of ambitious producer Douglas and his relations with actress Lana Turner, writer William Powell and director Barry Sullivan

The Clown (MGM) d.Robert Z Leonard: Tim Considine, Red Skelton. Thinly disguised remake of *The Champ* (1931) in which has-been comic Skelton is saved from pressing the self-destruct button by devoted son Considine

The Invitation (MGM) d.Gottfried Reinhardt: Ruth Roman, Dorothy McGuire. Glossy three-handkerchief women's picture in which Louis Calhern bribes Van Johnson to wed dying daughter McGuire. Disappointingly, a 'miracle cure' leads to a happy ending

The Las Vegas Story (RKO) d.Robert Stevenson: Vincent Price, Jane Russell. Flimsy murder yarn set in Nevada's gambling capital is redeemed only by Price and Russell's peculiar acting talents. Victor Mature co-stars

Moulin Rouge (UA) d.John Huston: Jose Ferrer, Jean Claudio. Biopic of the artist Toulouse-Lautrec, stunted by a childhood accident but carving his own niche in the Paris of the Belle Epoque

Stalag 17 (Paramount) d.Billy Wilder: Sig Ruman, William Holden. Wilder coaxes a thoroughly bad-tempered performance from Holden as a cynical POW camp black marketeer suspected of being a stoolie for the Germans

Macao (RKO) d.Josef von Sternberg: Jane Russell, Robert Mitchum. Drolly erotic picaresque thriller set in the gambling dens of the celebrated free port. A few bravura touches of *mise en scène* recall Sternberg's illustrious past

Affair in Trinidad (Columbia) d.Vincent Sherman: Alexander Scourby, Rita Hayworth, Glenn Ford. The Hayworth-Ford chemistry strikes sparks as torch singer and brother-in-law hunting down the murderer of Rita's husband

Jeopardy (MGM) d.John Sturges: Ralph Meeker, Barbara Stanwyck. Neat little programmer about a trapped man and a rising tide gives Stanwyck the chance to run through her repertoire of expressions of anguish and despair

Clash by Night (RKO) d.Fritz Lang: Robert Ryan, Marilyn Monroe. Turgid love triangle between nominal stars Barbara Stanwyck, Paul Douglas and Ryan takes second place to impact made by Monroe in breakthrough role

Because of You (Universal) d.Joseph Pevney: Jeff Chandler, Loretta Young. Unmitigated trash in which former dope-runner's moll Loretta becomes a nurse, marries neurotic pilot Jeff and then takes a powder with gangster boyfriend Alex Nicol

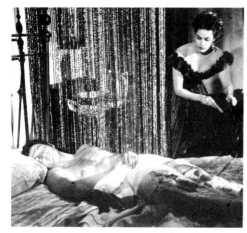

Scarlet Angel (Universal) d.Sidney Salkow: Rock Hudson, Yvonne de Carlo. Adventuress de Carlo swindles her way into New Orleans high society, then finds herself smitten with pangs of conscience

Five Fingers (Fox) d.Joseph L Mankiewicz: James Mason. Feline performance from Mason as 'Cicero', the British embassy valet in Ankara who sold secrets to the Germans in the Second World War

Carrie (Paramount) d.William Wyler: Laurence Olivier, Jennifer Jones. Olivier's obsessive love for actress Jones leads to his progressive disintegration in moving adaptation of Theodore Dreiser's 'Sister Carrie'

Deadline USA (Fox) d.Richard Brooks: Humphrey Bogart. Unfazed by the imminent closure of his newspaper, crusading editor Bogart goes after criminal big fish Martin Gabel

Don't Bother to Knock (Fox) d.Roy Baker: Richard Widmark, Donna Corcoran, Marilyn Monroe. Persuasive performance from Monroe as unbalanced babysitter who displays both suicidal and homicidal tendencies

The Greatest Show on Earth (Paramount) d.Cecil B DeMille: James Stewart, Gloria Grahame. Compulsive hokum with Stewart as the clown who hides his criminal past beneath several layers of make-up, Gloria the elephant girl, Charlton Heston the ring master

COMEDY

Has Anybody Seen My Gal? (Universal) d.Douglas Sirk: Rock Hudson, Piper Laurie. Eccentric millionaire Charles Coburn provides an old flame's family with an unexpected windfall in bouncy outing wittily scripted by Joseph Hoffman

Never Wave at a WAC (RKO) d.Norman Z McLeod: Marie Wilson, Rosalind Russell. Feeble farce plunges socialite Russell into the rigors of army life. Wilson delightful as scatterbrained ex-showgirl

No Time for Flowers (RKO) d.Don Siegel: Ilka Windisch, Viveca Lindfors, Paul Christian. Weak comedy drama, with echoes of *Ninotchka* (1939), in which Czech Party members Lindfors and Christian succumb to the capitalist delights of the West

No Room for the Groom (Universal) d.Douglas Sirk: Tony Curtis, Piper Laurie. GI Tony attempts to find solitude with wife Piper in a house crammed with relatives who are, as yet, unaware that they are married

Sally and Saint Anne (Universal) d.Rudolph Maté: Kathleen Hughes, Palmer Lee, Ann Blyth. Simple-minded comedy in which an Irish family invoke divine help to outwit a conniving town alderman

Son of Paleface (Paramount) d.Frank Tashlin: Bob Hope, Roy Rogers. Bob finds himself in bed with Trigger in jaunty reworking of *Paleface* (1948) formula. Pleasantly ironic performance from Rogers

We're Not Married (Fox) d.Edmund Goulding: Jane Darwell, Ginger Rogers, Fred Allen, Victor Moore. A legal loophole undoes the marriages of several couples. Ginger and Fred are radio stars whose wedded bliss is just a sham

Sky Full of Moon (MGM) d.Norman Foster: Jan Sterling, Carleton Carpenter. Green as grass cowpoke Carpenter romances shady lady Stirling amongst the jangling one-arm bandits of Las Vegas

A Girl in Every Port (RKO) d.Chester Erskine: William Bendix, Marie Wilson, Groucho Marx. Bendix and Groucho attempt to clean up at the races, wind up capturing a pair of saboteurs in dimwitted farce

What Price Glory? (Fox) d.John Ford: James Cagney, Corinne Calvet, Dan Dailey. Self-indulgent comedy-drama remake of the 1926 silent classic in which bumptious Captain Flagg (Cagney) and 'ornery Sergeant Quirt (Dailey) brawl their way up and down the trenches in World War I

Road to Bali (Paramount) d.Hal Walker: Bob Hope, Bing Crosby. Standard 'Road' fare beginning to look a little tired as the boys save Dorothy Lamour from assorted jungle perils. The only series entry in color

Where's Charley? (Fox) d.David Butler: Ray Bolger. Frantic musical version of 'Charley's Aunt' with Bolger in hyperactive form as the unlikeliest of Oxford undergraduates, decked out in drag

Monkey Business (Fox) d.Howard Hawks: Marilyn Monroe, Cary Grant. Staid couple Grant and Ginger Rogers take an accidental swig of Cary's rejuvenation elixir B-4 and reveal the anarchy lurking just below the surface of conventional life. Monroe the secretary described by Ginger as 'half child, but not the half that shows'

Ma and Pa Kettle on Vacation (Universal)
d.Charles Lamont; Marjorie Main, Percy Kilbride.
The hillbilly couple are treated to a trip to Paris,
where they become involved in the spy plot
obligatory in all such jaunts

Confidentially Connie (MGM) d.Edward
Buzzell: Louis Calhern, Janet Leigh. Calhern
blusters away as pregnant Leigh's father-in-law,
alarmed that her hard-up household budget
doesn't run to steak

The Lady Wants Mink (Republic) d.William A
Seiter: Gene Lockhart, Dennis O'Keefe, Hillary
Brooke. Pleasant little programmer in which Ruth
Hussey becomes a mink breeder with her eyes
on a luxury coat

Abbott and Costello Meet Captain Kidd
(Warner) d.Charles Lamont: Charles Laughton,
Lou Costello, Bud Abbott. All aboard for Skull
Island as Laughton wearily levers himself into
extremely low farce, managing to score a victory
on points over the increasingly ragged A and C

Francis Goes to West Point (Universal)
d.Arthur Lubin: Otto Hallett, Les Tremayne,
Donald O'Connor. Donald saves an atom plant
from sabotage and becomes a military cadet
while the mule helps West Point win a crunch
football game in lively series entry

Belles on Their Toes (Fox) d.Henry Levin:
Debra Paget, Hoagy Carmichael, Myrna Loy.
Cheerful sequel to *Cheaper by the Dozen* (1950)
in which Loy gamely takes on the engineering
business of dead husband Clifton Webb

Here Come the Marines (Monogram)
d.William Beaudine: Huntz Hall, Leo Gorcey. The
ageing delinquents lock horns with the military
life in ultra-cheapie directed by the maestro of
the zero budget

Jumping Jacks (Paramount) d.Norman Taurog:
Mona Freeman, Jerry Lewis. Dean and Jerry play
a pair of song and dance men who become
paratroopers with the usual chaotic results. Nice
mime sequence in which Lewis tries to pack a
parachute

Dreamboat (Fox) d.Claude Binyon: Clifton
Webb, Ginger Rogers. Long-forgotten silent star
Ginger cashes in on the TV success of her old
films to the alarm of former co-star Webb, now a
respected academic. Great fun

The Four Poster (Columbia) d.Irving Reis: Rex
Harrison, Lilli Palmer. Principals pull out all the
stops in adaptation of Jan de Hartog play
following the progress of a marriage. Later
became the musical 'I Do! I Do!'

MUSICALS

Lili (MGM) d.Charles Walters: Leslie Caron. Fetching carnival waif Caron quickens love in self-pitying puppeteer Mel Ferrer. Contains hit song 'Hi-Lili, Hi-lo'

Stars and Stripes Forever (Fox) d.Henry Koster: Clifton Webb, Robert Wagner, Ruth Hussey. Listless celebration of the life of march wizard John Philip Sousa, impersonated by a haughtily bewhiskered Webb with Hussey as his level-headed wife

Skirts Ahoy! (MGM) d.Sidney Lanfield: Joan Evans, Esther Williams, Vivian Blaine. Our three heroines join the Waves, sing 'What Good is a Guy Without a Gal?' and, of course, Esther swims. Debbie Reynolds, Bobby Van guest as themselves

Rainbow Round My Shoulder (Columbia) d.Richard Quine: Charlotte Austin, Arthur Franz. Charlotte Austin nurses dreams of movie stardom in spite of opposition from guardian Ida Moore. Solid programmer also features Frankie Laine, Billy Daniels

Singin' in the Rain (MGM) d.Gene Kelly, Stanley Donen: Gene Kelly. Joyous satire on the early days of talkies. Among many delights are Donald O'Connor's 'Make 'Em Laugh' routine, Kelly and Charisse in 'The Broadway Ballet' and Jean Hagen's silent star undone by her Bronx accent

Meet Me at the Fair (Universal) d.Douglas Sirk: Dan Dailey, Diana Lynn, Chet Allen. Easygoing huckster Dailey befriends runaway orphan Allen and saves him from the clutches of DA Hugh O'Brian in relaxed period piece

She's Working Her Way Through College (Paramount) d.Norman Taurog: Virginia Mayo, Ronald Reagan. Musical remake of *The Male Animal* (1942) with Mayo hogging the action as a burlesque queen with academic aspirations

The Stars Are Singing (Paramount) d.Norman Taurog: Bob Williams, Tom Morton, Rosemary Clooney, Anna Maria Alberghetti. Clooney's debut, trying to promote the singing career of illegal immigrant Alberghetti. Songs include her smash hit 'Come-On-A-My-House'

Lovely to Look At (MGM) d.Mervyn LeRoy: Ann Miller, Red Skelton. Remake of *Roberta* (1935) with Skelton playing an American comic who inherits a share in a bankrupt Paris fashion salon run by Kathryn Grayson and Marge Champion

Everything I Have Is Yours (MGM) d.Robert Z
Leonard: Marge and Gower Champion. Mild
musical domestic comedy only comes alive when
Marge and Gower shut up and start dancing

Hans Christian Andersen (RKO) d.Charles
Vidor: Danny Kaye. Goldwyn box-office smash
with Kaye in restrained mood as the tale-spinning
cobbler yearning for ballerina Jeanmaire.
Delightful Frank Loesser score includes
'Thumbelina' and 'The Ugly Duckling'

Just For You (Paramount) d.Elliott Nugent: Bing
Crosby. Broadway producer Bing enlists the help
of fiancée Jane Wyman in attempt to relate to his
frightful children, with complicated results.
Among the numbers, 'Zing a Little Song' and 'On
the 10.10 from Ten-Ten-Tennessee'

Bloodhounds of Broadway(Fox) d.Harmon
Jones: Mitzi Gaynor, Scott Brady, Wally Vernon.
Energetic Damon Runyan based tale of bent New
York bookie Brady falling for hoofin' hayseed
Gaynor

Million Dollar Mermaid (MGM) d.Mervyn
LeRoy: Esther Williams. Esther takes the titles role
in biopic of Annette Kellerman, Australian aqua
star and inventor of the 'one piece' bathing
costume. Two baroque water ballets from Busby
Berkeley

With a Song in My Heart (Fox) d.Walter Lang:
Susan Hayward. Susan socks it to 'em in
tearjerking biopic of singer Jane Froman, fighting
back after a crippling air accident. Songs dubbed
by Froman

The Merry Widow (MGM) d.Curtis Bernhardt:
Fernando Lamas, Lana Turner. Over-upholstered
Ruritanian romance lacks the sparkle of
Lubitsch's 1934 version. Turner dubbed by Trudy
Erwin

I Dream of Jeannie (Republic) d.Allan Dwan:
Muriel Lawrence, Lynn Bari, Eileen Christy. Dull
ramble through the life of Stephen Foster (Bill
Shirley) enlivened by Ray Middleton as Minstrel
Man E P Christy

About Face (Warner) d.Roy Del Ruth: Dick
Wesson, Eddie Bracken, Gordon MacRae.
Retread of the studio's army comedy *Brother Rat*
(1938) features early appearance by Joel Gray

Down Among the Sheltering Palms (Fox) d.Edmund Goulding: William Lundigan, Gloria de Haven, Lyle Talbot. Straitlaced soldier Lundigan is chased all over a Pacific atoll by journalist de Haven, Jane Greer and Mitzi Gaynor. Gloria sings 'All of Me'

The Girl Next Door (Fox) d.Richard Sale: June Haver, Dan Dailey. Broadway star Haver falls for cartoonist neighbor Dailey, providing excuse for charming UPA animated sequence

The Desert Song (Warner) d.H Bruce Humberstone: Kathryn Grayson, Gordon MacRae. Ramshackle Jazz Age hit falls apart in everybody's hands as Riff chieftain MacRae saves the Foreign Legion from evil sheik Raymond Massey, wins hand of general's daughter Grayson

WESTERNS

Ride the Man Down (Republic) d.Joseph Kane: Ella Raines, Rod Cameron. Talky Western in which ranch foreman Cameron tries to save Raines' cattle empire from the clutches of Forrest Tucker and Brian Donlevy after the death of her father

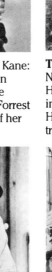

The Outcasts of Poker Flat (Fox) d.Joseph M Newman: Dale Robertson, Anne Baxter, Miriam Hopkins. Third screen version of Bret Harte tale in which snowbound characters – saloon singer Hopkins, gambler Robertson, whore Baxter – trawl through their pasts

Springfield Rifle (Warner) d.André de Toth: Paul Kelly, Gary Cooper, Guinn 'Big Boy' Williams. Cooper is a Union officer deliberately cashiered to infiltrate a gang of Confederates rustling horses during the Civil War

High Noon (UA) d.Fred Zinnemann: Lon Chaney, Gary Cooper. Much-lauded movie now seems a little labored, although writer Foreman's device of making screen time correspond with real time – as sheriff Cooper waits for the four gunmen – still generates tension

Montana Belle (RKO) d.Allan Dwan: Forrest Tucker, Scott Brady, Jane Russell. Big Jane overwhelms the masculine world of the Western with spirited performance as Belle Starr. Veteran director Dwan nudges this engaging movie on in lively style

The Naked Spur (MGM) d.Anthony Mann: James Stewart, Janet Leigh. Mann extracts a feverish performance from Stewart as the self-styled bounty hunter tracking Robert Ryan through the majestic scenery of the Rockies

Viva Zapata! (Fox) d.Elia Kazan: Marlon Brando. Kazan achieves vivid recreation of Mexican revolution but the shadow of McCarthyism hangs heavy over Brando's portrayal of Zapata as a 'man of individual conscience' rather than the socialist revolutionary penciled into the original script

Ride Vacquero! (MGM) d.John Farrow: Robert Taylor, Howard Keel, Anthony Quinn. Exuberantly demented performance from Quinn as the ruthless bandido determined to hang on to his land. Taylor the half-brother with divided loyalties

Valley of Fire (Columbia) d.John English: Gene Autry (r). Poker-faced Gene is the mayor of Quartz Creek, riding to the rescue of a wagon train of mail-order brides. Cf *Westward the Women* (1951)

Untamed Frontier (Universal) d.Hugo Fregonese: Suzan Ball, Scott Brady. Standard range war fare lifted by excellent cast, including Joseph Cotten, Shelley Winters and silent star Antonio Moreno

The Treasure of Lost Canyon (Universal) d.Ted Tetzlaff: Henry Hull, Tommy Ivo, William Powell. Robert Louis Stevenson story in which doctor Powell befriends an orphan and goes looking for treasure in uneasy partnership with Hull

The Big Sky (Winchester) d.Howard Hawks: Elizabeth Threatt, Kirk Douglas, Dewey Martin. Underrated Hawks film in which a trappers' trek up the Missouri is counterpointed by the relationship between youngster Martin and his happy-go-lucky idol Douglas

The Savage (Paramount) d.George Marshall: Charlton Heston, Joan Taylor. Heston is the orphan brought up by the Sioux who experiences double rejection by the white man and the tribe who raised him

Rancho Notorious (RKO) d.Fritz Lang: Marlene Dietrich, Arthur Kennedy. Expressionist tale of 'hate, murder and revenge' dominated by Dietrich as the ageing but still highly desirable saloon bar queen Altar Keane

The Raiders (Universal) d.Lesley Selander: Viveca Lindfors, Hugh O'Brian. Richard Conte leads a band of miners and homesteaders against grasping landgrabber Morris Ankrum. Lindfors wildy miscast as a Mexican spitfire

Denver and Rio Grande (Paramount) d. Byron Haskin: J Carrol Naish, Laura Elliot, Edmond O'Brien, Dean Jagger. Brisk tale of railroad race to cross the Rockies contains spectacular crash with real rolling stock

The Iron Mistress (Warner) d.Gordon Douglas: Alan Ladd. Workmanlike biopic of Jim Bowie, inventor of the wickedly double-edged knife, with Ladd impassive as ever in the title role

The Half-Breed (RKO) d.Stuart Gilmore: Jack Buetel, Robert Young, Janis Carter. Evil Reed Hadley is determined to drive the Indians off gold-bearing land in plodding programmer rendered tolerable by Ms Carter's more spectacular outfits

Horizons West (Universal) d.Budd Boetticher: Robert Ryan. Rock Hudson and Ryan are half-brothers whose choice of different paths after the Civil War brings them into conflict

Way of a Gaucho (Fox) d.Jacques Tourneur: Rory Calhoun. Rory conducts a one-man war against the coming of 'civilization' in quirky, visually inventive 'Western' set on the Argentine pampas

The Duel at Silver Creek (Universal) d.Don Siegel: Susan Cabot, Audie Murphy. Pacy if implausible actioner featuring Faith Domergue and Gerald Mohr as claimjumpers and Murphy as the fast gun on their trail

The Lawless Breed (Universal) d.Raoul Walsh: Dick Wessel, Julia Adams, Rock Hudson. Elegantly plotted, flashback-framed life of the legendary outlaw John Wesley Hardin (Hudson), yearning for domesticity but driven beyond the law

Battle at Apache Pass (Universal) d.George Sherman: Jay Silverheels, Susan Cabot, Jeff Chandler. Jeff dons the mantle of Cochise again, helping the US Cavalry defeat Silverheels' Geronimo and bring a crooked Indian agent to book

ROMANCE

Love is Better than Ever (MGM) d.Stanley Donen: Larry Parks, Elizabeth Taylor, Gene Kelly. Talent scout Parks spots the divine Liz and then decides to marry her. Can you blame him?

The Quiet Man (Republic) d.John Ford: Maureen O'Hara, Victor McLaglen, John Wayne, Barry Fitzgerald. Sentimental compendium of Irish clichés as Irish-American boxer Wayne returns to the land of his fathers to romance feisty O'Hara and take on McLaglen in a epic cross-country brawl

My Wife's Best Friend (Fox) d.Richard Sale: Anne Baxter, Macdonald Carey. Marital comedy in which Carey's admission of mild infidelity stirs Baxter's fertile imagination

Pat and Mike (MGM) d.George Cukor: Aldo Ray, Katharine Hepburn. Kate is the fearsomely talented athlete, Spencer Tracy her hardboiled manager, Aldo Ray a charmingly dense boxer in delightful Ruth Gordon, Garson Kanin comedy

My Pal Gus (Fox) d.Robert Parrish: Joanne Dru, Richard Widmark. Tycoon Widmark's romance with teacher Dru is interrupted by the return of his viperish wife Audrey Totter, claiming custody of their son

My Man and I (MGM) d.William Wellman: Ricardo Montalban, Shelley Winters. Montalban is the man, a kindly Mexican migrant worker, and Winters is I, a lady with a drink problem

Washington Story (MGM) d.Robert Pirosh: Patricia Neal, Van Johnson. Newshound Neal arrives to dig the dirt on Congressman Johnson but, as is ever the way in Hollywood, falls in love with the boring boob

AMERICANA

Carbine Williams (MGM) d.Richard Thorpe: James Stewart, Wendell Corey. Stewart well cast as the inventor of the celebrated gun in straightforward account of his brushes with the law and homespun family life

The Girl in White (MGM) d.John Sturges: James Arness, June Allyson. June soldiers her way through thankless role as the first woman doctor in New York. Arness' tattoo proves more interesting than the movie

Here Come the Nelsons (Universal) d.Frederick de Cordova: Gale Gordon, Lillian Bronson, Ozzie Nelson. America's first TV Family hit the big screen in mild comedy of misunderstandings with Rock Hudson and Piper Laurie providing a dash of romance

Come Back Little Sheba (Paramount) d.Daniel Mann: Richard Jaeckel, Shirley Booth, Terry Moore. Booth repeats her stage *tour de force* in the William Inge play, enlisting our sympathy for the ugly, stupid, slovenly Lola, lumbered with drunken husband Burt Lancaster

The Lusty Men (RKO) d.Nicholas Ray: Robert Mitchum, Susan Hayward. Touching performance from Hayward as the wife of rodeo rider Arthur Kennedy, battling to preserve a semblance of home life. Mitchum excellent as Kennedy's grizzled mentor

The Winning Team (Warner) d.Lewis Seiler: Doris Day, Eve Miller. Serviceable biopic of the baseball star Grover Cleveland Alexander (Ronald Reagan) who secretly suffers from double vision and epilepsy. Day the worried wife convinced he's an alcoholic

The President's Lady (Fox) d.Jean Negulesco: Charlton Heston, Susan Hayward. Heston looks suitably heroic as the future President Andrew Jackson while Hayward emotes furiously as his wife Rachel in account of their stormy marriage which makes fairly free with the facts

My Son John (Paramount) d.Leo McCarey: Robert Walker, Helen Hayes. Dean Jagger and his wife Hayes harbor suspicions that son Walker is a Communist in fascinating period piece which leaves a rancid taste in the mouth. Walker died before filming finished and a number of shots are spliced in from *Strangers on a Train* (1950)

O Henry's Full House (Fox) d.Henry Koster, Henry Hathaway, Jean Negulesco, Howard Hawks, Henry King: Marilyn Monroe, Charles Laughton. Five short stories from the master of the twist in the tale. This one is 'The Cop and the Anthem'

The Story of Will Rogers (Warner) d.Michael Curtiz: Eddie Cantor, Will Rogers Jr. Smoothly handled tribute to the rodeo star from Oolagah, Indian Territory, who became the definitive American folk hero, conquering the movies and journalism in the process

The Lion and the Horse (Warner) d.Louis King: Sherry Jackson, Steve Cochran. Efficient little B, from a master of the tight budget, focusing on the great outdoors and a gallant horse's battle with a mountain lion. Aimed at children and the first film released in WarnerColor

BRITISH AND FOREIGN

Meet Me Tonight (Rank) d.Anthony Pelissier: Kay Walsh, Ted Ray. Three Noel Coward one-act plays transferred to the screen. Walsh and Ray are the music hall has-beens 'The Red Hot Peppers'

Miss Robin Hood (Group 3) d.John Guillermin: Margaret Rutherford, Richard Hearne. Modest Ealing-influenced comedy in which dotty Rutherford and meek writer Hearne career after a stolen whisky formula

Folly to be Wise (London) d.Frank Launder: Peter Martyn, Janet Brown, Alastair Sim, Martita Hunt. Sim recreates stage role as the hapless army chaplain whose camp concert brains trust blows up in his lugubrious face

The Penny Princess (Rank) d.Val Guest: Reginald Beckwith, Dirk Bogarde, Yolande Donlan. American shopgirl Donlan inherits the tiny European state of Lampidorra, whose national dish is an alcoholic cheese. One suspects Bogarde would rather forget this one

Derby Day (British Lion) d.Herbert Wilcox: Michael Wilding, Anna Neagle. Stilted portmanteau film involving a disparate bunch of characters attending Britain's most famous horse race

Where No Vultures Fly (Ealing) d.Harry Watt: Dinah Sheridan, Anthony Steel. Sunnily patronizing account of a young couple's struggles to establish a a game reserve in Kenya. Proved an immense box-office hit

The Importance of Being Earnest (Rank) d.Anthony Asquith: Margaret Rutherford, Michael Redgrave. Superb cast glide through immaculate adaptation of Oscar Wilde's comedy of manners, with Edith Evans imperiously in command as Lady Bracknell

Top Secret (ABPC) d.Mario Zampi: Oscar Homolka, George Cole. Broad farce, lampooning Cold War paranoia, in which half-witted sanitary engineer Cole is kidnapped by the KGB who think he is a top nuclear scientist

Mandy (Ealing) d.Alexander Mackendrick: Mandy Miller, Phyllis Calvert, Jack Hawkins. Intensely moving account of a deaf child's fight to communicate. A key film in the later Ealing cannon

The Card (Rank) d.Ronald Neame: Alec Guinness, Glynis Johns. Guinness turns in delightful performance as Arnold Bennett's provincial hero Denry Machin, floating to fame and fortune on a cloud of charm

The Planter's Wife (Rank) d.Ken Annakin: Ram Gopal, Claudette Colbert, Jack Hawkins. Hangdog rubber planter Jack's marriage to Claudette is heading for the rocks while outside the compound the natives are getting distinctly restless

Pool of London (Ealing) d.Basil Dearden: Earl Cameron, Bonar Colleano. Accomplished film, full of documentary-style location shooting, follows seamen Cameron, Colleano on an eventful weekend shore leave

24 Hours of a Woman's Life (ABPC) d.Victor Saville: Merle Oberon, Leo Genn. Dreary film version of Stefan Zweig novel in which Oberon drifts into an affair with doomed gambler Richard Todd. Very lush, very slow

The Long Memory (Rank) Robert Hamer: Eva Bergh, John Mills. Glum thriller more likely to induce a permanent state of amnesia as ex-con Mills goes after the men who framed him for murder

The Sound Barrier (London) d.David Lean: Ralph Richardson, Ann Todd, Nigel Patrick. A war film in disguise in which designer Richardson's obsessive quest for a supersonic aircraft blights everything around him

The Gentle Gunman (Ealing) d.Basil Dearden: Robert Beatty, Dirk Bogarde, John Mills. Stiff adaptation of stage drama about the IRA with Bogarde and Mills extremely ill at ease as Irish brothers

Cosh Boy (Romulus) d. Lewis Gilbert: James Kenney, Joan Collins. Nasty piece of work Kenney gets Joan pregnant in deliriously bad exposé of teenage 'razor gangs' tearing the fabric of society apart

Trent's Last Case (British Lion) d.Herbert Wilcox: Orson Welles, John McCallum. Reporter turned detective Michael Wilding delves into the mysterious death of financier Welles in verbose remake of thriller filmed in 1929 by Howard Hawks

The Man Who Watched Trains Go By (Eros) d.Harold French: Herbert Lom, Marius Goring, Claude Rains. Gloomy *film noir* in which Rains' discovery of fraud by his boss Lom leads to murder and mental disintegration

I Believe in You (Ealing) d.Basil Dearden: Laurence Harvey, Joan Collins. Joan provides a streak of frank sexual allure, rare in British cinema of the period, in portmanteau film built around the clients of probation officer Cecil Parker

Angels One Five (ABPC) d.George More O'Ferral: John Gregson, Jack Hawkins. Gregson is the endearingly awkward young Hurricane pilot whose painful Battle of Britain apprenticeship and budding romance are cut short in a dogfight over southern England

Time Bomb (MGM) d.Ted Tetzlaff: Glenn Ford. Glenn is the unhappily married engineer roped in to defuse a bomb hidden on a trainload of naval mines by saboteur Victor Maddern

The Ringer (London) d.Guy Hamilton: William Hartnell, Herbert Lom. Sprightly Edgar Wallace story in which Donald Wolfit hams it up in the title role, playing the master of disguise ensuring that crooked lawyer Lom gets his just desserts

Stolen Face (Hammer) d.Terence Fisher: Lizabeth Scott, Paul Henreid. Early excursion into horror by Fisher with po-faced Henreid cast as a mad scientist remodeling the face of a psychopath to resemble ex-girlfriend Scott

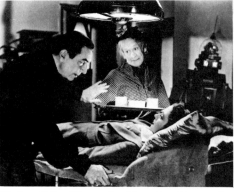

Mother Riley Meets the Vampire (Renown) d.John Gilling: Bela Lugosi, Arthur Lucan. Lesson No. 1 in the perils of typecasting. On his last legs, Bela totters through grisly comedy with music hall drag star Lucan. Very painful viewing

Decameron Nights (Film Locations) d.Hugo Fregonese: Joan Fontaine. Robust collection of Boccacio tales linked by suave Louis Jourdan as the writer, romancing the lovely Fontaine

The Pickwick Papers (Renown) d.Noel Langley: Noel Purcell, James Hayter, Harry Fowler. Zesty screen version of Dickens' tales of the Pickwick Club, crammed with juicy performances all of which hover on the right side of caricature. Nigel Patrick surprisingly good as Mr Jingle

Ikiru (Japan) d.Akira Kurosawa: Takashi Shimura. Full-fledged masterpiece in which Shimura gives breathtaking performance as an elderly civil servant finding belated fulfilment in his life before succumbing to cancer

Imbarco a Mezzanotte (Italy) d.Andrea Forzano: Paul Muni. Muni anguished as a down and out drawn into murder. Forzano was in fact the pseudonym for Hollywood exile Joseph Losey

Stazione Termini (Italy) d.Vittorio de Sica: Jennifer Jones, Montgomery Clift. Originally slated for Ingrid Bergman and Gérard Philipe, the movie focuses on a protracted leavetaking, at a Rome railroad station, between married woman Jones and lover Clift

Le Casque d'Or (France) d.Jacques Becker: Serge Reggiani, Simone Signoret. Serge and Simone are underworld lovers clutching at one last idyllic fling in the country. Title refers to Signoret's hairstyle in the movie

1953

It was the year of wide screens and 3-D as Hollywood launched an all-out offensive against television. The first film in CinemaScope, with its aspect ratio of 2.55:1, was Fox's *The Robe*, a biblical epic based on Lloyd C Douglas' novel about the aftermath of the Crucifixion. The film was shot by Fox's leading cameraman Leon Shamroy in both CinemaScope and a standard version, so that it could be given big-screen presentations and also released in conventional 16mm prints. Throughout filming Shamroy struggled with a lens which was not yet perfected and when the film was released it was clear that its journeyman director Henry Koster had not fully exploited the potential offered by CinemaScope's aspect ratio. Nevertheless, Fox's gamble with the process, in which they held the rights, paid off and *The Robe* was a huge hit at the box-office, prompting a sequel, *Demetrius and the Gladiators* (1954). The major studios also adopted 3-D, used to spectacular effect by André de Toth in Warner's *House of Wax*, a slice of artful Grand Guignol starring Vincent Price. Hard on its heels followed about 20 3-D features. The process proved a useful means of enhancing spacious settings – the deserts in *Hondo* and *Inferno* and the valley over which a cable car is suspended in the climax of *Second Chance*. But directors usually preferred to employ 3-D merely as a gimmick with missiles of every description erupting from the screen at the audience.

Contemporary photographs of audiences sitting in the dark wearing their special polaroid spectacles have a curiously science fiction quality, and two classics of the genre were released in 1953. Jack Arnold's *It Came from Outer Space*, another 3-D feature, was a small triumph of mood over budget; and George Pal's lavish updating of H G Wells' *The War of the Worlds* was full of striking imagery as sleek, predatory Martian war machines glided over the devastated California landscape like monstrous Manta rays.

Other outstanding films of the year included Joseph L Mankiewicz's stylish *Julius Caesar*; Sam Fuller's Cold War melodrama *Pickup on South Street*; *The Hitch Hiker*, a pulsating B-movie directed by Ida Lupino; and Fritz Lang's *The Big Heat*, in which idealistic cop Glenn Ford's campaign against svelte mobster Alexander Scourby turns into a personal vendetta after his wife is murdered with a car bomb. Ford's performance is one of the most blazingly intense portrayals of righteous vengeance in cinema and the perfect expression of his screen persona. Vincente Minnelli's *The Band Wagon* was one of the most glitteringly sophisticated musicals of the decade, marking a triumphant return to the screen by British star Jack Buchanan after an absence of 13 years. Alan Ladd, discarded by Paramount, suddenly found himself back in the big league in the title role of George Stevens' *Shane*, in which the

director's meticulously composed frames were hacked and elongated so that the film could open at the Radio City Music Hall as a wide-screen attraction.

The Motion Picture Academy voted Fred Zinnemann's *From Here to Eternity* the year's Best Picture and Zinnemann the Best Director. William Holden won the Best Actor Oscar for the splendidly bad-tempered performance which Billy Wilder coaxed from him in *Stalag 17*. Audrey Hepburn's novel gamine charms secured a rather generous Best Actress Award for her American debut in William Wyler's *Roman Holiday*, playing an incognito princess romancing newsman Gregory Peck. Best Supporting Actor and Actress were Frank Sinatra and Donna Reed for *From Here to Eternity*. Sinatra, on the brink of bankruptcy and a retirement forced by a hemorrhage of blood vessels in his vocal apparatus, had accepted the part of Private Maggio for a paltry $8,000 and in the process saved his career. All resemblance to *The Godfather*'s Johnny Fontaine is, of course, entirely coincidental. Laslo Benedek's *The Wild One*, essentially an old-fashioned 'problem' picture with leather trimmings, created a stir and was immediately banned in Britain by the Board of Film Censors (absurdly, it did not receive a certificate until 1967). In Howard Hawks' *Gentlemen Prefer Blondes* Marilyn Monroe told diamond magnate Charles Coburn, 'It's a terrible thing to be lonely, especially when you're in a crowd,' which of course was always Marilyn's problem.

Notable debuts included those by Jack Lemmon in *It Should Happen to You*; Julie Harris, repeating her stage success in *The Member of the Wedding*; and Anthony Perkins as Jean Simmons' shy boyfriend in *The Actress*. Other new faces were Edmund Purdom, Harry Belafonte and the spectacularly constructed Swedish beauty queen Anita Ekberg.

Death took William Farnum, silent star of the original version of *The Spoilers* (1914); and Lewis Stone, veteran character actor and MGM's Judge Hardy, who collapsed with a fatal heart attack after chasing a gang of youths who were throwing rocks at his Beverly Hills home.

RKO continued to generate more lawsuits than movies. Howard Hughes regained control at the beginning of the year, as chairman of the board and managing director of production, but the studio remained the sick man of Hollywood.

In Britain Norman Wisdom made his debut in *Trouble in Store*, the first of a string of immensely profitable slapstick comedies. Ealing studios agonized long and hard over whether to let Jack Hawkins cry in *The Cruel Sea*. Later Hawkins recalled that the scene in which his corvette captain broke down was played in three ways on three successive days before the decision was taken to let the tears flow.

ACTION

Hell Below Zero (Columbia) d.Mark Robson: Alan Ladd, Jill Bennett. Filleted version of a Hammond Innes best-seller despatches Ladd on an Antarctic whale hunt. Some high-voltage villainy from Stanley Baker makes the long voyage bearable

The Glory Brigade (Fox) d.Robert D Webb: Lee Marvin, Victor Mature, Richard Egan. Korean War drama casts Big Vic as a Greek-American volunteering to help a Greek regiment across a river and into enemy territory

Thunder Bay (Universal) d.Anthony Mann: Joanne Dru, James Stewart. Dan Duryea and Stewart are a pair of ex-GIs drilling for black gold off the storm-lashed Louisiana coast. Gilbert Roland sails over the horizon as shrimp boat captain.

Take the High Ground (MGM) d.Richard Brooks: Richard Widmark. Widmark snarls away in his own inimitable fashion as a tough training sergeant putting recruits through hell at Fort Bliss

Sailor of the King (Fox) d.Roy Boulting: Jeffrey Hunter. Mediterranean-set World War II actioner, based on a C S Forrester story, in which lone sailor Hunter takes on the might of the Kriegsmarine and prevails

Arena (MGM) d.Richard Fleischer: Barbara Lawrence, Gig Young, Robert Horton. Story of rodeo star Young's rocky marriage takes second place to lively action sequences filmed on location in Arizona and originally in 3-D

Island in the Sky (Warner) d.William Wellman: James Lydon, Hal Baylor, John Wayne. Wayne is the civilian pilot of an Army Transport Command 'plane which crash lands in Labrador. Marred by some mushy musing on the eternal verities of man and the elements

The Steel Lady (UA) d.E A Dupont: Tab Hunter, John Dehner, Rod Cameron, Richard Erdman. Inventive programmer, in which our four heroes are stranded in the desert and stumble across an abandoned World War II tank

Destination Gobi (Fox) d.Robert Wise: Richard Widmark. Offbeat war adventure, based on fact, in which Chief Petty Officer Widmark leads a group of Navy weathermen across the Mongolian desert and then on to Okinawa in a Chinese junk

City Beneath the Sea (Universal) d.Budd Boetticher: Anthony Quinn, Suzan Ball, Robert Ryan. Quinn and Ryan are a pair of dare-devil deep-sea divers hunting for gold bullion in the Caribbean and smashing up every bar in sight

Blowing Wild (Warner) d.Hugo Fregonese: Anthony Quinn, Barbara Stanwyck, Gary Cooper. Underrated tale of oil wildcatters down Mexico way. Stanwyck heaves with the middle-aged hots for a reluctant Cooper

The Desert Rats (Fox) d.Robert Wise: Richard Burton. James Mason turns up briefly as Rommel in tribute to the 8th Army's defence of Tobruk in which true Brit Burton wins the respect of the Australians under his command

Inferno (Fox) d.Roy Baker: Henry Hull, Robert Ryan. The studio's first in 3-D leaves millionaire playboy Ryan deliberately stranded in the desert by heartless wife Rhonda Fleming and business associate William Lundigan. He survives. Watch out, Rhonda!

Sea of Lost Ships (Republic) d.Joseph Kane: Wanda Hendrix, John Derek. Or Sea of Lost Scripts as rival coastguards Derek and Richard Jaeckel battle it out for Wanda

ADVENTURE AND FANTASY

Yankee Pasha (Universal) d.Joseph Pevney: Mamie Van Doren, Rhonda Fleming. The luscious Rhonda is kidnapped by Barbary pirates and sold into a Moroccan harem, enlivened by the busty presence of slave girl Mamie. Jeff Chandler comes to the rescue. For lovers of camp everywhere

Fair Wind to Java (Republic) d.Joseph Kane: Fred MacMurray, Vera Ralston. South Seas treasure hunt ends in time-honored volcanic climax. Ralston acquits herself surprisingly well as the native love interest

White Witch Doctor (Fox) d.Henry Hathaway: Robert Mitchum, Susan Hayward. No-nonsense Hayward rams modern medicine down the throats of understandably sceptical African tribesmen while Mitchum, Walter Slezak hunt jungle treasure

The Naked Jungle (Paramount) d.Byron Haskin: Charlton Heston, Eleanor Parker. Minor action classic in which plantation owner Heston and mail-order bride Parker battle a well-organized army of termites. Some laconic dialogue and a great deal of fuzzy process work

Botany Bay (Paramount) d.John Farrow: Alan Ladd. Windswept Ladd is Australia-bound on convict ship captained by silkily villainous James Mason. Patricia Medina provides the love interest in an eventful voyage

Back to God's Country (Universal) d.Joseph Pevney: Marcia Henderson, Rock Hudson. Game Henderson, injured sea captain husband Rock and a Great Dane career over the snowbound Canadian landscape pursued by vengeful Steve Cochran in creaking actioner first filmed in 1919

East of Sumatra (Universal) d.Budd Boetticher: Anthony Quinn, Jeff Chandler. Tin miner Jeff finds problems aplenty on Pacific isle ruled by the truculent Quinn. No prizes for guessing the winner of this off-beat encounter

Killer Ape (Columbia) d.Spencer Gordon Bennet: Carol Thurston. The lovely Thurston is disturbed by a large, er, thing in yet another sublimely surreal Jungle Jim offering crammed with random chunks of stock footage

The Beggar's Opera (Warner) d.Herbert Wilcox: Laurence Olivier. Larry sings pleasantly and swashbuckles energetically as John Gay's amorous highwayman Macheath but for all that this is not one of his happier efforts

All the Brothers Were Valiant (MGM) d.Richard Thorpe: Lewis Stone, Robert Taylor. Taylor and Stewart Granger are about as animated as a pair of salt-caked smokestacks as they play a pair of implausible whalers slugging it out on the storm-lashed expanses of the studio tank. Thar she blows!

King of the Khyber Rifles (Fox) d.Henry King: Guy Rolfe, Tyrone Power. Half-caste Power finds it heavy going in the famous regiment, particularly when he falls for CO Michael Rennie's daughter. Rolfe is the boyhood friend turned enemy in what is basically a remake of John Ford's *The Black Watch* (1929)

Elephant Walk (Paramount) d.William Dieterle: Abraham Sofaer, Elizabeth Taylor. The inevitable elephant stampede comes not a moment too soon in windy melodrama set on a Ceylon tea plantation. Taylor replaced Vivien Leigh, who can be seen in some of the long shots

Appointment in Honduras (RKO) d.Jacques Tourneur: Zachary Scott, Ann Sheridan. Usual mixed bunch of characters crashing around in the alligator-infested jungle, all for no clearly discernible reason

Treasure of the Golden Condor (Fox)
d.Delmer Daves: Leo G Carroll, Cornel Wilde.
Reworking of *Son of Fury* (1942) in which
dastardly George Macready cheats Wilde out of
his birthright, forcing him to join Finlay Currie in
a Guatemalan treasure hunt

Peter Pan (Disney) d.Hamilton Luske, Clyde
Geronimi, Wilfred Jackson. Disney version of
J M Barrie's fairy tale is an object lesson in the
animator's art, although it inevitably dispenses
with some of the more sinister Freudian
undertones of the original

Diamond Queen (Columbia) d.John Brahm:
Arlene Dahl, Sheldon Leonard. Part of the 1953-
Dahl mini-festival features the divine Arlene in
the title role while Fernando Lamas and Gilbert
Roland fight over her favors

The Neanderthal Man (UA) d.E A Dupont:
Robert Shayne. Mad scientist Shayne's miracle
serum has the usual unexpected side-effects in
rock-bottom variation on the Jekyll and Hyde
theme helmed by a half-forgotten master of silent
cinema

Sangaree (Paramount) d.Edward Ludwig:
Arlene Dahl, Fernando Lamas. Paramount
entered the 3-D stakes with this glossy version of
a Frank Slaughter yarn, in which a slave inherits
a plantation owner's fortune. Dahl looks ravishing
in Technicolor

Knights of the Round Table (MGM) d.Richard
Thorpe: Mel Ferrer, Robert Taylor. The studio's
first wide-screen movie resulted in a visually
sumptuous but otherwise pedestrian romance
set in the court of King Arthur. Shot on location
in England

House of Wax (Warner) d.André de Toth: Phyllis
Kirk. Moody 3-D remake of *Mystery of the Wax
Museum* (1933) established Vincent Price as the
leading horror star of the 1950s

Tarzan and the She Devil (RKO) d.Kurt
Neumann: Joyce MacKenzie, Lex Barker. Slinky
Monique van Vooren is the wicked lady of the
title, trying to get her talons on an ivory horde but
winding up as a doormat for a herd of stampeding
elephants

Fort Ti (Columbia) d.William Castle: Ben Astar,
Joan Vohs, George Montgomery. Tedious 3-D
programmer set during the Indian War of the
1760s and full of hurtling gimmickry

The Sword and the Rose (RKO) d.Ken Annakin:
Richard Todd, Glynis Johns. Dashing if
diminutive Todd is captain of the palace guard,
wooing Princess Mary Tudor (Johns) in opulent-
looking swashbuckler which never really catches
fire. James Robertson Justice enjoys himself as
King Henry VIII

Julius Caesar (MGM) d.Joseph L Mankiewicz: Marlon Brando, James Mason. Smooth Shakespearean adaptation, produced by John Houseman, in which Brando – as Mark Antony – more than held his own against Mason and Gielgud

Salome (Columbia) d.William Dieterle: Stewart Granger, Rita Hayworth. All-star cast wade valiantly through cliché-strewn celebration of the Bible's most famous striptease routine

The Robe (Fox) d.Henry Koster: Victor Mature. Roman tribune Richard Burton wins Christ's robe in the dice game at the Crucifixion. Big Vic is his slave Demetrius in vigorous adaptation of the Lloyd C Douglas blockbuster and the first film in CinemaScope

Perilous Journey (Republic) d.R G Springsteen: Scott Brady, Vera Ralston. Enjoyable programmer in which a shipful of women set sail for California in search of husbands

Desert Legion (Universal) d.Joseph Pevney: Alan Ladd, Arlene Dahl. Foreign Legionnaire Ladd saves Dahl's Lost City from the machinations of Richard Conte in slow-moving slice of hokum

The Golden Blade (Universal) d.Nathan Juran: Rock Hudson. Someone seems to have strapped Rock to a stuffed horse as he battles wicked Grand Vizier George Macready with a little help from the magic sword of Damascus

Prisoners of the Casbah (Columbia) d.Richard Bare: Turhan Bey, Gloria Grahame. Gloria has good reason to look glum in low-budget costumer providing fleeting refuge for fading stars Bey and Cesar Romero

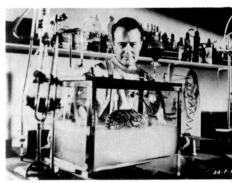

Donovan's Brain (UA) d.Felix Feist: Lew Ayres. Brain surgeon Ayres keeps a dead millionaire's brain alive in his lab with not entirely happy results. Ayres conveys his possession by the thing in the bottle with real conviction

The Magnetic Monster (UA) d.Curt Siodmak: Richard Carlson. Competent low-budgeter in which a ravenous radioactive isotope gobbles energy and doubles its size every 12 hours until Carlson provides the high-voltage climax

The Lost Planet (Columbia) d.Spencer Gordon Bennet: Michael Fox, Judd Holdren, Forrest Taylor. Last of the SF serials in which invisibility rays and thermic disintegrators run riot as alien beings from the planet Ergo embark on a power-crazed conquest of the Universe

Riders to the Stars (UA) d.Richard Carlson: William Lundigan. Labored documentary-style approach to megaboffin Herbert Marshall's attempt to catch a meteor for the greater glory of science and the infinite boredom of the audience

Invaders from Mars (UA) d.William Cameron Menzies: Leif Erickson, Hillary Brooke, Jimmy Hunt, Helena Carter, Walter Sande. Minor SF classic in which a Martian take-over of a small town is seen through the eyes of the terrified Hunt. Dreamily atmospheric art direction recalls Menzies' great days as a production designer

The Beast from 20,000 Fathoms (Warner) d.Eugene Lourié. Animator Ray Harryhausen's first major project marked the beginning of the decade's awakening monster cycle as a dinosaur's Arctic slumbers are disturbed by an A-bomb test. Based on a Ray Bradbury story, The Fog Horn

Spaceways (Hammer) d.Terence Fisher: Howard Duff, Eva Bartok. Duff and Bartok discover love across a crowded space probe in plodding British mixture of SF and Cold War thriller which borrowed sequences from *Rocketship X-M* (1950)

It Came From Outer Space (Universal) d.Jack Arnold: Richard Carlson. Arnold's first SF project, in which an alien space craft lands in the Arizona desert. Arnold exploits the bleak other-worldliness of the location to brilliant effect

War of the Worlds (Paramount) d.Byron Haskin: Ann Robinson, Gene Barry. H G Wells' classic is updated to 1950s California, complete with appearance by the Northrop 'Flying Wing', as sinister Martian warships reduce LA to rubble. Splendid special effects

MELODRAMA

Thy Neighbor's Wife (Fox) d.Hugo Haas: Cleo Moore, Ken Carlton. Downbeat drama of infidelity and murder set in a 19th-century Moravian village. By the end of the final reel all the principals have met sorry ends

The System (Warner) d.Lewis Seiler: Frank Lovejoy, Dan Seymour. Improbable tale of ruthless racketeer Lovejoy's redemption by the love of a good woman as his organization falls under the scrutiny of the Crime Investigation Committee

Little Boy Lost (Paramount) d.George Seaton: Bing Crosby, Christian Fourcade. Newsman Bing searches the orphanages of postwar France for his lost son. Sniffle, sniffle

Vicki (Fox) d.Harry Horner: Jeanne Crain, Jean Peters, Elliott Reid. Inferior remake of *noir* classic *I Wake up Screaming* (1942) in which Crain and Reid are hounded by psychopathic cop Richard Boone, in the role originally played with flesh-crawling panache by Laird Cregar

Plunder of the Sun (Warner) d.John Farrow: Francis L Sullivan, Patricia Medina. An ill-assorted bunch of crooks, drunks, archaeologists, and insurance investigator Glenn Ford, go flat out in pursuit of Aztec treasure in stylish jungle nonsense

Man on a Tightrope (Fox) d.Elia Kazan: Gloria Grahame, Fredric March. Czech circus boss March plans a bid for freedom in the West while assailed on all sides by family problems. Filmed in Germany

Titanic (Fox) d.Jean Negulesco: Barbara Stanwyck, Richard Basehart. Stanwyck and snobbish husband Clifton Webb rather unwisely book a cabin on the Titanic, ensuring a torrid voyage in lumbering disaster movie which sank without trace

Pickup on South Street (Fox) d.Sam Fuller: Jean Peters, Thelma Ritter. Pickpocket Richard Widmark gets more than he bargained for when he lifts Peters' purse. Definitive performance from Ritter as an exhausted underworld informer

The Maze (UA) d.William Cameron Menzies: Richard Carlson, Veronica Hurst. Intriguing 3-D cheapie, beautifully designed by Menzies, in which Carlson inherits a Scottish castle and with it the care of a monstrous 200-year-old ancestor

Miss Sadie Thompson (MGM) d.Curtis Bernhardt: Rita Hayworth, Jose Ferrer. Rita is a little overextended as Somerset Maugham's South Seas floozie tangling with hellfire preacher Ferrer. Filmed as *Rain* in 1928 and 1932 with, respectively, Gloria Swanson and Joan Crawford

Niagara (Fox) d.Henry Hathaway: Marilyn Monroe, Joseph Cotten. Faithless Monroe's plans to bump off husband Cotten go terminally awry in flashy suspenser gaudily photographed by Joe MacDonald

Split Second (RKO) d.Dick Powell: Jan Sterling, Stephen McNally. Powell's directing debut is high-octane prison-break meller which reaches a violent climax in a ghost town on the edge of an atom-test site

Trouble Along the Way (Warner) d.Michael Curtiz: John Wayne, Tom Tully. Sentimental vehicle for Wayne as a shady character who comes to the rescue of a bankrupt college

The Man in the Attic (Fox) d.Hugo Fregonese: Constance Smith, Jack Palance. Florid remake of *The Lodger* (1944) with knife-wielding psychopath Palance prowling the fog-bound streets of Old London Town in search of female prey

The All-American (Universal) d.Jesse Hibbs: Mamie Van Doren, Richard Long. Mamie well cast as a beer-hall floozie luring college football players to their doom in soapy drama starring Tony Curtis as a mixed-up gridiron hero

I Confess (Warner) d.Alfred Hitchcock: Montgomery Clift. Priest Clift takes a murderer's confession and is then accused of the crime. Although a minor work, it goes to the heart of Hitch's troubled Catholic conscience

Houdini (Paramount) d.George Marshall: Tony Curtis. Tony's first big success, and proof that he could act a bit, in highly fictionalized biopic of the great escapologist

Executive Suite (MGM) d.Robert Wise: Fredric March, Barbara Stanwyck, Walter Pidgeon, William Holden. Slick boardroom drama with an outstanding performance from Stanwyck in one of her last good films

Affair with a Stranger (RKO) d.Roy Rowland: Victor Mature, Jean Simmons. Will the marriage of writer Vic and model Jean survive a determined attempt to deep-six it by chanteuse Monica Lewis?

All I Desire (Universal) d.Douglas Sirk: Barbara Stanwyck, Richard Carlson. Stanwyck walks out on husband Carlson but her reappearance ten years later leads only to more angst and a shooting

The Juggler (Columbia) d.Edward Dmytryk: Kirk Douglas. Strong performance from Douglas as a Jewish refugee finding a new life in Israel after the horror of the concentration camps

From Here to Eternity (Columbia) d.Fred Zinnemann: Burt Lancaster, Tim Ryan. Burt strafes Zeros out of the sky at Pearl Harbor, takes a tumble in the surf with genteel Deborah Kerr in Oscar-laden version of James Jones best-seller

Bad for Each Other (Columbia) d.Irving Rapper: Marjorie Rambeau, Charlton Heston, Lizabeth Scott. Crusading doctor Heston clashes with the snobbish smart set in a Pennsylvania mining town

A Blueprint for Murder (Fox) d.Andrew L Stone: Jean Peters, Joseph Cotten. Cotten's affection for sister-in-law Peters is modified by a growing suspicion that she is a poisoner

Girls in the Night (Universal) d.Jack Arnold: Glenda Farrell, Harvey Lembeck, Patricia Hardy. So-so teenage delinquency drama boosted by presence of Farrell, the brassiest, quickest-talking gold-digger of the 1930s

The Blue Gardenia (Warner) d.Fritz Lang: Anne Baxter, Raymond Burr. Baxter slugs lecherous Burr with a poker and finds herself on a murder rap in engaging meller with strong '40s feel. Lovely performance from Ann Sothern as Baxter's wisecracking room-mate

Forbidden (Universal) d.Rudolph Maté: Tony Curtis, Joanne Dru. Small-time mobster Curtis escorts crime baron's widow Dru back to the States from Macao and then saves her from his compromised colleagues

The Hitch Hiker (RKO) d.Ida Lupino: Frank Lovejoy, William Talman, Edmond O'Brien. Pulsating thriller in which kill-crazy Tallman holds vacationing O'Brien, Lovejoy hostage in a nightmare drive across Mexico

The Glass Web (Universal) d.Jack Arnold: Marcia Henderson, John Forsythe, Edward G Robinson. 3-D chiller, set in a TV studio, where unhinged researcher Edward G goes on the rampage

City That Never Sleeps (Republic) d.John Brahm: Gig Young, Mala Powers. Bent cop Young slithers into the pocket of crooked businessman Edward Arnold in serviceable little B filled with off-beat touches

The Bigamist (Film Makers) d.Ida Lupino: Edmond O'Brien, Ida Lupino. Anguished O'Brien in the title role as the salesman with two wives – Lupino and Joan Fontaine – and a problem with adoption agency official Edmund Gwenn

The Big Heat (Columbia) d.Fritz Lang: Gloria Grahame, Glenn Ford. Gloria infinitely touching as the gangster's moll helping cop Ford to avenge the killing of his wife and receiving a boiling hot cup of coffee in the face for her pains from hoodlum Lee Marvin

Count the Hours (RKO) d.Don Siegel: Adele Mara, Macdonald Carey, Jack Elam. Attorney Carey fights to free an itinerant ranch hand from the death cell while taking flak from all sides

COMEDY

How to Marry a Millionaire (Fox) d.Jean Negulesco: Marilyn Monroe. Gold diggers Monroe, Lauren Bacall and Betty Grable rent a plush Manhattan penthouse as the first move in a determined manhunt

It Should Happen to You (Columbia) d.George Cukor: Jack Lemmon, Judy Holliday. Lemmon's debut as brash actress Holliday's nervously sincere chum, attempting to restrain her extravagant self-publicizing urges

Off Limits (Paramount) d.George Marshall: Mickey Rooney, Bob Hope. Rooney replaced an ailing Alan Young in this sassy Army comedy. Familiar support from chanteuse Marilyn Maxwell

Beat the Devil (Romulus) d.John Huston: Robert Morley, Mario Tulli, Peter Lorre, Humphrey Bogart. Stylish send-up of *The Maltese Falcon* (1941), co-written by Huston and Truman Capote, whose underhand humor completely eluded audiences of the day

Taxi (Fox) d.Gregory Ratoff: Dan Dailey, Constance Smith. Harassed bachelor cabbie Dan is pressganged by Irish immigrant Smith into a hunt for her missing heel of a husband

Forever Female (Paramount) d.Irving Rapper: William Holden, Ginger Rogers. Delicious comedy in which Ginger plays a Broadway star who refuses to face the fact that she's getting just a little too old to play pert little ingenues

South Sea Woman (Warner) d.Arthur Lubin: Burt Lancaster, Chuck Connors, Virginia Mayo. Galumphing Pacific-set farce featuring the AWOL antics of Marines Lancaster and Connors and brassy showgirl Mayo

Knock on Wood (Paramount) d.Norman Panama: Danny Kaye. The stolen plans of a secret weapon wind up in ventriloquist Danny's dummy in springheeled spy caper liberally sprinkled with routines from Kaye and featuring a charming performance by Mai Zetterling

Abbott and Costello Go To Mars (Universal) d.Charles Lamont: Lou Costello, Mari Blanchard, Budd Abbott. But, as every addict of movie trivia knows, they land on Venus, where they encounter the voluptuous Mari ruling over a matriarchy of US beauty queens

The Moon is Blue (Paramount) d.Otto Preminger: Maggie McNamara, William Holden. Screen version of a Broadway hit, considered a piquant novelty in its day, with McNamara making a point of flaunting her virginity

Casanova's Big Night (Paramount) d.Norman Z McLeod: Basil Rathbone, Bob Hope, Joan Fontaine. Hope in excellent form in his customary role of cowardly blowhard, masquerading as Casanova (Vincent Price!) and romancing Fontaine along the canals of Venice

The Caddy (Paramount) d.Norman Taurog: Jerry Lewis, Fred Clark. Dean and Jerry shuttle madly back and forth between the worlds of pro golf and showbiz. Laid-back Dino eases his way through 'That's Amore', which became a big hit

Scared Stiff (Paramount) d.George Marshall: Dean Martin, Jerry Lewis, Lizabeth Scott. Remake of Bob Hope's *Ghost Breakers* (1940) teams Lewis with Carmen Miranda in paranormal hijinks on a Caribbean isle. One of the less resistible Lewis-Martin efforts

MUSICALS

She's Back on Broadway (Warner) d.Gordon Douglas: Steve Cochran, Virginia Mayo. Hollywood sexpot Mayo goes for broke in a Broadway show called 'Breakfast in Bed'

Kiss Me Kate (MGM) d.George Sidney: Keenan Wynn, James Whitmore, Kathryn Grayson, Howard Keel. Witty, elegantly plotted version of the Cole Porter Broadway smash in which a musical version of *The Taming of the Shrew* is paralleled by the cast's backstage shenanigans. Ann Miller superb in 'Too Darn Hot'

Let's Do It Again (Columbia) d.Alexander Hall: Ray Milland, Jane Wyman, Leon Ames. But not a case of Let's See It Again as stars sleepwalk through pedestrian remake of the studio's splendid *The Awful Truth* (1937)

The Band Wagon (MGM) d.Vincente Minnelli: Cyd Charisse, Fred Astaire. Sophisticated tribute to the backstage musical with Fred cast as a fading movie star going through hell at the hands of demented Broadway director Jack Buchanan. Among many highlights, 'Dancing in the Dark' and 'A Shine on Your Shoes'

Calamity Jane (Warner) d.David Butler: Doris Day. 'Whip Crack Away' with a frenzied Day as the Calamitous One and Howard Keel as Wild Bill Hickock. Score includes Doris' big hit 'Secret Love'

Tonight We Sing (Fox) d.Mitchell Leisen: David Wayne, Isaac Stern. Wayne plays the great impresario Sol Huroc in gaudy biopic bolstered with stars from the worlds of opera, ballet and classical music. Heavy going

Here Come the Girls (Paramount) d.Claude Binyon: Bob Hope, Rosemary Clooney. Tangle-footed hoofer Hope is catapulted to stardom when leading man Tony Martin has a spot of bother with mobster Robert Strauss

Those Redheads from Seattle (Paramount) d.Lewis R Foster: Rhonda Fleming, Agnes Moorehead, Gene Barry. The frozen Yukon provides the backdrop to a modest outing aptly described as a '3-D musical with 2-D characters and a 1-D plot'

Small Town Girl (MGM) d.Leslie Kardos: Jane Powell, S Z 'Cuddles' Sakall, Bobby Van. Playboy Farley Granger runs into trouble with the law while speeding through Duck Creek and then falls for Powell. Van is a delight dancing 'Take Me to Broadway'

Dangerous When Wet (MGM) d.Charles Walters: Jack Carson, Esther Williams, Fernando Lamas. The one in which the athletic Esther swims the English Channel and cavorts with cartoon characters Tom and Jerry. Pleasant songs by Arthur Schwartz and Johnny Mercer

The Affairs of Dobie Gillis (MGM) d.Don Weis: Debbie Reynolds, Bobby Van. Lively campus romp in which the romance between chemistry students Van and Reynolds has literally explosive results

The French Line (RKO) d.Lloyd Bacon: Mary McCarty, Jane Russell. Husband-hunting oil heiress Russell stalks the boulevards of Gay Paree, romancing Gilbert Roland, displaying the famous bosom in 3-D and singing a couple of startlingly direct songs

The I-Don't-Care Girl (Fox) d.Lloyd Bacon: Mitzi Gaynor, Oscar Levant. Mitzi takes the title role in biopic of flamboyant Broadway star Eva Tanguay. Contains some truly ferocious tap routines choreographed by Seymour Felix

The Eddie Cantor Story (Warner) d.Alfred E Green: Tristram Coffin, Keefe Brasselle, Marie Windsor. Studio's attempt to repeat success of *The Jolson Story* (1946) is torpedoed by miscasting of Brasselle as the legendary eye-popping vaudevillian

I Love Melvin (MGM) d.Don Weis: Debbie Reynolds, Donald O'Connor. Sprightly tale of photographer's assistant O'Connor bluffing star-struck Reynolds that he can get her on the cover of *Look* magazine

The Farmer Takes a Wife (Fox) d.Henry Levin: John Carroll, Thelma Ritter, Betty Grable. Remake of 1935 Janet Gaynor/Henry Fonda vehicle. Set on the banks of the Erie Canal in the 1800s with Carroll and Dale Robertson vying for Grable's hand

The Jazz Singer (Warner) d.Michael Curtiz: Danny Thomas, Peggy Lee. Updated version of the 1927 smash with Korean War vet and cantor's son Thomas hitting Broadway to the alarm of Dad. Almost as ghastly as the 1980 Neil Diamond version

Because You're Mine (MGM) d.Alexander Hall: James Whitmore, Mario Lanza. Portly Mario is drafted into the army where he is befriended by opera-loving Sergeant Whitmore. He might have done better with Bilko

Call Me Madam(Fox) d.Walter Lang: Ethel Merman, George Sanders. Utterly unstoppable Ethel blasts everybody off the set as Mrs Stanley Adams, 'the hostess with the mostest' and ambassadress to Lichtenberg. Sanders reveals a pleasant tenor voice

Easy to Love (MGM) d.Charles Walters: Tony Martin, Esther Williams. Florida-set aqua spectacular features some glorious kitsch engineered by Busby Berkeley and a perfunctory plot involving Esther's unrequited yen for Van Johnson

Gentlemen Prefer Blondes (Fox) d.Howard Hawks: Jane Russell, Marilyn Monroe. Jane and Marilyn are the two big girls from Little Rock in superb adaptation of Anita Loos musical comedy. Jane relaxes among serried ranks of adoring musclemen, Marilyn sings 'Diamonds Are a Girl's Best Friend'

Torch Song (MGM) d.Charles Walters: Gig Young, Joan Crawford. Joan's first for MGM for 10 years is glorious farrago in which she plays a tough Broadway star clinging to her perch at the top (in other words herself). Michael Wilding is the blind piano accompanist who tames her

By the Light of the Silvery Moon (Warner) d.David Butler: Russell Arms, Doris Day, Gordon MacRae. More small-town nostalgia from a Booth Tarkington short story, with soldier MacRae and fiancée Day coping with life after World War I. Excellent support from Leon Ames, Rosemary De Camp

So This is Love (Warner) d.Gordon Douglas: Kathryn Grayson, Fortunio Bonanova. Competent biopic of opera star Grace Moore, who went from log cabin to the Met. Merv Griffin plays one of her boyfriends

Three Sailors and a Girl (Warner) d.Roy Del Ruth: Gordon MacRae, Jack Leonard, Jane Powell, Gene Nelson. Three of the US Navy's finest attempt to turn an out-of-town flop into a Broadway smash in one of several versions of a much-filmed George S Kaufman play, The Butter and Egg Man

WESTERNS

Texas Bad Man (Allied Artists) d.Lewis Collins: Elaine Riley, Wayne Morris, Myron Healey. Energetic oater with Morris as a sheriff bedeviled by his crooked father, who's out to steal a bullion shipment from the local mine

Pony Express (Paramount) d.Jerry Hopper: Rhonda Fleming, Charlton Heston, Jan Sterling. Celebration of the opening of the mail route to the West with Heston in virile form as Buffalo Bill, Forrest Tucker slightly less so as Wild Bill Hickock

The Moonlighter (Warner) d.Roy Rowland: Fred MacMurray, Barbara Stanwyck. Strange little Western in which Stanwyck is sworn in as a deputy and sets out on the trail of bank-robbing former boyfriend MacMurray

War Arrow (Universal) d.George Sherman: Jeff Chandler, Maureen O'Hara. Cavalryman Jeff plods around recruiting Seminole Indians to deal with the troublesome Kiowas in the teeth of oppositon from CO John McIntyre

The Last Posse (Columbia) d.Alfred Werker: Wanda Hendrix, John Derek. Broderick Crawford turns up as the once heroic sheriff whose nerve has been shriveled by drink. Derek is cattle baron Charles Bickford's son called in to right a raft of wrongs in this stylish outing crisply directed by Werker

Powder River (Fox) d.Louis King: Cameron Mitchell, Rory Calhoun. Sheriff Calhoun discovers that his doctor friend Mitchell is the murderer for whom he is searching. Final shoot-out is resolved by twist ending

Arrowhead (Paramount) d.Charles Marquis Warren: Charlton Heston, Katy Jurado. Heston is a swaggering, thoroughly disagreeable Indian scout whose exploits are based on the life of the legendary Al Seiber. Film used the sets from *The Savage* (1952)

Taza, Son of Cochise (Univeral) d.Douglas Sirk: Rock Hudson. Or Rock, son of Jeff Chandler, as peaceloving Hudson finds himself caught between the US cavalry and his bellicose brother. Originally shot in 3-D

The Stranger Wore a Gun (Columbia) d.André de Toth: Ernest Borgnine, Randolph Scott, Lee Marvin. Another 3-D Western in which Scott strolls through as a Quantrill raider trying to mend his ways, tangling with snarling heavy George Macready in all-action saloon bar gun battle

Seminole (Universal) d.Budd Boetticher: Rock Hudson. West Pointer Rock and Seminole chief Anthony Quinn dance a wary gavotte around each other through the swamplands, in search of peace and Barbara Hale. Some witty touches enliven an otherwise routine actioner

Gun Fury (Columbia) d.Raoul Walsh: Rock Hudson, Donna Reed. Demented bandit Phil Carey abducts Reed and the chase is on for increasingly shredded husband Hudson

Escape from Fort Bravo (MGM) d.John Sturges: John Forsythe, William Holden. Rugged cavalry captain Holden has his hands full dealing with escaped Confederate prisoners, marauding Indians and femme fatale Eleanor Parker in effective actioner based on a story by veteran Hollywood character actor Michael Pate

Hondo (Wayne-Fellows) d.John Farrow: John Wayne, Geraldine Page. Despatch rider Wayne rescues Page and her son from the Apache in superior movie which deals sympathetically with the Indians and gives the Wayne character an unexpected psychological depth

Topeka (Allied Artists) d.Thomas Carr: 'Wild Bill' Elliott, Rick Vallin. One of the best of Elliott's final series, crammed with exuberant crane shots, in which he plays the classic 'good bad man', hired to clean up a town and resisting the temptation to take it over himself

The Charge at Feather River (Warner) d.Gordon Douglas: Guy Madison. Tomahawks hurtle straight for your head in gimmicky 3-D spectacular with Madison rescuing Vera Miles from the Indians in biggest grossing Western of the year

The Man from the Alamo (Universal) d.Budd Boetticher: Glenn Ford. Superior B in which Ford escapes from the Alamo to warn Texas families of the impending defeat and is thereafter branded a coward. Superb cinematography by Russell Metty

Shane (Paramount) d.George Stevens: Van Heflin, Jean Arthur, Brandon de Wilde, Alan Ladd. Buckskin-clad Ladd is the guardian angel protecting homesteaders from hired killer Jack Palance in classic Western which mingles realism – the mud-splattered death of Elisha Cook Jr – with myth in equal measure

The Boy from Oklahoma (Warner) d.Michael Curtiz: Clem Bevans, Anthony Caruso, Nancy Olson. Will Rogers Jr stars as a lawyer turned sheriff of Bluerock in gently paced sagebrush comedy

City of Bad Men (Fox) d.Harmon Jones: Richard Boone, Don Hagerthy, Dale Robertson. Off-beat Western in which adventurer Robertson plans to lift the receipts from the 1897 Jim Corbett-Bob Fitzsimmons prizefight in Nevada City, but is kept on the straight and narrow by old girlfriend Jeanne Crain

The Marshal's Daughter (UA) d.William Berke: Laurie Anders, Hoot Gibson. Novelty Western with TV star Anders, enlisting Hoot's help to corral villain Bob Duncan between bouts of range warbling. Jimmy Wakeley, Johnny Mack Brown, Tex Ritter also guest

Wings of the Hawk (Universal) d.Budd Boetticher: Van Heflin, Julia Adams. Julia looks incredibly sexy as the Mexican revolutionary joining forces with dispossessed miner Heflin in lively Western originally shot in 3-D

Ride Clear of Diablo (Universal) d.Jesse Hibbs: Dan Duryea, Audie Murphy. Duryea in splendid form as the flamboyant gunman helping Audie to track down the killers of his father and kid brother in confidently handled low-budgeter

The Yellow Tomahawk (UA) d.Lesley Selander: Peter Graves, Peggie Castle, Rory Calhoun. Rory is an Indian guide hell bent on protecting settlers from marauding redskins

The Woman They Amost Lynched (Republic) d.Allan Dwan: Joan Leslie, Audrey Totter. Sly Western parody in which Eastern girl Leslie inherits a whole heap of trouble from Totter and the townsfolk of Border City

ROMANCE

Roman Holiday (Paramount) d.William Wyler: Audrey Hepburn, Gregory Peck. Charming if featherweight tale of runaway princess Hepburn falling in love with reporter Peck in the Eternal City

Mogambo (MGM) d.John Ford: Clark Gable, Ava Gardner. Full-blooded remake of *Red Dust* (1932) with Gable repeating his roguish role, Gardner substituting splendidly for Jean Harlow and Grace Kelly less happy in the part originally played by Mary Astor

Never Let Me Go (MGM) d.Delmer Daves: Clark Gable, Gene Tierney. Gable is the resourceful journalist set on smuggling ballerina Tierney out of Russia. Ironically made at a time when MGM were on the brink of terminating the King's contract

Something for the Birds (Fox) d.Robert Wise: Victor Mature, Patricia Neal. Romantic comedy in which conservation lobbyist Neal collides head-on with oil man Mature. Edmund Gwenn steals the film as an ingenious society party gate crasher

Latin Lovers (MGM) d.Mervyn LeRoy: Ricardo Montalban, Louis Calhern, Lana Turner. Heiress Lana is all of a dither worrying whether men will love her for her $37 million or just for her beautiful self. Ricardo feels strongly attracted to both

Second Chance (RKO) d.Rudolph Maté: Robert Mitchum, Linda Darnell. South American affair between prizefighter Mitchum and mobster's mol Darnell reaches an exciting climax in a crippled cable car shared by hit man Jack Palance

Dream Wife (MGM) d.Sidney Sheldon: Betta St John, Cary Grant, Deborah Kerr. Quizzical Cary's eye falls on Eastern princess St John but his marriage proposal causes a diplomatic stir

Rhapsody (MGM) d.Charles Vidor: Elizabeth Taylor, Vittorio Gassman. Vittorio tries hard to keep his eyes on the strings and off rich bitch Liz's cleavage in romance triangle completed by pianist John Ericson

Return to Paradise (UA) d.Mark Robson: Roberta Hayes, Gary Cooper. South Seas yarn in which beachcomber Cooper falls in love with native girl Hayes. Loosely based on a James Michener story and filmed on Samoa

AMERICANA

Main Street to Broadway (MGM) d.Tay Garnett: Agnes Moorehead, Tallulah Bankhead. Flimsy tale of struggle for success on the Great White Way is embellished with a small army of guest stars including Tallulah (naturally, Daaaaaaahling!) Helen Hayes, Rex Harrison

The Wild One (Columbia) d.Laslo Benedek: Mary Murphy, Marlon Brando. Marlon creates an enduring, if ever so slightly camp, image for leather lovers everywhere as the bike gang leader terrorizing a small town

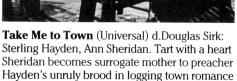

A Lion Is in the Streets (Warner) d.Raoul Walsh: Anne Francis, James Cagney, Lon Chaney, Sara Haden. Cagney plays a swamp peddler who metamorphoses into a Huey Long-type politician in feature which inevitably suffers in comparison with *All the King's Men* (1949)

Take Me to Town (Universal) d.Douglas Sirk: Sterling Hayden, Ann Sheridan. Tart with a heart Sheridan becomes surrogate mother to preacher Hayden's unruly brood in logging town romance

The Sun Shines Bright (Republic) d.John Ford: Charles Winninger, Russell Simpson. Ford's favorite film is re-working of his *Judge Priest* (1934) and a reactionary, damp-eyed celebration of Southern mythology

The Mississippi Gambler (Universal)
d.Rudolph Maté: Tyrone Power. Glossy adventure
set in ante-bellum New Orleans mingles romance
and swashbuckling in equal measure

Gypsy Colt (MGM) d.Andrew Marton: Ward
Bond, Frances Dee, Larry Keating. Equine
tearjerker in the style of *Lassie Come Home*
(1943) in which a much-loved steed is sold to a
racing stable by its needy owners

The Glen Miller Story (Universal) d.Anthony
Mann: June Allyson, James Stewart. Exemplary
biopic of the Big Band giant gave Allyson her best
role as Stewart/Miller's wife. Watch out for Gene
Krupa, Louis Armstrong playing 'Basin Street
Blues'

The Actress (MGM) d.George Cukor: Anthony
Perkins, Jean Simmons. Perkins' screen debut as
Simmons re-enacts Ruth Gordon's experiences
as a young thespian. Spencer Tracy plays her
irascible father

Big Leaguer (MGM) d.Robert Aldrich: Edward
G Robinson, Vera-Ellen. Standard sporting fare
of college-boy attracting the attention of the big-
time talent scouts

So Big (Warner) d.Robert Wise: Jane Wyman,
Sterling Hayden. Third screen version of Edna
Ferber's story of a country teacher (Wyman)
devoting her life to home and the raising of an
adored son

Member of the Wedding (Columbia) d.Fred
Zinnemann: Julie Harris, Ethel Waters. Harris
repeats her stage performance as a gawky young
girl edging out of childhood as her brother's
wedding approaches. She's great but miles too
old for the part

BRITISH AND FOREIGN

The Weak and the Wicked (ABPC) d.J Lee Thompson: Diana Dors. Gambling debts land Glynis Johns in jail whose denizens include 'good time girl' Dors, taking the rap for her boyfriend. No wonder she seems a trifle distressed.

Desperate Moment (Rank) d.Compton Bennett: Mai Zetterling, Dirk Bogarde. Under the mistaken impression that girlfriend Mai is dead, Bogarde confesses to a murder he did not commit. When she reappears he breaks out of jail and together they track down the real killer. Improbable, to say the least

The Net (Rank) d.Anthony Asquith: James Donald, Noel Willman. Hapless aero engineer Donald risks losing his wife to smooth colleague Herbert Lom and his spanking new jet aircraft to a Soviet spy ring

The Heart of the Matter (British Lion) d.George More O'Ferrall: Trevor Howard, Peter Finch. Unrelentingly sombre adaptation of Graham Greene novel with Howard excellent as an unpopular colonial police officer entrapped by a blackmailer and contemplating suicide

Trouble in Store (Rank) d.John Paddy Carstairs: Margaret Rutherford, Norman Wisdom. Huge hit for mawkish clown Wisdom whose put-upon 'little man' reduces a store to chaos and its elegant manager Jerry Desmonde to despair

The Square Ring (Ealing) d.Basil Dearden:
Robert Beatty, Kay Kendall. A hectic night of
action at an East End boxing promotion crammed
with all the stock characters of the genre. Beatty
is the punched-out champ trying to claw his way
back into the big time

Four-Sided Triangle (Hammer) d.Terence
Fisher: Stephen Murray, James Hayter. Mad
doctor Murray sets about duplicating Barbara
Payton after she leaves him for colleague John
Van Eyssen. It all ends in the usual lab blaze

The Captain's Paradise (British Lion)
d.Anthony Kimmins: Alec Guinness, Yvonne de
Carlo. Mild comedy in which sea captain
Guinness maintains two wives – frumpy Celia
Johnson in Gibraltar and tempestuous spitfire de
Carlo in North Africa. In the end they both leave
him

The Titfield Thunderbolt (Ealing) d.Charles Crichton: George Relph,
Godfrey Tearle. The villagers of Titfield resurrect an ancient locomotive in
a bid to stop the closure of their local railway line. Ironically, the sentimental
celebration of picturesquely obsolete machinery can be seen as an
unconscious metaphor for the studio's decline

Meet Mr Lucifer (Ealing) d.Anthony Pelissier: Gordon Jackson, Kay
Kendall. Fanciful satire on TV in which the devil decides that people are
getting too much pleasure from the idiot box. But his plans to remedy the
situation backfire

Three Steps to the Gallows (Eros) d.John
Gilling: Mary Castle, Scott Brady. Formula thriller
in which American merchant seaman Brady
docks in London to find his brother in the death
cell, framed by a diamond-smuggling ring

The Cruel Sea (Ealing) d.Charles Frend: Donald
Sinden, Jack Hawkins. As corvette captain
Ericson, Hawkins is allowed a brief moment of
uncharacteristic emotion after depth-charging a
U-boat in waters which contain the helpless
survivors of one of its victims

The Man Between (British Lion) d.Carol Reed:
James Mason, Claire Bloom. Mason is the shady
contact man, smuggling wanted West Berliners
from the East in moody thriller re-exploring the
territory mapped out in *The Third Man* (1949)

The Million Pound Note (Rank) d.Ronald Neame: Gregory Peck, Reginald Beckwith. Two wealthy brothers bet on whether a man could live on the note of the title without spending any of it. Seaman Peck is the guinea pig

The Red Beret (Warwick) d.Terence Young: Harry Andrews, Alan Ladd. The diminutive one plays a Yank with a past who joins the British Parachute Regiment in boisterous World War II actioner

The Malta Story (Rank) d.Brian Desmond Hurst: Anthony Steel, Alec Guinness. A feast of stern jaws, steady gazes and knobbly knees in which stalwart British cast make sure that the George Cross Island stays in Allied hands

Hobson's Choice (British Lion) d.David Lean: John Mills, Brenda de Banzie, Charles Laughton. Charming version of the Harold Brighouse play in which prosperous bootmaker Laughton's refusal to provide dowries for his three daughters stirs strong-willed eldest de Banzie into radical action, marrying impoverished Mills

They Who Dare (British Lion) d.Lewis Milestone: Dirk Bogarde. The Special Boat Squadron raid Axis-held islands in the Aegean in muddled actioner which, according to Bogarde, the cast, crew and director made up as they went along

Ugetsu Monogatari (Japan) d. Kenji Mizoguchi: Kinuyo Tanaka. Eloquent fusion of fantasy and reality as war in medieval Japan sets two potters and their families on tragically divergent paths. Ends with one of the most moving shots in cinema

Rob Roy, the Highland Rogue (RKO) d.Harold French: Richard Todd, Archie Duncan. Todd is the deshabillé Highland freebooter in zesty, simple-minded Scottish 'Western' from the Disney stable

Saikaku Ichidai Onna (Japan) d.Kenji Mizoguchi: Kinuyo Tanaka. One of the imperishable masterpieces of cinema, chronicling the decline of a courtesan in 18th-century Japan

Un Acte d'Amour (France) d.Anatole Litvak: Barbara Laage, Kirk Douglas. Heavy-breathing love story in which Kirk plays a GI in liberated Paris, romancing Dany Robin

Le Salaire de la Peur (France) d.Henri-Georges Clouzot: Yves Montand, Charles Vanel. Pulsating melodrama, with the bleakest of resolutions, follows four desperate characters driving trucks loaded with nitroglycerine through rough country in South America. Remade by William Friedkin in 1977

Destinées (France) d.Jean Delannoy, Marcello Pagliero, Christian-Jaque: Michele Morgan. Historical three-parter on women in war with Morgan as Joan of Arc, Martine Carol as Lysisistra and Claudette Colbert as a gal of the 20th century

Touchez Pas au Grisbi (France) d.Jacques Becker: Dora Doll, Jeanne Moreau, Jean Gabin. Thieves fight it out over the loot in flavorful story of Paris low life in which Gabin invests his gangster character with a characteristically world-weary warmth

Therese Raquin (France) d.Marcel Carné: Simone Signoret, Raf Vallone. Signoret and Vallone are the guilty lovers in powerful updating of the Zola classic

Le Carrosse d'Or (France) d.Jean Renoir: Anna Magnani. Bitter-sweet meditation on the interrelation of theater and life centered on a Commedia dell'arte troupe touring in 18th-century Peru

Gycklarnas Afton (Sweden) d.Ingmar Bergman: Anders Ek. A shabby little circus provides the arena for a sensitive allegory about the eternal joys and despairs of love and marriage

I Vitelloni (Italy) d.Federico Fellini: Alberto Sordi. Picaresque study of the kind of exotic layabouts who seem so dear to Fellini's heart

Il Maestro di Don Giovanni (Italy) d.Milton Krims: Errol Flynn, Gina Lollobrigida. The voluptuous Lollo stirs the old reprobate into a semblance of his former self in a project into which Flynn sank, and lost, much of his dwindling funds

Howard Hughes acquired total control of RKO for $23.5 million. Warner entered television production with a weekly hour-long series of programs called Warner Brothers Presents. The most successful was *Cheyenne*, developed from an old Warner property and starring Clint Walker, which ran for seven seasons. The Warner studio and distribution were now operating separately from their theaters, leaving only MGM-Loew's holding out against the US government's divorcement order. The major studios followed Fox into the wide-screen arena. RKO adopted SuperScope, first used in the United Artists release *Vera Cruz*, later renaming it RKO-Scope. Republic chose a process modeled on the French Cinépanoramique system called Naturama. Warner, in some confusion, annouced WarnerScope, then went one better with WarnerSuperScope, before subsiding into CinemaScope. CinemaScope's biggest rival was VistaVision, a system developed for Paramount which used a larger negative area to achieve better definition of the image. Paramount's *White Christmas*, the year's biggest grosser, was the first film shot in VistaVision. However, the process proved extremely expensive and was eventually abandoned in the 1960s.

The year belonged to Marlon Brando. He won the Best Actor Oscar for his performance as the washed-up boxer Terry Molloy in Elia Kazan's *On the Waterfront* and also picked up the New York Critics' Award. It was a remarkable performance and begetter of one of cinema's most quoted lines, 'I coulda been a contender.' Much of the effect was created by Brando's deployment of a formidable battery of technical tricks – a tendency he shares with Laurence Olivier –and it is difficult to watch the film today without being distracted by the mechanics of the performance. The Best Actress Award was won by Grace Kelly, slumming it in a shabby cardigan and dowdy hairdo in *The Country Girl*, a classic example of a star successfully trading her Diors for Sears Catalogue and an Oscar. In truth the Award should have gone to Judy Garland for her performance in George Cukor's *A Star is Born*, in which she showed her intuitive grasp of the drama in musicals, deeply inhaling the toxic aroma of her own unhappy greasepaint life.

Edmond O'Brien won the Best Supporting Actor Award or his performance as Oscar Muldoon, millionaire Warren Stevens' sycophantic aide in Joseph L Mankiewicz's *The Barefoot Contessa*. Newcomer Eva Marie Saint, Brando's wanly beautiful prop in *On the Waterfront*, won the Best Supporting Actress Award. *On the Waterfront* was also voted the Best Picture and Elia Kazan Best Director. A highly mannered film, mixing Grand Guignol with Hollywood neo-realism, *On the Waterfront* has not worn well with time. Hindsight lends Brando's decision to inform on the mob running the docks, and Kazan's willingness to co-operate with the HUAC, an irony not immediately apparent at the time.

Among the key films of the year were *The Creature from the Black Lagoon*, Jack Arnold's monster on the loose classic; *Rear Window*, Hitchcock's meditation on the voyeuristic nature of cinema; and *Bad Day at Black Rock*, in which John Sturges made brilliant use of CinemaScope to enhance the desert setting and the isolation of Spencer Tracy. Humphrey Bogart gave a mesmerizing performance in *The Caine Mutiny* as Captain Queeg, second cousin to his Fred C Dobbs in *The Treasure of the Sierra Madre* (1948), a man rent assunder by suspicion and paranoia. Warner's biggest grosser was the 'insect invasion' classic *Them!*

In Hitchcock's *To Catch a Thief*, elegant Grace Kelly offered Cary Grant a chicken picnic and in the same breath enquired, 'breast or leg?' Audrey Hepburn's elfin beauty in *Sabrina* provided a welcome antidote to the growing obsession with heavy-breasted leading ladies. Director Billy Wilder observed, 'Titism has taken over the country, but Audrey Hepburn singlehandedly may make bosoms a thing of the past.' She didn't.

James Dean arrived as the original Mixed-up Kid in Elia Kazan's *East of Eden*, adapted from part of a novel by John Steinbeck. Hedda Hopper, who had seen them all come, and helped not a few of them to go, raved, 'I couldn't remember having seen a young man with such power . . . so much sheer invention.' Nicholas Ray's *Johnny Guitar,* starring Joan Crawford, was a magnificently baroque Western, artfully exploiting its leading lady's basilisk humorlessness. *Seven Brides for Seven Brothers* was a delightful musical, bursting with hyper-energetic ensemble playing. Paul Newman made his debut in *The Silver Chalice*, an ill-fated epic; Angie Dickinson, fantasy mate of many a film critic, had a small part in *Lucky Me*; muscleman Steve Reeves turned up in *Athena*. Biggest box-office star of the year was durable John Wayne, followed by Dean Martin and Jerry Lewis, Gary Cooper, James Stewart, Marilyn Monroe, Alan Ladd, Bing Crosby, Jane Wyman and Marlon Brando. Clark Gable's contract with MGM ran out and was not renewed.

Death took directors Irving Pichel and William K Howard, Lionel Barrymore, crusty patriarch of MGM, and Sydney Greenstreet.

In Britain director Henry Cornelius had a huge hit with *Genevieve*, a charming comedy starring Kenneth More, Kay Kendall, John Gregson and Dinah Sheridan. Cartoonist Ronald Searle's truculent, anarchic schoolgirls made their first screen appearance in Launder and Gilliat's *The Belles of St Trinians*. The pig-tailed horrors of St Trinians would have proved more than a match for the medieval Japanese swordsmen in Akira Kurosawa's *Shichinin No Samurai*, starring Toshiro Mifune, which enjoyed an immense international success. Anthony Quinn's brutal street performer Zampano in Federico Fellini's *La Strada* won critical acclaim but with the passing of the years seems increasingly self-indulgent. In Poland director Andrzej Wajda emerged as a major talent with *Pokolenie*, a study of young Resistance workers.

ACTION

Bamboo Prison (Columbia) d.Lewis Seiler: Brian Keith, Robert Francis. Another Korean War POW camp drama in which intelligence agent Francis poses as a Communist collaborator with help from fellow undercover man Keith

Prisoner of War (MGM) d.Andrew Marton: Steve Forrest, Dewey Martin, Ronald Reagan. One of a rash of films dealing with the maltreatment and brainwashing of American POWS in the Korean War

Dragnet (Warner) d.Jack Webb: Richard Boone, Jack Webb. Webb is the stonefaced, seedily insufferable cop Joe Friday solving a murder in humdrum spin-off from hit TV series

Crime Wave (Warner) d.André de Toth: Ted de Corsia, Gene Nelson. Ex-con Nelson's attempt to go straight runs into trouble when he discovers a former inmate of St Quentin dying outside his home

Beachhead (UA) d.Stuart Heisler: Tony Curtis, Mary Murphy, Frank Lovejoy. Curtis and Lovejoy perform feats of derring-do behind enemy lines in brisk Pacific war actioner with a climax worthy of a Saturday-morning serial

Johnny Dark (Universal) d.George Sherman:Piper Laurie, Tony Curtis. Energetic racing car designer Curtis wins the Canada-to-Mexico race and the hand of Laurie. Remade in 1964 as *The Lively Set*

Unchained (Warner) d.Hall Bartlett: Elroy Hirsch. Old-fashioned social concern movie, redolent of the studio's past, focusing on attempts to reform the prison system

The Fast and the Furious (Palo Alto) d.John Ireland. Dorothy Malone, John Ireland. On the lam from a murder frame-up, Ireland uses some heavy persuasion to become Malone's driver in a sports car race over the border

Strategic Air Command (Paramount) d.Anthony Mann: James Stewart. Baseball star Stewart's recall to air duties puts a strain on his marriage in Cold War tub-thumper brashly hymning America's military might

Men of the Fighting Lady (MGM) d.Andrew Marton: Van Johnson. Gung-ho Korean air adventure strays into schoolboy fantasy when Johnson guides blinded fellow pilot Dewey Martin down to a safe landing on the Fighting Lady's heaving deck

Betrayed (MGM) d.Gottfried Reinhardt: Brian Smith, Victor Mature, Lana Turner. Stodgy World War II resistance drama set in Holland and starring a weary-looking Clark Gable

Riot in Cell Block 11 (Allied Artists) d.Don Siegel: Whit Bissell, Neville Brand. Pulsating performance from Brand as the baleful former military man reluctantly leading violent prison flare-up in protest against inhuman conditions

Hell and High Water (Fox) d.Sam Fuller: Victor Francen, Bella Darvi, Cameron Mitchell. Wild and woolly Cold War melo in which scientist Francen and mercenary submarine commander Richard Widmark thwart Communist atom plans in the Pacific

Hell's Island (Paramount) d.Phil Karlson: John Payne, Francis L Sullivan, Sandor Szabo. Hardboiled Payne pursues a stolen gem in freewheeling remake of *The Maltese Falcon* (1941) with the bulbous Sullivan filling the Sydney Greenstreet slot

Battle Cry (Warner) d.Raoul Walsh: Mona Freeman, Tab Hunter. Cliché-crammed tribute to the Marines in the Pacific, full of stereotypes from the all-American college boy to the tough sergeant with the heart of gold

The Bridges at Toko-Ri (Paramount) d.Mark Robson: Mickey Rooney. Thoughtful treatment of the effect of the Korean War on men and their families with Rooney outstanding as eccentric helicopter pilot rescuing downed jet ace William Holden. Won special effects Oscar for flying sequences

ADVENTURE AND FANTASY

The Silver Chalice (Warner) d.Victor Saville: Paul Newman, Virginia Mayo. Newman's debut as the slave who designs a stand for the cup used in the Last Supper. Stiff-jointed epic is enlivened by Mayo as sorcerer Jack Palance's curvacious apprentice

The Adventures of Hajji Baba (Fox) d.Don Weis: Elaine Stewart, John Derek. Chisel-featured Derek is the Barber of Bagdad, or some such nonsense, romancing princess Stewart in cheerfully camp adventure

The Egyptian (Fox) d.Michael Curtiz: Victor Mature, Edmund Purdom, Peter Ustinov. Victor's intriguing headgear provides light relief in agonizingly tedious epic charting Purdom's pre-Christian progress towards the concept of the One God

Demetrius and the Gladiators (Fox) d.Delmer Daves: Susan Hayward, Victor Mature. Sequel to *The Robe* (1953) with Big Vic condemned to the arena and getting kinda playful with Hayward's slinky Messalina while Jay Robinson hurtles over the top as Caligula

Princess of the Nile (Fox) d.Harmon Jones: Jeffrey Hunter, Debra Paget. Swordstress Debra takes up the scimitar against nasty Bedouin Michael Rennie in girl-crammed slice of hokum

Prince Valiant (Fox) d.Henry Hathaway: Robert Wagner, James Mason. The Viking cartoon hero springs to life in the virile form of Wagner, complete with Louise Brooks haircut and foiling the evil designs of Mason's Black Knight in the good old days of King Arthur

King Richard and the Crusaders (Warner) d.David Butler: Virginia Mayo, Laurence Harvey, George Sanders. Rambling adaptation of Walter Scott's *The Talisman* casts an uneasy Rex Harrison as Saladin, Sanders as Richard the Lionheart and Mayo, somewhat improbably, as his cousin the Lady Edith

Sign of the Pagan (Universal) d.Douglas Sirk: Jack Palance. Misplaced intellectual pretensions overwhelm leaden epic as Palance's hirsute, Christ-obsessed Attila the Hun chews up the scenery and threatens to devour the cast of thousands

Men of Sherwood Forest (Hammer) d.Val Guest: Eileen Moore, Don Taylor. Don swaps the mean streets of the Naked City for the sun-dappled glades of Sherwood in robust low-budgeter shot in England

The Black Shield of Falworth (Universal) d.Rudolph Maté: Tony Curtis, Janet Leigh. Tony pouts prettily as the peasant boy who's really the son of the banished Earl of Falworth, declaring in broadest Bronx, 'Yondah lies da cassle of my faddah!'

The Saracen Blade (Columbia) d.William Castle: Betta St John, Ricardo Montalban. Unintentionally hilarious script defeats the cast's gallant attempts to make sense of medieval tale of romance and revenge

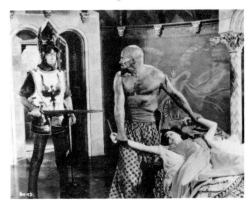

The Black Knight (Columbia) d. Tay Garnett: Alan Ladd, Patricia Medina. A low point in Ladd's career as he exchanges trenchcoat for some preposterous property department armor in clodhopping tale of the Knights of the Round Table

Underwater! (RKO) d.John Sturges: Richard Egan, Jane Russell, Robert Keith, Gilbert Roland, Lori Nelson. Russell is poured into clinging swimwear for inspection in 3-D Superscope as she dives for sunken treasure in shark-infested Caribbean waters

20,000 Leagues Under the Sea (Disney) d.Richard Fleischer: James Mason. Stylish version of Jules Verne classic casts Mason as a memorably sardonic Captain Nemo cruising the ocean depths in the baroque submarine Nautilus

Panther Girl of the Congo (Republic) d.Franklin Adreon: Myron Healey, Phyllis Coates. Phyllis is the eponymous serial heroine, battling the claw monsters' and deadly nerve gas, protecting evil scientist Arthur Space's diamond mine

Passion (RKO) d.Allan Dwan: Cornel Wilde, Raymond Burr. Dark tale of vengeance in old California, distinguished by Van Nest Polglase's art direction and Dwan's characteristically vigorous, uncomplicated approach

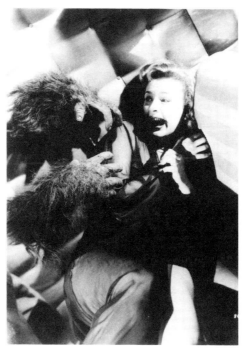

Phantom of the Rue Morgue (Warner) d.Roy Del Ruth. 3-D remake of *Murders in the Rue Morgue* (1932) induces more laughs than chills as Karl Malden hams it up wildly in the role originally played to sinister effect by Bela Lugosi

Valley of the Kings (MGM) d.Robert Pirosh: Robert Taylor, Eleanor Parker. Is he trying to tell us something? Taylor and Parker try to crack the secrets of the Pharaohs in meandering tale of archaeological intrigue

Untamed (Fox) d.Henry King: Hope Emerson, Susan Hayward. Boer leader Tyrone Power competes with rugged Richard Egan for tempestuous Irish immigrant Hayward in South African epic which rather sticks in the craw today

Khyber Patrol (UA) d.Seymour Friedman: Richard Egan, Dawn Addams, Donald Randolph. Egan and Addams compare pectorals in so-so actioner set on the Northwest Frontier

Green Fire (MGM) d.Andrew Marton: Grace Kelly, Paul Douglas, Stewart Granger. Emerald prospector Granger and coffee planter Kelly clash in the Colombian jungle before tumbling into the time-honored embrace in the final reel

Long John Silver (Fox) d.Byron Haskin: Robert Newton. Cost-conscious spin-off from Newton's Disney success as the peg-legged pirate, filmed in Australia and featuring a young Rod Taylor in a small part

Creature from the Black Lagoon (Universal) d.Jack Arnold: Ben Chapman, Julia Adams. Monster-on-the-loose masterpiece generates powerful erotic charge from the Gill-Man's understandable fascination with the lissom Adams and provided the inspiration from the opening sequence of *Jaws* (1975)

The Conquest of Space (Paramount) d.Byron Haskin. Based on Werner von Braun's book *The Mars Project*, this marked the end of the 'realist' cycle of space films until it was revived by *2001: A Space Odyssey* (1968)

Tobor the Great (Republic) d.Lee Sholem: Billy Chapin. Small scientific genius Chapin strikes up a telepathic relationship with his big robot buddy and foils a Communist spy plot. At the end poor old Tobor is shot off into space

Them! (Warner) d.Gordon Douglas. Atom tests in Nevada nourish a race of giant ants which come jingling out of the desert to infest the Los Angeles sewers before meeting the usual fiery end

Gojira (Toho) d.Inoshiro Honda: Godzilla. Aka *Godzilla, King of the Monsters*, this Japanese epic introduced a new tall, dark, fire-breathing leading man to the screen, doing what a 400ft Tyrannosaurus Rex has just gotta do

MELODRAMA

Six Bridges to Cross (Universal) d.Joseph Pevney: Tony Curtis, George Nader. Hoodlum Curtis graduates from petty offences to the criminal big-time in documentary-style rerun of the Boston Brinks robbery. Nader is the concerned cop who fails to reform him

Life in the Balance (Fox) d.Harry Horner: Anne Bancroft, Ricardo Montalban. Pint-sized sleuth Jose Perez tracks psychopathic killer Lee Marvin across Mexico City, placing himself in deadly peril in efficient location-shot thriller

Women's Prison (Columbia) d.Lewis Seiler: Jan Sterling, Ida Lupino, Cleo Moore, Vivian Marshall. Minor camp classic with Lupino as the sadistic superintendent of a prison bursting with B-movie favorites

Playgirl (Universal) d.Joseph Pevney: Shelley Winters, Richard Long. Colleen Miller is the Nebraskan innocent whose downward spiral from cover girl to party girl is halted by a repentant Winters

The Shanghai Story (Republic) d.Frank Lloyd: Marvin Miller, Ruth Roman. Ruth is the *femme fatale* suspected by interned Europeans of being in cahoots with slimy Communist police chief Miller

Las Vegas Shakedown (Allied Artists) d.Sidney Salkow: Coleen Gray, Dennis O'Keefe. Diverting programmer in which O'Keefe hits heavy trouble when he tries to run an honest gambling house in Sin City, Nevada – surely a logical impossibility

Rear Window (Paramount) d.Alfred Hitchcock: James Stewart. Tetchy Stewart is the wheelchair-bound lensman spying on his neighbors, and stumbling on murder, in rich metaphor for the impulses and fantasies released in the darkened shrine of cinema

Miami Story (Columbia) d.Fred F Sears: Beverly Garland, Barry Sullivan. Reformed mobster Sullivan infiltrates a Florida crime syndicate in routine gangster pic graced by the presence of the state's real-life Senator, one A Smathers

Suddenly (UA) d.Lewis Allen: Nancy Gates, Frank Sinatra. Frank in fine form as the rat-like leader of a trio of assassins lying in wait for the US President in the sleepy little town of the title

The Long Wait (UA) d.Victor Saville: Mary Ellen Kay, Anthony Quinn. Hackneyed meller in which anguished amnesiac Quinn discovers that he's been framed for a series of crimes

Shield for Murder (UA) d.Edmond O'Brien: Marla English. Two-timing cop O'Brien shoots a bookie and robs him of a bundle. Unknown to him the crime has been witnessed by a deaf mute!

The Mad Magician (Columbia) d.John Brahm: Vincent Price, Mary Murphy. Engagingly dotty 3-D *Grand Guignol* in which crazed illusionist Price's tricks eventually backfire on him

Naked Alibi (Universal) d.Jerry Hopper: Gloria Grahame, Sterling Hayden. Disgraced detective Hayden tracks cop-killer Gene Barry to a Mexican border town, where he's lying low with saloon singer Gloria at her flooziest

Witness to Murder (UA) d.Roy Rowland: Barbara Stanwyck. Standard Stanwyck slide into hysteria as she fails to convince anyone that sinister neighbor George Sanders is a strangler

A Bullet is Waiting (Columbia) d.John Farrow: Jean Simmons, Brian Aherne. A plane crash strands Sheriff Stephen McNally and his prisoner Rory Calhoun in fey Simmons' remote ranch

Private Hell 36 (Film Makers) d.Don Siegel: Steve Cochran, King Donovan. Tight little Ida Lupino-produced low-budgeter in which cops Cochran and Howard Duff succumb to temptation after recovering stolen money, with predictably distressing results

Pushover (Columbia) d.Richard Quine: Fred MacMurray, Kim Novak. Kim is the gangster's moll for whom infatuated cop MacMurray strays from the straight and narrow

Gorilla at Large (Fox) d.Harmon Jones: Anne Bancroft, Cameron Mitchell. Florid 3-D murder shocker, set in an amusement park whose main attraction – a ferocious gorilla - goes satisfyingly berserk in the final reel

Rogue Cop (MGM) d.Roy Rowland: Anne Francis, Robert Taylor. Effectively sour performance from Taylor as a cop in the pocket of the Mob tracking down his brother's killer

Dial M for Murder (Warner) d.Alfred Hitchcock: Robert Cummings, Grace Kelly. Claustrophobic 3-D version of stage hit with suave Ray Milland planning 'perfect crime' to dispose of wealthy wife Kelly

Mr Arkadin (Warner) d.Orson Welles: Robert Arden, Orson Welles. A rambling coda to *Citizen Kane* (1941) in which Orson plays a mysterious financier attempting to obliterate his shady past. Aka *Confidential Report*

Woman's World (Fox) d.Jean Negulesco: Lauren Bacall, Cornel Wilde. Tartly observed excursion into the sexual politics of the business world as three applicants for a top executive job parade themselves and their wives before auto baron Clifton Webb

Bad Day at Black Rock (MGM) d.John Sturges: Spencer Tracy, Ernest Borgnine. Tracy is the grizzled one-armed stranger rattling the skeleton in the closet of a dusty little desert town, and giving Borgnine a terrific beating in the process

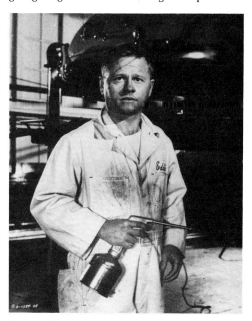

Drive a Crooked Road (Columbia) d.Richard Quine: Mickey Rooney. Strong performance from Rooney as a gullible auto mechanic conned into a bank robbery by Dianne Foster and playboy-turned-criminal Kevin McCarthy

The Barefoot Contessa (UA) d.Joseph L Mankiewicz: Ava Gardner. Ava is the Spanish gypsy girl who is maneuvered into screen stardom by sourly cynical director Humphrey Bogart

The Caine Mutiny (Columbia) d.Edward Dmytryk: Fred MacMurray, Humphrey Bogart, Robert Francis. Bogart unforgetable as the paranoid minesweeper skipper Captain Queeg whose mental collapse forces subordinates Francis and Van Johnson to extreme measures and a court martial

Black Tuesday (UA) d.Hugo Fregonese: Peter Graves, Jean Parker, Edward G Robinson. Edward G stirs memories of his heyday at Warner in old-fashioned prison break drama full of gunplay and hardboiled dialogue

The Big Combo (Allied Artists) d.Joseph H Lewis: Brian Donlevy, Richard Conte, Steve Mitchell. Gripping low-budget *film noir* in which cop Cornel Wilde's obsessive pursuit of racketeer Conte is fueled by a pathetic infatuation with his classy moll Jean Wallace

Human Jungle (Allied Artists) d.Joseph M Newman: Jan Sterling, Gary Merrill. Fast-moving B-movie retread of *Detective Story* (1951) follows a crowded day in a police precinct house

Highway Dragnet (Allied Artists) d.Nathan Juran: Richard Conte, Mary Beth Hughes. The cops want to question hitch-hiking ex-Marine Conte for the murder of B-girl Hughes. But a twist lies in store when he accepts a lift from Joan Bennett and Wanda Hendrix

Dangerous Mission (RKO) d.Louis King: Vincent Price, Victor Mature, Piper Laurie, William Bendix. Laurie is the witness of a gangland killing pursued to Glacier National Park by Price, who's out to kill her, and Mature, who's determined to bring her back alive

Black Widow (Fox) d.Nunnally Johnson: Van Heflin. Philandering Broadway producer Heflin finds little minx Peggy Ann Garner dead in his apartment. Could bitchy star Ginger Rogers be the lethal lady of the title?

Magnificent Obsession (Universal) d.Douglas Sirk: Jane Wyman, Rock Hudson. Exquisitely textured weepie with Rock as the playboy who redeems himself by training as a surgeon after accidentally blinding Wyman. Originally filmed in 1935 with Robert Taylor, Irene Dunne

Night People (Fox) d.Nunnally Johnson: Gregory Peck, Anita Bjork. Location-shot Cold War drama, set in Berlin, in which intelligence officer Peck defuses crisis caused by Communist kidnapping of a US soldier

Human Desire (Columbia) d.Fritz Lang: Broderick Crawford, Gloria Grahame, Glenn Ford. Gritty remake of Renoir's *La Bête Humaine* (1938) in which sultry Gloria ensnares Ford in a plot to do away with her homicidal husband Crawford

End of the Affair (Columbia) d.Edward Dmytryk: Deborah Kerr, Van Johnson. Frightful hash of a gloomy Graham Greene novel miscasts Van Johnson and Kerr as a pair of star-crossed lovers in wartime London

The Flame and the Flesh (MGM) d.Richard Brooks: Bonar Colleano, Lana Turner. Curious Italian-set remake of a 1937 French melo, *Naples au Baiser du Feu,* in which it takes Carlos Thompson an age to realize Lana's a tramp

Bait (Columbia) d.Hugo Haas: Cleo Moore, Hugo Haas, John Agar. Typically morbid Haas tale of double-cross and retribution with a weird prologue by Cedric Hardwicke as the Devil

The High and the Mighty (Warner) d.William Wellman: William Campbell, Wally Brown, John Wayne, Doe Avedon, Robert Stack. Group jeopardy yarn in which an airliner loses an engine on flight from Honolulu to San Francisco. All-star supporting cast keeps the tension boiling

The Country Girl (Paramount) d.George Seaton: Grace Kelly, Bing Crosby, William Holden. Mournful Crosby gives an immensely assured performance as a broken-down singer attempting a comeback encouraged by director Holden. Kelly his dowdy wife

This Is My Love (RKO) d.Stuart Heisler: Hal Taylor, Dan Duryea, Linda Darnell. Angst-drenched domestic drama in which fantasist Darnell and sister Faith Domergue tangle over handsome Rick Jason. Duryea is Faith's crippled husband

COMEDY

Susan Slept Here (RKO) d.Frank Tashlin: Anne Francis, Dick Powell, Debbie Reynolds. Teenage spitfire Debbie is dumped on bachelor scriptwriter Powell to help with a screenplay on juvenile delinquency

We're No Angels (Paramount) d.Michael Curtiz: Aldo Ray, Humphrey Bogart, Peter Ustinov. Three escaped convicts from Devil's Island come to the aid of the French family with whom they find refuge

Living It Up (Paramount) d.Norman Taurog: Jerry Lewis, Sheree North. Slapdash remake of screwball classic *Nothing Sacred* (1937) with Lewis in the Lombard role as suspected radiation victim exploited by publicity-hungry newshound Janet Leigh

Phffft! (Columbia) d.Mark Robson: Jack Lemmon, Kim Novak. Which is the sound of Lemmon and Judy Holliday's marriage breaking up in characteristically knowing George Axelrod comedy

The Long Long Trailer (MGM) d.Vincente Minnelli: Desi Arnaz, Lucille Ball. Lucy and Desi embark on an incident-packed honeymoon shackled to the monstrous vehicle of the title. A big box-office hit

Fireman Save My Child (Universal) d.Leslie Goodwins: Hugh O'Brian, Buddy Hackett. High-speed period farce originally slated for Abbott and Costello features manic participation from the immortal Spike Jones and His City Slickers as the San Francisco Fire Service is motorized

Ma and Pa Kettle at Home (Universal) d.Charles Lamont: Percy Kilbride, Marjorie Main, Brett Halsey. An agricultural scholarship beckons for bright young Kettle brat Halsey but it hangs on an inspection of their ramshackle farm by finicky judges Alan Mowbray, Ross Elliott

The Atomic Kid (Republic) d.Leslie Martinson: Robert Strauss, Mickey Rooney. Uranium prospector Rooney survives an atomic blast with comic results in far-off days when radiation was considered good for a laugh

She Couldn't Say No (RKO) d.Lloyd Bacon: Jean Simmons, Robert Mitchum. Scatterbrained rich girl Simmons' determination to repay her debt to a small Arkansas town provides complications galore. Arthur Hunnicutt droll as the local lush

Three-Ring Circus (Paramount) d.Joseph Pevney: Zsa Zsa Gabor, Dean Martin. Sexy trapeze artist Zsa Zsa and nice Joanne Dru compete for big-headed Dean while Jerry Lewis clowns around. Elsa Lanchester turns up as the Bearded Lady

Francis Joins the WACs (Universal) d.Arthur Lubin: Lynn Bari, Chill Wills, Julia Adams. A clerical error consigns Donald O'Connor and the talkative mule to the WACs, with Wills doubling in usual role of Francis' gravelly voice and as Army bigwig

The Trouble with Harry (Paramount) d.Alfred Hitchcock: Shirley MacLaine, John Forsythe, Mildred Natwick, Edmund Gwenn. MacLaine's debut, as the young widow, in fat Alfred's gleefully black comedy about a troublesome corpse disturbing the tranquil tenor of a New England community drenched in the ravishing colors of autumn

Bowery to Bagdad (Allied Artists) d.Edward Bernds: Huntz Hall, Joan Shawlee, Leo Gorcey, Eric Blore. The usual cut-rate shenanigans, distinguished by the presence of the droll Blore, slumming it rather at the end of his career

Paris Playboys (Allied Artists) d.William Beaudine: Leo Gorcey, Huntz Hall. Ferret-faced Hall takes the place of a French scientist lookalike to foil an assassination attempt and invents a new explosive

MUSICALS

Young at Heart (Warner) d.Gordon Douglas: Frank Sinatra, Doris Day. Musical remake of *Four Daughters* (1938) with Day as the prim schoolteacher marrying embittered songwriter Sinatra on the rebound

So This Is Paris (Universal) d.Richard Quine: Mara Corday, Tony Curtis. Three American matelots find romance on the boulevards of Gay Paree in dull imitation of *On the Town* (1949)

Red Garters (Paramount) d.George Marshall: Guy Mitchell, Rosemary Clooney. Vigorous Western spoof gave Clooney and Buddy Ebsen the chance to score a big hit with 'Brave Man'

The Glass Slipper (MGM) d.Charles Walters: Leslie Caron. Michael Wilding, looking very unhappy in leotards, is discreetly guided by Caron through plush version of the Cinderella story, which includes two ballet sequences choreographed by Roland Petit

Brigadoon (MGM) d.Vincente Minnelli: Cyd Charisse, Barry Jones, Gene Kelly. Airless, stagebound fantasy in which New Yorkers Kelly and Van Johnson stumble across the fairytale Scottish village of Brigadoon, which appears only once every 100 years

Lucky Me (Warner) d.Jack Donohue. Doris Day, Phil Silvers. A troupe of entertainers is stranded in Miami. Filmed in WarnerColor, it marked the debut of Angie Dickinson

Seven Brides for Seven Brothers (MGM) d.Stanley Donen: Howard Keel, Jane Powell. The seven Pontipee brothers set about securing wives in feast of dynamic dancing exhilaratingly choreographed by Michael Kidd

A Star Is Born (Warner) d.George Cukor: Judy Garland. Luminous remake of 1937 Janet Gaynor/ Fredric March vehicle with Judy at her most quiveringly vulnerable as Vicki Lester, singing 'The Man that Got Away'. James Mason harrowing as fading star Norman Maine. One of the all-time greats

White Christmas (Paramount) d.Michael Curtiz: Danny Kaye, Bing Crosby. The year's top money-maker and first in VistaVision. Danny and Bing are the song and dance men saving Dean Jagger's ski resort hotel from bankruptcy by putting on the inevitable show. Rosemary Clooney, Vera Ellen co-star

There's No Business Like Show Business (Fox) d.Walter Lang: Marilyn Monroe, Donald O'Connor, Mitzi Gaynor. You might disagree after enduring Johnnie Ray opting for the priesthood in gaudy tale of vaudeville family built around Irving Berlin evergreens. Monroe at her sexiest in 'Heat Wave'

Deep in My Heart (MGM) d.Stanley Donen: Helen Traubel, Jose Ferrer. Star-packed biopic of composer Sigmund Romberg (Ferrer) includes the 'Leg of Mutton Rag' – shown here– and many of Sig's greatest hits

Hit the Deck (MGM) d.Roy Rowland: Debbie Reynolds. Remake of a 1930 RKO flop pitches three sailors into a complicated love tangle. Choreography by Hermes Pan and some pleasant Vincent Youmans songs

Three for the Show (Columbia) d.H C Potter: Betty Grable. CinemaScope remake of *Too Many Husbands* (1940) with Grable discovering she's married to dancer Gower Champion and to composer Jack Lemmon, who returns from the dead

The Seven Little Foys (Paramount) d.Melville Shavelson: Bob Hope, James Cagney. Somewhat heartless biopic of vaudevillian and father of seven Eddie Foy springs to life when Cagney puts on his hoofing shoes as George M Cohan

Rose Marie (MGM) d.Mervyn LeRoy: Ann Blyth, Howard Keel. Studio's third version of Rudolf Friml's operetta and first musical made in CinemaScope. For all those who thrill to the sound of 'The Indian Love Call'

Jupiter's Darling (MGM) d.George Sidney: Howard Keel, Esther Williams. The one with the pink elephants, Howard Keel as Hannibal and George Sanders as Esther's fiancé Fabius Maximus. The sum total is a kitsch classic

Carmen Jones (Fox) d.Otto Preminger: Dorothy Dandridge, Harry Belafonte. Update of Bizet's Spanish opera turns Dandridge's Carmen into a parachute factory girl and Don José into GI Belafonte. Both stars' singing was dubbed

WESTERNS

Sitting Bull (UA) d.Sidney Salkow: J Carrol Naish. Relatively accurate account of events leading up to the Battle of the Little Big Horn. Iron Eyes Cody played Crazy Horse and acted as the technical adviser

They Rode West (Columbia) D.Phil Karlson: May Winn, Robert Francis. Cavalry medic Francis hits trouble when he decides to treat an epidemic on a Kiowa reservation

Three Hours to Kill (Columbia) d.Alfred Werker: Dana Andrews. Accomplished programmer in which Andrews survives a lynching for a murder he did not commit to become an embittered roving gunfighter searching for the real killer

Cattle Queen of Montana (RKO) d.Allan Dwan: Lance Fuller, Barbara Stanwyck, Chubby Johnson. Ronald Reagan is the mysterious gunman (and undercover agent) riding to rancher Stanwyck's rescue. The incomparably professional Stanwyck did all her own stunts

Track of the Cat (Warner) d.William Wellman: Robert Mitchum, William Hopper. Ambitious psychological Western counterpoints the hunt for an unseen cougar with a family drama in a snowbound North California farmhouse

Two Guns and a Badge (Allied Artists) d.Lewis Collins: Bob Wilke, Wayne Morris, Roy Barcroft. The last of the series Westerns features Morris as an ex-convict mistaken for a sheriff. Beverly Garland provides the romantic interest

River of No Return (Fox) d.Otto Preminger: Rory Calhoun, Marilyn Monroe. Feckless gambler Calhoun abandons saloon singer wife Monroe to the tender mercies of a sulky Robert Mitchum and a river-raft ride through Indian territory

Jubilee Trail (Republic) d.Joseph Kane: Vera Ralston, Forrest Tucker. Dance-hall queen Ralston teaches Easterner Joan Leslie the tricks of frontier life, romances grizzled trader Tucker in flamboyant would-be epic

Destry (Universal) d.George Marshall: Audie Murphy, Mari Blanchard. Impoverished remake of Marshall's 1939 hit *Destry Rides Again* with Murphy and Blanchard in the Stewart/Dietrich roles. Some salty cameos from Edgar Buchanan, Thomas Mitchell, Wallace Ford

The Naked Dawn (Universal) d.Edgar G Ulmer: Arthur Kennedy, Betta St John. Kennedy superb as a swaggering bandido in fatalistic ultra-cheapie high on gloomy atmospherics

Run for Cover (Paramount) d.Nicholas Ray: John Derek, James Cagney. Eloquently fraught essay on 'father and son relationship' in which Sheriff Cagney and crippled deputy Derek head towards a fatal confrontation

Drum Beat (Warner) d.Delmer Daves: Alan Ladd, Charles Bronson. In his first major role Bronson plays 'Captain Jack', the treacherous Modoc chief brought to book by Ladd in handsomely photographed adventure

Vera Cruz (UA) d.Robert Aldrich: Burt Lancaster, Gary Cooper, Sarita Montiel. Burt is the wolfishly grinning villain in double-cross extravaganza which heavily influenced the Westerns of Sergio Leone

Tall Man Riding (Warner) d.Lesley Selander: Dorothy Malone. Tightly controlled programmer in which Randolph Scott joins forces with Malone to settle accounts with her swindling cattle baron father Robert Barrat

The Lone Gun (UA) d.Ray Nazarro: George Montgomery, Dorother Malone. Routine oater in which disillusioned Marshal Montgomery turns in his badge but is soon obliged to deal with obnoxious outlaws Neville Brand and Douglas Kennedy

Saskatchewan (Universal) d.Raoul Walsh: Alan Ladd, Shelley Winters, Jay Silverheels. Good-looking but sluggish tale of Indian-reared Mountie Ladd snuffing out renegade Sioux north of the border after the Battle of the Little Big Horn

Tennessee's Partner (RKO) d.Allan Dwan: Ronald Reagan, Rhonda Fleming. Another little gem from Dwan, set in a gold rush town, where Fleming's 'Duchess' runs a Marriage Market for prospectors and sells them caviar at $1,000 a portion and doughnuts slightly cheaper at $5 each. Rhonda's a girl who knows the score

The Americano (RKO) d.William Castle: Ursula Thiess, Glenn Ford. Western-style action in a Brazilian setting as cowboy Ford delivers a consignment of prize Brahma bulls to an opulent South American ranchero and runs into some heavy gunplay

The Bounty Hunter (Warner) d.André de Toth: Marie Windsor Randolph Scott. Stonefaced Scott trails robbers Howard Petrie, Dub Taylor and Windsor, who are masquerading as solid citizens

Silver Lode (RKO) d.Allan Dwan: John Payne, Dolores Moran. Low-budget masterpiece encloses anti-McCarthy tract in standard tale of Payne trying to clear himself of murder charge while the object of a manhunt led by Dan Duryea

Johnny Guitar (Republic) d.Nicholas Ray: Joan Crawford, Sterling Hayden. Stylized, surreal, neurotic Western stands all the genre's conventions on their heads as guntotin' Crawford slugs it out with cattle queen Mercedes McCambridge. Among many delights an astonishingly virtuosic opening sequence

The Far Country (Universal) d.Anthony Mann: Corinne Calvet, Walter Brennan. Elegant, formally perfect Western in which cattleman James Stewart is the cantankerous loner hero and John McIntyre the paradoxically affable villain. Filmed in the majestic setting of the Canadian Rockies

Ten Wanted Men (Columbia) d.H Bruce Humberstone: Richard Boone, Randolph Scott. A rare Western from veteran B hand Humberstone in which Scott attempts to bring a measure of law and order to a vast tract of Arizona territory

Broken Lance (Fox) d.Edward Dmytryk: Robert Wagner. Western remake of *House of Strangers* (1949) with cattle baron Spencer Tracy as the overbearing paterfamilias leaving psychological claw marks all over his inadequate sons

The Black Dakotas (Columbia) d.Ray Nazarro, Noah Beery Jr, Gary Merrill. Confederate agent Merrill tries to foment an Indian uprising and steal their gold in solid B-movie with a Civil War setting

The Far Horizons (Paramount) d.Rudolph Maté: William Demarest, Fred MacMurray, Donna Reed. MacMurray co-stars with Charlton Heston in limply inaccurate account of the Lewis and Clark expedition of 1803. Reed the shapely Indian guide over whom the explorers fall out

The Desperado (Allied Artists) d.Thomas Carr: James Lydon, Wayne Morris. Excellent performance from Lydon, best remembered as Henry Aldrich, teaming up with wanted killer Morris to end carpetbagger Rayford Barnes' Texas reign of terror

Outlaw's Daughter (Fox) d.Wesley Barry: Jim Davis, Kelly Ryan. Convinced that Sheriff Davis has killed her reformed outlaw father, Dalton girl Ryan takes to crime unaware that one of her companions is the real killer

Four Guns to the Border (Universal) d.Richard Carlson: Rory Calhoun. Bank robbers Calhoun, George Nader and Jay Silverheels rescue Colleen Miller and Walter Brennan from the Apache . Features a surprisingly torrid love scene between Miller and Calhoun

Seminole Uprising (Columbia) d.Earl Bellamy: Karin Booth, George Montgomery. The Indians are on the warpath again in studio-bound low-budgeter long on words and short on action

Apache (UA) d.Robert Aldrich: Jean Peters, Burt Lancaster. Hard-hitting piece with Lancaster as one of Geronimo's braves who wages a one-man war against the US cavalry. Marred by an upbeat ending inserted on the studio's insistence

Drums Across the River (Universal) d.Nathan Juran: Audie Murphy, Hugh O'Brian. Troublemaking Lyle Bettger fans the flames of an Indian war to get his hands on reservation gold and also finds time to frame Audie for a bullion robbery

The Command (Warner) d.David Butler: Joan Weldon, Guy Madison. The studio's first in CinemaScope stars Madison as the inexperienced commander of a troop-laden wagon train in darkest Wyoming. Sam Fuller had a hand in the script

Garden of Evil (Fox) d.Henry Hathaway: Gary Cooper, Susan Hayward. Three adventurers – Cooper, Richard Widmark, Cameron Mitchell – set out to rescue Hayward's husband Hugh Marlowe, who's trapped in a gold mine deep in Mexican bandit territory

The Gambler from Natchez (Fox) d.Henry Levin: Dale Robertson, Debra Paget. Colorful Louisiana adventure, set in the 1800s, in which Robertson tracks down his father's killers and succumbs to lusty river girl Paget

Davy Crockett, King of the Wild Frontier (Buena Vista) d.Norman Foster: Buddy Ebsen, Fess Parker. Entertaining story of the celebrated Indian scout assembled from Disney TV series. Started a rage for funny furry hats

The Violent Men (Columbia) d.Rudolph Maté:
Barbara Stanwyck, Brian Keith. Stanwyck is the
ranchhouse Regina Giddens carrying on with
Keith, killing disagreeable husband Edward G
Robinson in a fire by hanging on to his crutches
in hand-me-down version of *Jubal* (1956)

Stranger on Horseback (UA) d.Jacques
Tourneur: Joel McCrea, Kevin McCarthy. McCrea
is the austere judge who is forced to buckle on
his gunbelt in order to set justice straight and
bring a murderer to trial

Rails into Laramie (Universal) d.Jesse Hibbs:
John Payne. Workmanlike oater in which Mari
Blanchard enterprisingly organizes an all-woman
jury to help Payne convict crooked saloonkeeper
Dan Duryea, who's trying to keep out the railroad

ROMANCE

Three Coins in the Fountain (Fox) d.Jean
Negulesco: Louis Jourdan, Maggie McNamara,
Clifton Webb. Three American girls working in
Rome toss coins in the Trevi fountain and wish
for romance. The fountain delivers. Jule Styne-
Sammy Cahn title song won an Oscar

To Catch a Thief (Paramount) d.Alfred
Hitchcock: Cary Grant, Grace Kelly. Cat burglar
Carey prowls smoothly around ultra-chic Kelly in
Riviera-set caper larded with sophisticated sexual
innuendo

About Mrs Leslie (Paramount) d.Daniel Mann:
Robert Ryan, Shirley Booth. Flashback tale of
affair between rooming house owner Booth and
business tycoon Ryan benefits from the offbeat
casting of the two stars

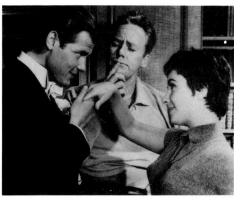

The Last Time I Saw Paris (MGM) D.Richard
Brooks: Roger Moore, Van Johnson, Elizabeth
Taylor. Glossy but bathetic F Scott Fitzgerald
adaptation set among the disillusioned smart set
in postwar Paris

Sabrina (Paramount) d.Billy Wilder: William
Holden, Audrey Hepburn. Hepburn is romanced
by middle-aged tycoon Humphrey Bogart to keep
her out of the clutches of happy-go-lucky younger
brother Holden. Watch out for Francis X
Bushman in small role

Desirée (UA) d.Henry Koster: Jean Simmons,
Marlon Brando. Perfectly idiotic historical
romance with Brando as Napoleon, Simmons in
the title role as the love who forsakes him for
Michael Rennie's Count Bernadotte and Merle
Oberon as a glacial Josephine. Brando recalled,
'I played it for laughs'

The Student Prince (MGM) d.Richard Thorpe: Louis Calhern, Edmund Gwenn, Edmund Purdom. Mario Lanza's throbbingly dubbed voice emerges disconcertingly from pretty-boy Purdom's lips as he woos barmaid Ann Blyth in old Heidelberg

Athena (MGM) d.Richard Thorpe: Steve Reeves, Debbie Reynolds, Jane Powell. Weird musical romance celebrating the joys of healthy living with Reeves displaying the male body beautiful, Vic Damone warbling 'The Girl Next Door'

AMERICANA

The Long Gray Line (Columbia) d.John Ford: Maureen O'Hara, Tyrone Power. Turgid story of West Point athletic trainer Power qualifies as the longest, grayest movie to which Ford ever put his hand

The Bob Matthias Story (Allied Artists) d.Francis D Lyon: Ward Bond, Bob Matthias. Routine biopic of the great Olympic athlete with Matthias turning in an engagingly self-effacing performance as himself

Prince of Players (Fox) d.Philip Dunne: Richard Burton, John Derek. The story of the acting Booths, with Burton as Edwin, Derek as Lincoln's assassin John, and Raymond Massey as their crazy old drunk of a father

On the Waterfront (Columbia) d.Elia Kazan: Rod Steiger, Marlon Brando. Celebrated naturalistic melodrama, groaning under the weight of powerful performances, in which washed-up pug Brando ensures bloody martyrdom when he informs on the Mob running the docks

East of Eden (Warner) d.Elia Kazan: Julie Harris, James Dean. High-class Steinbeck weepie with Dean affectingly hesitant as Raymond Massey's unloved son Cal, Jo Van Fleet his brothel-keeping mother

BRITISH AND FOREIGN

Radio Cab Murder (Eros) d.Vernon Sewell: Lana Morris, Jimmy Hanley. Former safecracker Hanley agrees to act as the police's 'inside man' to bust open a crime syndicate

Romeo and Juliet (Rank) d.Renato Castellani: Laurence Harvey, Susan Shentall. Ravishingly photographed but in all other respects undistinguished stab at Shakespeare. Shentall's first and last film

Duel in the Jungle (ABPC) d.George Marshall: Jeanne Crain, Dana Andrews. Adventurer David Farrar fakes his own death but is followed into the jungle by fiancée Crain and stolid insurance investigator Andrews

A Kid for Two Farthings (British Lion) d.Carol Reed: Diana Dors, Jonathan Ashmore, Sid James. Sentimental Cockney fairytale in which Ashmore's 'unicorn' brings good luck to the people of Petticoat Lane

Star of India (Eros) d.Arthur Lubin: Cornel Wilde, Jean Wallace. Returning to France after five years in India, Wilde finds his estate confiscated by nasty Herbert Lom, who has also stolen the priceless diamond of the title

The Master Plan (Grand National) d.Cy Endfield: Norman Wooland, Wayne Morris. Wooland and Morris lurch around in pursuit of a spy ring, a quest complicated by Wayne's blackout problem

Lease of Life (Ealing) d.Charles Frend: Adrienne Corri, Robert Donat. Touching performance from Donat as a dull dog of a clergyman given a year to live and deciding to speak his mind

Beau Brummell (MGM) d.Curtis Bernhardt: Peter Ustinov, Stewart Granger. Granger excellent in the title role as the Regency's most outrageous dandy. Ustinov enjoys himself as the fatuous Prince of Wales

The Beachcomber (Rank) d.Muriel Box: Robert Newton. The pop-eyed one is Maugham's bibulous remittance man redeeming himself in South Seas cholera epidemic. Remake of *Vessel of Wrath* (1938)

Knave of Hearts (ABPC) d.René Clement: Gérard Philipe, Joan Greenwood. Acerbic sex comedy in which philandering Philipe plays fast and loose with the ladies but is confined to a wheelchair in mordant conclusion

West of Zanzibar (Ealing) d.Harry Watt: Anthony Steel. Gamewarden Steel rounds up an ivory-poaching ring while his wife Sheila Sim adorns the African bush with an astonishingly varied wardrobe

Meet Mr Callaghan (Eros) d.Charles Saunders: Derrick de Marney, Delphi Lawrence. Thick-ear private eye Slim Callaghan solves a murder mystery in British poverty row version of *The Thin Man*

The Purple Plain (Rank) d.Robert Parrish: Gregory Peck, Lyndon Brook. Gripping drama, set in 1945, in which rehabilitated pilot Peck endures nightmare journey through the Burmese jungle after his plane comes down

The Sea Shall Not Have Them (Eros) d.Lewis Gilbert: Michael Redgrave, Dirk Bogarde. Archetypal war drama casts four survivors from a crashed plane adrift in a North Sea minefield. One of them has vital information about German V-weapons

The Sleeping Tiger (Anglo-Amalgamated) d.Joseph Losey: Dirk Bogarde, Alexis Smith. Feverish melodrama in which psychiatrist Alexander Knox's attempts to analyze hoodlum Bogarde end in spectacular tragedy

One Good Turn (Rank) d.John Paddy Carstairs: Norman Wisdom, Thora Hird. Odd-job man Wisdom saves an orphanage from a greedy speculator with a series of heroically comic feats

The Seekers (Rank) d.Ken Annakin: Noel Purcell, Jack Hawkins. Misfiring British attempt at a 'Western', set in the pioneering days of New Zealand, moves glumly towards a bloody climax

The Rainbow Jacket (Ealing) d.Basil Dearden: Fella Edmonds, Bill Owen. Solid horse racing drama in which Edmonds is introduced to the hard facts of the racing game by disgraced jockey Owen

Lilacs in the Spring (Republic) d.Herbert Wilcox: Anna Neagle, David Farrar, Errol Flynn. Stagy cavalcade of Neagliana which allows the star to fantasize herself into a number of roles, including Nell Gwynn and Queen Victoria

The Maggie (Ealing) d.Alexander Mackendrick: Tommy Kearins, Paul Douglas, Alex Mackenzie. A cargo of bathroom fittings bound for the Scottish vacation home of vulgar American millionaire Douglas is hijacked by the the foxy old captain of the rusting coastal puffer of the title

Seagulls Over Sorrento (MGM) d.John and Roy Boulting: Gene Kelly, John Justin. Uneasy mixture of comedy and drama as British and American scientists develop a dangerous experimental torpedo at a remote wartime research station

Doctor in the House (Rank) d.Ralph Thomas: Dirk Bogarde, Donald Sinden, Kenneth More. Colossal comedy hit followed the erratic progress of four medical students at St Swithins Teaching Hospital at whose apex stands the impressive figure of James Robertson Justice as Sir Lancelot Spratt

The Love Lottery (Ealing) d.Charles Crichton: Herbert Lom, David Niven. Matinée idol Niven is persuaded to offer himself as first prize in a giant lottery run by a sinister/comic international organization. Humphrey Bogart turns up in a cameo at the end

The Colditz Story (British Lion) d.Guy Hamilton: John Mills, Eric Portman. Wartime drama set in high-security castle bulging with hardened Allied escapers. Much twitting of bumbling Germans by effortlessly superior British types

The Man Who Loved Redheads (British Lion) d.Harold French: Moira Shearer, John Justin. Romantic comedy in which elderly Justin's lifetime infatuation with a succession of redheads – all played by Shearer – finally catches up with him

Genevieve (Rank) d.Henry Cornelius: Kay Kendall, Kenneth More. Sophisticated British version of an American-style marital comedy centers on the rivalry between vintage car owners More and John Gregson

Beautiful Stranger (British Lion) d.David Miller: Stanley Baker, Ginger Rogers. Ginger becomes a murder suspect in labyrinthine thriller by the end of which it is almost impossible to know why any of the characters are doing anything

You Know What Sailors Are (Rank) d.Ken Annakin: Akim Tamiroff, George Coulouris. Tipsy Navy Lieutenant Donald Sinden's practical joke leads to an international scramble for a supposedly deadly weapon in cheerfully slapdash romp

The Belles of St Trinians (British Lion) d.Frank Launder: George Cole, Alastair Sim. Rollicking farce in which the most anarchic girls' academy in the world is presided over by Sim's stately headmistress, Miss Fritton

Forbidden Cargo (Rank) d.Harold French: Nigel Patrick, Terence Morgan. Birdwatcher Joyce Grenfell puts suave customs man Patrick on the track of smuggling siblings Elizabeth Sellars and Terence Morgan

An Inspector Calls (British Lion) d.Guy Hamilton: Alastair Sim, Bryan Forbes, Brian Worth. J B Priestley's tart Edwardian morality tale in which Sim's mysterious 'inspector' lays bare the hypocrisy of a rich industrialist's family

The Divided Heart (Ealing) d.Charles Crichton: Cornell Borchers, Armin Dahlen. All stops out tug-of-love drama in which a war orphan becomes the subject of a legal battle when his real mother is found to be still alive

Father Brown (Columbia) d. Robert Hamer: Alec Guinness, Joan Greenwood. Guinness is G K Chesterton's whimsical priestly sleuth on the trail of master criminal Peter Finch in comedy-drama full of felicitous touches

The Green Scarf (British Lion) d.George More O'Ferrall: Michael Redgrave, Kieron Moore. Whiskery French lawyer Redgrave takes on the seemingly hopeless case of a shipboard murder to which deaf and blind mute Moore has already confessed

The Good Die Young (British Lion) d.Lewis Gilbert: Joan Collins, Richard Basehart. Psychotic playboy Laurence Harvey, appropriately called Rave, persuades a sad bunch of characters to pull a mail van heist. It goes wrong

The Constant Husband (British Lion) d.Sidney Gilliat: Kay Kendall, Rex Harrison, Cecil Parker. Brittle comedy in which lawyer Harrison recovers from amnesia to discover that he is married to seven wives. First British movie to have US premiere on TV. Did you catch it?

Double Exposure (Rank) d.John Gilling: Gary Marsh, John Bentley. Private dick Bentley's routine assignment turns into a case of murder in promising B-movie which never quite delivers

Animal Farm (ABPC) d.John Halas, Joy Batchelor. Powerful full-length cartoon version of George Orwell's political fantasy is marred by changed ending in which the animals stage a counter-revolution against Napoleon and his pigs

Devil Girl from Mars (Danzigers) d.David Macdonald: Patricia Laffan, Adrienne Corri, Hugh McDermott, Joseph Tomelty, Hazel Court. Laffan is PVC-clad spacegirl Nyah scouring the Scottish countryside for British beefcake to service her Martian matriarchy. Deliriously awful Z-budget stab at space opera

Du Rififi Chez les Hommes (France) d.Jules Dassin: Marie Sabouret, Jean Servais. Celebrated silent robbery sequence provides highlight of cynical saga of jewel thieves falling out over the loot

Les Diaboliques (France) d.Georges-Henri Clouzot: Vera Clouzot, Simone Signoret. The ultimate spine-tingler in which a hateful schoolmaster is killed by his wife and mistress. But is he really dead? The seedy private school setting, with its weed-clogged pool, is rank with poisonous imagery

Le Rouge et Le Noir (France) d.Claude Autant-Lara: Gérard Philipe, Danielle Darrieux. Measured version of the Stendhal classic gave Darrieux her favorite role as Madame de Renal

Madame de . . . (France) d.Max Ophuls: Vittorio de Sica, Danielle Darrieux. Lady of fashion Darrieux pawns her earrings which are retrieved by husband Charles Boyer and given to his mistress. In turn she sells them and they are bought by diplomat de Sica who presents them to Madame de . . .

Shichinin No Samurai (Japan) d.Akira Kurosawa: Toshiro Mifune. A 16th-century Japanese village hires a band of professional warriors to defend it against marauding outlaws. Technically brilliant, visually superb and full of ambiguities and ironies absent from the Hollywood remake *The Magnificent Seven* (1960)

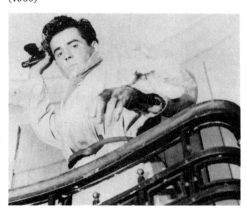

Pokolenie (Poland) d.Andrzej Wajda. Wajda's debut with an assured if overly romantic treatment of the growth to personal and political maturity of a young working-class layabout

Ulisse (Italy) d.Mario Camerini: Kirk Douglas. Bemused Kirk fills the title role, voyaging home to Penelope after the Trojan War in enjoyably random mish-mash of classical myth on which a small army of screenwriters labored seemingly in vain

La Strada (Italy) d.Federico Fellini: Giulietta Masina, Anthony Quinn. Huge success for Quinn as the brutal street performer Zampano. Whether his performance was great acting or inspired hamming depends on your point of view

Senso (Italy) d.Luchino Visconti: Alida Valli, Farley Granger. Surprisingly good performance from Granger as the worthless Austrian soldier who betrays the aristocratic Valli

Mambo (Italy) d.Robert Rossen: Silvana Mangano, Vittorio Gassman. Co-production in which Hollywood's heavy hand hovers over tale of salesgirl Mangano whose life is complicated by Gassman's penniless gambler and Michael Rennie's sickly count as she metamorphoses into a famous dancer

1955

Hollywood's big guns continued to fire broadside after broadside at the elusive target of television. *Oklahoma!*, the screen version of the Rodgers and Hammerstein Broadway hit, was the first picture in the new Todd-AO process, but teething toubles led to considerable distortion of the frame.

A series of musclebound spectaculars, set in varying anachronistic versions of Ancient Greece and Egypt were levered off the production line. Among them were *Alexander the Great, Helen of Troy* and *Land of the Pharaohs*, the last blessed with a script by William Faulkner located more closely to Memphis, Tennessee, than Memphis, Egypt. RKO's *The Conqueror*, starring John Wayne as Genghis Khan, was one of the decade's most deliciously wayward pieces of casting.

The small screen's telling reply came in the shape of *Marty*, an adaptation of a Paddy Chayevsky television play, costing a mere $350,000 and originally intended as a tax write-off. Directed by a veteran of TV drama, Delbert Mann, *Marty* starred Ernest Borgnine as the plug-ugly Bronx pork butcher sadly resigned to bachelorhood, the aimless rituals of male cameraderie and the demands of his elderly mother. He meets and woos sweet but plain teacher Betsy Blair, telling her, 'Dogs like us, we're not such dogs as we think we are.' This self-deprecating line of chat won Marty his girl and Borgnine the Best Actor Award. The film was also voted Best Picture and prompted a string of so-called 'clothesline dramas', medium-budget explorations of working-class life which owed much to Italian neo-realism and were scripted and directed by men who had learned their craft in live TV's 'Golden Age'; among them Rod Serling, Gore Vidal, Abby Mann, Robert Mulligan, Martin Ritt and John Frankenheimer.

Marty's oafish buddies were all fans of pulp maestro Mickey Spillane. In sharp contrast to Delbert Mann's earnest efforts to capture the everyday essence of the lives of unremarkable people was Robert Aldrich's brilliantly stylized *Kiss Me Deadly*, in which Ralph Meeker gave the performance of his life as the swaying, strutting PI Mike Hammer, a stunning portrayal of self-sufficient brutality. *Kiss Me Deadly*'s B-movie structure reverberates with echoes of ancient myth and the paranoia of the nuclear age, fixing it on the borderline between rough-neck thriller and science fiction *film noir*. This mood of unease was caught by Don Siegel's *Invasion of the Body Snatchers*, and the film has often been cited both as a classic anti-McCarthy tract and as a distillation of the decade's anti-Communist dread.

Drug addiction also came in for dramatic treatment in Otto Preminger's *The Man with the Golden Arm*, in which jazz man Frank Sinatra's skills as a poker dealer gave his needle-punctured 'golden arm' the quality of ironic metaphor. In a lighter vein Sinatra was teamed with Marlon Brando in *Guys and Dolls*, which gave the latter the chance to demonstrate that he could sing and dance as well as glower and mumble. In *The Seven Year Itch*, Billy Wilder unforgettably captured Marilyn Monroe's calculatedly innocent sexuality and her air of being the totally unconscious agent provocateuse of all the male preenings and posturings surrounding her.

James Stewart's final collaboration with Anthony Mann, *The Man from Laramie*, was a taut revenge Western full of flawless landscape photography, Stewart's suppressed malevolence and the friendly treachery of Arthur Kennedy. Roger Corman made a less distinguished directing debut with a Z-budget Western *Five Guns West*. Charles Laughton's first and only film as a director, *Night of the Hunter*, was a lyrical masterpiece in which Robert Mitchum gave one of the most hypnotic studies of evil in American cinema. Audie Murphy relived his wartime exploits in *To Hell and Back*; and Vic Morrow made a memorable screen debut as a snarling punk in *The Blackboard Jungle*, the first film to feature rock 'n' roll and to give its teenage characters a healthy measure of 'heptalk'.

Youth confronted adult incomprehension in Nicholas Ray's *Rebel Without a Cause*, in which James Dean formed a touching trio with Sal Mineo and Natalie Wood. On 30 September Dean was killed driving his Porsche shortly before filming of George Stevens' *Giant* finished. Death was, perhaps, the shrewdest of career decisions, freezing Dean in the sullenly romantic image of the lost leader of the beat generation.

Death also claimed promising young leading man Robert Francis, killed in a plane crash; Carmen Miranda, exotic star of many a Technicolor Fox extravaganza; John Hodiak, lantern-jawed leading man who had enjoyed a brief vogue in the war years; and Theda Bara, silent cinema's greatest vamp and the first star to be presented as an object of sexual fantasy.

Jack Lemmon's performance as the wily, lecherous Ensign Pulver in *Mister Roberts* won him the Best Supporting Actor Oscar. Best Supporting Actress was Jo Van Fleet, who played James Dean's brothel-keeping mother in East of Eden, a marvellously sardonic performance and her screen debut. Anna Magnani won the Best Actress Award with one of her favorite roles, the mourning widow succumbing to lusty Burt Lancaster in Tennessee Williams' *The Rose Tattoo*.

The number of feature films made in Hollywood was inexorably declining – the eight major studios' output was 215 films, compared with over 400 in 1951. The weekly average of cinema attendances in the United States dropped to 45.8 million, half that of the all-time high achieved in 1946.

Satyajit Ray became the first Indian film-maker to achieve an international reputation with *Pather Panchali*, the first of a great trilogy, which won the Grand Prix at Cannes. In Britain there was a rush of war films, the best of which was Michael Anderson's *The Dam Busters*, celebrating Bomber Command's heroic raid on the Ruhr dams. Alexander Mackendrick's *The Ladykillers* was the last great Ealing comedy, a surreal masterpiece in which Alec Guinness' gang of thieves was paralyzed by the moral innocence of sweet old lady Katie Johnson.

ACTION

The Looters (Universal) d.Abner Biberman: Julie Adams, Ray Danton, Thomas Gomez, Rory Calhoun, Frank Faylen. Riproaring B-movie throwback involves a crashed aircraft, a rescue party and a tempting bundle of loot

A Prize of Gold (Columbia) d.Mark Robson: Nigel Patrick, Richard Widmark. British-shot thriller in which USAF sergeant Widmark assembles a hand-picked team to lift a bullion consignment. But the best laid schemes. . .

Blood Alley (Warner) d.William Wellman: Lauren Bacall, John Wayne. Big John continues to biff the Commies, navigating a ferry-boat full of refugees to safety in Hong Kong

Big House USA (UA) d.Howard W Koch: Broderick Crawford, Ralph Meeker. Brutal prison break drama whose principal characters exhibit unrelieved villainy throughout, not least William Talman as Machine Gun Mason

To Hell and Back (Universal) d.Jesse Hibbs: Audie Murphy. Surprisingly good account of Murphy's progress from Texas farmboy to the most decorated US soldier of World War II. Contrives to avoid most of the usual clichés

The Racers (Fox) d.Henry Hathaway: Cesar Romero, Kirk Douglas. Driven Grand Prix ace Kirk's obsession with winning alienates fellow drivers and girlfriend Bella Darvi before he reforms

The Square Triangle (Universal) d.Jerry Hopper: Tony Curtis, John Day. Tony pulls on the gloves to raise money for alcoholic father Jim Backus. Naturally he punches his way to the top

Jump into Hell (Warner) d.David Butler: Jacques Sernas, Peter Van Eyck, Norman Dupont, Leon Lontok. Earnest lowbudgeter deals with the French military disaster at Dien Bien Phu in 1954, which marked the end of their colonial rule in Indochina

Hell on Frisco Bay (Warner) d.Frank Tuttle: Alan Ladd, Rod Taylor, Tina Carver. Old-fashioned waterfront melo finds Edward G Robinson in sinister form as the gang boss framing ex-cop Ladd

The Sea Chase (Warner) d.John Farrow: John Wayne, Lana Turner. World War II actioner with Wayne miscast as a 'good German' sailing a rusty old freighter from Sydney to the North Sea

Bhowani Junction (MGM) d.George Cukor: Stewart Granger, Ava Gardner. Ava is the half-caste in love with British officer Granger in confident version of John Masters' novel of the turbulent partition of India in 1947

Five Against the House (Columbia) d.Phil Karlson: Kim Novak, Guy Madison. Five friends set out to rob a casino in Reno, Nevada, in one of the most enjoyable minor movies of the decade

Foxfire (Universal) d.Joseph Pevney: Jane Russell, Jeff Chandler. East coast socialite Russell experiences severe culture shock when she marries half-breed Apache mining engineer Jeff and goes to live in an Arizona ghost town

ADVENTURE AND FANTASY

Diane (MGM) d.David Miller: Roger Moore, Lana Turner, Pedro Armendariz. If you can believe in Lana as Diane de Poitiers and Pedro as King Francis, you will love this costumer in whose script Christopher Isherwood had a hand

The Conqueror (RKO) d.Dick Powell: John Wayne, Susan Hayward. Mongol leader Wayne tells Susan: 'I shall keep you, Bortai, in response to my passion. Your hatred will kindle into love'. Need we say any more?

That Lady (Fox) d.Terence Young: Christopher Lee, Olivia de Havilland, Francoise Rosay. Olivia is the exotic Spanish powerbroker Anna de Mendoza, fatally falling for her protegé Gilbert Roland

The King's Thief (MGM) d.Robert Z Leonard: Ann Blyth, David Niven. Baroque costumer casts an ill-at-ease Niven as the scheming Duke of Brampton in tale of intrigue at the court of an exceptionally languid Charles II played by George Sanders

Alexander the Great (UA) d.Robert Rossen: Harry Andrews, Richard Burton. Virile Burton gets a blonde perm and most of the known world in dull, would-be serious account of history's greatest conqueror

Moonfleet (MGM) d.Fritz Lang: Joan Greenwood, George Sanders, Stewart Granger. Lang's first in CinemaScope is an immensely stylish 18th-century smuggling yarn, full of Gothic touches, with Greenwood and Sanders in feline form as the heavies

Helen of Troy (Warner) d.Robert Wise: Rosanna Podesta. Minor '50s icon Podesta, her features unclouded by thought, is the Face that Launched a Thousand Ships in Hollywood assault on Homer's Iliad

The Purple Mask (Universal) d.H Bruce Humberstone: Tony Curtis. Cheerfully idiotic French Revolution adventure loses its head with casting of Curtis as effete second cousin to the Scarlet Pimpernel

Lady Godiva (Universal) d.Arthur Lubin: Maureen O'Hara. Fiery Saxon noblewoman Maureen goes ever so discreetly naked through the streets of Coventry to prove the loyalty of her people in comic strip slice of medieval myth

The Prodigal (MGM) d.Richard Thorpe: Lana Turner. Lana sashays around menacingly as the evil high priestess of love, corrupting Edmund Purdom, who plays the Biblical ne'er do well with all the charisma of Zeppo Marx

Quentin Durward (MGM) d.Richard Thorpe: Kay Kendall, Robert Taylor. The lovely Kendall is reason enough to watch this handsome Walter Scott tale with Taylor in the title role, swashbuckling through medieval France

The Virgin Queen (Fox) d.Henry Koster: Richard Todd, Bette Davis. Imperious Davis reprise to her 1939 triumph as crafty Queen Bess, whose gimlet gaze falls fondly on Todd's small but perfectly formed Sir Walter Raleigh

Son of Sinbad (RKO) d.Ted Tetzlaff: Dale Robertson, Vincent Price. Spirited Arabian Nights burlesque with dashing Dale, the Forty (female) Thieves and Price as Omar Khayyam defeating the forces of Tamerlane the Cruel

Desert Sands (UA) d.Lesley Selander: John Carradine, Marla English, Keith Larsen. Foreign Legion farrago in which fanatic Carradine tricks English and Larsen into blind hatred of all Legionnaires with bloody consequences in desert fort climax

Land of the Pharaohs (Warner) d.Howard Hawks: Jack Hawkins, Kerima. Screenwriter William Faulkner's notions of how a Pharaoh might have talked enliven blockbuster in which the Great Pyramid and petulant, power-hungry Joan Collins compete for harassed Hawkins' attention

The Scarlet Coat (MGM) d.John Sturges: Cornel Wilde, Bobby Driscoll. Glossy War of Independence epic in which secret agent Wilde unmasks the traitor Benedict Arnold

Kiss of Fire (Universal) d.Joseph M Newman: Barbara Rush, Jack Palance. Jack is dispossessed nobleman El Tigre, escorting princess Rush from Santa Fe to Monterey in 16th-century Western

Captain Lightfoot (Universal) d.Douglas Sirk: Henry Hull, Rock Hudson. The brogue gets the better of Rock as he essays the role of a 19th-century Irish rebel tormenting the dastardly English

The Magnificent Matador (Fox) d.Budd Boetticher: Anthony Quinn, Maureen O'Hara, Thomas Gomez. Wolfishly grinning Quinn fills the title role, pursued by omens of death and a lustful O'Hara in colorful celebration of the corrida

Tarzan's Hidden Jungle (RKO) d.Harold Schuster: Gordon Scott. Tarzan helps UN medics Peter Van Eyck and Vera Miles and thwarts hunter Jack Elam's crazy plan to amass 2,000 barrels of animal fat and a small mountain of ivory and lion skins

The Left Hand of God (Fox) d.Edward Dmytryk: Lee J Cobb, Humphrey Bogart. World War II yarn, set in China, in which downed US pilot Bogart becomes warlord Cobb's adviser before taking a powder disguised as a priest

Pearl of the South Pacific (RKO) d.Allan Dwan: Virginia Mayo, Dennis Morgan. A trio of rogues pass off Virginia as a missionary to steal a cache of pearls guarded by the regulation giant octopus

Secret of the Incas (Paramount) d.Jerry Hopper: Charlton Heston, Nicole Maurey. Firm-jawed Chuck sets off in search of fabled treasure in fast-moving actioner

Escape to Burma (RKO) d.Allan Dwan: Robert Ryan, Barbara Stanwyck, David Farrar. More like trapped on the backlot as runaway Ryan takes refuge on Stanwyck's teak plantation followed by dogged policeman Farrar

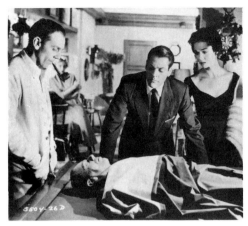

Invasion of the Body Snatchers (UA) d.Don Siegel: King Donovan, Kevin McCarthy, Dana Wynter. Parasite aliens replace human inhabitants of a sleepy California town with soulless simulacra in definitive evocation of '50s unease. You're next!

Tarantula (Universal) d.Jack Arnold: John Agar, Leo G Carroll, Mara Corday. Carroll's experiments in 'accelerated tissue growth' produce a monster spider and rearrange his own physiognomy in minor SF classic with eerie desert backdrop

It Came From Beneath the Sea (Columbia) d.Robert Gordon. Master animator Ray Harryhausen's 'quintopus' rises from the deep to topple the Golden Gate Bridge before being zapped with an atom-tipped torpedo

Revenge of the Creature (Universal) d.Jack Arnold: Lori Nelson. The Gill-Man is imprisoned in a Florida oceanarium where ichthyologists Nelson and John Agar try to teach him to speak. Mercifully, he escapes

King Dinosaur (Zigmor) d.Bert I Gordon: Bill Bryant, Wanda Curtis. Primitive SF exploiter, shot in a weekend. Made lavish use of stock footage from *One Million BC* (1940) and enlarged photographs of comatose lizards

The Day the World Ended (Golden State) d.Roger Corman: Paul Blaisdell, Lori Nelson. Mutants run amok in Corman's first SF movie, a post-holocaust drama with semi-conscious Biblical overtones struggling to surmount its poverty row limitations

This Island Earth (Universal) d.Joseph M Newman: Faith Domergue, Rex Reason, Jeff Morrow. Intriguing mixture of poetry and pulp, illuminated by superb special effects, as the inhabitants of the planet Metaluna enlist earthlings' help in their battle with the Zahgons

Creature with the Atom Brain (Columbia) d.Edward L Cahn: Richard Denning. Investigating police doctor Denning stumbles across an atom-powered zombie in surreal Curt Siodmak-scripted shocker which randomly combines gangsters, Nazis and the baleful effects of radiation

Gigantis (Toho) d.Motoyoshi Oda. Once again an A-blast revives Godzilla, who obliterates Osaka with much serious stomping of models before being buried under an avalanche

MELODRAMA

Murder is My Beat (Allied Artists) d.Edgar G Ulmer: Paul Langton, Barbara Payton. Another bizarrely disordered voyage into Ulmer's world of low-budget limbo in which a woman convicted of murder sees the man she is supposed to have killed apparently alive and well. To rank alongside the remarkable *Detour* (1945)

Lucy Gallant (Paramount) d.Robert Parrish: Charlton Heston, Claire Trevor. Oil-town sudser in which embittered career woman Jane Wyman dithers over dull rancher Heston. Trevor impeccable as ever in support

Slightly Scarlet (RKO) d.Allan Dwan: Arlene Dahl, Ted de Corsia. Flavorful James M Cain adaptation in which John Payne finds himself enmeshed in big city graft and corruption. Dahl entertaining as a tipsily man-hungry ex-con

The Shrike (Universal) d.Jose Ferrer: Jose Ferrer, June Allyson. Screen version of Ferrer's stage success as a Broadway director driven to collapse by supernag of a wife Allyson, here rather miscast

The Phenix City Story (Allied Artists) d.Phil Karlson: John Larch, Kathryn Grant. Raw, fast-moving indictment of an octopus-like syndicate, based on the real life clean up of 'Sin City' Alabama after the murder of a reforming attorney-general elect

There's Always Tomorrow (Universal) d.Douglas Sirk: Fred MacMurray, Barbara Stanwyck. Ross Hunter-produced remake of 1934 women's picture in which neglected husband Fred moons over old flame Stanwyck

The Naked Street (UA) d.Maxwell Shane: Farley Granger, Anne Bancroft. Racketeer Anthony Quinn engineers Granger's release from the death cell to marry pregnant sister Bancroft, after which things become a little complicated

New York Confidential (Warner) d.Russell Rouse: Richard Conte, Anne Bancroft. Busy Bancroft is mobster Broderick Crawford's daughter, Conte his hitman Nick Magellan in hard-hitting 'syndicate' thriller whose authenticity was vouched for by the city's Anti-Crime Committee

Tight Spot (Columbia) d.Phil Karlson: Ginger Rogers, Brian Keith. The situation in which Ginger finds herself when she is persuaded by DA Edward G Robinson to testify against her old boyfriend, racketeer Lorne Greene

The Night Holds Terror (Columbia) d.Andrew L Stone: John Cassavetes, Hildy Parks, Vince Edwards, Jack Kelly. Three hoodlums, led by the menacing Cassavetes, hold Kelly to ransom when they discover he has a wealthy father. Taut police procedure drama

Trial (MGM) d.Mark Robson: Arthur Kennedy, Katy Jurado. Pseudo-liberal drama in which Kennedy plays a crypto-Communist cynically using a young Mexican's murder trial to inflame racial hatred.Glenn Ford is the patsy he hires to act for the defence

All That Heaven Allows (Universal) d.Douglas Sirk: Rock Hudson, Jane Wyman, Agnes Moorehead. Wyman's infatuation with her gardener Hudson outrages family and friends in stylish entry in Sirk's masterly series of weepies

I Died a Thousand Times (Warner) d.Stuart Heisler: Lee Marvin, Earl Holliman, Shelley Winters. Misfiring remake of *High Sierra* (1941), with Jack Palance in the role that made Bogart a star

Storm Fear (UA) d. Cornel Wilde: Cornel Wilde, Jean Wallace. Gloomy thriller in which three fugitives from justice seek refuge in a snowbound cabin

Violent Saturday (Fox) d.Richard Fleischer: Stephen McNally, J Carrol Naish, Lee Marvin. Off-beat thriller in which McNally's plans for a smalltown bank heist have a dramatic effect on a number of the locals, including Richard Egan, Victor Mature, Sylvia Sidney and Ernest Borgnine

The Man With the Golden Arm (UA) d.Otto Preminger: Frank Sinatra. Dated but still powerful study of drug addiction with Frank as the jazz man stuck on the needle, Kim Novak the girl locking herself up with him on a crash cure

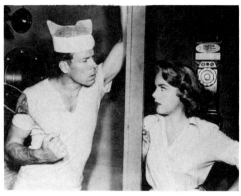

Shack Out on 101 (Allied Artists) d.Edward Dein: Lee Marvin, Terry Moore. Keenan Wynn's greasy beanery is the location for schlock classic in which Moore fights Communism and the lecherous advances of every man within miles. Marvin plays a spy called Slob

Not As a Stranger (UA) d.Stanley Kramer: Lon Chaney, Robert Mitchum. Portentous screen version of a best-seller following the rise of priggishly ambitious doctor Mitchum. Chaney touching as his alcoholic father. Kramer's debut as a director

The Man Who Knew Too Much (Paramount) d.Alfred Hitchcock: Doris Day, James Stewart, Richard Wattis. Hitch's remake of 1934 classic is disappointingly flat, with Doris' trilling of 'Que Sera Sera' calculated to dissipate the tension

Queen Bee (Columbia) d.Ranald MacDougall: Barry Sullivan, Joan Crawford. MacDougall ingeniously exploits Crawford's 'bitch on wheels' screen persona as the manipulative Southern belle everyone wants to murder, with some justification. Fay Wray turns up in a small part as one of her victims

Bedeviled (MGM) d.Mitchell Leisen: Anne Baxter, Steve Forrest. Implausible Paris-shot thriller in which trainee priest Forrest wrestles with temptations of the flesh while protecting fugitive murderer Baxter. A well-placed bullet resolves all his doubts

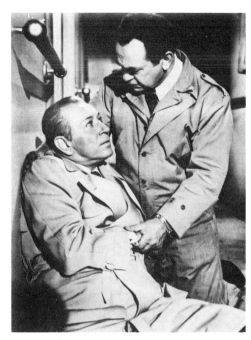

A Bullet for Joey (UA) d.Lewis Allen: George Raft, Edward G Robinson. Washed-up gangster Raft is lured out of Lisbon retirement to kidnap atom scientist George Dolenz. Viperish Audrey Totter is one of his old gang

The Blackboard Jungle (MGM) d.Richard Brooks: Vic Morrow, Sidney Poitier, Glenn Ford. Schoolteacher Glenn comes to grips with a classful of decidedly over-age delinquents in adaptation of an Evan Hunter novel which also features Bill Haley's 'Rock Around the Clock'

The Big Knife (UA) d.Robert Aldrich: Ida Lupino, Jack Palance. Aldrich slyly catches Palance unawares as the anxiety-riddled movie star on the slide in Clifford Odets' bitter tale of Hollywood folk. Studio boss Rod Steiger is a fearsome amalgam of Louis B Mayer and Harry Cohn

Cult of the Cobra (Universal) d.Francis D Lyon: Jack Kelly. Camp '50s favorite Faith Domergue is the leader of a coven of snake worshippers, loosing a plague of serpents on a hapless bunch of GIs

A Kiss Before Dying (UA) d.Gerd Oswald: Mary Astor, Virginia Leith, Robert Wagner. Minor masterpiece, based on an Ira Levin novel, with Wagner perfectly cast as a boyish psychopath and Astor outstanding as his doting mother

Illegal (Warner) d.Lewis Allen: Jayne Mansfield, Edward G Robinson, Nina Foch (r). Remake of *The Mouthpiece* (1932) with compromised former DA Edward G risking the wrath of the Mob when he defends his ex-assistant Foch on a murder rap

Running Wild (Universal) d.Abner Biberman: Kathleen Case, William Campbell, Mamie Van Doren, Jan Merlin. Undercover cop Campbell poses as a crook to pin the rap on Keenan Wynn, a modern Fagin running a gang of adolescent car thieves. Much jive talk

The Crooked Web (Columbia) d.Nathan Juran: Mari Blanchard, Frank Lovejoy, Richard Denning. Undercover agents Blanchard and Denning aim to trick café-owner Lovejoy into confessing a wartime murder in Germany. Mari's methods seem a little obvious

No Man's Woman (Republic) d.Franklin Adreon: Jill Jarmyn, Richard Crane, Marie Windsor. Marie is the hard-faced wrecker of sundry lives whose violent decease puts estranged husband John Archer in the frame for murder

The Rains of Ranchipur (Fox) d.Jean Negulesco: Lana Turner, Richard Burton. Remake of 1939 Tyrone Power vehicle in which Indian doctor-prince Burton is torn between his people and wealthy Lana. Earthquakes and monsoons concentrate his mind

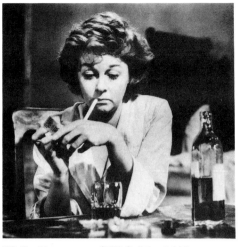

I'll Cry Tomorrow (MGM) d.Daniel Mann: Susan Hayward. Susan socks it to us in powerhouse portrayal of alcoholic singer Lillian Roth, effectively combining her performances in *My Foolish Heart* (1949) and *With a Song in My Heart* (1952)

Kiss Me Deadly (UA) d.Robert Aldrich: Gaby Rodgers. Ralph Meeker's Mike Hammer struts through a remarkable transformation of Spillane pulp into stylishly inspired allegory of violence, fascism and corruption in America. One of the key films of the decade

Killer's Kiss (UA) d.Stanley Kubrick: Jamie Smith, Irene Kane. Kubrick's second is a tight little low-budget revenge melodrama, the making of which provided the inspiration for an arty film of the 1980s, *Stranger's Kiss*

House of Bamboo (Fox) d.Sam Fuller: Robert Stack, Robert Ryan. Slammin' Sam serves up a great steaming hunk of raw cinema as detective Stack pursues master criminal Ryan through postwar Tokyo

The Cobweb (MGM) d.Vincente Minnelli: Gloria Grahame, Richard Widmark. Personal and professional frustrations boil over in a private mental hospital where the emotional temperature runs way over normal. Lillian Gish is one of the more engagingly dotty inmates

The Desperate Hours (Paramount) d.William Wyler: Fredric March, Humphrey Bogart. Bogie oozes sour, middle-aged malevolence as a gang of escaped convicts terrorize a classically Middle American family headed by an anguished March

The View from Pompey's Head (Fox) d.Philip Dunne: Dana Wynter, Richard Egan. Steamy Southern meller in which lawyer Egan's investigation into the apparently disappearing royalties of author Sidney Blackmer uncovers a scandal

Female on the Beach (Universal) d.Joseph Pevney: Jeff Chandler, Joan Crawford. Widow Joan's impetuous marriage to personable beach bum Jeff looks like buying her a one-way ticket to the morgue

The Girl in the Red Velvet Swing (Fox) d.Richard Fleischer: Joan Collins, Ray Milland. Overwrought account of a notorious society scandal of 1906 in which showgirl Collins' passion for architect Milland drives her demented playboy husband Farley Granger to murder

Hold Back Tomorrow (UA) d.Hugo Haas: John Agar. Characteristically morbid Haas cocktail in which condemned man Agar gets married on the night of his execution

COMEDY

You're Never Too Young (Paramount) d.Norman Taurog: Jerry Lewis, Mitzi McCall. Vague echoes of Billy Wilder's *The Major and the Minor* (1942) as halfwit Lewis poses as a 12-year-old to escape vengeful racketeer Raymond Burr

The Seven Year Itch (Fox) d.Billy Wilder: Marilyn Monroe, Tom Ewell. Ewell is the Walter Mittyish Don Juan manqué fantasizing about devastatingly ingenue neighbor Marilyn, a girl who can recognize classical music because 'there isn't a vocal'

How to Be Very Very Popular (Fox)d.Nunnally Johnson: Sheree North. Zippy approximation of '30s screwball as burlesque dancers North and Betty Grable escape from a murderer in Charles Coburn's co-ed college. North spends most of the film in an hypnotic trance, as you can see

The Private War of Major Benson (Universal) d.Jerry Hopper: Charlton Heston, Tim Hovey, Julie Adams. Heston proves that his forte is not comedy as a fierce disciplinarian humiliatingly placed in charge of a juvenile West Point staffed by nuns

Forever Darling (MGM) d.Alexander Hall: James Mason, Lucille Ball. Elegant guardian angel Mason gently steers Lucy's faltering marriage away from the rocks in mild comic fantasy

The Lieutenant Wore Skirts (Fox) d.Frank Tashlin: Sheree North, Tom Ewell. Vulgar Tashlin outing in which TV writer Ewell tries to convince his wife North that she is insane to obtain her discharge from the air force. You'll have to see the film to discover how she got there in the first place

Mister Roberts (Warner) d.John Ford, Mervyn LeRoy: James Cagney, William Powell, Jack Lemmon, Henry Fonda. Raucously sentimental celebration of Navy life in the Pacific. Cagney is the oafish captain, Powell the ironic 'Doc', Lemmon the libidinous loafer Ensign Pulver, and Fonda the officer of the title, tragically yearning for action. Sequel *Ensign Pulver* (1964)

The Tender Trap (MGM) d.Charles Walters: David Wayne, Celeste Holm, Frank Sinatra, Debbie Reynolds. Heartless romantic comedy in which womanizing theatrical agent Sinatra is finally tamed by ferociously naive young actress Reynolds

Francis in the Navy (Universal) d.Arthur Lubin: Donald O'Connor, Martha Hyer. The talking mule faces the indignity of being auctioned off as navy surplus. Not a moment too soon for flagging series

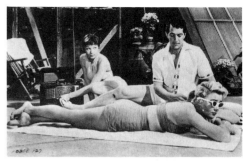

Artists and Models (Paramount) d.Frank Tashlin: Shirley MacLaine, Dean Martin, Dorothy Malone. Frantic Dean and Jerry outing in which jibbering Jerry's nightmares attract the attentions of a spy ring when they're reproduced in Dean's comic strip

Abbott and Costello Meet the Mummy (Universal) d.Charles Lamont: Bud Abbott, Lou Costello. A and C go in search of the Big Bandaged One and the untold wealth of the Pharaohs, hotly pursued by scheming Marie Windsor

MUSICALS

Daddy Long Legs (Fox) d.Jean Negulesco: Fred Astaire, Leslie Caron. Millionaire Fred sponsors French orphan Caron's education and finds altruism leading to romance in third film version of 1912 Jean Webster novel. Best song Johnny Mercer's 'Something's Gotta Give'

The Court Jester (Paramount) d.Norman Panama, Melvin Frank: Danny Kaye. Danny dances foolish attendance on wicked Basil Rathbone in uninhibited medieval farce graced by the eccentric presence of Mildred Natwick as the necromancer Griselda

Love Me or Leave Me (MGM) d.Charles Vidor: James Cagney, Doris Day. Doris is Ruth Etting, the singer unhappily married to the simply appalling Martin 'the Gimp' Snyder, played with relish by Cagney

Sincerely Yours (Warner) d.Gordon Douglas: Dorothy Malone, Liberace. Hypnotically ghastly remake of an old George Arliss film, *The Man Who Played God* (1932), with Liberace as an egomaniac pianist who becomes a reformed character when he loses his hearing

It's Always Fair Weather (MGM) d.Stanley Donen, Gene Kelly: Michael Kidd, Gene Kelly, Dan Dailey. Three wartime buddies meet up ten years later only to find they have nothing in common any more. Kelly sings 'I Like Myself' while gliding around on rollerskates

The Vagabond King (Paramount) d.Michael Curtiz: Oreste, Kathryn Grayson. VistaVision hokum was the fourth screen version of a Rudolf Friml warhorse based on the adventurous life of the French medieval poet François Villon

Oklahoma! (MGM) d.Fred Zinnemann: Gordon MacRae, Charlotte Greenwood. The corn is quite literally as high as an elephant's eye in Todd-AO version of Rodgers and Hammerstein's 1943 smash. Outstanding support from Gloria Grahame as Ado Annie, Rod Steiger as Jud Fry

Guys and Dolls (MGM) d.Joseph L Mankiewicz: Sheldon Leonard, Stubby Kaye, Marlon Brando. Stubby stops the show with 'Sit Down You're Rocking the Boat' in colorful pastiche of Damon Runyan's world of hoods and golden-hearted hookers. Brando sings convincingly as Skye Masterson, the gambler falling for missionary lady Jean Simmons

Gentlemen Marry Brunettes (UA) d.Richard Sale: Jane Russell, Jeanne Crain. Showbiz sisters Russell and Crain cut a swathe through the Continent in the Roaring Twenties, playing hell with a small army of helpless males including the wonderful Rudy Vallee as himself

The Second Greatest Sex (Universal) d.George Marshall: Jeanne Crain, George Nader. Kansas ladies withhold their favors Lysistrata-style to put a stop to all that tiresome male feuding. Lots of acrobatic dancing in the style of *Seven Brides for Seven Brothers* (1954)

Ain't Misbehaving (Universal) d.Edward Buzzell: Rory Calhoun, Jack Carson, Piper Laurie. Rich Rory falls for chorus girl Piper while his hardboiled minder Carson tries hard to protect his charge's fortune

My Sister Eileen (Columbia) d.Richard Quine: Betty Garrett, Kurt Kasznar, Janet Leigh. Garrett and Leigh are the lively girls from Ohio living it up in Greenwich Village in property with a complicated past which includes a joyous 1942 screen comedy version starring Rosalind Russell

Kismet (MGM) d.Vincente Minnelli: Dolores Gray, Howard Keel, Sebastian Cabot. Gray a delight as Wazir Cabot's Wife of Wives, Keel the poet-beggar Haaj in handsome if slow-moving Arabian Nights romance previously filmed in 1930, 1942

Interrupted Melody (MGM) d.Curtis Bernhardt: Eleanor Parker, Glenn Ford. Strong central performance from Parker in moving biopic of the great dramatic soprano Marjorie Lawrence, struck down by poliomyelitis at the height of her career. Her vocals were dubbed by Eileen Farrell

High Society (MGM) d.Charles Walters: Frank Sinatra, Grace Kelly. Smooth as silk remake of *The Philadelphia Story* (1940). Frank and Bing Crosby sing 'Now You Have Jazz'. Kelly's fine, if you haven't seen Hepburn in the original

Bring Your Smile Along (Columbia) d.Blake Edwards: Frankie Laine, Keefe Brasselle. Lyric-writing out-of-towner Constance Towers finds romance and smash hits in the Big Apple with tunesmith Brasselle. Frankie bellows away throughout

Girl Rush (Paramount) d.Robert Pirosh: Eddie Albert, Rosalind Russell. Ros inherits a flyblown Las Vegas gambling house but is soon involved with handsome Fernando Lamas, owner of the money-spinning Golden Flamingo

Pete Kelly's Blues (Warner) d.Jack Webb: Jack Webb, Peggy Lee. Musical melodrama, set in the 1920s, with trumpeter Webb taking on the racketeers, Lee touching as a singer succumbing to the booze

WESTERNS

Smoke Signal (Universal) d.Jerry Hopper: Dana Andrews, Piper Laurie. A small cavalry patrol attempt to evade an Indian war party on their trail by way of uncharted river rapids

Many Rivers to Cross (MGM) d.Roy Rowland: Eleanor Parker, Victor McLaglen, Robert Taylor. Enjoyable frontier comedy-drama, set in 18th-century Kentucky, with McLagen in fine knockabout form as Parker's ruffianly father

The Last Frontier (Columbia) d.Anthony Mann: Victor Mature, Robert Preston. Mann's restless camera follows the changes brought to the life of heroically naive trapper Mature when 'civilization' comes to the wilderness in the form of a cavalry outpost commanded by martinet Preston

Texas Lady (RKO) d.Tim Whelan: Barry Sullivan, Claudette Colbert. Romance between crusading newspaperwoman Claudette and gambler Sullivan was veteran director Whelan's last. Title song gave Les Paul and Mary Ford a big hit

Wichita (Allied Artists) d.Jacques Tourneur: Vera Miles, Joel McCrea. Relaxed McCrea is Wyatt Earp, cleaning up a railhead cow town in stylish Western with strong supporting cast

Man With the Gun (UA) d.Richard Wilson: Robert Mitchum. Weary gunman Mitchum cleans up Sheridan City in an attempt to win back his estranged wife Jan Sterling

Man Without a Star (Universal) d.King Vidor: Kirk Douglas, Jeanne Crain. Kirk is the drifter who suppresses his hatred of barbed wire on the range to lead small ranchers against scheming cattle queen Crain. Lovely performance from Claire Trevor as a hardbitten saloon queen with a heart of gold

The Tall Men (Fox) d.Raoul Walsh: Jane Russell, Clark Gable. Ruthlessly ambitious Robert Ryan and mature realist Gable compete for an assured Russell on an epic cattle drive from Texas to Montana. Leisurely storytelling, superb cinemaphotography, relaxed playing in masterful Western

The Spoilers (Universal) d.Jesse Hibbs: Anne Baxter, Jeff Chandler, Barbara Britton. Fifth screen version of Rex Beach's Klondike adventure preserves the spectacular slugfest, this time between Chandler and Rory Calhoun, but offers little else beyond a weird performance from Ray Danton as a sinister gunslinger

Tribute to a Bad Man (MGM) d.Robert Wise: Don Dubbins, James Cagney, Royal Dano. Cagney, now noticeably portly, plays an irascible horse-breeder, owner of the 'JR' ranch, at constant war with rustlers and his spirited Greek housekeeper Irene Papas

Strange Lady in Town (Warner) d.Mervyn LeRoy: Greer Garson, Dana Andrews. Doctor Garson battles with male prejudice in Santa Fe but contrives to treat Billy the Kid, Lew Wallace and Geronimo in easygoing oater full of striking locations

Five Guns West (Palo Alto) d.Roger Corman: Dorothy Malone, John Lund. Corman's first movie with Confederate officer Lund leading a band of paroled criminals in search of a Northern gold shipment and a traitor

The Last Hunt (MGM) d.Richard Brooks: Robert Taylor, Russ Tamblyn. Taylor is the Indian-hating hunter obsessed with slaughtering the dwindling buffalo herds, who meets an icy end, frozen inside a buffalo carcass

The Rawhide Years (Universal) d.Rudolph
Maté: Arthur Kennedy, Tony Curtis. Riverboat
gambler Curtis is framed for murder and pursued
by the law and the baddies in the form of amiable
Kennedy and menacing Peter Van Eyck

Lawless Street (Columbia) d.Joseph H Lewis:
Angela Lansbury, Warner Anderson. Town-tamin'
Marshall Randolph Scott cleans up Medicine
Bend and is reunited with wife Lansbury in
characteristically superior Lewis offering

Comanche (UA) d.George Sherman: Kent Smith,
Linda Cristal. Strange little movie pursues 'White
Man and Red Man Must be Brothers' theme with
some highly original casting, including Mike
Mazurki as an Indian brave

Rage at Dawn (RKO) d.Tim Whelan: Randolph
Scott. Undercover agent Scott tracks down the
Reno brothers – Forrest Tucker, Myron Healey, J
Carrol Naish – while romancing their sister Mala
Powers. Ends with a lynching

The Man from Laramie (Columbia) d.Anthony
Mann: James Stewart. Mann's last collaboration
with Stewart grafts elements of King Lear on to
the time-honored theme of revenge. The scene
in which Alex Nicol shoots Stewart pointblank in
the hand is one of the most shockingly brutal in
all Westerns

The Return of Jack Slade (Allied Artists)
d.Harold Schuster: Mari Blanchard, John Ericson.
To settle his father's debt to society, Ericson pins
on a badge in serviceable programmer

Great Day in the Morning (RKO) d.Jacques
Tourneur: Virginia Mayo, Robert Stack. North-
South tensions reach breaking point as gold-
hungry prospectors tangle with the townsfolk of
Denver on the eve of the Civil War

The Indian Fighter (UA) d.André de Toth: Kirk
Douglas, Elsa Martinelli. Scout Douglas saves a
wagon train from Indian massacre and Martinelli
takes a celebrated naked dip in sub-Fordian
exercise hustled along with some brio by de Toth

Mohawk (Renown) d.Kurt Neumann: Scott
Brady. Deranged John Hoyt stirs up an Indian war
which is skilfully defused by traveling artist Brady
whose reward is lithe chief's daughter Rita Gam

Chief Crazy Horse (Universal) d.George
Sherman: Suzan Ball, Victor Mature. Mature plays
the victor of the Little Big Horn determined to
unite the tribes against the white man but dying
at the hands of renegade half-caste Little Big Man,
played by Ray Danton

Apache Woman (Golden State) d.Roger Corman: Joan Taylor, Lance Fuller. Half-breed Taylor is forced to choose between Indian affairs agent Lloyd Bridges and her outlaw brother Fuller in another primitive but lively Corman Western

Gunpoint! (Allied Artists) d.Alfred Werker: Fred MacMurray, Walter Brennan. Peaceloving storekeeper MacMurray brings down a bank robber with a lucky shot. But a grateful town has second thoughts about helping him out when the dead man's brothers swear revenge

The Last Command (Republic) d.Frank Lloyd: Sterling Hayden, Ernest Borgnine. Hayden plays Jim Bowie in workmanlike account of the siege of the Alamo which makes fairly free with the facts in true Hollywood fashion

The Kentuckian (UA) d.Burt Lancaster: Burt Lancaster, Donald MacDonald. Backwoodsman Burt's journey to Texas is bogged down by a blood feud and a notably ferocious bull-whipping from no-good innkeeper Walter Matthau

The Road to Denver (Republic) d.Joseph Kane: Lee J Cobb, Skip Homeier, Lee Van Cleef (r). Brothers John Payne and Homeier find themselves on opposite sides of the law in robust programmer handled with as much verve as the low budget allowed

Red Sundown (Universal) d.Jack Arnold: Robert Middleton, Rory Calhoun. Briskly handled B in which reluctant gunman Calhoun buckles on his holster to prevent a range war. Martha Hyer provides the love interest

ROMANCE

Summertime (Lopert/Korda) d.David Lean: Rossano Brazzi, Katharine Hepburn. Leathery Hepburn softens under the gentle romantic glare of heartthrob Rossano in Venice-set affair handled with Lean's customary deliberation

The Lady and the Tramp (Disney) d.Hamilton Luske, Clyde Geronimi, Wilfred Jackson. Disney's first feature-length cartoon in CinemaScope. Highlight is a torch song – dubbed by Peggy Lee – performed by a mongrel floozie

Miracle in the Rain (Warner) d.Rudolph Maté: Paul Picerni, Jane Wyman, Eileen Heckart. Sentimental treatment of a briefly idyllic affair between Plain Jane Wyman and GI Van Johnson, who 'returns' after being killed in action

Marty (UA) d.Delbert Mann: Betsy Blair, Ernest Borgnine. Marvellous performance from Borgnine as the unprepossessing Bronx butcher who unexpectedly finds love. Originally a Paddy Chayevsky TV play

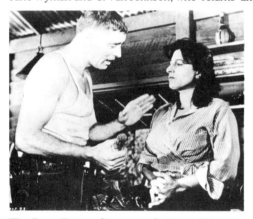

The Rose Tattoo (Paramount) d.Daniel Mann: Burt Lancaster, Anna Magnani. Magnani is splendidly earthy as the Gulf Coast widow romanced by roistering truck driver Burt in effective adaptation of a Tennessee Williams play

The Birds and the Bees (Paramount) d.Norman Taurog: David Niven, George Gobel, Mitzi Gaynor. Feeble remake of the 1941 Preston Sturges hit *The Lady Eve*, with Niven salvaging some honor in the role originally played by Charles Coburn

Love Is a Many Splendored Thing (Fox) d.Henry King: Jennifer Jones, William Holden. Married newsman Holden falls in love with beautiful Eurasian doctor Jones, the widow of a Chinese general, but gets himself conveniently killed in the Korean War. Title song won an Oscar

AMERICANA

Come Next Spring (Republic) d.R G Springsteen: Steve Cochran, Ann Sheridan. Unpretentious but affecting drama in which drunkard Cochran returns to the Arizona farm, wife and child he deserted to redeem himself as the hired hand

Night of the Hunter (UA) d.Charles Laughton: Robert Mitchum. Laughton's only film as a director is haunting, dreamlike allegory of innocence and evil, with Mitchum supplying the evil as cinema's most dementedly fraudulent man of God

Goodbye My Lady (Warner) d.William Wellman: Walter Brennan, Brandon de Wilde. Gently paced boy and dog story set in the Mississippi swamplands and directed with loving care by Wellman

The Court Martial of Billy Mitchell (Warner)
d.Otto Preminger: Ralph Bellamy, Gary Cooper.
Ponderous courtroom drama casts a taciturn
Cooper as the legendary champion of the bomber
who ultimately fell out with the US military
Establishment

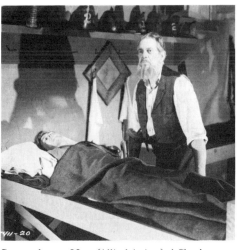

Seven Angry Men (Allied Artists) d.Charles
Marquis Warren: Raymond Massey. Strong
performance from Massey as John Brown, a part
he had already essayed to some effect in *Santa
Fe Trail* (1940)

The Eternal Sea (Republic) d.John H Auer:
Dean Jagger, Alexis Smith, Sterling Hayden. Low-
budget biopic of Admiral John Hoskins, played
rather glumly by Hayden, who overcame crippling
World War II injuries to pioneer the use of jet
aircraft on America's carriers

Picnic (Columbia) d.Joshua Logan: Cliff Robertson, William Holden.
Always at his best as a heel, drifter Holden steals Kim Novak from buddy
Robertson before moving on in fine screen version of a William Inge play

Rebel Without a Cause (Warner) d.Nicholas Ray: Sal Mineo, James Dean,
Natalie Wood. As Ray's disenchanted teenage alter ego Dean proves that to
achieve cult status your minimum requirements are a windcheater, spotless
white T-shirt and a great head of hair

A Man Called Peter (Fox) d.Henry Koster: Jean
Peters, Richard Todd. One of Todd's best
performances as the Scottish minister Peter
Marshall who rose to become chaplain to the US
Senate

Go Man Go (UA) d.James Wong Howe: Dane
Clark, Pat Breslin, Sidney Poitier. Pacy account
of the formation and rise to fame of the Harlem
Globetrotters basketball team directed by one of
cinema's greatest cameramen

The McConnell Story (Warner) d.Gordon
Douglas: June Allyson, Alan Ladd. Workmanlike
tribute to veteran pilot and Korean War jet ace
Captain Joseph McConnell. As ever, Allyson is
the understanding wife

BRITISH AND FOREIGN

The Deep Blue Sea (Fox) d.Anatole Litvak: Vivien Leigh, Kenneth More. Terence Rattigan's sombre play of a doomed romance between suicidal Leigh and feckless World War II fighter ace More, who turns in a quite flawless performance

The Dark Avenger (Fox) d.Henry Levin: Michael Hordern, Errol Flynn. Trapped inside his armor, Flynn looks badly in need of a drink as he lurches through the history books as the Black Prince, rescuing Joanne Dru from the clutches of French nobleman Peter Finch

Passage Home (Rank) d.Roy Baker: Peter Finch, Diane Cilento. Unwanted passenger Cilento raises the temperature on an unhappy merchant ship skippered by the grim Finch as it steams slowly homeward from South America

Footsteps in the Fog (Columbia) d.Arthur Lubin: Jean Simmons, Stewart Granger. Tangled period chiller in which poisoner Granger takes just a little too much of his own medicine in an attempt to rid himself of blackmailing housekeeper Simmons

Richard III (British Lion) d.Laurence Olivier: Claire Bloom, Laurence Olivier. Larry is mesmerically malevolent as Richard Crookback in superbly realized Shakespeare. An impeccable cast includes Stanley Baker as Henry Tudor

The Ship That Died of Shame (Ealing) d.Basil Dearden: Richard Attenborough, George Baker. Essay in postwar disillusionment as the crew of the decommissioned Motor Torpedo Boat 1087 describe a downward spiral from smuggling to murder before their boat 'rebels'

I Am a Camera (British Lion) d.Henry Cornelius: Julie Harris, Laurence Harvey. Tepid adaptation of Isherwood's autobiographical tales of 1930s Berlin, filtered through a John Van Druten play, with Harvey as Herr Issyvoo and Harris as Sally Bowles

Out of the Clouds (Ealing) d.Basil Dearden: Robert Beatty, James Robertson Justice. Old-fashioned portmanteau film revolving around incidents at a fogbound airport

Happy Ever After (ABPC) d.Mario Zampi: Barry Fitzgerald, David Niven. A collection of colorful Irish villagers plan to rid themselves of disagreeable new squire Niven, who turns out to be a rack renter who won't even stand a round of drinks

The Man Who Never Was (Fox) d. Ronald Neame: Robert Flemyng, Clifton Webb. Competent account of a 1943 British Intelligence triumph in which a body bearing 'secret' documents was used to convince the Germans that an invasion of Greece was about to be launched on the eve of the landings in Sicily

Albert RN (Dial) d.Lewis Gilbert: Jack Warner, Robert Beatty, Anthony Steel. True wartime adventure in which naval POWs devise a remarkably lifelike dummy – which can even smoke a cigarette – to cover an escape

Above Us the Waves (Rank) d.Ralph Thomas: William Russell, John Mills, Anthony Wager. Midget submarines attack the German pocket battleship Tirpitz moored menacingly in a Norwegian fjord

Cockleshell Heroes (Columbia) d.Jose Ferrer: Trevor Howard (1), Anthony Newley. Romanticized account of an heroic wartime operation in which a small group of Marines raid the Bordeaux docks with limpet mines in flimsy canoes

The Dam Busters (ABPC) d.Michael Anderson: Robert Shaw, Richard Todd. Key British war film recounting the development by Barnes Wallis (Michael Redgrave) of the 'bouncing bomb' and its use against the Ruhr dams by an elite Bomber Command squadron led by Wing Commander Guy Gibson (Todd)

An Alligator Named Daisy (Rank) d.J Lee Thompson: Diana Dors, Donald Sinden. Amiable frolic finds harassed songwriter Sinden attempting to cope with the web-footed leading lady and his busty heiress fiancée Dors

Carrington VC (British Lion) d.Anthony Asquith: Noelle Middleton, David Niven, Raymond Francis. Niven plays a war hero whose battles with military bureaucracy lead to a court-martial

Simba (Rank) d.Brian Desmond Hurst: Donald Sinden, Dirk Bogarde. Forceful drama, set in East Africa during the time of the Mau Mau rebellion. One of the more thoughtful attempts to come to terms with the end of the British Empire

Storm Over the Nile (British Lion) d.Terence Young, Zoltan Korda: Mary Ure, Anthony Steel. Stolid remake of Korda's 1939 imperial classic *The Four Feathers* casts Steel as the British officer branded a cad and a coward who chooses a strange way of redeeming himself in the Sudan

The Feminine Touch (Ealing) d.Pat Jackson: Belinda Lee, Mandy Miller. Anemic soaper, badly in need of a blood transfusion, set in a busy hospital where Lee finds romance with handsome doctor George Baker

Timeslip (Anglo-Amalgamated) d.Ken Hughes: Peter Arne, Gene Nelson. Ingenious SF thriller in which scientist Arne helps Nelson and Faith Domergue to foil a sabotage plot after surviving a murder attempt which leaves his brain working seven seconds ahead of time

Cast a Dark Shadow (Rank) d.Lewis Gilbert: Margaret Lockwood, Dirk Bogarde, Kathleen Harrison. Stagy thriller in which slimy Bogarde bumps off his first wife Mona Washbourne and then plans to rid himself of No. 2 Lockwood

Simon and Laura (Rank) d.Muriel Box: Ian Carmichael, Peter Finch, Kay Kendall. Comedy making much play of 'live' TV which catches out feuding couple Kendall and Finch in front of several million viewers

Josephine and Men (British Lion) d.Roy Boulting: Peter Finch, Jack Buchanan. Limp comedy in which dizzy Glynis Johns ricochets between struggling writer Finch and embattled businessman Donald Sinden

Doctor at Sea (Rank) d.Ralph Thomas: Dirk Bogarde, Brigitte Bardot. Bogarde is the young ship's doctor whose voyage to South America is complicated by delicious nightclub singer Bardot in second of money-spinning series

1984 (Holiday) d.Michael Anderson: Edmond O'Brien. Orwell's savage satire on totalitarianism is heavily watered down with O'Brien as Winston Smith, the clerk in the Ministry of Truth who rebels, and Jan Sterling as his lover. Michael Redgrave chilling as the agent of Big Brother

Value for Money (Rank) d.Ken Annakin: John Gregson, Diana Dors. Bluff North Country millionaire Gregson is ensnared by showgirl Diana in lively variation on an old-fashioned theme

King's Rhapsody (British Lion) d.Herbert Wilcox: Anna Neagle, Errol Flynn, Martita Hunt. Errol escapes from his armor but still looks well and truly zonked as he gingerly negotiates his way through a preposterous Ruritanian romance adapted from an Ivor Novello musical

The Prisoner (Columbia) d.Peter Glenville: Jack Hawkins, Alec Guinness. Stark political melodrama, set in a nameless East European country, pits Cardinal Guinness against remorseless interrogator Hawkins

The Quatermass Xperiment (Hammer) d.Val Guest: Richard Wordsworth. Astronaut Wordsworth is invaded by a malevolent alien vegetable but civilization as we know it is saved by Brian Donlevy's fast-talking Professor Quatermass

The Ladykillers (Ealing) d.Alexander Mackendrick: Cecil Parker, Danny Green, Herbert Lom, Alec Guinness, Peter Sellers, Katie Johnson. A bizarre gang of crooks, led by a sabre-toothed Guinness, find their plans unhinged by the moral innocence of the old lady in whose lop-sided house they plot a robbery

Oh, Rosalinda!! (ABPC) d.Michael Powell: Michael Redgrave, Ludmilla Tcherina, Anton Walbrook. Powell's legendary quirkiness gets the better of him in whimsical version of Strauss' *Die Fledermaus* set in postwar Vienna

Attila Flagello di Dio (Italy) d.Pietro Francisci: Sophia Loren, Anthony Quinn. Tony is Zorba the Hun, setting his sights on the sack of Rome in spectacularly inept spectacular

Mio Figlio Nerone (Italy) d.Steno: Alberto Sordi, Gloria Swanson. Gloria's umpteenth comeback, as Agripina, in weird satire on costume epics which also features Brigitte Bardot and Vittorio de Sica. A curiosity to be savored

Donna Piu' Bella del Mondo (Italy) d.Robert Z Leonard: Gina Lollobrigida, Vittorio Gassman. Biopic of the soprano Lina Cavalieri with Gassman as her princely lover and Robert Alda as her jealous music master

Il Bidone (Italy) d.Federico Fellini: Richard Basehart, Broderick Crawford. Grim Maupassant-like *conte* in which con-men Basehart and Crawford masquerade as priests, but Crawford's belated spiritual awakening costs him his life

Les Grandes Manoeuvres (France-Italy) d.René Clair: Gérard Philipe, Michele Morgan. Dragoons officer Philipe wagers that he will make the next woman who walks into the room fall in love with him. Fortunately for all concerned it is not Phyllis Diller but the lovely Morgan

Napoléon (France) d.Sacha Guitry: Daniel Gélin. Star-packed celebration of one of history's biggest egos with the striking Gélin as the young Bonaparte metamorphosing unconvincingly into Raymond Pelegrin. Michele Morgan is Josephine

Futures Vedettes (France) d.Marc Allégret: Jean Marais, Brigitte Bardot. A prophetic title for BB, still a brunette as she plays a music student romancing opera singer Marais

Les Huis Clos (France) d.Jacqueline Audry: Arletty, Gaby Sylvia. The film version of Jean-Paul Sartre's perfectly reasonable theory that hell is other people. Arletty dominates the proceedings as the scathing lesbian Inez

French Can Can (France) d.Jean Renoir: Jean Gabin, Francoise Arnoul. Gabin plays the impressario of the Moulin Rouge cabaret where the famous dance was invented in colorful celebration of the French *Belle Epoque*

Lola Montes (France) d.Max Ophuls: Peter Ustinov, Martine Carol. Ophuls' last film in which he follows the life of the legendary courtesan through a series of complex flashbacks from the circus act in which she later toured. A superb exercise in cinema

Les Carnets du Major Thompson (France) d.Preston Sturges: Martine Carol, Jack Buchanan. The elegant Buchanan is the British diplomat in Sturges' heartbreakingly botched attempt to turn his exile in France to advantage. A sad example of what happens when genius dries up

Elena et les Hommes (France) d.Jean Renoir: Jean Marais, Ingrid Bergman. Impoverished Polish princess Bergman drifts through romantic intrigues with Marais and Mel Ferrer in disappointing fantasy exquisitely photographed by Claude Renoir

Sommarnattens Leende (Sweden) d.Ingmar Bergman: Gunnar Bjornstrand, Eva Dahlbeck. Beautifully played period sex comedy which just lacks the warmth and sadness that prevents irony from sliding into schematic cynicism

Ikimono no Kiroku (Japan) d.Akira Kurosawa: Toshiro Mifune. Tour de force by Mifune as an aging industrialist who wants to move his family to Brazil to escape the A-bomb but is committed to an insane asylum

Pather Panchali (India) d.Satyajit Ray: Subir Bannerjee. Slow-moving, painstakingly detailed chronicle of life in a poor Bengal village owes much to Renoir. A big hit at the Cannes Film Festival but, surprisingly, Truffaut walked out

1956

Two blockbusters dominated the box-office: Mike Todd's *Around the World in 80 Days* and Cecil B DeMille's remake of *The Ten Commandments*. *Around the World in 80 Days* was a triumph of packaging, if little else. Under the rather uncertain direction of Michael Anderson, 44 stars appeared in cameo roles, and the film's principle pleasure is spotting them as they flit across the screen. The deployment of an impressive array of logistics was sufficient to secure an otherwise vulgar wide-screen extravaganza the Best Picture Award. In his last film DeMille showed that he had lost none of his tasteless exuberance, blending sex, sadism and religiosity in equal measure. As Moses, Charlton Heston provided the monumental focus for a succession of spectacular setpieces, ageing from warrior prince to Old Testament prophet, mane of hair and bushy beard streaming in the wind in apocalyptic splendor. Thereafter he became irrevocably associated with the epic film.

Humphrey Bogart, ravaged by cancer bowed out with *The Harder They Fall*, playing a washed-up journalist who finds integrity in the final reel. James Dean made a posthumous appearance in *Giant*, ageing – not wholly convincingly– from a young cowhand to a middle-aged oil tycoon threshing about in a rage of wasted energies. Fritz Lang brought his Hollywood career to an end with two superb examples of the *film noir, Beyond a Reasonable Doubt* and *While the City Sleeps*. Frank Tashlin's *Hollywood or Bust* marked the end of the partnership between Dean Martin and Jerry Lewis.

The title *Hollywood or Bust* was a none too subtle play on Hollywood's increasing obsession with big-breasted leading ladies, in this case the well-upholstered Anita Ekberg, whose mammaries constantly threatened to crowd out the rest of the cast. In a class of her own, however, was Jayne Mansfield, star of Frank Tashlin's *The Girl Can't Help It*. Tashlin began his career in 1928 as an animator with Max Fleischer, and in Mansfield he found the closest approximation to a 'cartoon woman', around whose over-developed anatomy he sprayed machine-gun bursts of cruelly mocking sight gags.

Elvis Presley made his screen debut in a Western, *Love Me Tender*, tangling with brother Richard Egan over Debra Paget. Another Western, *Seven Men from Now*, marked the beginning of a remarkable series of assured, austere low-budget films directed by Budd Boetticher, produced by Harry Joe Brown and starring Randolph Scott.

Rock'n'roll was now infiltrating Hollywood. *The Girl Can't Help it* had been enlivened by Fats Domino, The Platters, Gene Vincent and Little Richard, all of whom were to feature in the wave of exploitation movies which hit the screen. Among them were Edward L Cahn's *Shake, Rattle and Roll* and *Rock Around the Clock*, directed by B wizard Fred F Sears, king of the quickies in a business where time was of the essence.

The mood was infectious. Schlockmeister Roger Corman, who had moved into the SF field in 1955 with *The Day the World Ended*, now changed into a higher gear. In his *It Conquered the World* Lee Van Cleef played host to a fanged cucumber from Venus; and Corman's supremely inventive *Not of This Earth* cast gravel-voiced Paul Birch as a business-suited alien whose dark glasses concealed a pair of ping-pong eyeballs which scrambled his victims' brains.

Carroll Baker created a sensation as the heedlessly erotic child bride in *Baby Doll*, sucking her thumb in an unconscious reminder of the perversely sucked toe in Buñuel's *L'Age d'Or* (1930). *Baby Doll* also gave Karl Malden his best movie part as the cuckolded Archie Lee Meighan. Yul Brynner repeated his stage triumph as the autocratic King of Siam in Rodgers and Hammerstein's *The King and I*. Then he co-starred in *Anastasia* with Ingrid Bergman, whose portrayal of the pretender to the Tsarist fortune won her a 'come back, all is forgiven' Best Actress Award. Dorothy Malone was voted Best Supporting Actress for *Written on the Wind*, in which she was the poor little rich girl hopelessly in love with Rock Hudson and trying to forget her misery with drink and men. The Best Supporting Actor Oscar went to Anthony Quinn for his Paul Gauguin in Vincente Minnelli's *Lust for Life*.

Keen to exploit Grace Kelly's impending marriage to Prince Rainier III of Monaco, MGM dusted off an old Molnar warhorse and cast Kelly as a Princess-to-be-Married in *The Swan*. Soon afterwards she became Princess Grace of Monaco in a spectacular marriage ceremony held in the principality.

Death took two great directors: the Russian Alexander Dovzhenko and the Japanese Kenji Mizoguchi; cheerful B-movie veteran B Reeves Eason; the German silent master E A Dupont, who had gone to Hollywood in the '30s and declined to second features; and Alexander Korda, self-ordained Khan of the British film industry. Also leaving the stage were actors Edward Arnold, George Bancroft, Jean Hersholt, eye-rolling Robert Newton and, saddest of all, a wraith-like Bela Lugosi.

In Britain John and Roy Boulting's *Private's Progress* was the first of a series which lobbed a few mildly satirical grenades over the battlements of various British institutions, in this case the Army. A young Michael Caine made his debut in *A Hill in Korea,* the only notable British film to deal with the Korean War. Another war film, *Reach for the Sky*, contained a moving central performance for Kenneth More as the legless fighter ace Douglas Bader, which cemented his position as one of Britain's most popular leading men and exemplar of the cinema of understatement and restraint. There was nothing remotely restrained about Roger Vadim's *Et Dieu Créa La Femme*, the movie which turned brunette starlet Brigitte Bardot into pouting blonde bombshell BB, playing fast and loose in the fashionable Mediterranenan resort of St Tropez.

ACTION

Between Heaven and Hell (Fox) d.Richard Fleischer: Frank Gorshin, Robert Wagner. Stock footage provides most of the action in tale of heartless Southern gentleman Wagner discovering the meaning of comradeship in the wartorn Pacific. Broderick Crawford hams it up more than a little as a crazed commanding officer

Men in War (UA) d.Anthony Mann: Aldo Ray. Anti-heroic Korean War actioner, struggling to reconcile realism and humanism, with strong central performances from Ray and Robert Ryan

Away All Boats (Universal) d.Joseph Pevney: Jeff Chandler. 'Get Away from My Ship!' bellows iron man Jeff as Japanese Kamikaze planes barrel in towards the USS Belinda

Attack! (UA) d.Robert Aldrich: Jack Palance. Strident attempt to strip away the glamor of the war machine as war-weary Palance clashes with cowardly officer Eddie Albert during the Battle of the Bulge

Run for the Sun (UA) d.Roy Boulting: Trevor Howard. Competent retread of *The Most Dangerous Game* (1932) with literary types Richard Widmark and Jane Greer falling into the sadistic clutches of huntsman Howard, who's after human prey

Screaming Eagles (Allied Artists) d.Charles Haas: Jacqueline Beer, Tom Tryon (r). Mixed-up outsider Tryon is regenerated by the comradeship of battle as a crack unit fights its way bloodily through the hedgerows of Normandy

The Wings of Eagles (MGM) d.John Ford: Louis Jean Heydt, John Wayne. Uneven blend of virtual slapstick and drama celebrating the life of Frank 'Spig' Wead, a pioneer aviator who became a screenwriter after a crippling accident. Ward Bond turns up as film director 'John Dodge' in what appears to be an affectionate parody of Ford

D-Day, the 6th of June (Fox) d.Henry Koster: Richard Todd. Gray rehash of the likes of *A Yank in the RAF* (1941) in which Todd and Robert Taylor share the favors of ice maiden Dana Wynter before Todd goes out with a big bang on the Normandy beach-head

Battle Hymn (Universal) d.Douglas Sirk: Rock Hudson. Sentimental biopic of Colonel Dean Hess, a priest-cum-fighter pilot who atoned for his accidental bombing of a German orphanage in World War II by airlifting 100 mites to safety in the Korean conflict

The Mountain (Paramount) d.Edward Dmytryk: Robert Wagner, Spencer Tracy. Cinema's unlikeliest brothers, Wagner and Tracy, climb in search of a crashed airliner, but Wagner's lust for loot ensures his doom

The Bold and the Brave (RKO) d.Lewis R Foster: Wendell Corey, Mickey Rooney. The adventures of three soldiers in the Italian campaign of 1944. Hopelessly compromised by priggish Don Taylor's toe-curling affair with prostitute Nicole Maurey

Soldier of Fortune (Fox) d.Edward Dmytryk: Clark Gable, Danny Chang, Susan Hayward. Gable is engaged by Hayward to find her husband Gene Barry and the search takes him into Red China. Might have been more convincing in 1936 as Gable was getting a little elderly for this kind of thing

Trapeze (UA) d.Carol Reed: Burt Lancaster, Gina Lollobrigida, Tony Curtis. Turbulent love triangle between aerialists Burt, Gina and Tony is pursued as dramatically in the air as on the ground

Nightfall (Columbia) d.Jacques Tourneur: Aldo Ray, Anne Bancroft. Snowbound chase thriller as murder suspect Ray is hunted by the cops and a pair of bank robbers, one of whom has a fatal encounter with a snowplough

Hold Back the Night (Allied Artists) d.Allan Dwan: John Payne. Discover the secret of grizzled World War II veteran Payne's unopened bottle of whiskey as he commands a fighting retreat in Korea

Toward the Unknown (Warner) d.Mervyn LeRoy: Lloyd Nolan, William Holden. Is ace test pilot Holden more interested in his magnificently phallic Bell X-C rocket plane or co-star Virginia Leith? Lloyd Nolan ponders this vital question

Hot Rod Girl (Nacirema) d.Leslie Martinson: Lori Nelson. Disillusioned John Smith pulls out of the hell that is hotrodding, but a manslaughter rap is waiting in the wings. Dire stuff

ADVENTURE AND FANTASY

Around the World in 80 Days (UA) d.Michael Anderson: Shirley MacLaine, David Niven, Cantinflas, Buster Keaton. Niven is Jules Verne's unflappable hero Phileas Fogg, careering round the world in star-crammed but exceptionally stodgy spectacular. Ingenious Saul Bass titles arrive at the end of an interminable three hours

The Living Idol (MGM) d.Albert Lewin: Liliane Montevecchi. Outlandish Mexico-set adventure in which archaeologist James Robertson Justice, wearing one of the silliest pieces of headgear in cinema, conjures up a centuries-old Mayan jaguar god

Beyond Mombasa (Columbia) d.George Marshall: Cornel Wilde, Donna Reed, Ron Randell, Leo Genn. Wilde rampages through the African bush, seeking his brother's killers and a hidden uranium mine

The Ten Commandments (Paramount) d.Cecil B DeMille: Charlton Heston. Moses goes up the mountain, meets God, acquires a startling new hairstyle, parts the Red Sea and generally comes up trumps in disarmingly tuppence-colored epic of epics

Safari (Columbia) d.Terence Young: Victor Mature, Janet Leigh. Fatuous Warwick actioner in which white hunter Mature's obsessive pursuit of Mau Mau terrorists is matched by aristocratic Roland Culver's manic ambition to shoot the rogue lion Hatari

Congo Crossing (Universal) d.Joseph Pevney: Virginia Mayo, Peter Lorre, George Nader. Sultry murder suspect Mayo fetches up in steamy Congatonga where a weary-looking Lorre contemplates the heart of darkness

Back from Eternity (RKO) d.John Farrow: Rod Steiger, Robert Ryan, Anita Ekberg. A plane crash deposits a mixed bunch of characters in the middle of head hunter territory. Disappointing remake of Farrow's 1939 B classic *Five Came Back*. But which five is it to be?

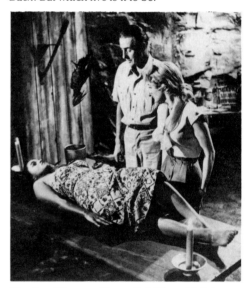

Voodoo Woman (Carmel) d.Edward L Cahn: Tom Conway, Mary Ellen Kaye. Power-crazed medic Conway uses voodoo and science to create a cross between man and beast to kill by telepathic command

War and Peace (Ponti-de Laurentiis) d.King Vidor: Audrey Hepburn, Vittorio Gassman. Reader's Digest version of Tolstoy. Henry Fonda, as Pierre, is the only member of the cast who seems to have read the book. John Mills acutely embarrassing as a Russian peasant with a Cockney accent

Earth Versus the Flying Saucers (Columbia) d.Fred F Sears. Ray Harryhausen's dreamlike stop-motion special effects distinguish tale of alien invaders whose fatal weakness is a sensitivity to high-frequency noise and a 100 per cent allergy to B people Hugh Marlowe, Harry Lauter and Morris Ankrum

The Mole People (Universal) d.Virgil Vogel: Cynthia Patrick. John Agar's scientific expedition discovers a lost underground city whose albino inhabitants hold the dreaded Mole People in thrall. Screenplay by the egregiously named Laszlo Gorag

Zarak (Columbia) d.Terence Young: Anita Ekberg, Victor Mature. Anita's belly dance has to be seen to be believed in terminal Warwick trash supposedly set on the Northwest Frontier

Moby Dick (Warner) d.John Huston: Gregory Peck. Superb cinematography by Oswald Morris distinguishes doom-laden adaptation of Melville's great novel in which peg-leg Peck sails the Pequod across the seven seas in search of the Great White Whale. Orson Welles puts in a telling appearance as Father Mapple

Rodan (Toho) d.Inoshiro Honda. Supersonic pterodactyl Rodan's spectacularly destructive Eastmancolor progress is finally halted by an erupting volcano in smash hit Japanese Total Mobilization epic full of excellent special effects

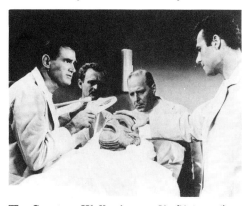

The Creature Walks Among Us (Universal) d.John Sherwood: Jeff Morrow. Further indignities are inflicted on the Gill-Man by crass scientist Morrow who experiments on his red corpuscle count in order to breed a new species

Not of This Earth (Allied Artists) d.Roger Corman: Beverly Garland. Wryly inventive Z-budgeter in which gravel-voiced Paul Birch dons a pair of shades to play a blood-sucking alien loose in Beverly Hills. Immortal cameo from Dick Miller as a crazed door-to-door vacuum cleaner salesman

Attack of the Crab Monsters (Allied Artist) d.Roger Corman: Pamela Duncan. Monstrously mutated crabs chew their way through the usual team of scientists in Corman cheapie whose peculiar sense of disequilibrium triumphs over the tatty production values

World Without End (Allied Artists) d.Edward Bernds: Lisa Montell, Rod Taylor. Hugh Marlowe's scientific team fall through a time warp to land on Earth in AD 2058 and find it devastated by nuclear war. Plot-line similar to H G Wells' 'The Time Machine', eventually filmed in 1960 with Taylor as the Time Traveler

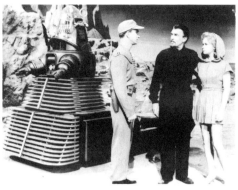

The Forbidden Planet (MGM) d.Fred M Wilcox: Robby the Robot, Leslie Nielsen, Walter Pidgeon, Anne Francis. Enchanting free adaptation of The Tempest, full of witty effects, with Pidgeon as an intergalactic Prospero, Francis a fetching Miranda, Robby a deadpan Ariel and Caliban a destructive ray

The Black Sleep (UA) d.Reginald LeBorg: Tor Johnson, Lon Chaney, George Sawaya, John Carradine. A silent Bela Lugosi and mad doctor Basil Rathbone join a cast who had seen better days in brain transplant farrago directed by B-movie veteran LeBorg

It Conquered the World (AIP) d.Roger Corman: Beverly Garland. As the master observed when directing this film, 'Always make sure that the monster is bigger than your leading lady'. Cucumber things from Venus, and their deadly Bat Mites, threaten all we hold dear

The Pharaoh's Curse (UA) d.Lee Sholem: Kurt Katch, Alvaro Guillot. An ancient mummy rises from the slumber of centuries to threaten a hapless archaeological expedition

Bride of the Monster (Exclusive) d.Edward D Wood: Bela Lugosi. Poor old Bela's atom-ray machine produces a sad gallery of grotesques before a giant octopus (borrowed from Paramount's prop department) puts an end to his agony in one of Wood's surreal home movies

MELODRAMA

The Great Man (Universal) d.Jose Ferrer: Jose Ferrer, Julie London. Gritty behind-the-microphone radio drama in which investigative reporter Ferrer delves into a 'great man's' murky past. London sings 'The Meaning of the Blues'

Crime of Passion (UA) d.Gerd Oswald: Barbara Stanwyck, Raymond Burr. Pushy policeman's wife Stanwyck will stop at nothing to ensure husband Sterling Hayden's promotion. But it all ends in floods of tears

Strange Intruder (Allied Artists) d.Irving Rapper: Ida Lupino, Edmund Purdom. Strained meller in which unhinged ex-POW Purdom strikes an imprudent bargain to kill Lupino's children

Crime in the Streets (Allied Artists) d.Don Siegel: Sal Mineo, Mark Rydell, John Cassavetes. A 1950s *Dead End* (1937) in which teenage crime Tsar Cassavetes is hauled back from the brink of murder by the love of his little brother. Adapted from a TV play

Four Boys and a Gun (UA) d. William Berke: Frank Sutton (r). Four young thugs plan a sports stadium robbery but wind up with a dead cop on their hands

Swamp Women (Woolner) d.Roger Corman: Touch (later Michael) Connors, Marie Windsor (r). It's alligator al fresco time as Marie's statuesque band of escaped female cons, and undercover cop Beverly Garland, run riot over the swamplands in search of buried loot. Absolutely not to be missed

The Big Boodle (UA) d.Richard Wilson: Errol Flynn. Havana-set gangster caper serves only to emphasize the speed and totality of Flynn's vertiginous decline

A Woman's Devotion (Republic) d.Paul Henreid: Rosenda Monteros, Ralph Meeker. Like many a B-feature couple before them, vacationing Meeker and Janice Rule are plunged into a Mexican murder mystery

The Wild Party (UA) d.Harry Horner: Anthony Quinn. Hamfisted attempt at naturalistic drama in which washed-up football star Quinn decides to let it all hang out in a shabby roadside dance hall

The Killing (UA) d.Stanley Kubrick: Elisha Cook Jr, Marie Windsor. Tight racetrack heist thriller, slightly marred by hectoring voice-over. Made before Kubrick was overtaken by galloping elephantiasis. Riveting performance from Timothy Carey as an ultra-cool paraplegic killer

The Harder They Fall (Columbia) d.Mark Robson: Humphrey Bogart, Rod Steiger. Bogart's last film as the has-been sportswriter-turned press agent clutching at integrity in the final reel of Budd Schulberg's exposé of the corrupt underbelly of the fight game

Edge of the City (MGM) d.Martin Ritt: Sidney Poitier, John Cassavetes. Grim waterfront drama in which Poitier and army deserter Cassavetes run up against union racketeer Jack Warden. Still packs a punch

Beyond a Reasonable Doubt (RKO) d.Fritz Lang: Sidney Blackmer, Dana Andrews. Lang's last US film. Andrews is the writer persuaded by newspaper proprietor Blackmer to expose the dangers of circumstantial evidence by planting clues which implicate him in a murder. He is convicted and sentenced to death, but Blackmer dies before he can reveal the fraud

The Power and the Prize (MGM) d.Henry Koster: Burl Ives, Robert Taylor. Facile big business drama in which Taylor has his cake and eats it, marrying European refugee Elisabeth Mueller and ousting odious boss Ives

The Leather Saint (Paramount) d.Alvin Ganzer: John Derek. A melange of prayers and pugilism as priest Derek becomes pro fighter Kid Sunday (what else?) raising money to fight a polio epidemic

The Boss (UA) d.Byron Haskin: John Payne (c). Positively Payne's finest hour in hard-driving low-budgeter based on the infamous life and times of 'Boss' Pendergast, whose political machine controlled Kansas City

Ransom! (MGM) d.Alex Segal: Donna Reed, Glenn Ford. Ford radiates controlled misery and dogged tenacity as his refusal to meet the demands of his son's kidnappers leaves him isolated but ultimately vindicated. Another filmed TV play

While The City Sleeps (RKO) d.Fritz Lang: Rhonda Fleming, James Craig. Lang's penulti-mate US movie is rancid *film noir* in which reporters on the *New York Sentinel* ruthlessly compete for the editorship of the paper by solving a series of brutal sex murders. Most of them emerge as more objectionable than the pathetic murderer John Barrymore Jr

Behind the High Wall (Universal) d.Abner Biberman: Betty Lynn, John Gavin. Remake of *The Big Guy* (1939) gives bent prison warder Tom Tully the choice between ill-gotten gains and saving convict Gavin from the chair. Sylvia Sidney touching as Tully's crippled wife

The Revolt of Mamie Stover (Fox) d.Raoul Walsh: Agnes Moorehead, Jane Russell. Jane gets ahead as one of the girls in Moorehead's Hawaian 'dance hall', singing 'Keep Your Eyes on the Hands' to the clients in sanitized but oddly vulgar version of William Bradford Huie's novel

The Price of Fear (Universal) d.Abner Biberman: Merle Oberon, Lex Barker. Lex is framed for two crimes – a hit and run incident and a murder – each of which might provide him with an alibi for the other

Istanbul (Universal) d.Joseph Pevney: Cornell Borchers, Errol Flynn. *Singapore* (1947) was taken off the shelf and dusted down for Errol, playing a pilot chasing a diamond cache and bumping into amnesiac wife Borchers

Anastasia (Fox) d.Anatole Litvak: Yul Brynner, Ingrid Bergman. Ingrid's first US film for seven years as the girl groomed by Russian emigré Brynner to pose as the daughter of the Tsar Nicholas to collect the $10 million held in her name in the Bank of England

Nightmare (UA) d. Maxwell Shane: Kevin McCarthy. Serviceable remake of Shane's *Fear in the Night* (1947) in which jazz musician McCarthy commits murder under hypnosis. Edward G Robinson, some legendary jazz men and the New Orleans setting round out a satisfying programmer

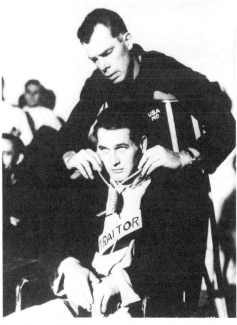

The Rack (MGM) d.Arnold Laven: Lee Marvin, Paul Newman. Korean War hero and POW Newman is court-martialled for collaborating with the enemy. Based on a TV play by the prolific Rod Serling

Written on the Wind (Universal) d.Douglas Sirk: Rock Hudson, Dorothy Malone. A torrent of oil money fails to bring happiness to the filthy rich Hadley family, not least Robert Stack's profligate Kyle and his sexy sister Malone, who sublimates her unrequited love for Rock in a series of casual affairs

The Bottom of the Bottle (Fox) d.Henry Hathaway: Bruce Bennett, Van Johnson, Robert Adler. Or bottom of the barrel, perhaps, as escaped convict Van Johnson pays an unexpected call on his lawyer brother Joseph Cotten's border ranch. Cotten is none too pleased to see him

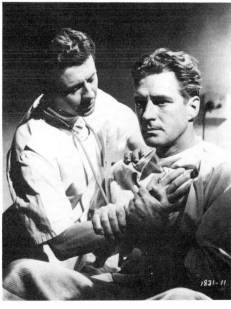

I've Lived Before (Universal) d.Richard Bartlett: Phil Harvey, Jock Mahoney. Airline pilot Mahoney emerges from a plane crash convinced that he is a dead World War I fighter pilot. Ann Harding excellent as the dead ace's ageing girlfriend, convinced that the soul of her lover lives on

Slander (MGM) d.Roy Rowland: Van Johnson, Harold J Stone. Overheated exposé of 'yellow' journalism as sleazy scandal magazine editor Steve Cochran reveals popular TV puppeteer Johnson's criminal past

Julie (MGM)d.Andrew L Stone: Louis Jourdan, Doris Day. Doris discovers that unbalanced husband Jourdan has killed his first wife and now has similar plans for her. Idiotic climax on board an aeroplane

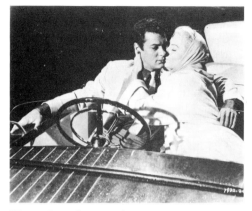

Mister Cory (Universal) d.Blake Edwards: Tony Curtis, Martha Hyer. Chicago slum kid Curtis makes good as a gambler but fails to snare classy Hyer. Enjoyably energetic performance from Curtis as a determined opportunist

The Cruel Tower (Allied Artists) d.Lew Landers: Charles McGraw, John Ericson. The old circus trapeze triangle is transferred to the macho world of steeplejacks, with Ericson nearly taking a fatal tumble over homicidal McGraw's brassy mistress Mari Blanchard

These Wilder Years (MGM) d.Roy Rowland: James Cagney, Barbara Stanwyck, Betty Lou Keim. Industrialist Cagney's search for his illegitimate son leads to his adoption of unmarried mother Keim

Teenage Rebel (Fox) d.Edmund Goulding: Betty Lou Keim, Ginger Rogers. Unloved Keim is reunited with her mother Rogers after eight years with her divorced father. Love and good old-fashioned family values break down her surly exterior

Lust for Life (MGM) d.Vincente Minnelli: Kirk Douglas. Kirk unleashes his limitless capacity for mutilation and suffering in his impersonation of Van Gogh, a portrayal of creativity and crippling personal inadequacy cleverly manipulated by Minnelli. Anthony Quinn's Gaugin is less impressive, although his performance won him an Oscar

Patterns (UA) d.Fielder Cook: Van Heflin, Everett Sloane. Rod Serling drama of executive power struggle features well-observed performance by Ed Begley as a manager hounded to death by the Machiavellian Sloane

23 Paces to Baker Street (Fox) d.Henry Hathaway: Van Johnson, Vera Miles, Cecil Parker. Suspenseful thriller, set in Sherlock Holmes' old stamping ground, in which blind writer Van Johnson solves a kidnap mystery in style worthy of the Master

Outside the Law (Universal) d.Jack Arnold: Grant Williams, Ray Danton, Leigh Snowden. Underpowered showcase for three of the studio's minor lights. Danton plays an ex-GI with a criminal past rounding up a gang of counterfeiters when they kill one of his buddies

The Bad Seed (Warner) d.Mervyn LeRoy: Patty McCormack, Nancy Kelly. Chilling adaptation of Maxwell Anderson play, with small psychopath McCormack running amok, is compromised by a feeble ending. Kelly repeats her stage performance as the murderous mite's anguished mother

Autumn Leaves (Columbia) d.Robert Aldrich: Ruth Donnelly, Joan Crawford. At this stage in her career Joan was forever being menaced by younger men. Here it is husband Cliff Robertson, who turns out to be not quite all he seems

Death of a Scoundrel (RKO) d.Charles Martin: Zsa Zsa Gabor, George Sanders. Penniless European conman Sanders uses a succession of female dupes as stepping stones to Stateside success. At the time Zsa Zsa was his real-life partner. His brother Tom Conway also appears in a small part

Gaby (MGM) d.Curtis Bernhardt: John Kerr, Leslie Caron. Third time around for *Waterloo Bridge* (1931,'40) in which ballerina Caron falls in love with Kerr across a crowded World War II air raid shelter

The Wrong Man (Warner) d.Alfred Hitchcock: Henry Fonda, Vera Miles. Fonda is the musician Manny Balastrero, a Kafkaesque victim whose life is shattered after being arrested for a hold-up he did not commit. Based on the real life story told in Maxwell Anderson's 'A Case of Identity'

The Bachelor Party (Paramount) d.Delbert Mann: Don Murray, Carolyn Jones. Adaptation of Paddy Chayevsky TV play revolving around a stag night before Philip Abbott's wedding. Everyone acts out of their skins, particularly Jones as a philosophical nymphomaniac

Hilda Crane (Fox) d.Philip Dunne: Jean Simmons, Jean-Pierre Aumont. Simmons is the small-town vamp of the title, suggesting a passionate, thwarted woman at odds with the frequently anodyne female images of the period

Cry in the Night (Warner) d.Frank Tuttle: Natalie Wood, Richard Anderson. Thudding psychological thriller in which Peeping Tom Raymond Burr makes off with Wood, hotly pursued by her policeman father Edmond O'Brien

Bigger than Life (Fox) d.Nicholas Ray: Barbara Rush, Walter Matthau, James Mason. Acerbic view of the ambiguous benefits of 'wonder drugs' as a course of treatment turns teacher Mason into a homicidal maniac bent on killing himself and his family

The Girl in Black Stockings (UA) d.Howard W Koch: John Dehner, Lex Barker, Anne Bancroft. A murder epidemic grips a smart Utah resort hotel. Could the maniac at large be the lovely Bancroft? Perish the thought!

The Unguarded Moment (Universal) d.Harry Keller: Dani Crayne, John Saxon. Highschool teacher Esther Williams becomes involved with classroom heartthrob Saxon (in the days before his hairstyle resembled a Brillo pad). Unfortunately he turns out to be a psychopathic nightstalker

COMEDY

The Girl He Left Behind (Warner) d.David Butler: Jessie Royce Landis, Tab Hunter. Tab is teamed with Natalie Wood in busy comedy about a pampered pain-in-the-neck peacetime draftee turned into a man by the Army

The Ambassador's Daughter (UA) d.Norman Krasna: Edward Arnold, Adolphe Menjou, Myrna Loy. Idiotic Senator Menjou goes to France on a military fact-finding mission, decides that naughty-naughty Paris should be placed off limits to all service personnel

Everything But the Truth (Universal) d.Jerry Hopper: John Forsythe, Tim Hovey, Frank Faylen, Maureen O'Hara. Hovey's addiction to the truth leads to embarrassing revelations about a crooked real-estate deal

The Teahouse of the August Moon (MGM) d.Daniel Mann: Marlon Brando, Glenn Ford. Delightful comic performances from Brando and Ford as a wily Japanese interpreter and harassed US Army officer in postwar Okinawa. Scripted by John Patrick from his Broadway hit

The Girl Can't Help It (Fox) d.Frank Tashlin: Jayne Mansfield, Tom Ewell. For all you semiologists out there Jayne gives a little demonstration of the separation of form and function in raucous comedy tricked out with rock'n'rollers Fats Domino, Gene Vincent and Little Richard, who tears through the title song

The Happy Road (MGM) d.Gene Kelly: Michael Redgrave, Barbara Laage, Gene Kelly. Two runaway children draw single parents Kelly and Laage together in pleasant romantic comedy shot in France

Our Miss Brooks (Warner) d.David Weisbart: Robert Rockwell, Eve Arden. Amiable comedy, spun off from Arden's TV show, in which she's a teacher setting her cap at biology master Rockwell

Francis in the Haunted House (Universal) d.Charles Lamont: Mickey Rooney. Rock-bottom for Rooney as we say farewell to the loquacious quadruped in last of the series. Paul Frees takes over from Chill Wills as His Mule's Voice

Crashing Las Vegas (Allied Artists) d.Jean Yarbrough: Leo Gorcey, Mary Castle, Huntz Hall. A violent electric shock fails to eliminate the ferret-faced Hall but gives him the power to predict winning numbers. The Bowery Boys head for Nevada

Toy Tiger (Universal) d.Jerry Hopper: Jeff Chandler, Tim Hovey. Jeff finds that he's been 'adopted' by Hovey to back up tall tales about his Dad in inferior remake of the 1938 Deanna Durbin hit *Mad About Music*. It does not appear that Chandler is exactly mad about Hovey

Kelly and Me (Universal) d.Robert Z Leonard: Van Johnson, Piper Laurie. Song and dance man Johnson's faithful hound becomes a Rin Tin Tin-style movie star in cheerful outing set in the early days of talkies

That Certain Feeling (Paramount) d.Norman Panama: Bob Hope, Eva Marie Saint, George Sanders. For once Hope is allowed to build a role rather than spray one-liners around, playing a neurotic cartoonist ghosting for more celebrated but less talented artist Sanders. Saint provides the romantic complications

Full of Life (Columbia) d.Richard Quine: Richard Conte, Judy Holliday. Hard-up writer and pregnant wife Holliday fight a plague of termites with the help of sentimental father-in-law Salvatore Baccaloni

Pardners (Paramount) d.Norman Taurog: Dean Martin, Jerry Lewis. A trace of irony in the title as the duo were motoring fast towards a bust-up. Jerry is a Manhattan millionaire taming a Western town in remake of an old Bing Crosby vehicle *Rhythm on the Range* (1936)

Hollywood or Bust (Paramount) d.Frank Tashlin: Anita Ekberg, Jerry Lewis. The bust presumably being Ekberg's as Lewis and Dean crash Tinsel Town in their last film together

The Little Hut (MGM) d.Mark Robson: Ava Gardner, Stewart Granger, David Niven. Dismal version of stage success shipwrecks society types on a desert island where mild sexual shenanigans ensue

Dance With Me Henry (UA) d.Charles Barton: Sheree Alberoni, Lou Costello. A and C bow out in threadbare effort revolving around an amusement park which is about as run down as their screen partnership

The Solid Gold Cadillac (Columbia) d.Richard Quine: Paul Douglas, Judy Holliday. Small stockholder Holliday outmaneuvers a bunch of corporate villains in sprightly adaptation of George S Kaufman play

MUSICALS

Bundle of Joy (RKO) d.Norman Taurog: Eddie Fisher, Debbie Reynolds. Sacked salesgirl Debbie finds a surprise Christmas package in a doorway in witless remake of *Bachelor Mother* (1939)

The Best Things in Life are Free (Fox) d.Michael Curtiz: Ernest Borgnine, Gordon MacRae, Sheree North, Dan Dailey. Old-fashioned biopic of tunesmiths Buddy De Sylva (MacRae), Ray Henderson (Dailey), and Lew Brown (Borgnine). Sheree's a wow doing the 'Black Bottom' with Jacques d'Amboise

Cha-Cha-Cha Boom! (Columbia) d.Fred F Sears: Bankrupt musical talent scout Steve Dunne travels to Cuba to look for new material

The Benny Goodman Story (Universal) d.Valentine Davies: Donna Reed, Steve Allen. Pedestrian attempt to repeat the success of *The Glen Miller Story* (1954) fails to catch fire although the music remains in the capable hands of the likes of Lionel Hampton, Harry James and Gene Krupa

Invitation to the Dance (MGM) d.Gene Kelly: Tamara Toumanova, Gene Kelly. The strain shows in ambitious three-part dance extravaganza on which work began in 1952. This still is from 'Ring Around the Rosy', with music by André Previn. The final segment, 'Sinbad the Sailor', combines live action with Hanna-Barbera cartoon characters

Serenade (Warner) d.Anthony Mann: Joan Fontaine, Mario Lanza. Fiery Sarita Montiel and chic Fontaine compete for paunchy Mario, the California vineyard worker-turned opera star in free (to say the least) adaptation of a James M Cain novel

The King and I (Fox) d.Walter Lang: Yul Brynner, Deborah Kerr. Rodgers and Hammerstein smash hit musicalization of *Anna and the King of Siam* (1946) provides showcase for Brynner as the Eastern monarch at cultural cross purposes with indomitable governess Kerr. Songs include 'Shall We Dance', 'Hello Young Lovers' and 'Getting to Know You'

Carousel (Fox) d.Henry King: Shirley Jones, Gordon MacRae. Superb widescreen version of Rodgers and Hammerstein's adaptation of 'Liliom' with MacRae as the carnival barker Billy Bigelow, falling for cotton mill girl Jones. Best song 'If I Loved You'

Anything Goes (Paramount) d.Robert Lewis: Jeanmaire, Bing Crosby, Mitzi Gaynor, Donald O'Connor. End of Bing's 21 years at Paramount in retread of 1936 Cole Porter hit set on a round-the-world cruise. Bing croons 'You're the Top'

The Opposite Sex (MGM) d.David Miller: Joan Blondell, Dolores Gray. Musical version of Claire Booth Luce's running cat fight *The Women*, first filmed in 1939, with June Allyson, Joan Collins respectively in the roles originally played by Norma Shearer and Joan Crawford

Beau James (Paramount) d.Melville Shavelson: Bob Hope, Jimmy Durante. Floperoo for Bob as the cheerful scallywag Jimmy Walker, colorful Mayor of New York. Narrated by Walter Winchell

Funny Face (Paramount) d.Stanley Donen: Fred Astaire, Audrey Hepburn. Fashion photographer Fred whisks mousy Greenwich Village bookseller Audrey to Paris where she blossoms into a top model in sumptuously staged romance. The Astaire character based on Richard Avedon

The Eddy Duchin Story (Columbia) d.George Sidney: Tyrone Power, Kim Novak. Power takes the title role in maudlin biopic of the pianist/ bandleader of the '30s and '40s whose life was by no means a bowl of cherries. Novak looks ravishing as his first wife

Meet Me in Las Vegas (MGM) d.Roy Rowland: Winona Smith, Dan Dailey, Cyd Charisse, Cora Williams. Gambling rancher Dan finds a leggy good luck charm in the shape of ballerina Charisse. Guest appearances from Lena Horne, Jerry Colonna, Frank Sinatra, Tony Martin, Debbie Reynolds

Rock Around the Clock (Columbia) d.Fred F Sears: Bill Haley (1). First of the rock'n'roll exploiters features Haley and the Comets, the Platters and Tony Martinez and his Band.

Shake, Rattle and Roll! (American International) d.Edward L Cahn: Fats Domino. Fats eases his benign bulk through rickety cheapie in which Tom Connor sets up a rock'n'roll center in the teeth of opposition from the usual collection of old fuddy-duddies

WESTERNS

The Proud Ones (Fox) d.Robert D Webb: Jeffrey Hunter, Robert Ryan. Many a nod in the direction of *High Noon* (1952) as uncompromising Marshal Ryan deals with vengeful Hunter – whose father he killed in the line of duty – and wheeler-dealer Robert Middleton

Love Me Tender (Fox) d.Robert D Webb: Richard Egan, Debra Paget, Elvis Presley. Elvis' first is a confused post-Civil War Western in which he contrives to get shot by Neville Brand. The final ghostly image of the Pelvis, superimposed over tombstone and mourners, strumming and singing away, will appeal to lovers of the grotesque

Johnny Concho (UA) d.Don McGuire: Frank Sinatra. Cowardly Frank is driven out of Cripple Creek when his gunman brother is killed by William Conrad. He returns to redeem himself

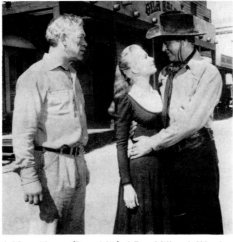

A Man Alone (Republic) d.Ray Milland: Ward Bond, Mary Murphy, Ray Milland. Although Milland never looked entirely happy in a stetson, this is an interesting oater in which he plays an outlaw who enlists the help of sheriff Bond's daughter Murphy in exposing the corrupt businessmen running a town

Jubal (Columbia) d.Delmer Daves: Glenn Ford, Felicia Farr. Brooding, sexually charged Western version Othello in which Rod Steiger's whining, Iago-like ranch foreman Pinky ('He don't like nobody – not even himself') sets off a bloody chain of events

The Maverick Queen (Republic) d.Joseph Kane: Barbara Stanwyck, Barry Sullivan. Republic's first in Naturama features Stanwyck in the title role and Sullivan as the Pinkerton man posing as a bandit to break up the Wild Bunch

The Man from Del Rio (UA) d.Harry Horner: Anthony Quinn. Drunken Mexican gunfighter Quinn makes good as a sheriff in spite of the bigotry of the townsfolk who hire him

The Last Wagon (Fox) d.Delmer Daves: Richard Widmark, Felicia Farr. Widmark is the half-breed Comanche Todd, wanted for murder, who leads a wagon train to safety on a painful voyage of self-discovery

The Lonely Man (Paramount) d.Henry Levin: Robert Middleton, Jack Palance. Interesting reworking of *The Shepherd of the Hills* (1941) in which reformed outlaw Palance returns home to make peace with his embittered son Anthony Perkins

Gunfight at the OK Corral (Paramount) d.John Sturges: Kirk Douglas. Handsome assault on Western myth whose impressive production values crowd out incisive characterization. Douglas is Doc Holliday and Burt Lancaster the legendary Wyatt Earp

Bandido! (UA) d.Richard Fleischer: Ursula Thiess, Robert Mitchum, Zachary Scott. Roguish Mitchum and gunrunning Zach go through their paces in colorful Mexican Civil War adventure burdened with a clunking Max Steiner score

Rebel in Town (UA) d.Alfred Werker: Ruth Roman, John Payne. Literate, atmospheric B-movie in which Payne and Roman ride out for revenge after Southern patriarch J Carrol Naish accidentally kills their small son

Pillars of the Sky (Universal) d.George Marshall: Jeff Chandler, Dorothy Malone. Trouble erupts when the US Cavalry start to build a fort on land granted to the Indians by treaty. Adapted from Will Henry's novel 'Frontier Fury'

The Tall T (Columbia) d.Budd Boetticher: Maureen O'Sullivan, Randolph Scott, Richard Boone. Superbly assured Western which moves from sly parody of *Shane* (1952) to tragic climax as stonefaced Scott and flamboyant Boone move inexorably towards the climactic shoot-out

The Searchers (Warner) d.John Ford: Jeffrey Hunter, Natalie Wood. Moving, mysterious account of nomad John Wayne's five-year hunt for his niece Wood, kidnapped by the Indian chief Scar. Landscape is perfectly married to theme and the closing moments are among the most melancholy in Western cinema

The First Traveling Saleslady (RKO) d.Arthur Lubin: Clint Eastwood, Carol Channing. Bankrupt corset entrepreneur Ginger Rogers runs into trouble way out West when she moves into the barbed wire business. Spotty comedy now chiefly notable for Eastwood's callow presence

Seven Men From Now (Warner) d.Budd Boetticher: Randolph Scott, Gail Russell. First in the resonant collaboration between Boetticher, Scott, screenwriter Burt Kennedy and producer Harry Joe Brown. Scott is the man on the trail of the outlaws who killed his wife

The Burning Hills (Warner) d.Stuart Heisler: Tab Hunter, Natalie Wood. Drab Tab sets out to avenge the killing of his brother by cattle baron's son Skip Homeier and finds a fetching companion in the form of Mexican spitfire Wood

The Fastest Gun Alive (MGM) d.Russell Rouse: Broderick Crawford, John Dehner, Chris Olson. Glenn Ford is the peaceable storekeeper saddled with his father's legendary reputation as a gunman in modest oater which turned out to be one of the studio's biggest grossers of 1956

Dakota Incident (Republic) d.Lewis R Foster: Regis Toomey, Linda Darnell, Dale Robertson. A group of stagecoach passengers is pinned down by the Apache in a desert gulley and then picked off one by one. Convention demands that Dale and Linda survive

Canyon River (Allied Artists) d.Harmon Jones: Marcia Henderson, Richard Eyer, George Montgomery. Rancher Montgomery romances Henderson, fights off rustlers as he drives a herd of Herefords from Oregon to Texas

The First Texan (Allied Artists) d.Byron Haskin: Felicia Farr, Joel McCrea. Respectful, stilted biopic of Sam Houston with McCrea playing the hero who had greatness thrust upon him

Backlash (Universal) d.John Sturges: Donna Reed, Richard Widmark. Much snarling and snapping as gunman Widmark searches for the father he never knew (John McIntyre), only to find a man who sold out his partners to the Apache for $60,000 in gold

Tension at Table Rock (RKO) d.Charles Marquis Warren: Richard Egan, Dorothy Malone. Egan stars as a Shane-like gunman taming the town of Table Rock in uneven programmer salvaged in part by the presence of Royal Dano

Gun the Man Down (UA) d.Andrew V McLaglen: Harry Carey Jr, Emile Meyer. The first from Ford clone McLagen casts James Arness as a betrayed bank robber exacting lingering revenge on his former partners in crime. Angie Dickinson brightens things up

Westward Ho the Wagons (Disney) d.William Beaudine: Fess Parker, Kathleen Crowley. Amiable but routine outing from a king of the Bs is salvaged by a dramatic battle with the Indians staged by stuntman-supreme Yakima Canutt

The Treasure of Pancho Villa (RKO) d.George Sherman: Rory Calhoun, Shelley Winters. American adventurer Calhoun negotiates a minefield of treachery and double-dealing to lift the gold of the title in pacy adventure set in the Mexican Civil War

The Guns of Fort Petticoat (Columbia) d.George Marshall: Audie Murphy. Highminded Audie deserts rather than take part in the Sand Creek massacre and then returns to Texas to save a group of women on whom the Indians will seek their revenge. Murphy's first independent production

The Black Whip (Fox) d.Charles Marquis Warren: Paul Richards, Coleen Gray. Entertaining quickie in which wimpish way station manager Hugh Marlowe saves saloon girls Gray, Adele Mara, Dorothy Schuyler and the divine Angie Dickinson from Richards' band of outlaws

The Brass Legend (UA) d.Gerd Oswald: Hugh O'Brian: Poker-faced lawman O'Brian brings baddie Raymond Burr to book in exuberantly handled actioner climaxing in a ferocious gunfight on horseback

Three Violent People (Paramount) d.Rudolph Maté: Charlton Heston, Anne Baxter. Presumably to demonstrate his versatility Heston followed Moses with the swinish Colt Sanders, fighting with his brother Tom Tryon, ex-prostitute wife Baxter and sundry carpetbagging landgrabbers

ROMANCE

Spring Reunion (UA) d.Robert Pirosh: Dana Andrews, Betty Hutton. Low-budget soaper in which Andrews and Hutton poke around in the sputtering embers of an old affair at a high school reunion. Hutton's mother played by silent star Laura La Plante

Bus Stop (Fox) d.Joshua Logan: Marilyn Monroe, Don Murray. Marilyn's touchingly blowsy saloon chantoosie Cherie – the nearest she came to a completely realized character – is pursued by whoop-it-up cowpoke Murray in charming adaptation of William Inge play. Watch it just to see Marilyn's magically awful version of 'That Old Black Magic'

The Proud and the Profane (Paramount) d.George Seaton: Deborah Kerr, Thelma Ritter. Echoes of *From Here to Eternity* (1953) reverberate when nurse Kerr is seduced by rough and ready William Holden – 'My pleasures are physical . . . the men call me the Beast'. And well they might

The Rainmaker (Paramount) d.Joseph Anthony: Katharine Hepburn, Burt Lancaster. Adaptation of N Richard Nash's play, with Burt as the traveling conman providing first, and temporary love for aging spinster Hepburn

Hot Blood (Columbia) d.Nicholas Ray: Jane Russell, Cornel Wilde. Gypsy temptress Jane shakes her tambourines and drives whip-wielding Cornel wild in outrageous adventure reminiscent of the heyday of Maria Montez

The Swan (MGM) d.Charles Vidor: Grace Kelly, Alec Guinness. Creaking old Molnar warhorse, previously filmed in 1925 and '30, in which Grace is betrothed to princeling Guinness but takes to flirting with handsome tutor Louis Jourdan

Ten Thousand Bedrooms (MGM) d.Richard
Thorpe: Dean Martin, Eva Bartok. Dino's first
without Jerry Lewis in which he plays the owner
of a luxury hotel chain (10,000 bedrooms,
geddit?) romancing sisters Bartok and Anna Maria
Alberghetti in the Eternal City. Virtually
unendurable

Love in the Afternoon (Allied Artists) d.Billy
Wilder: Audrey Hepburn, Maurice Chevalier.
Paris-set May-December romance between
Hepburn and Gary Cooper is delicately handled
by Wilder in self-conscious homage to Lubitsch.
Also Wilder's first collaboration with screenwriter
I A L Diamond

Never Say Goodbye (Universal) d.Jerry Hopper:
Rock Hudson, Cornell Borchers, George Sanders.
Lachrymose remake of *This Love of Ours* (1945)
in which a street accident reunites physician
Rock with long-lost wife Borchers

You Can't Run Away From It (Columbia) d.Dick Powell: June Allyson,
Jack Lemmon. The picture says it all. This was the second musical remake
of *It Happened One Night* (1934), the first being *Eve Knew Her Apples*
(1945). But it might have been better for all concerned if they had run away
from it – fast

Tea and Sympathy (MGM) d.Vincente Minnelli: Deborah Kerr, John Kerr.
The two principals recreate their Broadway success in Robert Anderson's
play, with Deborah playing the teacher's wife genteelly offering herself to
Kerr, who's worried that he might be gay

AMERICANA

The Catered Affair (MGM) d.Richard Brooks:
Debbie Reynolds, Ernest Borgnine, Bette Davis.
One of the many 'clothesline' features of the
period, with Davis as the Bronx-Irish wife of cab-
driver Borgnine determined to give daughter
Debbie a ruinously expensive wedding breakfast.
From a Paddy Chayevsky play

Giant (Warner) d.George Stevens: Mercedes
McCambridge, James Dean. Stevens' sympathetic
handling of a powerful cast gives some shape to
a sprawling saga of Texas cattle barons the
Benedicts and the sudden oil wealth acquired by
their former ranch hand Dean

Glory (RKO) d.David Butler: Walter Brennan,
Margaret O'Brien. Will O'Brien's filly win the
Kentucky Derby? You do not need to be psychic
to guess the result

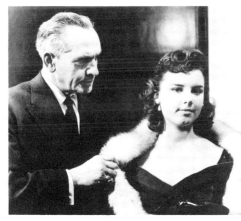

The Man in the Gray Flannel Suit (Fox)
d.Nunnally Johnson: Fredric March, Gigi Perreau.
Glossy critique of the American Dream in which
thrusting corporate speechwriter Gregory Peck is
persuaded by March to forsake the greasy
executive pole to devote more time to his family

The Great American Pastime (MGM)
d.Herman Hoffman: Tom Ewell, Anne Francis.
Ewell's lopsided charm injects a modicum of life
into programmer about Little League baseball and
its effects on suburban families

Fear Strikes Out (Paramount) d.Robert
Mulligan: Anthony Perkins. The Hollywood debut
of director Mulligan and producer Alan J Pakula
is quietly handled drama based on baseball
player Jimmy Piersall and the father fixation
which drove him to a breakdown. Perkins is
appropriately intense throughout

Baby Doll (Warner) d.Elia Kazan: Carroll Baker.
Carroll is the thumb-sucking child-bride married
to blustering Karl Malden and playing around with
rival Eli Wallach in Tennessee Williams
adaptation shot on location in the sweltering
Mississippi back country. The movie created a
boom in 'baby doll' pyjamas and called down the
wrath of the League of Decency

Somebody Up there Likes Me (MGM) d.Robert
Wise: Paul Newman, Everett Sloane. Outstanding
performance from Newman as Rocky Graziano
the slum kid who became a boxing champ.
Excellent script by Ernest Lehman and an Oscar
for cinemaphotographer Joseph Ruttenberg

Friendly Persuasion (Allied Artists) d.William
Wyler: Gary Cooper, Richard Eyer, Anthony
Perkins. A Quaker family struggles to keep its
identity during the Civil War. Full of warm playing
and with a splendid score by Dimitri Tiomkin.
Won the Grand Prix at Cannes

BRITISH AND FOREIGN

Private's Progress (British Lion) d.John
Boulting: Peter Jones, Ian Carmichael. Wide-eyed
innocent Carmichael joins the sloppiest unit in
the British Army before being pitched into a cloak-
and-dagger operation to snatch looted art
treasures from the Germans. Delightful dig at the
British establishment full of comically
disagreeable characters.

A Town Like Alice (Rank) d. Jack Lee: Virginia
McKenna, Takagi. Atmospheric adaptation of
Nevil Shute novel about the deprivations suffered
by a group of women in Malaya on a cruel forced
march to a Japanese internment camp

Ill Met by Moonlight (Rank) d.Michael Powell:
Marius Goring, David Oxley, Dirk Bogarde.
Idiosyncratic account of the wartime capture in
Crete of a German general (Goring) by Major
Patrick Leigh Fermor (Bogarde)

Seven Waves Away (Columbia) d.Richard Sale: Tyrone Power, Mai Zetterling. Relentlessly grim drama in which Power takes command of a lifeboat carrying the excitable survivors of a sunken luxury liner

The Battle of the River Plate (Rank) d.Michael Powell: Ian Hunter, Anthony Quayle. Much laconic British banter on the bridge as the Royal Navy corners the German pocket battleship *Graf Spee* off Montevideo. Peter Finch appropriately anguished as her doomed captain

A Hill in Korea (British Lion) d.Julian Amyes: Stanley Baker, George Baker. The only notable British film about the Korean War cannot quite struggle free from the genre clichés of ill-assorted patrol caught behind enemy lines. Provides a check list of British actors of the '50s most at home in uniform, plus a small part for Michael Caine

The Iron Petticoat (British Lion) d.Ralph Thomas: Alan Gifford, Katharine Hepburn, Bob Hope. Tired effort to update *Ninotchka* (1939) in which humorless Soviet flying ace Hepburn touches down in the West to encounter Hope and the blessings of American civilization. The stars click surprisingly well, which is more than can be said for the script

The Good Companions (ABPC) d.J. Lee Thompson: Hugh Griffith, Eric Portman. Portman, Celia Johnson and John Fraser come to the rescue of a fifth-rate concert party, the Dinky Doos, in energetic second screen version of the J B Priestley classic

Abdullah the Great (British Lion) d.Gregory Ratoff: Kay Kendall, Gregory Ratoff. The lovely Kendall slums it as a model kidnapped by Oriental potentate Ratoff. Made in Egypt, and looks like it

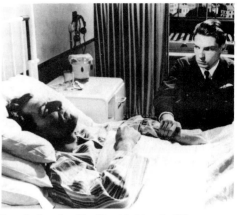

Reach for the Sky (Rank) d.Lewis Gilbert: Kenneth More, Lyndon Brook. Pivotal British war film pays tribute to the legless Battle of Britain fighter ace Douglas Bader. Subsequently much maligned as a crass piece of myth-making, it nevertheless contains a moving central performance from More

The Baby and the Battleship (Rank) d.Jay Lewis: Lisa Gastoni, Richard Attenborough. Money-spinning service comedy in which naval ratings Attenborough and John Mills smuggle an Italian infant on board ship and try to keep it hidden from the top brass

The Long Arm (Ealing) d.Charles Frend: John Stratton, Jack Hawkins. Glum, gray police procedure drama, capturing the pinched mood of Britain in mid-decade, in which rookie cop Stratton and old hand Hawkins track down ingenious safecracker Richard Leech

Brothers in Law (British Lion) d.Roy Boulting: Ian Carmichael, Terry-Thomas. Hopelessly naive barrister Carmichael is tossed to the legal wolves in sprightly sequel to *Private's Progress* (1956)

Charley Moon (British Lion) d.Guy Hamilton: Max Bygraves. Meandering musical in which Max hits the showbiz heights only to give it all up and join a traveling circus. Songs include the hit 'Out of Town'

Town on Trial! (Columbia) d.John Guillermin: John Mills. The murder of a small-town good-time girl brings Inspector John Mills screeching down from Scotland Yard in his Wolsely, to launch a bullying investigation in which he suspects everybody but the real killer

Yangtse Incident (British Lion) d.Michael Anderson: William Hartnell, James Kenney, Richard Todd, Richard Leech. Tense treatment of a postwar incident in which the British cruiser *Amethyst* was bottled up by the Chinese on the Yangste and forced to run the gauntlet of their artillery

X the Unknown (Hammer) d.Leslie Norman: William Lucas, Dean Jagger. A primeval mud monster, adapted to feed off radiation, slithers across the Scottish moors in fine example of the sober realist tradition of British SF movies

Fire Maidens from Outer Space (Criterion) d.Cy Roth: Anthony Dexter, Susan Shaw. In sharp contrast, star trekker Dexter discovers the descendants of the lost continent of Atlantis on the 13th moon of Jupiter in magnificently incompetent cheapie

Three Men in a Boat (Remus) d.Ken Annakin: Campbell Cotts, George Woodbridge, Laurence Harvey, Jimmy Edwards, David Tomlinson. Diverting adaptation of Jerome K Jerome's comedy of three stalwarts' boat trip up the Thames with their dog Montmorency

Port Afrique (Columbia) d.Rudolph Maté: Pier Angeli, James Hayter. Crippled flier Phil Carey returns to Morocco to find his wife dead in suspicious circumstances. His investigations lead him to the sobering truth

Yield to the Night (ABPC) d.J. Lee Thompson: Yvonne Mitchell, Diana Dors. Anti-capital punishment drama, loosely based on the Ruth Ellis case, in which a deglamorized Dors winds up in the death cell after shooting her lover's mistress

Who Done It? (Rank) d.Basil Dearden: Benny Hill, Belinda Lee. Now get this – ice-rink sweeper Hill wins £100 and a bloodhound, so he sets up a detective agency. Soon he's involved with an Iron Curtain hit squad. Variety strong-girl Lee comes to the rescue. You'll love it

Tiger in the Smoke (Rank) d.Roy Baker: Tony Wright, Donald Sinden. Screen version of Margery Allingham's remarkable thriller kicks off to brilliant noirish start but then falls away. Sinden becomes involved in the hunt for loot stashed away after a wartime commando raid

Let's Be Happy (ABPC) d.Henry Levin: Tony Martin, Vera-Ellen. Imported American stars plug away gamely in remake of *Jeannie* (1941), in which Vera-Ellen spends a legacy on a trip to Scotland and is romanced by Martin and penniless laird Robert Flemyng

The Intimate Stranger (Anglo-Amalgamated) d.Joseph Losey: Richard Basehart, Mervyn Johns. Sacked film producer Johns sets about wrecking the life of his wunderkind successor Basehart

Biruma No Tategoto (Japan) d.Kon Ichikawa: Shoji Yasui. Wartime story of a young Japanese soldier, wounded and separated from his unit, who becomes a Buddhist monk committed to wandering the countryside and burying the unknown dead. A heady, over-emotional plea for humanity and peace, contrasting the horrors of war with pastoral lyricism

The Hunchback of Notre Dame (France) d.Jean Delannoy: Anthony Quinn. Quinn suffers mightily as Hugo's bell-ringing hunchback but the shades of Charles Laughton hover in the wings. Gina Lollobrigida plays Esmeralda

Le Notti di Cabiria (Italy) d.Federico Fellini: Guilietta Massina, François Périer. Masina's portrayal of a waif-like, wistfully optimistic prostitute provided the basis for Neil Simon's play 'Sweet Charity', filmed in 1969 with Shirley MacLaine

Kanal (Poland) d.Andrzej Wajda: Vladek Sheybal. The film which brought Wajda into the international limelight. A group of partisans take to the sewers during the Warsaw uprising of 1944, and are trapped and killed in eloquent expression of Polish martyrdom

Et Dieu Créa La Femme (France) d.Roger Vadim: Jean-Louis Trintignant, Brigitte Bardot. Or rather Svengali-like Vadim creates BB, sultry symbol of beckoning postwar affluence and sexual permissiveness, playing fast and loose with all the available menfolk in St Tropez

Un Condamné à Mort s'est Echappé (France): d.Robert Bresson. Uniquely austere evocation of the spirit of the Resistance concentrated in telling detail on an escape from a Gestapo prison in Lyons. The economic visuals and dispassionate voice-over are brilliantly counter-pointed by a lush Mozart score

For the first time in its history MGM showed a loss, slipping $455,000 into the red. RKO reached the end of the line. Universal took over the distribution of the studio's remaining important pictures and production ceased. In the autumn RKO's Gower Street and Culver City film-making plants were sold to two of the studio's former contract players, Lucille Ball and Desi Arnaz, stars since 1951 of the hugely succesful 'I Love Lucy' TV series. The RKO studios were now given over to the production of television programs.   Hollywood's sour attitude was caught by Manhattan copywriter Tony Randall in *Will Success Spoil Rock Hunter?*, Frank Tashlin's rancid satire on the advertising business. Muses Randall, 'What has success to do with talent? If it had, Brooks Brothers would go out of business, and TV studios would be turned into supermarkets.' A ferocious frontal assault on TV hucksterism was made by Elia Kazan's *A Face in the Crowd*, in which Andy Griffith made his debut.

Distractedly Hollywood began to rummage around in its own past, with biopics of Buster Keaton, Jeanne Eagels and Lon Chaney. As the doomed silent star in *Jeanne Eagels*, Kim Novak was barely adequate. The casting of Donald O'Connor in the title role in *The Buster Keaton Story* seems like Hollywood's last attempt to bury one of its greatest geniuses in a welter of anachronistic slapstick. In *Man of a Thousand Faces*, James Cagney attacked the role of Lon Chaney with all his customary energy, transcending Joseph Pevney's flat direction to hint at the strange, masochistic fires which drove the master of the grotesque.

The most successful picture of the year was *The Bridge on the River Kwai*, produced by Sam Spiegel, directed by David Lean and starring Alec Guinness, William Holden and Jack Hawkins. It was a monument to the Spiegel method: the meticulous preparation of an ostensibly solemn subject swaddled in a suffocating blanket of production values with its hint of radicalism kept firmly in its place by the tidy impersonality of David Lean's direction. *Bridge on the River Kwai* edged gingerly away from the stereotypes of wartime heroism but ultimately managed to deliver little more than the banal message that war is 'madness'. Nevertheless, *Bridge on the River Kwai* emerged with a total of seven Oscars. Best Picture, Director and Actor (Guinness as the tragically obsessed Colonel Nicholson), Cinematograhy (Jack Hildyard), Editing (Peter Taylor), Scoring (Malcolm Arnold) and Screenplay (Carl Foreman and Michael Wilson). As both Foreman and Wilson were still on the blacklist, the script was credited to Pierre Boulle, on whose book the script was based, but who spoke no English!

Stanley Kubrick's *Paths of Glory*, set in World War I, also sought to demonstrate the futility of war, not so much on the the battlefield – where he confined himself to a single bravura set-piece – but in the cynical coils of general staff politics, which demands random executions after the failure of a suicidal attack.

Another aspect of service life – the hot house atmosphere of a cadet school – was given a remarkable resonance in *The Strange One* by Ben Gazzara's performance as the fetishistic Jocko de Paris, a role he had originally created in the Actors Studio. It was an arresting debut, but Gazzara's subsequent career has failed to fulfil the promise of the casually harbored hostility he generated in *The Strange One*. Joanne Woodward was equally impressive in *The Three Faces of Eve*, winning the Best Actress Oscar as the young Southern woman afflicted with multiple personality. Red Buttons and Miyoshi Umeki won the Best Supporting Actor and Actress Awards as the unhappy lovers in *Sayonara*.

Audie Murphy was intriguingly cast in the title role of *The Quiet American*, an adaptation of a Graham Greene novel set in contemporary French Indo-China. Graham Greene disowned the film. His critique of American intervention in Vietnam had been twisted by the director Joseph L Mankiewicz into a characteristic Fifties tale of Communists conniving against Murphy, the representative of a shadowy, semi-official economic aid mission who is negotiating with a disaffected Vietnamese general to set up a 'third force'.

The Quiet American gave Audie Murphy some respite from the long grind of formula Westerns in which the only thing that changed was the horses. Notable contributions to the genre included Arthur Penn's *The Left-Handed Gun*, in which a modern American youth – Paul Newman – was substituted for a mythical Billy the Kid; *3:10 to Yuma*, a formal masterpiece directed by Delmer Daves; and Sam Fuller's baroque extravaganza, *Forty Guns*, dominated by a black-clad Barbara Stanwyck.

In a flash of crazy brilliance a young exploitation producer, Herman Cohen, grafted two classic elements of the horror film on to the teen agony movie to give us *I Was a Teenage Werewolf* and *I Was a Teenage Frankenstein*. These gleefully tacky drive-in smashes mark the point at which the horror film, dormant since the early Forties, began to assert itself over the science fiction cycle. In the same year a small British studio, Hammer, released *The Curse of Frankenstein*, starring a feverish Peter Cushing as the demon Baron and Christopher Lee as his monstrous creation.

Ironically, death took the English director James Whale, who had made Boris Karloff a horror star in *Frankenstein* (1931). Also bowing out were silent star Norma Talmadge; Erich von Stroheim, frustrated genius and all-round megalomaniac; Louis B Mayer, exhausted by his struggle with Loew's; production designer and director William Cameron Menzies; veteran director Tim Whelan; Oliver Hardy, from a heart attack; and 'King of the Quickies' Fred F Sears. After a long illness, borne with great fortitude and humor, Humphrey Bogart succumbed to throat cancer.

ACTION

The Brothers Rico (Columbia) d.Phil Karlson:
Richard Conte. Pacy Simenon adaptation in
which ex-mobster's accountant Conte is used by
the syndicate to finger his brothers

Baby Face Nelson (UA) d.Don Siegel: Mickey
Rooney, Leo Gordon. Rooney is like a crazy little
clockwork doll running wild as the pint-sized
Prohibition gangster finally put out of his misery
by girlfriend Carolyn Jones

Underwater Warrior (MGM) d.Andrew Marton:
Dan Dailey. Slim effort, based on the real-life
exploits of an American diving pioneer, follows
Dailey's adventures from Korea to the hazardous
retrieval of documents from an aircraft ditched at
sea

Legend of the Lost (UA) d.Henry Hathaway:
Sophia Loren, Rossano Brazzi. Protracted Sahara
adventure in which Brazzi and John Wayne
search for the lost city of Timgad, tangle over
ravishing slave girl Loren. Virtually a parody of
Hathaway's action style

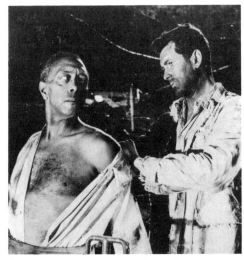

Something of Value (MGM) d.Richard Brooks:
Juano Hernandez, Rock Hudson. Portentous
attempt to deal with the Mau Mau rebellion in
Africa pits tolerant settler Hudson against
boyhood chum Sidney Poitier, who has become
a guerrilla leader. From a Robert Ruark novel

House of Numbers (MGM) d.Russell Rouse:
Jack Palance, Harold J Stone. Palance in dual role
as a vicious San Quentin lifer and the twin brother
who devises an ingenious scheme to engineer
his escape

Girl in the Kremlin (Universal) d.Russell
Birdwell: Zsa Zsa Gabor. Glorious slice of tara-
diddle in which Zsa Zsa plays twin sisters on
opposite sides when Soviet dictator Josef Stalin
turns up in Greece, his faced transformed by
plastic surgery

Lafayette Escadrille (Warner) d.William
Wellman: Tab Hunter. Perfunctory programmer,
lacking any sense of period feel, in which
Wellman pays tribute to the celebrated World War
I fighter squadron of which he was a member

Darby's Rangers (Warner) d.William Wellman:
Jack Warden, James Garner. The men of an élite
US commando unit spend more time chasing the
local women than the enemy as they work up for
action in wartime Britain

Jet Pilot (RKO) d.Josef von Sternberg: Janet Leigh, John Wayne. Much-delayed Cold War drama soars into previously uncharted realms of the ridiculous as US pilot Wayne falls in love with defecting Soviet jet ace Leigh. Many laughs, all of them unintentional

Bail Out at 43,000 (UA) d.Francis D Lyon: Paul Kelly, John Payne. Air ace Payne spends most of the movie fretting about whether his nerve will hold up when it comes to testing a new ejector seat for the USAF's bombers

Bombers B-52 (Warner) d.Gordon Douglas: Efrem Zimbalist Jr, Karl Malden. Routine romance between CO Zimbalist and resentful veteran Sergeant Malden's daughter Natalie Wood is interwoven with excellent footage of jet maneuvers

The Enemy Below (Fox) d.Dick Powell: Curt Jurgens, Theodore Bikel. Honorable, war-weary U-boat commander Jurgens and destroyer captain Robert Mitchum play a deadly game of cat and mouse in the Atlantic

Hellcats of the Navy (Columbia) d.Nathan Juran: Ronald Reagan, Arthur Franz. Cut-rate actioner in which submarine commander Reagan torpedoes his way through thousands of tons of Japanese shipping, teaches Franz the meaning of command decisions, romances Nancy Davis, his future First Lady

China Gate (Fox) d.Sam Fuller: Angie Dickinson, Gene Barry. A band of adventurers attack a Communist ammunition dump in Indochina in dynamic, rough-hewn actioner set in pre-Vietnam days when everything seemed so much simpler. Required viewing for all Ollie North fans

ADVENTURE AND FANTASY

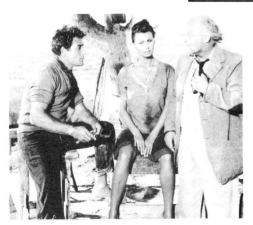

Boy on a Dolphin (Fox) d.Jean Negulesco: Jorge Mistral, Sophia Loren, Laurence Naismith. Visually handsome Aegean adventure in which sponge-diver Loren and archaeologist Alan Ladd save a priceless statue from the clutches of feline connoisseur Clifton Webb

Johnny Tremain (Disney) d.Robert Stevenson: Richard Beymer, Hal Stalmaster. Energetic adaptation of an Esther Forbes novel, set in the Revolutionary War, happily confuses fiction and fact

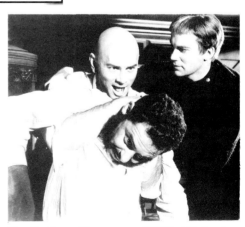

The Brothers Karamazov (MGM) d.Richard Brooks: Yul Brynner, William Shatner. Brooks also scripted solemn but only partially successful attempt to capture the emotional intensity of the Dostoevsky masterpiece. Hollywood at its most pathetically eager to appear respectable

The Story of Mankind (Warner) d. Irwin Allen: Anthony Dexter, Chico Marx. Mankind is put on trial in weird historical pageant, adapted from Henrik van Loon's ineffably simple-minded stroll through the past; notable chiefly for some engagingly off-beat casting, including Chico as Isaac Newton, Hedy Lamarr as Joan of Arc and Francis X Bushman as Moses

Saint Joan (UA) d. Otto Preminger: Jean Seberg, Richard Widmark. Big-budget, Graham Greene-scripted version of George Bernard Shaw play thrown off course by Seberg's tentative performance in the title role

Omar Khayyam (Paramount) d.William Dieterle: John Derek. Colorful costumer, set in medieval Persia, contains a strikingly crazy performance from cult favourite Yma Sumac. Cornel Wilde stars in the title role

The Pride and the Passion (UA) d.Stanley Kramer: Cary Grant. As ever looking ill-at-ease in costume, British naval officer Grant manhandles a huge artillery piece across Spain in C S Forester yarn of the Peninsular War. Frank Sinatra, disastrously miscast as a Spanish guerrilla, is out-acted by the not unpersonable cannon

From Hell It Came (Allied Artists) d.Dan Milner: Tina Carver, Tod Andrews. Radiation raises poor old Gregg Palmer from the dead as a walking tree stump determined to dispose of those who con-demned him to death. Once again cut-rate monster maker Paul Blaisdell does his worst

Macabre (Allied Artists) d.William Castle: Howard Hoffman, Jacqueline Scott. Low-budget murder shocker, tricked out with all the usual Castle gimmicks, including an unrepeatable offer to insure moviegoers against being frightened to death

Viking Women and the Voyage to the Waters of the Sea Serpent (AIP) d. Roger Corman. The longest title, and probably the lowest budget in the book. This one will leave scholars of the Dark Ages scratching their heads as a band of Viking women set sail in search of their menfolk to encounter whirlpools, terrifying Grimault warriors and the hungry serpent of the title

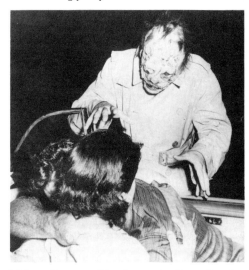

I Was a Teenage Frankenstein (Santa Rosa) d.Herbert L Strock: Gary Conway. Zany old Whit Bissell is at it again, assembling a monster from the limbs of dead hot rodders, exulting 'Even the tear ducts work!' as he surveys his handiwork

Plan 9 from Outer Space (Reynolds) d.Edward D Wood : Vampira. Aliens attempt to conquer Earth by raising the dead as zombies. A spectral Bela Lugosi, spliced in from Wood's *Tomb of the Vampire*, makes a harrowing posthumous appearance. Virtually unwatchable film with a fleeting, fragmentary hallucinatory charm

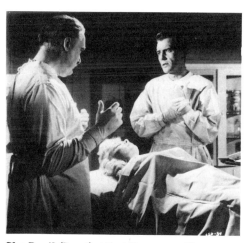

She Devil (Regal) d.Kurt Neumann: Albert Dekker, Mari Blanchard, Jack Kelly. Shades of Jekyll and Hyde as Kelly's new serum gives TB victim Blanchard distressingly homicidal tendencies which are signaled every time her hair changes from blonde to brunette

I Was a Teenage Werewolf (Sunset) d.Gene Fowler Jr: Michael Landon. Why has pensive Landon, star student at Rockwell High School, started to eat his steak raw? Mad scientist Whit Bissell attempts to solve the problem by hurling the hapless youth back to his 'primitive state', producing a teenage werewolf who sprouts hair and fangs every time the class bell rings

Invasion of the Saucermen (American International) d.Edward L Cahn: Gloria Castillo, Steve Terrell. Bizarre comedy mixture of SF and teen agony exploiter as alien visitors meet their doom in the headlights of the movie's dragster heroes

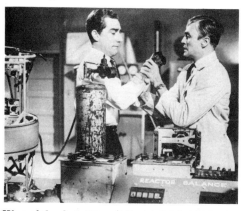

War of the Satellites (Allied Artists) d.Roger Corman: Richard Devon (1). Fast-on-the-draw exploiter, filmed in eight days, to cash in on the Sputnik launch. An alien super-intelligence attempts to stop foolish Earthlings from venturing into space

The Incredible Shrinking Man (Universal) d.Jack Arnold: Grant Williams. Masterful evocation of 1950s unease as diminishing radiation victim Williams finds the familiar features of domestic life transformed into malevolent agents of destruction. Adapted by Richard Matheson from his own novel

20 Million Miles to Earth (Columbia) d.Nathan Juran. The Ymir, a space beast brought back to Earth by a manned expedition to Venus, is the first of master animator Ray Harryhausen's truly memorable creations

The Black Scorpion (Warner) d.Edward Ludwig. Radiation rears a swarm of mutated monsters, all of which are eaten by the Black Scorpion before it sets out for Mexico City and a film contract. Some of the animation sequences were borrowed from an unfinished Willis O'Brien project

The Amazing Colossal Man (American International) d.Bert I Gordon: Cathy Downs, William Hudson (c). Army officer Glenn Langan shoots up to 50ft after exposure to radiation in an A-bomb test. The big syringe is one of many futile, and unintentionally hilarious attempts to save him

The Monolith Monsters (Universal) d.John Sherwood: Grant Williams, Lola Albright. Geologist Williams discovers an alien element, brought to Earth in a meteorite shower, which invades human bodies, first turning them into stone and then expanding into gigantic shards of crystal which threaten to engulf the planet

The Monster That Challenged the World (UA) d.Arnold Laven. One of the decade's most enjoyable low-budget creature features in which Tim Holt deals with a plague of prehistoric caterpillers thrown up by an earthquake

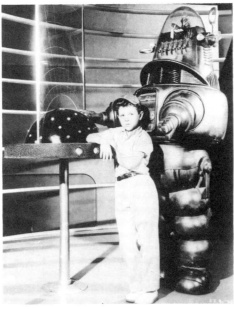

The Invisible Boy (UA) d.Herman Hoffman: Richard Eyer, Robby the Robot. Philip Abbott's super-computer rebuilds Robby and then uses him in a bid for world domination. The action is seen from the point of view of 10-year-old Eyer in a fashion which anticipates *ET* (1982)

The Night the World Exploded (Clover) d.Fred F Sears: Tristram Coffin, Kathryn Grant, William Leslie. Seismologist Leslie stumbles on E-112, a new element in the Earth's crust which is triggering a potentially catastrophic series of earthquakes. The movie is slightly less earth-shattering

Kronos (Fox) d.Kurt Neumann: Jeff Morrow, Barbara Lawrence, George O'Hanlon. A 100ft-high alien robot lumbers across California, gorging itself on the power stations in its path and gobbling up the USAF's atom bombs like a performing seal at feeding time

The Deadly Mantis (Universal) d.Nathan Juran: William Hopper, Alix Talton, Craig Stevens. The installation of an early warning system near the North Pole wakes a monster insect which wings its way south, creating havoc along America's eastern seaboard before being gassed to death in an underground parking lot

The Land Unknown (Universal) d.Virgil Vogel: Shawn Smith, Jock Mahoney. A stray pterodactyl brings Jock's helicopter crashing into an Antarctic Land That Time Forgot, peopled by prehistoric monsters and crazy Henry Brandon, a Ben Gunn figure trapped after a similar accident

MELODRAMA

Paths of Glory (UA) d.Stanley Kubrick: Kirk Douglas, Wayne Morris. Douglas is the idealistic French officer caught in the cynical toils of general staff politics when three of his men are randomly singled out for court-martial and execution after the failure of a suicidal attack

Until They Sail (MGM) d.Robert Wise: Jean Simmons, Paul Newman. Glossy treatment of US servicemen abroad in wartime New Zealand and their traumatic effect on the lives of the four Leslie sisters, Simmons, Piper Laurie, Joan Fontaine and Sandra Dee

The Abductors (Fox) d.Andrew V McLaglen: Victor McLaglen. Ex-con McLaglen sets out to steal Lincoln's body from the tomb in Springfield in roundabout bid to secure a stash of counterfeit money

Time Limit (UA) d.Karl Malden: Martin Balsam, Rip Torn, Richard Widmark. Efficient adaptation of a Broadway drama in which Richard Basehart is court-martialled for collaboration with the Reds in the Korean War

Witness for the Prosecution (UA) d.Billy Wilder: Marlene Dietrich. Agatha Christie courtroom drama dominated by Charles Laughton as the QC defending murder suspect Tyrone Power. Sadly, Marlene's Cockney impersonation gives the whole game away

The Quiet American (UA) d.Joseph L Mankiewicz: Audie Murphy, Michael Redgrave. Intriguing adaptation of a Graham Greene novel, minus its anti-Americanism, with Murphy excellent as the US intelligence man fatally attempting to impose his own naive solutions on the Indochina conflict. A bitter foretaste of what was to come in the 1960s

Zero Hour (Paramount) d.Hall Bartlett: Linda Darnell, Dana Andrews. Arthur Hailey drama in which glum ex-fighter pilot Andrews takes the controls of an airliner after the crew are laid low by food poisoning. Estranged wife Darnell also lends a hand

Tarnished Angels (Universal) d.Douglas Sirk: Dorothy Malone, Rock Hudson. Malone is simply marvellous as the languorous self-destructive wanton married to barnstorming stunt flyer Robert Stack, flirting with drunken reporter Hudson. From William Faulkner's 'Pylon'

The Strange One (Columbia) d.Jack Garfein: Ben Gazzara. Remarkable debut by Gazzara as the fetishistic military cadet Jocko de Paris in screen version of Calder Willingham's 'End as a Man'. Originally an Actor's Studio production with Gazzara in the lead

The Key (Columbia) d.Carol Reed: Sophia Loren, William Holden. Moody, metaphysical war drama in which Loren plays a mysterious refugee, the key to whose flat has been held by a succession of seamen, now all in Davy Jones' locker

The DI (Warner) d.Jack Webb: Jack Webb, Don Dubbins. Unintentionally camp Marine training drama in which grim drill instructor Webb licks over-emotional recruit Don Dubbins into shape

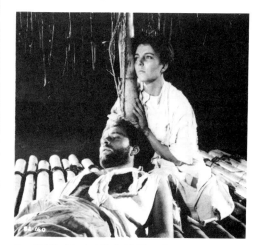

Sea Wife (Fox) d.Bob McNaught: Richard Burton, Joan Collins. RAF officer Burton and nun Collins are cast adrift in the Pacific when their ship is torpedoed by the Japanese. Burton falls in love unaware that Collins is in holy orders

Man Afraid (Universal) d.Harry Keller: Eduard Franz, Tim Hovey. Grief-stricken Franz decides to take revenge on clergyman George Nader after the latter has accidentally killed his teenage burglar son

Man on Fire (MGM) d.Ranald MacDougall: Inger Stevens, Bing Crosby. Little Malcolm Broderick effects a touching reconciliation between embittered Crosby and his ex-wife Stevens

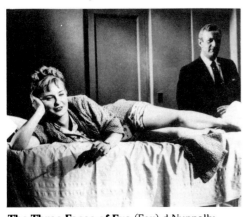

The Three Faces of Eve (Fox) d.Nunnally Johnson: Joanne Woodward, Lee J Cobb. Tour de force from Woodward as the young woman suffering from multiple personality. Cobb the psychiatrist who hypnotizes her back to health

A Hatful of Rain (Fox) d.Fred Zinnemann: Don Murray, Anthony Franciosa. Heart-rending performance from the underrated Murray as a junkie struggling to hide his addiction from his pregnant wife Eva Marie Saint

Lizzie (MGM) d.Hugo Haas: Eleanor Parker, Richard Boone. Adaptation of Shirley Jackson's 'The Bird's Nest' in which Parker is afflicted with similar problems to those of Joanne Woodward in *The Three Faces of Eve*, the success of which effectively buried this movie

The Vintage MGM d.Jeffrey Hayden: Pier Angeli, Leif Erickson, Michele Morgan. Mel Ferrer and John Kerr are the two incongruous Italians, on the run from the police, seeking refuge as grapepickers in Erickson's vineyard. The usual romantic complications ensue

Man in the Shadow (Universal) d.Jack Arnold: Orson Welles, Jeff Chandler. Newly appointed Sheriff Chandler hits trouble when he investigates the death of a Mexican laborer on local Mr Big Welles' ranch

Monkey on My Back (UA) d.André de Toth: Dianne Foster, Cameron Mitchell. Hard-driving biopic casts Mitchell as boxer and war hero Barney Ross, who became a drug addict after being treated with morphine for chronic malaria

The Tattered Dress (Universal) d.Jack Arnold: Jeanne Crain, George Tobias, Jeff Chandler. New York lawyer Chandler wins smalltown playboy Philip Reed's acquittal on a murder charge and then finds himself in the dock accused of bribery

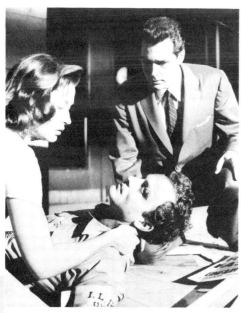

The Garment Jungle (Columbia) d.Vincent Sherman, Robert Aldrich: Gia Scala, Robert Loggia, Kerwin Matthews. Romantic interludes intrude on pacy exposé of union-gangster corruption in the dressmaking industry

The Unholy Wife (RKO) d.John Farrow: Rod Steiger, Diana Dors. Lamentable attempt to boost British sex bomb Dors as the platinum-blonde slut two-timing on winery owner Steiger and then plotting a murder which goes spectacularly wrong

Four Girls in Town (Universal) d.Jack Sher: Grant Williams, Elsa Martinelli. Elsa, Gia Scala and Julie Adams compete for a plum movie part in acerbic tale of Tinsel Town

The Burglar (Columbia) d.Paul Wendkos: Jayne Mansfield, Dan Duryea. Oddly effective little thriller in which Duryea and Mansfield join forces to lift a valuable jewel necklace from a rich old eccentric, then fall foul of a corrupt policeman

Johnny Trouble (Warner) d.John H Auer: Stuart Whitman, Carolyn Jones. Remake of *Someone to Remember* (1943) in which lonely widowed invalid Ethel Barrymore fantasizes that freshman Whitman is her grandson

No Down Payment (Fox) d.Martin Ritt: Cameron Mitchell, Tony Randall. There are slightly fewer than eight million stories in the naked suburbs of Sunrise Hills, where the strain of meeting the credit payments, racist bigotry and sexual frustration all take their toll

The Devil's Hairpin (Paramount) d.Cornel Wilde: Cornel Wilde, Jean Wallace. Swaggering former motor racing champ Wilde makes a comeback, beats his big rival and learns a little humility before being reunited with wife Wallace

Stake Out on Dope Street (Warner) d.Irvin Kershner. Three teenagers find a cache of heroin and decide to go into business as pushers in tight little semi-documentary programmer

A Farewell to Arms (Fox) d.Charles Vidor: Rock Hudson, Jennifer Jones. Rock is no match for Gary Cooper in the 1932 original, but he's thoughtful, sincere and gently romantic as Hemingway's World War I ambulance driver wounded in action and falling in love with nurse Jones

Hot Spell (Paramount) d.Daniel Mann: Shirley Booth, Anthony Quinn. Booth discovers that you can never go home as tensions within her disintegrating family reach flashpoint in a sweltering Southern summer

Flood Tide (Universal) d.Abner Biberman: Michael Ray, George Nader, Cornell Borchers. Insanely jealous youngster Ray pulls out all the stops in an attempt to wreck his mother Borchers' relationship with neighbor Nader

The Sun Also Rises (Fox) d.Henry King: Errol Flynn, Ava Gardner. Hemingways' account of the lost generation of Americans living in Europe after World War I. Flynn is wryly amusing as the gentlemanly roué Mike Campbell, touchingly trying to outrun the bulls in Pamplona. Also Tyrone Power's last completed film

Island in the Sun (Fox) d.Robert Rossen: Joan Fontaine, Harry Belafonte. Darryl F Zanuck's first as an independent producer is a turgid story of murder, politics and interracial love in the West Indies. From a novel by Alec Waugh

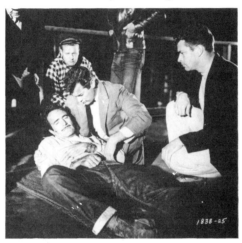

The Midnight Story (Universal) d.Joseph Pevney: Gilbert Roland, Tony Curtis. San Francisco cop Curtis goes freelance to solve the murder of the priest who helped bring him up. Roland the suspect he can't help liking, Marisa Pavan the love interest

Slaughter on Tenth Avenue (Universal) d.Arnold Laven: Richard Egan, Nick Dennis. Deputy DA Egan goes all out to break the code of silence imposed by New York's waterfront racketeers

Death in Small Doses (Allied Artists) d.Joseph M Newman: Mala Powers, Peter Graves. Undercover cop Graves poses as a truck driver to crack a drugs ring supplying 'stay awake' pills to truckers. Powers turns out to be the gang's Mrs Big

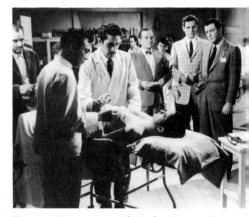

Tip on a Dead Jockey (MGM) d.Richard Thorpe: Martin Gabel (c), Jack Lord, Robert Taylor. Sluggish smuggling yarn adapted from a John O'Hara story

The Seventh Sin (MGM) d.Ronald Neame: Eleanor Parker, Jean-Pierre Aumont. Remake of Somerset Maugham's Far East story *The Painted Veil* (1934), starring Greta Garbo, in which unfaithful wife Parker redeems herself during an epidemic

Wild is the Wind (Paramount) d.George Cukor: Anna Magnani, Anthony Franciosa. Virtual remake of *They Knew What They Wanted* (1940). Italian sheep rancher Anthony Quinn marries his dead wife's sister Magnani, with handsome adopted son Franciosa completing a fraught triangle

The Careless Years (UA) d.Arthur Hiller: Natalie Trundy, Dean Stockwell. Trundy and Stockwell's plans to elope go badly awry in tale of gauche young lovers

No Time to Be Young (Columbia) d.David Lowell Rich: Robert Vaughn. Draft-dodging dropout Vaughn takes to a life of crime with fatal results

The Barretts of Wimpole Street (MGM) d.Sidney Franklin: Jennifer Jones, John Gielgud. Tepid remake of Franklin's 1934 movie, celebrating the romance between poets Elizabeth Barrett and a very muscular Robert Browning played by Bill Travers. Gielgud icily effective as Jones' domineering Papa

The Night Runner (Universal) d.Abner Biberman: Ray Danton, Colleen Miller. Psychopath Danton's premature release from a mental institution has predictably disastrous results before he sensibly turns himself over to the authorities

Motorcycle Gang (Golden State) d.Edward L Cahn: Anne Neyland, Steve Terrell. The comatose Terrell is goaded into a 'chicken run' by taunts of cowardice from hit-and-run biker John Ashley

Three Brave Men (Fox) d.Philip Dunne: Ray Milland, Dean Jagger, Ernest Borgnine. An innocent flirtation with a Communist front organization costs Navy civil servant Borgnine his job. Lawyer Milland and Assistant Secretary of the Navy Jagger come to his rescue

Valerie (UA) d.Gerd Oswald. Sterling Hayden, Anita Ekberg. Flashback drama in which Hayden and Jerry Barclay are charged with wounding Ekberg and murdering her parents

The Wayward Bus (Fox) d.Victor Vicas: Joan Collins, Jayne Mansfield. An equally wayward movie, based on a minor Steinbeck novel, in which an eventful journey effects a reconciliation between Rick Jason and Joan Collins and sparks unlikely romance between stripper Mansfield and traveling salesman Dan Dailey

Untamed Youth (Warner) d.Howard W Koch: Mamie Van Doren, Lori Nelson (with guitar). Hitchhikers Lori and Mamie wind up in a prison farm, run by lantern-jawed John Russell, whose inmates include cotton-pickin' rock 'n' roller Eddie Cochran

Sorority Girl (AIP) d.Roger Corman: Dick Miller, Susan Cabot. Female version of *The Strange One* (1957) in which twisted Cabot browbeats and blackmails her sorority sisters

Affair in Havana (Allied Artists) d.Laslo Benedek: Raymond Burr, John Cassavetes. Pianist Cassavetes falls in love with the lovely but selfish and luxury-loving wife of paralyzed Burr

Rock All Night (AIP) d.Roger Corman: Dick Miller (c), Russell Johnson (r). Gunsels a Go Go as a pair of hit men hold the terminally hip habitués of Al's Bar hostage before Miller wisecracks them into surrender. Music from the Platters and the appalling house band, the Blockbusters

The Young Stranger (RKO) d.John Frankenheimer: Whit Bissell, James MacArthur. Frankenheimer's first is a 'generation gap' drama in which puppyish newcomer MacArthur plays a talented teenager whose brush with the law eventually leads to a reconciliation with his film executive father

The Green-Eyed Blonde (Warner) d.Bernard Girard: Carla Merey, Beverly Long. The inmates of a girls' corrective institution attempt to hide a baby from the authorities. When it's discovered, all hell breaks loose

COMEDY

Designing Woman (MGM) d.Vincente Minnelli: Lauren Bacall, Dolores Gray. Sportswriter Gregory Peck and fashion designer Bacall clash head-on in marital comedy reminiscent of the best of the Tracy-Hepburn outings

Joe Butterfly (Universal) d.Jesse Hibbs: Burgess Meredith, Audie Murphy. Pale imitation of *Teahouse of the August Moon* (1956) in which Burgess' ingratiatingly streetwise interpreter helps an advance guard of US journalists set up a magazine in postwar Tokyo

Don't Go Near the Water (MGM) d.Charles Walters: Gia Scala, Glenn Ford. Limp Army comedy, set in the South Pacific, salvaged by Fred Clark as a bumbling, officious commanding officer

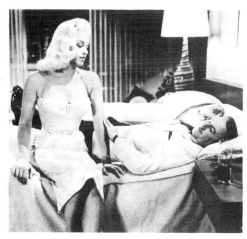

I Married a Woman (RKO) d.Hal Kanter: Diana Dors, George Gobel. It frequently helps. Mind-numbingly unfunny effort in which ad-man Gobel's career takes a nosedive after his marriage to beauty contest winner Dors. John Wayne pops up in a cameo role

This Could Be the Night (MGM) d.Robert Wise: J Carrol Naish, Jean Simmons. Jean is the prim but by no means naive teacher working as a secretary to night club-owning gangster Paul Douglas, romancing one of his associates Anthony Franciosa

My Man Godfrey (Universal) d.Henry Koster: June Allyson, David Niven. Damp remake of 1936 Carole Lombard/ William Powell screwball classic with Niven the urbane butler to Allyson's madcap family

The High Cost of Loving (MGM) d.Jose Ferrer: Gena Rowlands, Jose Ferrer. Comedy of middle-class insecurity as paranoid executive Ferrer frets about losing his job. Inventive opening sequence dispenses with dialogue

Kiss Them for Me (Fox) d.Stanley Donen: Jayne Mansfield, Cary Grant, Suzy Parker. Jayne's one-woman war effort consists of making as many servicemen as possible happy while Navy flier Cary organizes a non-stop party at San Francisco's Mark Hopkins Hotel on an eventful shore leave

No Time for Sergeants (Warner) d.Mervyn LeRoy: Nick Adams, Andy Griffith. Repeat of Griffith's Broadway hit as the trusting hayseed drafted into the Air Force to the dismay of his sergeant Myron McCormick

The Sad Sack (Paramount) d.George Marshall: Phyllis Kirk, Jerry Lewis, Shepperd Strudwick. Jerry plays the misfit GI in jerky screen verison of George Baker's comic strip. Peter Lorre wanders through mournfully as an Arab

Hear Me Good (Paramount) d.Don McGuire: Joe E Ross, Jean Willes, Hal March. Con-man March plans to fix the Miss Wide World beauty contest but the Mob intervenes

Escapade in Japan (RKO) d.Arthur Lubin: Roger Nakagawa, Jon Provost. Mild comedy-drama in which two young runaways are chased through Tokyo in simple-minded plea for mutual understanding between two wartime enemies

Operation Mad Ball (Columbia) d.Richard Quine: Dick York, Mickey Rooney, Jack Lemmon. Rooney does his best to inject a sense of accelerating chaos as a bunch of scheming soldiers plan a wild party off base

The Kettles on Old Macdonald's Farm (Universal) d.Virgil Vogel: Gloria Talbott, John Smith. Parker Fennelly takes over from Percy Kilbride as Pa Kettle, helping Marjorie Main to engineer a marriage between rich sophisticate Talbott and poor lumberjack Smith. Also Main's last film and last of the series

The Fuzzy Pink Nightgown (UA) d.Norman Taurog: Jane Russell, Ralph Meeker. Cracking cast come a cropper in grating Hollywood satire revolving around movie star Russell's transformation of her kidnapping into a publicity stunt

Oh Men! Oh Women! (Fox) d.Nunally Johnson: Ginger Rogers, Dan Dailey, David Niven. Deft comedy of manners in which suave psychiatrist Niven has a trying time sorting out his own problems and the sex lives of his patients. Tony Randall's feature debut

Will Success Spoil Rock Hunter? (Fox) d.Frank Tashlin: Jayne Mansfield, Tony Randall. Tashlin carries Mansfield's image to its logically absurd extreme as Rita Marlowe, the pneumatic film star endorsing Stay-Put lipstick for dazed ad-man Randall

MUSICALS

The Helen Morgan Story (Warner) d.Michael Curtiz: Ann Blyth. Lots of standards, dubbed by Gogi Grant, as Blyth plays the Prohibition-era torch singer launched on a unhappy road to stardom by unscrupulous hustler Paul Newman

Pal Joey (Columbia) d.George Sidney: Rita Hayworth, Frank Sinatra, Kim Novak. Cautious Hollywood tinkering dilutes the Richard Rodgers-Lorenz Hart-John O'Hara musical but the principals still combine in a heady cocktail with Sinatra perfectly cast as the moody, womanizing soft hearted heel-hero, singing 'The Lady is a Tramp'

The Joker Is Wild (Paramount) d.Charles Vidor: Mitzi Gaynor, Frank Sinatra. Frank stars as Joe E Lewis, the Prohibition nightclub singer who became a comedian after his vocal chords were slashed by the Mob. A wryly unsentimental performance undermined by a maudlin ending

Bop Girl Goes Calypso (UA) d.Howard W Koch: Judy Tyler. Psychologist Bobby Troup predicts that rock 'n' roll will lose its popularity to the calypso. Wrong again, Bobby!

Jailhouse Rock (MGM) d.Richard Thorpe: Elvis Presley. Tailor-made vehicle for the Pelvis as an ex-jail bird who becomes a rock star on his release. Best songs, 'Treat Me Nice' and 'Baby, I Don't Care'

The Pajama Game (Warner) d.George Abbott, Stanley Donen: Doris Day, John Raitt. A truly cinematic musical in which the camera joins in the fun as Day – contriving to look both sexy and wholesome in the garments of the title – organizes a wages dispute in a pajama factory

Silk Stockings (MGM) d.Rouben Mamoulian: Peter Lorre, Jules Munshin, Joseph Buloff, Cyd Charisse. Incomparable dancing from Fred Astaire and Charisse in musical remake of *Ninotchka* (1939) with Charisse in the Garbo role of frosty Soviet emissary unfrozen by the wicked ways of the West. Among many delights 'All of You' and 'Fated to be Mated'

Les Girls (MGM) d.George Cukor: Gene Kelly, Kay Kendall. *Rashomon* comes to the musical as showgirls Kendall, Mitzi Gaynor and Taina Elg give wildly varying evidence about their former boss Kelly in libel action in a London court-room. Words and music by Cole Porter

The Girl Most Likely (RKO) d.Mitchell Leisen: Jane Powell, Kaye Ballard. The last directed by Leisen is a so-so remake of *Tom, Dick and Harry* (1940) with Powell pursued by Cliff Robertson, Keith Andes and Tommy Noonan

The Seven Hills of Rome (MGM) d.Roy Rowland: Mario Lanza. Unwisely Lanza attempts playful imitations of Dean Martin, Frankie Laine and Louis Armstrong as an American TV star chasing heiress Peggie Castle to Rome but falling for Maria Alassio

Loving You (Paramount) d.Hal Kanter: Elvis Presley, Wendell Corey, Lizabeth Scott. Hustling press agent Scott promotes Aw Shucks country boy Elvis to stardom, but he'd rather swop those fancy-looking duds for a pair of faded jeans

April Love (Fox) Henry Levin: Dolores Michaels, Pat Boone, Shirley Jones. Boone is the highly unconvincing juvenile delinquent sent to his uncle's stud farm in Kentucky where he romances Jones and wins a trotting race

WESTERNS

Walk the Proud Land (Universal) d.Jesse Hibbs: Victor Millan, Anne Bancroft, Audie Murphy. Leisurely oater in which Murphy plays the real-life Indian agent who persuaded Geronimo (Jay Silverheels) to lay down his arms

Drango (UA) d.Hall Bartlett: Jeff Chandler, Joanne Dru, Milburn Stone. Chandler-produced film, set in the aftermath of the Civil War, in which Jeff becomes the new military governor of Georgia, still devastated after Sherman's March to the Sea

Decision at Sundown (Columbia) d.Budd Boetticher: Randolph Scott. A grim-faced Scott rides into town obsessed to the point of dementia with exacting revenge on hapless John Carroll for the death of his wife

The Dalton Girls (UA) d.Reginald LeBorg: Lisa Davis, Merry Anders. Merry leads her sisters into a life of banditry after their father is killed. Only one of them survives to the end of the outlaw trail

The Domino Kid (Columbia) d.Ray Nazarro: Rory Calhoun, Denver Pyle. Competent revenge Western, independently produced by Calhoun, in which he returns from the Civil War and sets out in search of the five outlaws who gunned down his father

Run of the Arrow (RKO) d.Sam Fuller: Charles Bronson, Rod Steiger, Sarita Montiel. Steiger is the Southerner who becomes a Sioux rather than accept defeat by the North in the Civil War. Also features the great Tim McCoy, while Montiel is dubbed by Angie Dickinson

The Ride Back (UA) d.Allen H Miner: Anthony Quinn. Lawman William Conrad escorts Quinn back to Texas to face a murder trial on a journey which quickly becomes one of self-discovery. The direction was supervised by Robert Aldrich

The Big Land (Warner) d.Gordon Douglas: Alan Ladd, Edmond O'Brien. Farsighted Ladd persuades Texas cattlemen and farmers to join forces with the railroad and outmaneuver crooked cattle buyer Anthony Caruso

The Hired Gun (Columbia) d.Ray Nazarro: Anne Francis, Rory Calhoun. Another indie from Rory in which he's a gunman hired to track escaped murderer Francis. She pursuades him to go after the real killers

Trooper Hook (UA) d.Charles Marquis Warren:
Pat O'Moore, Barbara Stanwyck, Terry Lawrence.
Cavalry Sergeant Joel McCrea arrives to claim
captured white woman Stanwyck from Indian
chief Rodolfo Acosta and return her to husband
John Dehner. But she refuses to leave her Indian
child behind. Title song by Tex Ritter

Ride Out for Revenge (UA) d.Bernard Girard:
Joanne Gilbert. Thoughtful Western pits heroic
Indians against he corrupt, drunken US Cavalry
led by Lloyd Bridges, in charge of an enforced
move of the Cheyenne from their ancestral lands

Fury at Showdown (UA) d.Gerd Oswald: John
Derek. Elegantly pared-down quickie belies its
five-day shooting schedule as embittered
gunslinger Derek finds it hard going straight while
crooked attorney Gage Clark is around

The Halliday Brand (UA) d.Joseph H Lewis:
Joseph Cotten, Ward Bond. A routine assignment
– Cotten's rebellion against his tyrannical lawman
father Bond – is given added resonance by Lewis'
penetrating direction

The Left-Handed Gun (Warner) d.Arthur Penn:
John Dehner (c), Paul Newman. Penn's first
feature and an adaptation of Gore Vidal's teleplay
about Billy the Kid. Newman plays the celebrated
teenage desperado as an illiterate victim of his
own pulp fiction legend. Dehner is a sternly
authoritarian father figure as Pat Garrett

Black Patch (Warner) d.Allen H Miner: George
Montgomery, Diane Brewster, Leo Gordon.
Offbeat programmer, scripted by Gordon, in
which he plays the friend turned bankrobber
whom lawman Montgomery is accused of
murdering for the money

The Tin Star (Paramount) d.Anthony Mann:
Anthony Perkins, Henry Fonda. Young sheriff
Perkins serves a tough apprenticeship at the
hands of bounty hunter and ex-lawman Fonda

The True Story of Jesse James (Fox)
d.Nicholas Ray: Robert Wagner, Jeffrey Hunter.
Rebel Without a Cause (1955) is never far away
as Wagner and Hunter, alias Frank and Jesse
James, behave like a pair of mixed-up Middle
American teenagers

3:10 to Yuma (Columbia) d.Delmer Daves:
Glenn Ford, Van Heflin. Formally immaculate if
slightly heartless classic, in which rancher Heflin
agrees to escort amiable but deadly outlaw Ford
to Yuma for a reward which exactly matches the
price he has to pay for water supplies to his
parched land

Forty Guns (Fox) d.Sam Fuller: Barbara Stanwyck, Dean Jagger(r). Feverish exercise, boasting more phallic imagery then the facade of a Hindu temple, in which Stanwyck queens it over Tombstone Territory until the arrival of Marshal Barry Sullivan

Quantez (Universal) d.Harry Keller: Dorothy Malone, John Gavin. Good-looking but listless Western in which a gang of outlaws led by John Larch are trapped in a ghost town by an Apache war party

The Tall Stranger (Allied Artists) d.Thomas Carr: Virginia Mayo, Joel McCrea. Resolutely old-fashioned Western, briskly nudged along by Carr, with wounded Union officer McCrea trying to mediate when Confederate homesteaders settle on the range ruled by his half-brother Barry Kelly

ROMANCE

Bonjour Tristesse (Columbia) d.Otto Preminger: David Niven, Jean Seberg. Riviera-set adaptation of Francoise Sagan's novel is given added bite by Preminger as malicious adolescent Seberg's attempt to frustrate widowed father Niven's affair with Deborah Kerr has tragic results

The Lady Takes a Flyer (Universal) d.Jack Arnold: Lana Turner, Richard Denning, Jeff Chandler. Husband and wife Jeff and Lana run a worldwide plane-ferrying service which hits problems when she has a baby

Heaven Knows, Mr Allison (Fox) d.John Huston: Deborah Kerr, Robert Mitchum. Tough Marine Sergeant Mitchum and Catholic nun Kerr are isolated on a Pacific island swarming with Japanese troops. He falls in love, but she emerges intact from their subsequent adventures

Sayonara (Warner) d.Joshua Logan: Marlon Brando, Red Buttons. A contemporary Madam Butterfly, based on a James A Michener best-seller, in which Korean War pilot Brando overcomes his native Southern prejudice to fall in love with Japanese actress Miiko Taka. Button's affair with Miyoshi Umeki has less happy results

The Prince and the Showgirl (Warner) d.Laurence Olivier: Laurence Olivier, Marilyn Monroe. Gratingly stagy performance from Larry as the Balkan princeling making a beeline for the tantalizingly gauche Monroe during the 1911 coronation of George V. From the Terence Rattigan play in which Olivier had originally starred on stage with Vivien Leigh

An Affair to Remember (Fox) d.Leo McCarey: Cary Grant, Deborah Kerr. Remake of Irene Dunne/Charles Boyer vehicle, *Love Affair* (1939), in which Grant and Kerr's shipboard romance runs into complications when they reach dry land

Top Secret Affair (Warner) d.H C Potter: Kirk Douglas, Susan Hayward. Adaptation of John P Marquand's 'Melville Goodwin USA', with Kirk as the eponymous military man, Hayward the newshound setting out to dig the dirt on him but ending up in his arms

Tammy and the Bachelor (Universal) d.Joseph Pevney: Leslie Nielsen, Debbie Reynolds. Backwoods girl Debbie saves wealthy drifter Nielsen from a 'plane crash in the Mississippi and then descends like a breath of fresh air on his stuffy plantation home

Desk Set (Fox) d.Walter Lang: Spencer Tracy, Katharine Hepburn. Computer-crazy efficiency expert Tracy invades a network TV company office presided over by starchy stick-in-the-mud Hepburn. Romance ensues but it's not a patch on their previous collaborations

AMERICANA

Slim Carter (Universal) d.Richard Bartlett: Jock Mahoney, Tim Hovey. Genial Hollywood satire in which bigheaded cowboy Mahoney becomes a star in his first film and is humanized by Hovey, the child who wins a month's stay with him in a contest

A Face in the Crowd (Warner) d.Elia Kazan: Andy Griffith. Skilful if flawed dissection of fascism in the TV age as drunken bum Griffith becomes a folksy national idol, flirting with a political group on the Neanderthal right. His downfall is dramatic if somewhat stagily engineered

Raintree County (MGM) d.Edward Dmytryk: Eva Marie Saint, Rod Taylor, Montgomery Clift. Sprawling, episodic saga of the South in the Civil War thrown off balance by an hysterical performance from Elizabeth Taylor as Clift's unhinged wife

Man of a Thousand Faces (Universal) d.Joseph Pevney: Robert Evans, James Cagney. Uninspired biopic of Lon Chaney skirts around the master of make-up's weirdly masochistic approach to his work but allows Cagney, in the title role, to indulge his remarkable talent for mime

Desire Under the Elms (Paramount) d.Delbert Mann: Sophia Loren, Burl Ives. Loren is the exotic intruder into Eugene O'Neill's dour New England landscape, marrying patriarch Ives and bearing his son Anthony Perkins' child

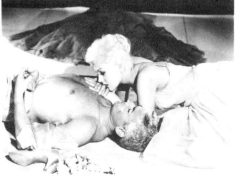

Jeanne Eagels (Columbia) d.George Sidney: Jeff Chandler, Kim Novak. Carefully staged biopic of the doomed silent star who died of drink and drugs propels Novak beyond her limited range. Better in the imagination than on the screen

Peyton Place (Fox) d.Mark Robson: Russ Tamblyn, Diane Varsi. Lumbering screen version of Grace Metalious' junky best-seller set in a small New England town. Some of the cast might have benefited from a bite on the bottom from *Old Yeller's* rabid wolf

The Spirit of St Louis (Warner) d.Billy Wilder: James Stewart. Colossal box-office disaster with Stewart suitably earnest as the pioneer aviator Charles Lindbergh flying the Atlantic to the strains of Franz Waxman's swelling symphonic score

Sweet Smell of Success (UA) d.Alexander Mackendrick: Tony Curtis, Burt Lancaster. 'Match me, Sidney!' Lancaster is the heartless, corrupt gossip columnist JJ Hunsecker, Curtis his groveling gopher Sidney Falco in a New York rancid with creeping hysteria and acid disenchantment

The Buster Keaton Story (Paramount) d.Sidney Sheldon: Donald O'Connor, Edward Wahrman, Peter Lorre. Casting O'Connor as brilliant beautiful Buster is little short of an insult to the great man, but at least this indifferent biopic, concentrating on Keaton's troubled private life, ensured that his last years were spent in comfort

Band of Angels (Warner) d.Raoul Walsh: Clark Gable, Sidney Poitier. Kentucky belle Yvonne de Carlo finds she has negro blood, is sold into slavery and bought by New Orleans blade Gable. Hilarious parade of every cliché of the Deep South from a novel by Robert Penn Warren

Old Yeller (Disney) d.Robert Stevenson: Tommy Kirk, Dorothy McGuire. Only the most flinty-hearted among you will forbear to sniffle when rancher Fess Parker has to shoot the shambling mongrel of the title, which has faithfully saved his masters from a series of wilderness perils before being bitten by a rabid wolf

Bernardine (Fox) d.Henry Levin: Richard Sargent, Janet Gaynor, Pat Boone. Boone's screen debut in piece of teenage fluff celebrating the pangs of young love, notably Sargent's passion for telephonist Terry Moore

12 Angry Men (UA) d.Sidney Lumet: E G Marshall. Lumet's feature film debut is gripping drama in which juryman Henry Fonda's lone dissenting voice wins over his fellow jurors one by one and secures the acquittal of a man accused of murder

BRITISH AND FOREIGN

The Bridge on the River Kwai (Columbia) d.David Lean: Alec Guinness, Sessue Hayakawa. Oscar-laden epic with Guinness as the stubbornly Blimpish British colonel unwittingly aiding the Japanese war effort as the POWs under his command labor to finish a vital railway bridge. Cynical William Holden is the escapee sent back to blow it up

The Camp on Blood Island (Hammer) d.Val Guest. Controversial exploitation movie in which the British inmates of a Japanese POW camp try desperately to keep the news of the end of the war from the brutal commandant, who has sworn to kill them all if Japan surrenders

No Time to Die (Columbia) d.Terence Young: Victor Mature. Hamfisted World War II actioner, set in Libya, in which escaped POW Mature goes through hell at the hands of a sheik in league with the Nazis

Seven Thunders (Rank) d.Hugo Fregonese: Stephen Boyd, Anna Gaylor, Tony Wright, Kathleen Harrison. Two escaped British POWs hide out in Marseilles, then fall into the homicidal clutches of bogus Resistance man James Robertson Justice

Windom's Way (Rank) d.Ronald Neame: Peter Finch, Mary Ure. Finch is the idealistic head of a Malay hospital striving to save his marriage and heal the wounds opened up by the exploitation of the local plantation workers

The One That Got Away (Rank) d.Roy Baker: Hardy Kruger, Alec McCowen. Kruger plays the cocksure German POW Franz von Werra, the only enemy serviceman to escape British hands in World War II

The Naked Earth (Fox) d.Vincent Sherman: Richard Todd, Juliette Greco. Morbid tale of turn-of-the-century Africa in which settler Todd takes to crocodile hunting after the failure of his tobacco crop. The crocs get the last laugh

Carve Her Name with Pride (Rank) d.Lewis Gilbert: Virginia McKenna. Inspirational account of the wartime exploits, capture and death of the British agent Violette Szabo with an exemplary central performance from McKenna

The Safecracker (MGM) d.Ray Milland: Ray Milland, Percy Herbert. Milland is the jailed thief of the title offered his freedom in 1940 in return for cracking a safe in Belgium containing a list of Nazi agents in London

The Shiralee (MGM) d.Leslie Norman: Peter Finch, Dana Wilson. Touching Australian outback drama in which itinerant swagman Finch goes walkabout with his enchanting little daughter Buster after discovering his wife with her lover

Interpol (Columbia) d.John Gilling: Trevor Howard. Enjoyable performance from Howard as a crackpot villain whose drugs ring is bust wide open by Interpol man Victor Mature

Fire Down Below (Columbia) d.Robert Parrish: Robert Mitchum, Bernard Lee, Jack Lemmon, Rita Hayworth. Smugglers Mitchum and Lemmon fall out over femme fatale Rita before effecting a touching reconciliation in the blazing, explosives-filled tanker hold where Lemmon lies trapped beneath a girder

Man in the Sky (Ealing) d.Charles Crichton: Jack Hawkins. Grizzled test pilot Hawkins battles with a blazing prototype and shrewish wife Elizabeth Sellars in hangdog drama which never leaves the runway

Manuela (British Lion) d.Guy Hamilton: Elsa Martinelli, Trevor Howard. Tramp steamer skipper Howard's infatuation with teenage half-caste Martinelli leads to the loss of his ship. A rare display, for British cinema of the period, of the corrosive effects of a hopeless passion

Time Without Pity (Eros) d.Joseph Losey: Paul Daneman, Leo McKern, Michael Redgrave. Stylish thriller in which pathetic alcoholic Redgrave has 24 hours to prove his son Alec McCowen innocent of murder. Towering performance from McKern as the power-crazed tycoon who's the real killer

Fortune is a Woman (Columbia) d.Sidney Gilliat: Arlene Dahl, Dennis Price, Jack Hawkins. Insurance assessor Hawkins marries shady lady Dahl after husband Price is burned to death. Soon a blackmailer is at work

Kill Me Tomorrow (Renown) d.Terence Fisher: Pat O'Brien, Lois Maxwell. Drunken newsman O'Brien confesses to a murder he did not commit to pay for an operation to save his son's life

High Tide at Noon (Rank) d.Philip Leacock: Betta St John, Flora Robson, Alexander Knox. Leaden melodrama, set in a fun-loving Nova Scotia lobster-fishing community, in which St John makes a big mistake when she marries William Sylvester

Across the Bridge (Rank) d.Ken Annakin: Rod Steiger. Interesting adaptation of a Graham Greene story in which crooked financier Steiger murders a lookalike and assumes his identity as he flees to Mexico, only to become ensnared in a trap of his own making

Chase a Crooked Shadow (ABPC) d.Michael Anderson: Anne Baxter, Herbert Lom. Heiress Baxter is exposed as a thief and a murderer after total stranger Richard Todd turns up at her Costa Brava villa claiming to be her brother

Violent Playground (Rank) d.Basil Dearden: David McCallum. Social-conscience thriller in which tearaway McCallum leads Liverpool copper Stanley Baker a merry dance committing arson, killing a van driver and taking two children hostage

The Story of Esther Costello (Columbia) d.David Miller: Joan Crawford, Heather Sears. Joan lets fly with furious emotion in a richly masochistic role, rescuing blind-deaf mute Sears and then seeing her charity campaign turned into a massively fraudulent money machine by husband Rossano Brazzi and grasping promoter Ron Randell

The Long Haul (Columbia) d.Ken Hughes: Victor Mature, Diana Dors. Ex-GI Mature is forced into a fur-smuggling racket by Patrick Allen's Joe Easy. Neither the busty presence of Dors nor several gallons of strong British tea can dispel his all-embracing ennui

Hell Drivers (Rank) d.Cy Endfield: Sean Connery, Sid James, Patrick McGoohan, Stanley Baker. Glorious celebration of boneheaded machismo in game British stab at an American-style high-octane road movie. Ex-con Baker joins a death-trap trucking business

Woman in a Dressing Gown (ABPC) d.J Lee Thompson: Yvonne Mitchell, Anthony Quayle. Quintessentially glum soaper of the '50s in which despairing husband Quayle threatens to leave the slatternly Mitchell for chic Sylvia Sims

The Spanish Gardener (Rank) d.Philip Leacock: Harold Scott, John Whiteley, Dirk Bogarde. Stuffy diplomat Michael Hordern decides to put an end to the budding friendship between his spoilt son Whiteley and the consulate gardener Bogarde. From a novel by A J Cronin

Action of the Tiger (MGM) d.Terence Young: Martine Carol, Sean Connery. Idiotic adventure yarn in which Carol hires mercenary Van Johnson to rescue her brother held captive in Albania. The cast plough doggedly through a steady drizzle of clichés

Blue Murder at St Trinians (British Lion) d.Frank Launder: Terry-Thomas, Joyce Grenfell. With its headmistress (Alastair Sim) in prison, and the British Army unable to control its gymslip-clad hordes, St Trinians ventures into Europe, where it wins a water polo tournament by its usual method of cheating and runs down a cache of stolen jewels. Plot very similar to the Will Hay classic *Boys Will Be Boys* (1935)

True as a Turtle (Rank) d.Wendy Toye: June Thorburn, John Gregson. All aboard Cecil Parker's yacht for an incident-packed trip across the Channel in shipshape comedy outing

Barnacle Bill (Ealing) d.Charles Frend: Alec Guinness. Sad echo of Ealing's golden days with Guinness as a bogus seadog in command of a rundown Victorian seaside pier. In a halfhearted nod to *Kind Hearts and Coronets* (1949), he also impersonates a long line of salty ancestors

The Naked Truth (Rank) d.Mario Zampi: Terry-Thomas, Peter Sellers. Cheerfully cynical comedy in which Dennis Price is the smooth blackmailer extorting money by threatening to expose public figures in his sleazy magazine

A King in New York (Archway) d.Charles Chaplin: Dawn Addams, Charles Chaplin. Chaplin is an exiled monarch adrift in the Big Apple, poking fun at modern mores and drenching the House Un-American Activities Committee with a fire hose, in belated riposte to the treatment he received at the hands of his adopted country

The Admirable Crichton (Columbia) d.Lewis Gilbert: Kenneth More. Efficient version of J M Barrie play in which butler More becomes the natural leader of querulous family of shipwrecked aristocrats. The social order is restored the moment they are rescued but Crichton has a last trick up his Jeevesian sleeve

The Smallest Show on Earth (British Lion) d.Basil Dearden: Peter Sellers, Bill Travers. Charming comedy in which Travers and Virginia McKenna inherit a crumbling fleapit of a cinema staffed by tipsy projectionist Sellers, Edwardian cashier Margaret Rutherford and doddering doorman Bernard Miles

The Doctor's Dilemma (MGM) d.Anthony Asquith: Dirk Bogarde, Leslie Caron. George Bernard Shaw play, shorn of much of its satirical bite, in which the inventor of a new treatment for TB must decide whether to treat a dull doctor or Bogarde's wayward genius of an artist

The Weapon (Eros) d.Val Guest: Lizabeth Scott, George Cole. Workmanlike thriller in which Scott's small son Jon Whiteley stumbles across a gun used by Cole in an unsolved murder

Lucky Jim (British Lion) d.John Boulting: Ian Carmichael. Carmichael takes the title role as Jim Dixon, a brash working-class lecturer at a provincial university in watered-down version of Kingsley Amis' barbed best-selling comedy of manners

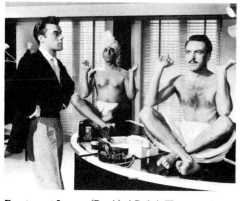

Doctor at Large (Rank) d.Ralph Thomas: Dirk Bogarde, Martin Benson, Donald Sinden. Third in Rank's successful series finds Bogarde at large in the fleshpots of Harley Street and the Riviera before he comes down to earth with a bump again at St Swithin's Hospital

Fiend Without a Face (Eros) d.Arthur Crabtree: Kim Parker. This is the fate which lies in store when you are attacked by a big blob of 'materialized thought' released by the machinations of scientist Kynaston Reeves. Marshall Thompson plods to the rescue

The Abominable Snowman (Hammer) d.Val Guest: Forrest Tucker. Botanist Peter Cushing and belligerent soldier of fortune Tucker mount a Himalayan expedition to find the legendary Yeti in intermittently atmospheric spine-tingler

It's Great to Be Young (British Lion) d.Cyril Frankel: John Mills. Cheerful comedy in which Mills plays a teacher whose pupils are just mad about music

Night of the Demon (Columbia) d.Jacques Tourneur: Dana Andrews. Moody version of M R James' classic chiller, 'The Casting of the Runes' in which occultist Niall MacGinnis summons up a demon – disappointingly revealed at the beginning of the movie – to deal with nosey psychologist Andrews

Dangerous Exile (Rank) d.Brian Desmond Hurst: Belinda Lee, Louis Jourdan. Dashing Jourdan is the Royalist French aristocrat, snatching the imprisoned Dauphin from under the noses of the Republicans and crossing the Channel in a balloon in handsome French Revolution adventure

The Moonraker (ABPC) d.David Macdonald: Sylvia Sims, George Baker. Baker is the mysterious Moonraker, alias the Earl of Dawlish, helping Prince Charles escape Cromwell's axe in lively Civil War swashbuckler

Quatermass II (Hammer) d.Val Guest: Bryan Forbes, Brian Donlevy. Once again alien invaders are on the march, taking over the British government Bodysnatchers style and building a secret advanced base on the eerie windswept expanses of Wytherton Flats. Donlevy's bristling Professor Quatermass battles the menace

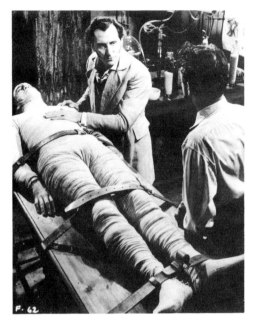

The Curse of Frankenstein (Hammer)
d.Terence Fisher: Christopher Lee, Peter Cushing.
Hammer's revival of Gothic horror with Cushing
outstanding as the demon Baron, an arrogant
aristocratic polymath whose blend of relentless
dandyism and sadism was in the true Byronic
tradition

Grip of the Strangler (Eros) d.Robert Day: Boris
Karloff. Novelist Karloff unwisely reopens the
case of the Haymarket Strangler, only to discover
the grip of the long-dead mass murderer reaching
out from beyond the grave

Donzoko (Japan) d.Akira Kurosawa: Toshiro
Mifune, Isuzu Yamada. Powerful adaptation of
the Lower Depths with Mifune as the thief. The
bleak dénouement is utterly true to Gorky's
harrowing original

Det Sjunde Inseglet (Sweden) d.Ingmar
Bergman: Bengt Ekerot, Max von Sydow.
Crusader von Sydow returns home to play chess
with Death while plague stalks the land. Grimly
beautiful evocation of medieval life, full of
stunning set pieces and a streak of ironic humor

Smultronstället (Sweden) d.Ingmar Bergman:
Victor Sjoström, Ingrid Thulin. Director Sjoström
plays an embittered Stockholm professor
reviewing the disappointments of his life on a
journey to collect an honorary degree. Bibi
Andersson portrays his first love and a modern
girl

Kumonosu-Jo (Japan) d.Akira Kurosawa:
Toshiro Mifune. Remarkable version of Macbeth
in which Mifune ends up like a pin-cushion. A
subtle, deadly performance from Isuzu Yamada
as his wife, her approach signalled by the sinister
swishing of her kimono

Les Espions (France) d.Henri-Georges Clouzot:
Curt Jurgens (r). Gérard Sety's seedy clinic is
plunged into a Kafkaesque nightmare with the
arrival of mysterious new patient Jurgens. Also
stars Peter Ustinov and Martita Hunt

Une Parisienne (France) d.Michel Boisrond:
Brigitte Bardot. Bardot is given numerous
opportunities to disrobe in a sagging soufflé
about a diplomat's wife who flirts with a foreign
prince. Co-starring Henri Vidal, Charles Boyer

Spanish Affair (Paramount) d.Don Siegel: Jose
Guardiola, Richard Kiley, Carmen Sevilla. One of
Siegel's minor efforts is little more than a
travelogue following American architect Kiley's
somewhat erratic progress through Spain

Le Fatichi di Ercole (Italy) d.Pietro Francisci:
Steve Reeves. The film that launched a thousand
rippling deltoids with Reeves as the mythical hero
flexing his muscles in a colorful comic strip
fantasy of Ancient Greece

Cinema audiences dropped to 40 million, a new low in Hollywood's history. The studios continued to ride a financial switchback: MGM struggled back into profit; Fox, aided by royalties from oil wells on its studio property, reported a $7.5 million profit; Paramount's profits leapt to $12.5 million, but Universal, Warner and Columbia all reported a loss.

Columbia also lost its tyrannical boss Harry Cohn, who died of a heart attack while dressing for dinner. Coarse, brutal and intuitive, he had literally left his mark on the movies. There are echoes of him in Broderick Crawford's Willie Stark in *All the King's Men* (1949) and the same actor's uncouth scrap metal king Harry Brock in *Born Yesterday* (1950). Even closer to home was Rod Steiger's fearsome movie mogul in *The Big Knife* (1957), borrowing the tantrums from Cohn and the tears from Louis B Mayer. Hollywood wags observed that most of the mourners attended Cohn's funeral just to make sure that the old monster was dead.

Almost as dead as Cohn was the Hollywood musical, but MGM rallied for one final flourish with *Gigi*, the last of its great musicals and deserved winner of eight Oscars including: Best Picture, Director (Vincente Minnelli), Screenplay (Alan Jay Lerner), Cinematography (Joseph Ruttenberg), Art Direction (William A Horning, Preston Ames, Henry Grace and Keogh Gleason), and Costume Design (Cecil Beaton). *Gigi* marked the end of an era. Its producer Arthur Freed, the genius who presided over the last great flowering of the MGM musical, was to make only one more, *The Bells Are Ringing* (1960). The year's Best Actor Award went to David Niven for his performance as the bogus major in *Separate Tables*, caught committing an indecent offence in a Bournemouth cinema. Susan Hayward was voted Best Actress for *I Want to Live!*, in which she slugged away gamely as a woman in the death cell. The Best Supporting Actor and Actress Awards went to Burl Ives and Wendy Hiller for their performances in, respectively, *The Big Country* and *Separate Tables*.

It was an eventful year for Lana Turner. In 1957 she had starred in *Peyton Place* as the mother of an illegitimate child. Now her life began to imitate Grace Metalious. On 4 April, 1958, Lana's teenage daughter Cheryl Crane attacked and killed her mother's mobster lover Johnny Stompanato with a kitchen knife. At Universal the wily producer Ross Hunter scented the public's lust for sensation and cast Turner as the ambitious actress who neglects her daughter in Douglas Sirk's *Imitation of Life*. Sirk brilliantly exploited Turner's hard, plastic quality – in itself an ironic comment on the film's title – and used her limited acting ability to give added resonance to her uneasy pursuit of respectability.

Another embattled Hollywood veteran, Robert Taylor, gave a memorably bitter twist to Nicholas Ray's *Party Girl*, playing a bent lawyer with a limp fretfully trying to break free from the grip of the Mob. Errol Flynn was heartbreakingly cast as John Barrymore, his long-dead drinking partner, in *Too Much Too Soon*. Robert Ryan gave one of his best performances in *God's Little Acre* as the Georgia farmer obsessed with finding gold. Orson Welles' *Touch of Evil* – much mangled by Universal – was packed with dazzling directorial pyrotechnics and ripe performances, not least Welles' crooked cop Hank Quinlan, mountainous, unshaven and sweat-sodden, gobbling candy bars and prompting Mexican madam Marlene Dietrich to observe that, 'He was some kind of a man,' as his bloated corpse bobs grotesquely in the shallows of the Rio Grande. In *Vertigo* Hitchcock caught the haunting tension between Kim Novak's almost desperately solemn concentration and shy blonde beauty.

There was a tragic aptness to Robert Donat's closing line in *The Inn of the Sixth Happiness* as he told Ingrid Bergman, 'We shall not meet again, I think.' He died shortly afterwards, wasted by chronic asthma and leaving only his fee for the film, £25,000. Death also took another perfect English gentleman, Ronald Colman, who had been one of the few stars to make a wholly successful transition from silents to sound. Other deaths included fussy, flustered character actor Franklin Pangborn; Edna Purviance, the first and most durable of Charlie Chaplin's young 'discoveries'; and Marshall Neilan, playboy director of the Twenties and canny handler of Mary Pickford, who had drunk himself into oblivion and eked out the last years of his life with bit parts and extra work. Poignantly, his last appearance had been in a small role in *A Face in the Crowd* (1957). While filming *Solomon and Sheba* in Spain, Tyrone Power suffered a fatal heart attack after a strenuous sword fight with George Sanders. Egomaniac producer Mike Todd died in a plane crash.

In Britain, *Carry on Sergeant*, a broad Army comedy, was the first in a hugely successful series – sustained by a gallery of familiar faces and outrageously smutty humor – which ran on at the rate of one a year into the Seventies. Hammer's triumph with *The Curse of Frankenstein* (1957) led to a spate of horror films, of which Terence Fisher's *Dracula*, starring Christopher Lee as a strikingly urbane vampire, was the most distinguished. In France, Jacques Tati's endearing Monsieur Hulot reappeared in *Mon Oncle*, trying as hard as ever to integrate himself into a world which could not accommodate his physical awkwardness and inner remoteness. *Mon Oncle* won the Special Jury Prize at Cannes and was celebrated by such critics of Cahiers du Cinéma as Francois Truffaut and Jean-Luc Godard, who as directors were soon to bring a stylistic revolution to French films. Claude Chabrol made his directing debut with *Le Beau Serge*, a film often used as a convenient starting point for the French 'New Wave'. In Poland an electrifying young actor, Zbigniew Cybulski, burst on to the international scene in Andrzej Wajda's *Popiol i Diament*. Comparisons were immediately made with James Dean, but Cybulski lingered longer, growing fat and debauched before dying under the wheels of a train in 1967.

ACTION

The Naked and the Dead (Warner) d.Raoul Walsh: Aldo Ray, Cliff Robertson. Norman Mailer's gritty portrait of a doomed platoon in the Pacific retains much of its macho vigor but at the expense of substituting stereotyping and cliché for the original's psychological insights

The Hunters (Fox) d.Dick Powell: Robert Mitchum. Korean War jet pilot Mitchum finds himself behind enemy lines in the trying company of panicky Lee Phillips and cocky Robert Wagner. May Britt provides the love interest off the battlefield

Run Silent, Run Deep (UA) d.Robert Wise: Clark Gable, Burt Lancaster. Old-fashioned meller lifted by painstaking attention to detail and the powerful pairing of Gable and Lancaster as incompatible but mutually respectful submariners

The Last Blitzkrieg (Columbia) d.Arthur Dreifuss: Van Johnson, Kerwin Matthews. Dull World War II drama about an English-speaking Nazi (Johnson) who sickens of the Hitler regime while operating behind enemy lines in US uniform during the Battle of the Bulge

Kings Go Forth (UA) d.Delmer Daves: Frank Sinatra, Tony Curtis. GI Tony spurns besotted Natalie Wood when he discovers she's half colored but conveniently and climactically sacrifices himself for buddy Frank Sinatra on a vital mission behind enemy lines

The Young Lions (Fox) d.Edward Dmytryk: Marlon Brando. Montgomery Clift and Brando vie for martyrdom as, respectively, a Jew beset by fierce anti-Semitism among his fellow Americans and a fiercely idealistic Nazi who sees the light

In Love and War (Fox) d.Philip Dunne: Bradford Dillman. Competent account of three Marines in World War II and the women they leave behind. Dillman is the regulation intellectual, Jeffrey Hunter the rugged sergeant and Robert Wagner the coward who finds courage on the battlefield

Imitation General (MGM) d.George Marshall: Glenn Ford, Red Butttons. Uneasy mixture of farce and straight war drama in which Sergeant Ford assumes the identity of a dead general to blunt a German attack

A Time to Love and a Time to Die (Universal) d.Douglas Sirk: John Gavin. A melancholy Erich Maria Remarque story in which Wehrmacht soldier Gavin marries his childhood sweetheart Lilo Pulver while on leave in Berlin before returning to the Eastern front where he is killed while exercising a new humane attitude towards the enemy

The Defiant Ones (UA) d.Stanley Kramer: Sidney Poitier, Tony Curtis. Typically portentous Kramer drama as escaped convicts Poitier and Curtis flee through the Southern bayous still shackled together. Splendid cameo from Lon Chaney as one of the characters they meet on the way

Revolt in the Big House (Allied Artists) d.R G Springsteen: Gene Evans, Timothy Carey. Routine prison-break yarn in which Robert Blake saves his cellmates from wholesale slaughter at the hands of scheming Evans

I, Mobster (Fox) d.Roger Corman: Steve Cochran. Gangland Tsar Cochran sings like a canary to the Feds in flashback tale of his life of crime

Torpedo Run (MGM) d.Joseph Pevney: Ernest Borgnine, Glenn Ford. Submarine skipper Ford corners a Japanese aircraft carrier in Tokyo Bay, but it is shielded by a freighter carrying prisoners of war, among them his wife and children

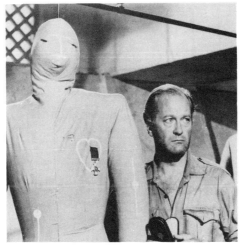

Bitter Victory (Columbia) d.Nicholas Ray: Curt Jurgens. Oddly cast Jurgens plays a British commander of a desert patrol who allows a scorpion to sting his wife's lover (Richard Burton) to death and then eliminates the only witness before returning to an ironic hero's welcome

Machine-Gun Kelly (AIP) d.Roger Corman: Charles Bronson. Grimy low-budgeter casts Bronson as the eponymous hitman, adrift in an American limbo of seedy hotels and greasy diners – Edward Hopper filtered through a B-movie lens

The Decks Ran Red (MGM) d.Andrew L Stone: Dorothy Dandridge, James Mason, Broderick Crawford. Crisp suspenser in which freighter captain Mason has to contend with murderous crew members Crawford and Stuart Whitman

The Trap (Paramount) d.Norman Panama: Richard Widmark. Desert-set drama in which attorney Widmark is forced into helping gangster Lee J Cobb flee across the border

Ten Seconds to Hell (UA) d.Robert Aldrich: Jack Palance, Jack and Jeff Chandler are a pair of improbable German bomb disposal experts competing for the languid attention of Martine Carol

The Deep Six (Warner) d.Rudolph Maté: Alan Ladd. World War II drama in which Quaker naval gunnery officer Ladd wrestles with his conscience before leading a hazardous shore mission

The Bonnie Parker Story (Nicholson/Arkoff) d.William Witney: Dorothy Provine. Modestly budgeted precursor of Arthur Penn's *Bonnie and Clyde* (1967) with Provine playing the Thompson gun-totin' Parker, whose criminal progress ends in a hail of bullets

Twilight for the Gods (Universal) d.Joseph Pevney: Rock Hudson, Cyd Charisse. A battered old brigantine, springing more leaks than British Intelligence, zig-zags across the Pacific with alcoholic Rock at the helm and a mixed bunch of passengers skulking below decks. Arthur Kennedy excellent as Rock's shifty second-in-command

The Gun Runners (UA) d.Don Siegel: Audie Murphy, Gita Hall, Eddie Albert. *To Have and Have Not* (1944) modified to the requirements of an undemanding programmer as Audie gets involved in gun-running to Cuba

ADVENTURE AND FANTASY

Tarzan's Fight for Life (MGM) d.H Bruce Humberstone: Gordon Scott, Eve Brent. Scott's running battle with sinister witch doctor James Edwards comes to an end when the latter unwisely takes a dose of his own medicine. Directed by one of Hollywood's great journeymen

Enchanted Island (RKO) d.Allan Dwan: Dana Andrews, Jane Powell. Low-budget version of Melville's 'Typee' in which seafarers Andrews and Don Dubbins are saved from ending up in the cannibals' pot by princess Powell

The Old Man and the Sea (Warner) d.John Sturges: Spencer Tracy. Hemingway's interior monologue turned into a vehicle for Tracy as the stubbly old fisherman battling the elements. Started by Fred Zinnemann and finished, mainly in the studio tank, by Sturges

The Buccaneer (Paramount) d.Anthony Quinn: Yul Brynner, Claire Bloom, Charles Boyer. Remake of DeMille's florid 1938 epic with Brynner as the privateer coming to the aid of Andrew Jackson (Charlton Heston) in the war of 1812. Lacks the crazy confidence of the original

The Roots of Heaven (Fox) d.John Huston: Errol Flynn, Juliette Greco. Idealistic Trevor Howard press gangs a bunch of no-hopers in a bid to save elephants from extinction and the story is made headline news by opportunistic reporter Orson Welles

Watusi (MGM) d.Kurt Neumann: George Montgomery, David Farrar, Taina Elg. Cut-rate jungle actioner, stitched together with footage left over from the 1950 version of *King Solomon's Mines*

Timbuktu (UA) d.Jacques Tourneur: Victor Mature. Gun-runner Vic throws in his hand with the French against rebellious Emir John Dehner in plodding actioner awash with sets of glaring artificiality

Maracaibo (Paramount) d.Cornel Wilde: Jean Wallace, Cornel Wilde. Dare-devil firefighter Wilde tames a Venezualan oil blaze and romances ex-girlfriend Wallace. Cheerfully uncomplicated

The Barbarian and the Geisha (Fox) d.John Huston: John Wayne, Eiko Ando. Wayne plays Townsend Harris, first US consul in Japan, winning the respect of the initially hostile locals and the love of geisha Ando

Zorro the Avenger (Disney) d.Charles Barton: Guy Williams, Henry Calvin. The apparently effete Williams is, of course, the masked avenger, dealing out summary justice to wicked Charles Korvin, who plans to sell California to a foreign power

The Vikings (UA) d.Richard Fleischer: Kirk Douglas. Kirk undergoes his usual quota of savage mutilations in handsome epic, tangling with Saxon rival Tony Curtis over busty Janet Leigh

The Naked Maja (MGM) d.Henry Koster: Anthony Franciosa. Misbegotten historical drama with Franciosa playing the 18th-century Spanish master painter Goya and Ava Gardner the Duchess of Alba, the sultry subject of one of his most celebrated paintings

Machete (UA) d.Kurt Neumann: Carlos Rivas, Mari Blanchard. The marvellous Mari is the discontented wife of plantation owner Albert Dekker whose plans for the future do not include her husband

The Inn of the Sixth Happiness (Fox) d.Mark Robson: Robert Donat, Ingrid Bergman, Curt Jurgens. Donat's last, touching appearance as the mandarin converted to Christianity by redoubtable missionary Bergman. Based on the real-life exploits of Gladys Aylward in the wartorn China of the 1930s

The Blob (Paramount) d.Irvin S Yeaworth Jr: Aneta Corseaut, Steve McQueen. Steve and his hot-rod gang battle a giant killer protoplasm from outer space. Sequel *Beware! the Blob* (1971)

The Fly (Fox) d.Kurt Neumann: Al Hedison, Patricia Owens. Scientist Hedison steps into his matter transmitter with a fly and emerges with the insect's head and claw. The insect buzzes off with his head and arm. Crude but not without its weirdly morbid moments. Breathtakingly remade in 1986 by David Cronenberg

Space Children (Paramount) d.Jack Arnold: Michael Ray. An alien intelligence takes control of the children of scientists and technicians at a US base, compelling them to sabotage a project to launch an H-bomb into space

The Seventh Voyage of Sinbad (Columbia) d.Nathan Juran. Kerwin Matthews takes the title role and animator Ray Harryhausen the honors in brilliant fantasy illuminated by the 'Dynamation' process. This is his Cyclops, adapted from the Ymir which appeared in *20 Million Miles to Earth* (1957)

The Return of Dracula (UA) d.Paul Landres: Francis Lederer. The vampire Bellac visits the United States in the body of a fugitive East European painter who is going to live with his sister in an archetypal small American town

Attack of the 50ft Woman (Allied Artists) d.Nathan Juran: Allison Hayes. Heiress Hayes' brief encounter with an outsized alien sends her shooting up to 50ft and on a murderous rampage in search of her wastrel husband William Hudson

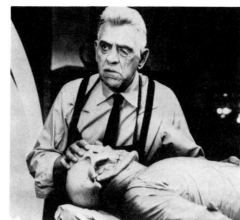

Frankenstein 1970 (Allied Artists) d.Howard W Koch: Boris Karloff. Boris is the Baron, using atom power to revive his monster and the limbs of a massacred TV crew to set him on his way

House on Haunted Hill (Allied Artists) d.William Castle: Caroline Ohmart. Cut-rate Castle chiller, full of the Maestro's scummy sets, whose special gimmick was a skeleton winging its way across the cinema auditorium as Vincent Price cranked a handle on screen

Missile Monsters (Republic) d.Fred C Brannon: Gregory Gay. Gay is Mota the malevolent Martian in re-edited version of the 1951 serial *Flying Disc from Mars*. Features stock footage from *The Purple Monster Strikes* (1945), *King of the Mounties* (1942), *G-Men Versus the Black Dragon* (1943), *Secret Service in Darkest Africa* (1943) and *King of the Rocket Men* (1949). Nothing if not eclectic

Attack of the Puppet People (AIP) d.Bert I Gordon: John Agar, June Kenney. Twisted dollmaster John Hoyt miniaturizes human beings to a tenth of their normal size. And that's about it

Teenage Caveman (Malibu) d.Roger Corman: Robert Vaughn, Darrah Marshall. Vaughn is the over-age teenager of the title, member of a post-nuclear holocaust tribe, in minor pulp triumph which combines stock footage from *One Million BC* (1940) with plot elements from *The Wizard of Oz* (1939)

Monster on the Campus (Universal) d.Jack Arnold: Arthur Franz, Troy Donahue. Arnold's least successful SF outing in which college professor Franz's experiments with a million-year-old fish turn him into a prehistoric ape-man. Perhaps we have overlooked some deeply subtle sub-text here

Queen of Outer Space (Allied Artists) d.Edward Bernds: Laurie Mitchell, Eric Fleming. Costumes and sets from *Forbidden Planet* (1956) and *Flight to Mars* (1951) and special effects from *World Without End* (1956) sustain bizarre essay in sexual politics in which Mitchell plays the deadly queen of a Venusian matriarchy and Zsa Zsa Gabor the free spirit who falls for spaced-out astronaut Fleming

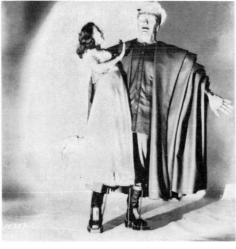

The Colossus of New York (Paramount) d.Eugene Lourié: Mala Powers, Ed Wolff. Interesting Expressionistic reworking of the Frankenstein theme in which surgeon Otto Kruger transplants the brain of a dead scientist into a mechanical monster which then runs amok in the United Nations

I Married a Monster from Outer Space (Paramount) d.Gene Fowler Jr. Stylish blend of Cold War drama and sexual politics in which Tom Tryon is kidnapped by monstrous aliens and linked to a machine which gives a look-alike his memory. Will his fiancée spot the difference after they are married?

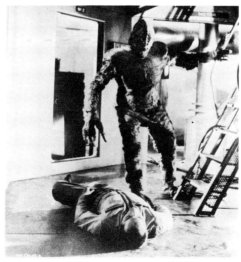

It! The Terror from Beyond Space (Vogue) d. Edward L Cahn: Ray 'Crash' Corrigan. Low-budget precursor of *Alien* (1979) in which a blood-drinking alien hitches a sanguinary ride with a spaceship returning from Venus

The Cosmic Man (Futura) d.Herbert Greene: Bruce Bennett (l). John Carradine is the eponymous alien appearing in negative to spread the word of love among suspicious earthlings

War of the Colossal Beast (Carmel) d.Bert I Gordon: Roger Pace. Tacky sequel to *The Amazing Colossal Man* (1957) which bursts into color during the high-voltage climax. Any moment now this page will turn puce

Night of the Blood Beast (Balboa) d.Bernard Kowalski. A monster from outer space invades human bodies in an attempt to colonize earth, only to meet the usual fiery end

The Most Dangerous Man Alive (Columbia) d.Allan Dwan: Ron Randell. Escaped convict Randell is exposed to a cobalt bomb explosion and transformed into a man of steel before achieving melt-down. The last movie directed by one of Hollywood's most engagingly durable professionals

MELODRAMA

Imitation of Life (Universal) d.Douglas Sirk: Sandra Dee, Lana Turner. Remake of a 1934 Claudette Colbert weepie with Turner as the ambitious actress neglecting daughter Dee, and Juanita Moore as the colored woman who shares her life and whose daughter Susan Kohner passes for white

Cry Terror (MGM) d.Andrew L Stone: Rod Steiger, Inger Stevens. Thudding thriller in which crazed Steiger uses a bomb to hold an airline to ransom and unwitting accomplice James Mason's family hostage

City of Fear (Columbia) d.Irving Lerner: Vince Edwards(r): Vince crashes out of jail with a canister he foolishly imagines to contain a million dollars. In fact it is throbbing with lethal radioactive cobalt 60

The Journey (MGM) d.Anatole Litvak: Deborah Kerr, Yul Brynner. Absurd drama, set at the time of the Hungarian uprising, in which English aristocrat Kerr yields to Russian major Brynner to save refugee Jason Robards from a one-way ticket back to the Gulag

I Want to Live ! (UA) d.Robert Wise: Susan Hayward. Quintessentially gutsy performance from Hayward as the goodtime girl turned murderer Barbara Graham moving towards a harrowing gas chamber climax

The Goddess (Columbia) d.John Cromwell: Lloyd Bridges, Kim Stanley. Kim endures a nightmare childhood and two catastrophic marriages before she metamorphoses into mixed-up movie star Rita Shaw

Home Before Dark (Warner) d.Mervyn LeRoy: Efrem Zimbalist Jr, Jean Simmons. Simmons returns home to Dan O'Herlihy from a mental institution only to find that the delusions for which she was committed were not wholly in the mind

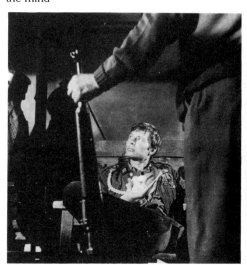

Verboten! (Columbia) d.Sam Fuller: Tom Pittman. Shrill Fuller exercise in hysteria, set in occupied postwar Berlin and revolving around a love affair between an embittered German girl and a US soldier

Short Cut to Hell (Paramount) d.James Cagney, Robert Ivers. Cagney tries his hand at directing with a competent remake of *This Gun for Hire* (1942)

China Doll (UA) d.Frank Borzage: Victor Mature, Li Li Hua. Romantic drama in which disillusioned World War II transport pilot Mature accidentallly acquires a Chinese wife who restores him to humanity and bears him a child before being killed in a Japanese air raid

The Fearmakers (UA) d.Jacques Tourneur: Veda Ann Borg, Dana Andrews. Lurid piece of anti-Red propaganda in which POW Andrews returns from the Korean War to find that his PR company has been taken over by sinister political activists

That Kind of Woman (Paramount) d.Sidney Lumet: Tab Hunter, Sophia Loren. Basically a remake of *Shopworn Angel* (1938) in which naive soldier James Stewart fell for worldly lady Margaret Sullavan. This time around it's paratrooper Tab improbably wresting kept woman Loren from millionaire George Sanders.

Cat on a Hot Tin Roof (MGM) d.Richard Brooks: Elizabeth Taylor, Paul Newman. Liz unsheaths her claws as Maggie the Cat, Newman blunders around as her emasculated jock of a husband Brick, while their predatory family hovers over Burl Ives' dying patriarch 'Big Daddy' in zesty Tennessee Williams adaptation

The Female Animal (Universal) d.Harry Keller: Jane Powell, Hedy Lamarr, Jan Sterling. Hedy is appropriately cast as an ageing star losing hunky Hollywood extra George Nader to adopted daughter Powell. Sterling splendid as a man-eating former child star

Anna Lucasta (UA) d.Arnold Laven : Sammy Davis Jr, Eartha Kitt. All-black remake of a 1949 Paulette Goddard film in which waterfront *fille de joie* Kitt is married off to an earnest young college boy for money

I Accuse! (MGM) d.Jose Ferrer: Jose Ferrer. Rehash of the Dreyfus scandal, with Gore Vidal screenplay, starring Ferrer as the innocent Jewish officer condemned to Devil's Island. Anton Walbrook is the raffishly elegant traitor Esterhazy

Violent Road (Warner) d.Howard W Koch: Perry Lopez, Merry Anders. Vigorous programmer, reminiscent of *Le Salaire de la Peur* (1953), with a cargo of explosives bumping its way over a rocky road and bringing the inevitable moments of truth

The Case Against Brooklyn (Columbia) d.Paul Wendkos: Darren McGavin(l). Rookie cop Darren endures the killing of his wife, the shooting of his partner, a brutal beating up and a spell in jail before putting a narcotics ring behind bars

Kathy O (Universal) d.Jack Sher: Mary Fickett, Patty McCormack. Patty is the spoilt child star, 'adored by millions yet loved by none', giving studio publicist Dan Duryea the run-around

My Gun is Quick (UA) d.George White: Jan Chaney, Robert Bray. But my brain is slow. Bray is Mickey Spillane's Mike Hammer, employing his subtle touch to clear up a murder and a jewel robbery as the corpses fall like ninepins

Never Love a Stranger (Allied Artists) d.Robert Stevens: John Barrymore Jr. Episodic meller following the progress of Jewish mobster Barrymore from the early 1900s to the Prohibition era. Steve McQueen is the boyhood chum now on the opposite side of the law

Screaming Mimi (Columbia) d.Gerd Oswald: Sol Garss, Anita Ekberg. Exotic dancer Ekberg is unhinged by a sex maniac's assault, and although apparently cured turns out to be a psychopathic killer

Party Girl (MGM) d.Nicholas Ray: Cyd Charisse, Robert Taylor. Crippled gangland lawyer Taylor falls for dancer Charisse in stylish thriller which has gathered a cult following. Taylor's last film for MGM on his long 24-year contract

Touch of Evil (Universal) d.Orson Welles: Marlene Dietrich, Orson Welles. Nightmarish, bravura performance from Welles as the rogue cop Hank Quinlan, a putrescent garbage bag of a man, tangling with Mexican narcotics agent Charlton Heston and his American wife Janet Leigh in a sleazy border town. The opening shot is a technical tour de force

The Lineup (Columbia) d.Don Siegel: Robert Keith, Eli Wallach. TV spin-off, embellished with a few arty touches, in which Wallach and Keith play a pair of equivocal dope ring bagmen – Julian and Dancer – whose assignment unravels before their eyes

The Middle of the Night (Columbia) d.Delbert Mann: Kim Novak, Fredric March. Turgid adaptation of a Paddy Chayevsky play in which March is the middle-aged man – an effective combination of crabbed age and lost youth – prepared to give up everything for Novak

Ten North Frederick (Fox) d.Philip Dunne: Suzy Parker, Gary Cooper. Disenchanted businessman turned politician Cooper finds fleeting comfort with the lovely Parker before a fatal illness pulls him back inside the family orbit

High School Hellcats (Indio) d.Edward Bernds: Yvonne Lime. Insecure Lime joins the Hellcats, run by a couple of teenage psychopaths, and nearly comes to a sticky end

The Nun's Story (Warner) d.Fred Zinnemann: Peter Finch, Audrey Hepburn. A radiant Hepburn as Sister Luke is caught in a spiritual tug-of-war between her vows and inner doubts. Finch the agnostic doctor she meets in the Congo. Craftsmanlike direction and photography and a superb supporting cast including Peggy Ashcroft, Mildred Dunnock and Colleen Dewhurst

The Party Crashers (Paramount) d.Bernard Girard: Frances Farmer, Connie Stevens. Cut-rate exploiter in which the usual pubescent gangs run riot. The last film made by two of Hollywood's saddest casualties, Farmer and Bobby Driscoll

Vertigo (Paramount) d.Alfred Hitchcock: James Stewart, Kim Novak. Stewart is the detective who loses his nerve and then becomes obsessed with two forms of a mythic Novak in dreamlike masterpiece which will keep writers on film busy for ever. Film-making always seemed an ordeal for Novak and never more so than in this rapt, trancelike performance

High School Confidential (MGM) d.Jack Arnold: Russ Tamblyn, Jan Sterling, Mamie Van Doren. Small masterpiece of camp in which sleazy Mamie plays hostess to her 'nephew', narcotics agent Tamblyn. 'Don't tell me you never rode in a hot rod or had a late date in the balcony?' she coos invitingly to an available male.

The Gift of Love (Fox) d.Jean Negulesco: Evelyn Rudie, Robert Stack, Lauren Bacall. Remake of *Sentimental Journey* (1946) in which dying Bacall adopts a little girl so that husband Stack will have someone to love him in the future

Live Fast, Die Young (Universal) d.Paul Henreid: Michael Connors. Teenage exploiter in which Mary Murphy tries to save sister Norma Eberhardt from a sordid life of crime. Co-stars Troy Donahue

Stage Struck (RKO) d.Sidney Lumet: Christopher Plummer, Henry Fonda. Remake of *Morning Glory,* which won Katharine Hepburn an Oscar in 1933, casts Susan Strasberg as the starry-eyed smalltown girl carving a niche for herself on Broadway

Separate Tables (UA) d.Delbert Mann: David Niven, Deborah Kerr. Terence Rattigan's study of failure and loneliness in a seedy-genteel seaside boarding house is given the Grand Hotel treatment with a starry cast and a set the size of the Ritz. Niven won an Oscar for his touching portrayal of a bogus major

Juvenile Jungle (Republic) d.William Witney. Teenage gang boss Cory Allen finds romance interfering with his plans to pull a liquor store heist

Dragstrip Girl (Golden State) d.Edward L Cahn: Frank Gorshin, Fay Spain. Hot-rodders Steve Terrell and John Ashley go full throttle for Spain but a hit-and-run killing complicates things on the eve of the big race

COMEDY

Geisha Boy (Paramount) d.Frank Tashlin: Jerry Lewis, Suzanne Pleshette. Jerry is a hamfisted magician, traveling to the Far East with farcical results

Teacher's Pet (Paramount) d.George Seaton: Doris Day, Gig Young, Clark Gable. Hardbitten newsman Gable accidentally enrols in perky Doris' journalism class and quickly moves on to some extra-mural activities. Gig Young impeccable in support

The Perfect Furlough (Universal) d.Blake Edwards: King Donovan, Janet Leigh. Sex-starved soldier Tony Curtis' reward for Arctic duties is a holiday in Paris with film star Linda Cristal, supervised by pert Army psychologist Leigh

The Tunnel of Love (MGM) d.Gene Kelly: Vikki Dougan, Richard Widmark. Jaunty outing wraps Widmark and Doris Day in miles of red tape, and sundry other distractions, as they set about adopting a child

The Mating Game (MGM) d.George Marshall: Tony Randall, Debbie Reynolds. Uptight attorney Reynolds finds romance with dithering Randall in the unlikely location of a birdwatching retreat

Me and the Colonel (Columbia) d.Peter Glenville: Curt Jurgens, Akim Tamiroff, Danny Kaye. Danny plays it uncharacteristically straight in screen version of 'Jacobowsky and the Colonel', about a Jewish refugee and an anti-Semitic Polish officer (Jurgens) thrown together by the war

A Nice Little Bank That Should Be Robbed
(Fox) d.Henry Levin: Tom Ewell, Mickey
Shaughnessy, Mickey Rooney. Ewell and Rooney
finance their gambling habit with a spot of larceny
and the calamitous advice of incompetent bookie
Shaughnessy

The Remarkable Mr Pennypacker (Fox)
d.Henry Levin: Dorothy McGuire, Dorothy
Stickney, Clifton Webb, Larry Gates, Ron Ely, Jill
St John. Adaptation of a Liam O'Brien play with
Webb as the suavely plausible bigamist,
businessman, free-thinker and father of 17

Rock-a-Bye Baby (Paramount) d.Frank Tashlin:
Connie Stevens, Jerry Lewis. Freewheeling
remake of Preston Sturges' *The Miracle of
Morgan's Creek* (1944) in which Jerry becomes
babysitter to movie star Marilyn Maxwell, who
doesn't want the public to know that she's got
triplets

Operation Petticoat (Universal) d.Blake
Edwards: Arthur O'Connell, Virginia Gregg. Cary
Grant's ramshackle submarine takes on an
explosive female cargo in cheerful World War II
comedy, with Tony Curtis in fine form as a
scheming subordinate

Auntie Mame (Warner) d.Morton DaCosta:
Rosalind Russell. Ros roars through energetic
adaptation of her stage smash as the eccentric
millionairess who believes that 'life is a banquet
and most poor suckers are starving to death'

Rally Round the Flag Boys (Fox) d.Leo
McCarey: Paul Newman, Joanne Woodward.
Confused critique of the American way of life in
which suburban wife Woodward's protests
against a proposed missile base drive husband
Newman into the arms of neglected Joan Collins

Once Upon a Horse (Universal) d.Hal Kanter:
Dick Martin, Martha Hyer. Scatterbrained comedy
Western featuring Rowan and Martin.
Afficionados of the genre will spot Tom Keene,
Bob Livingston, Bob Steele and Kermit Maynard.
Re-released in 1963 as *Hot Horse*

Bell, Book and Candle (Columbia) d.Richard
Quine: Elsa Lanchester, Jack Lemmon, Kim
Novak, Ernie Kovacs, James Stewart. Novak is at
her most bashfully beautiful as the witch yearning
to be human, charming soon-to-be married
publisher Stewart

The Reluctant Debutante (MGM) d.Vincente
Minnelli: Kay Kendall, Rex Harrison. Smooth
adaptation of a brittle, snobbish William Douglas
Home play in which Kay and Rex turn in perfectly
judged, self-mocking performances as the
harassed guardians of their lively American niece
Sandra Dee

Paris Holiday (UA) d.Gerd Oswald: Bob Hope. Bob co-stars with French funnyman Fernadel but their styles remain firmly at odds with each other. Features Preston Sturges in a small role

Houseboat (Paramount) d.Melville Shavelson: Sophia Loren, Cary Grant, Harry Guardino. Harassed father of three Grant is taken in hand by housekeeper Loren. Guardino delightful as the houseboat's handyman

Onionhead (Warner) d.Norman Taurog: Andy Griffith, Walter Matthau. Lovesick Okie Griffith joins the USS Periwinkle as a cook, serving under redoubtable master chef Matthau

MUSICALS

Damn Yankees (Warner) d.George Abbott, Stanley Donen: Tab Hunter, Gwen Verdon. A middle-aged baseball nut makes a pact with the Devil (marvellous Ray Walston) and turns into ace long-ball hitter Hunter. Verdon steals the show as Old Nick's erotic confederate Lola. Whatever Lola wants, Lola gets . . .

Mardi Gras (Fox) d.Edmund Goulding: Tommy Sands, Pat Boone, Gary Crosby, Richard Sargent. Hand-me-down version of MGM's *Best Foot Forward* (1943) in which military cadet Boone wins a date with Hollywood starlet Christine Carere

South Pacific (Fox) d.Joshua Logan: Mitzi Gaynor. Technicolor Todd-AO extravaganza from Richard Rodgers and Oscar Hammerstein II with Gaynor playing the nurse who falls for plantation owner Rossano Brazzi. Juanita Hall the only survivor of the stage show as Bloody Mary

Gigi (MGM) d.Vincente Minnelli: Louis Jourdan, Leslie Caron. The last of the studio's great musicals, set in *fin de siècle* Paris, in which Caron is the young girl brought up to be a courtesan, Jourdan her elegant suitor, Maurice Chevalier her worldly grandfather, thanking heaven for little girls. Stunning gowns by Cecil Beaton

Merry Andrew (MGM) d.Michael Kidd: Danny Kaye, Pier Angeli. Kaye is the schoolmaster turned circus artist in amiable outing enlivened by some sprightly Saul Chaplin-Johnny Mercer songs, including 'Salud'

St Louis Blues (Paramount) d.Allen Reisner: Eartha Kitt, Nat King Cole. Lackluster biopic of the jazz composer W C Handy (Cole) with Kitt as the woman he loved. Also features Mahalia Jackson, Ella Fitzgerald, Cab Calloway and Billy Preston as the young Handy

Tom Thumb (MGM) d.George Pal: Russ Tamblyn. Much trick photography, an energetic performance from Tamblyn as the tiny hero and strong support from Terry-Thomas and Peter Sellers as the villains of the piece

Sing, Boy, Sing (Fox) d.Henry Ephron: Nick Adams, Tommy Sands. Tommy is the simple Southern country boy promoted to big-bucks stardom by hustling agent Edmond O'Brien but tempted to return to the family trade of preaching

King Creole (Paramount) d.Michael Curtiz: Elvis Presley, Vic Morrow. One of the King's best efforts as the hustler out to make a fast buck in the sleazy nightclubs of New Orleans. Excellent support from Carolyn Jones, Walter Matthau and Dean Jagger

The Big Beat (Universal) d.Will Cowan: Andrea Martin (1), Rose Marie. A classical recording company is taken over by the boss' son (William Reynolds), a rock fanatic. Features George Shearing, Fats Domino, The Mills Brothers, Harry James, The Four Aces

Hot Rod Gang (Columbia) d.Lew Landers: Gene Vincent (r). Low-budget compendium of teenpix clichés as hot-rod-happy John Ashley joins Gene's band to raise money for the big race

WESTERNS

Ambush at Cimarron Pass (Fox) d.Jodie Copelan: Margia Dean, Scott Brady. Cavalry sergeant Brady has a tough time escorting a prisoner across Apache territory, including a brush with Clint Eastwood over Dean

Gunman's Walk (Columbia) d.Phil Karlson: Van Heflin, Tab Hunter. Father and son conflict between Van Heflin and Hunter moves remorselessly towards the final shoot-out

Good Day for a Hanging (Columbia) d.Nathan Juran: Robert Vaughn. Teenage gunman Vaughn is as guilty as hell but almost succeeds in charming his way out of the death cell before reverting to his true colors

Fort Dobbs (Warner) d.Gordon Douglas: Virginia Mayo, Clint Walker. Ponderous man-mountain Clint is the oulaw who rescues Mayo from the Comanche and then masterminds the defence of Fort Dobbs to clear his name

The Fiend Who Walked the West (Fox) d.Gordon Douglas: Hugh O'Brian, Robert Evans. Western remake of *Kiss of Death* (1947), much criticized at the time for its violence, with O'Brian and Evans stepping into the roles vacated by Victor Mature and Richard Widmark

Last Train from Gun Hill (Paramount) d.John Sturges: Kirk Douglas, Anthony Quinn. Lawman Douglas' attempts to take in Earl Holliman, the man who raped and killed his wife, meets resistance from Holliman's father Quinn who, in the way of these things, happens to be Kirk's best friend

From Hell to Texas (Fox) d.Henry Hathaway: Diane Varsi, Chill Wills, Don Murray. Man on the run Murray finds refuge with Wills and Varsi while close behind rides R G Armstrong and his vengeful brood

Cowboy (Columbia) d.Delmer Daves: Victor Manuel Mendoza, Glenn Ford. Tenderfoot hotel clerk Jack Lemmon signs on for a rugged trail drive led by stern cattle boss Ford in warm adaptation of Frank Harris' imaginative memoir 'My Reminiscences as a Cowboy'

Westbound (Warner) d.Budd Boetticher: Michael Dante, Karen Steele, Michael Pate. Randolph Scott resurrects a stagecoach line to ship California gold to the Union forces in the Civil War. The formidable Steele was Boetticher's wife at the time this movie was made

King of the Wild Stallions (Allied Artists) d.R G Springsteen: Edgar Buchanan, Diane Brewster. Charmingly innocent oater, scripted by serial veteran Ford Beebe, which revolves around a hunt for the legendary horse of the title

The Sheriff of Fractured Jaw (Fox) d.Raoul Walsh: Jayne Mansfield, Kenneth More. Amiable English gunsmith More walks into a range war and seeks solace in the wide open spaces of Mansfield's cleavage in bizarre cross between *The Paleface* (1948) and *Ruggles of Red Gap* (1935). Shot, most unconvincingly, in England

Terror in a Texas Town (UA) d.Joseph H Lewis: Sterling Hayden, Victor Millan. Striking minimalist Western, famous for its final confrontation between harpoon-wielding Swede Hayden and Ned Young's laconic, black-clad kamikaze gunman

The Bravados (Fox) d.Henry King: Stephen Boyd. Grim-faced Gregory Peck sets out to kill the four men whom he believes to have raped and killed his wife. But a shock lies in store when he confronts his final victim, Henry Silva

Tonka (Disney) d.Lewis R Foster: Britt Lomond, Sal Mineo. Sioux brave Sal's attachment to the wild stallion of the title gives him a grandstand seat at the battle of the Little Big Horn

Man of the West (UA) d.Anthony Mann: Gary Cooper. Strikingly malevolent performance from Lee J Cobb as the crazed Doc Tobin, forcing reformed former henchman Cooper back into a reluctant life of crime

Saddle the Wind (MGM) d.Robert Parrish: John Cassavetes, Robert Taylor. Saloon singer Julie London is torn betwen retired gunman Taylor and his trigger-happy brother Cassavetes. Scripted by the prolific Rod Serling

The Sheepman (MGM) d.George Marshall: Glenn Ford, Shirley MacLaine. Lively comedy Western, from the director of *Destry Rides Again* (1939), with sheepman Ford muscling in on cattle country and stealing MacLaine from Leslie Nielsen. Wonderful performance from Edgar Buchanan as a local wind-bag

These Thousand Hills (Fox) d.Richard Fleischer: Don Murray, Stuart Whitman. Coldly ambitious cowboy Murray's route to the top includes standing by while old buddy Whitman is lynched by Richard Egan's posse

The Law and Jake Wade (MGM) d.John Sturges: Patricia Owens, Robert Taylor, Richard Widmark. Respectable Marshal Taylor's Quixotic decision to rescue former partner in crime Widmark from a hanging traps him in a hunt for buried loot

Warlock (Fox) d.Edward Dmytryk: Dorothy Malone, Richard Widmark. Ambitiously literate Western overreaches itself as monumental hired gun Henry Fonda rides into town, accompanied by crippled sidekick Anthony Quinn, to deal with the McQuann gang

Rio Bravo (Armada) d.Howard Hawks: Angie Dickinson, John Wayne. A great Western in which cantankerous loner sheriff Wayne reluctantly gathers a 'family' around him – old-timer Walter Brennan, drunken gunman Dean Martin, beardless youth Ricky Nelson and professional gambler Dickinson – in a bid to bring murderer Claude Akins to trial

Night Passage (Universal) d.James Neilson: James Stewart, Audie Murphy. Disappointing Western in which Stewart works for the railroad while crooked younger brother Murphy plans to lift the payroll it carries

Badman's Country (Warner) d.Fred F Sears: George Montgomery, Karin Booth. Playful poverty row outing with Montgomery cast as Pat Garrett, joining forces with Buster Crabbe's Wyatt Earp, Malcolm Atterbury's Buffalo Bill and Morris Ankrum's Bat Masterson for a final shoot-out with Neville Brand's Hole-in-the-Wall gang

Bullwhip (Allied Artists) d.Harmon Jones: Rhonda Fleming. Rhonda is the hot-headed half-breed heiress who goes through an unusual 'arranged marriage' with condemned man Guy Madison

The Big Country (UA) d.William Wyler: Charlton Heston, Charles Bickford. Overblown epic – with superb photography by Franz Planer and score by Jerome Moross – tosses sea captain Gregory Peck into a range war between Bickford and Burl Ives and a violent feud with vicious ranch foreman Heston

The Proud Rebel (MGM) d.Michael Curtiz: Alan Ladd, David Ladd. Family-angled film, set in the aftermath of the Civil War, with Ladd traveling the country to find a cure for his son's dumbness and becoming involved in Olivia de Havilland's fight against cattle baron Dean Jagger

Buchanan Rides Alone (Columbia) d.Budd Boetticher: Randolph Scott. Scott rides into Agrytown where everything – a steak, a bed, a bottle of whisky – costs $10 and the ruling Agry family are so corrupt that they spend most of their time trying to double cross each other. Corpse-strewn and cheerfully crazed finale

---

ROMANCE

Fraulein (Fox) d.Henry Koster: Dana Wynter, Mel Ferrer. Wynter is a genteel German in postwar Berlin, innocently registering as a prostitute in the US sector and then in falling in love with officer Ferrer

Green Mansions (MGM) d.Mel Ferrer: Audrey Hepburn, Anthony Perkins. Hepburn is Rima the Bird Girl in offbeam stab at W H Hudson's South American romance. Perkins remains perfectly puzzled throughout

Black Orchid (Paramount) d.Martin Ritt: Sophia Loren, Anthony Quinn. Bumbling businessman Quinn takes up with criminal's widow Loren but has trouble convincing their respective offspring that marriage is the best answer

Indiscreet (Warner) d.Stanley Donen: Cary Grant, Ingrid Bergman. Featherweight romantic comedy in which suave bachelor-diplomat Grant and worldly actress Bergman prowl around each other in a make-believe smart-set London

This Happy Feeling (Universal) d.Blake Edwards: Curt Jurgens, Debbie Reynolds. Debbie falls for retired matinée idol Curt but eventually settles for neighbor John Saxon. Troy Donahue flits through as a Method actor!

A Certain Smile (Fox) d.Jean Negulesco: Joan Fontaine, Christine Carere, Eduard Franz. A Francoise Sagan comedy of sexual errors in which Carere falls for middle-aged flirt Rossano Brazzi. Fontaine is his understanding wife

AMERICANA

Wind Across the Everglades (Warner) d.Nicholas Ray: Burl Ives, Christopher Plummer. Drink-sodden conservationist Plummer divides his time between a Miami bordello and forays against the developers encroaching on the swamplands. Laughable but looks good

Some Came Running (MGM) d.Vincente Minnelli: Shirley MacLaine, Frank Sinatra. Sinatra is at his most aggressive as James E Jones' idealistic hero in study of disillusionment in a small Midwestern town in the late 1940s

Thunder Road (UA) d.Arthur Ripley: Robert Mitchum, Gene Barry. The Devil got him first. Country backroads unreel in moonshining Mitchum's headlights as if in a dream in B classic produced by the star and directed by one of the poverty row's most intriguing talents

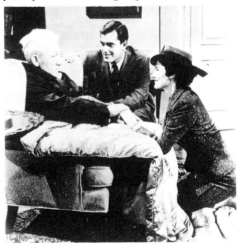

The Last Hurrah (Columbia) d.John Ford: Spencer Tracy, Tab Hunter, Dianne Foster. Affectionately handled version of an Edwin O'Connor novel, loosely based on the career of Boston's Mayor Curley, in which Tracy plays a wily old Tammany Hall politician fighting his final campaign

God's Little Acre (UA) d.Anthony Mann: Jack Lord, Tina Louise. Erskine Caldwell's feisty Georgia farm folk are brought to the screen, with Tina's bountiful charms proving all to much for lusty Lord

The Restless Years (Universal) d.Helmut Kautner: John Saxon, Sandra Dee. Oh, the shame of it! Smalltown girl Dee is ostracized after having an illegitimate baby. From the stage play 'Teach Me How to Cry'

The Long Hot Summer (Fox) d.Martin Ritt:
Orson Welles, Joanne Woodward. William
Faulkner tale of the steamy South in which virile
young drifter Paul Newman worms his way into
a bickering family whose patriarch is Welles' Big
Daddy-like tycoon. Atmospheric score from Alex
North

Too Much Too Soon (Warner) d.Art Napoleon:
Errol Flynn. Should be retitled 'Night of the Living
Dead' as a haggard Flynn plays his old drinking
partner John Barrymore – one of Hollywood's
most poignantly appropriate pieces of casting –
in melodrama based on the sad life of Diana
Barrymore (Dorothy Malone)

Lonelyhearts (UA) d.Vincent Donehue:
Montgomery Clift, Robert Ryan. A Dore Schary-
scripted and produced adaptation of Nathanael
West's minor classic 'Miss Lonelyhearts', with
Clift as the journalist haunted by the agony
column he writes

Andy Hardy Comes Home (MGM) d.Howard
W Koch: Teddy Rooney, Mickey Rooney. Mickey
rummages around in his past – and those of
millions of Middle American moviegoers – in
misfiring revival of the classic series which
provides a paradigm of his switchback
Hollywood career

Marjorie Morningstar (Warner) d.Irving
Rapper: Natalie Wood, Carolyn Jones. Wood is
the middle-class Jewish girl who falls for the
glamor of showbiz and the easy charm of
producer Gene Kelly. Splendid cast includes
Claire Trevor, Everett Sloane, Martin Balsam

All Mine to Give (RKO) d.Allen Reisner: Glynis
Johns, Cameron Mitchell. Lugubrious saga of
Scottish couple emigrating to America and
enduring the rigors and heartbreaks of
backwoods life

BRITISH AND FOREIGN

Blind Spot (Butchers) d.Peter Maxwell: Anne
Sharpe, Michael Caine. Remake of *Blackout*
(1950) in which blind Robert Mackenzie uncovers
a dope smuggling racket run by Sharpe and
Caine

Another Time, Another Place (Paramount)
d.Lewis Allen: Lana Turner, Sean Connery.
Wartime romance between journalists Turner and
Connery is cut short by the latter's death in a
'plane crash

Tread Softly Stranger (Renown) d.Gordon
Parry: George Baker, Diana Dors. Robbery,
murder, a blind witness and Dors as a sulphorous
sex bomb smouldering away in faintly ludicrous
thriller set in a Yorkshire town

Heart of a Child (Rank) d.Clive Donner: Willoughby Goddard, Donald Pleasance. Silly tearjerker involving Tyrolean youngster Richard Williams' struggle to keep his St Bernard dog from being turned into pet food by his miserable old Papa Pleasance

The Snorkel (Hammer) d.Guy Green: Peter Van Eyck. Suspenseful thriller in which Van Eyck devises an ingenious way of disposing of his wife but is finally hoist by his own petard

The Man Upstairs (British Lion) d.Don Chaffey: Richard Attenborough. Little Dicky goes bananas and barricades himself in his room before being persuaded to see sense by young housewife Dorothy Alison

Floods of Fear (Rank) d.Charles Crichton: Anne Heywood, Howard Keel. Raw drama in which convict Keel saves Heywood from a watery grave and a fate worse than death at the hands of Cyril Cusack

No Trees in the Street (ABPC) d.J Lee Thompson: Stanley Holloway. Teenage tearaway Melvyn Hayes drifts into a life of crime, rapidly moving from petty theft to murder in adaptation of a Ted Willis play

Intent to Kill (Fox) d.Jack Cardiff: John Crawford, Betsy Drake, Richard Todd. Brain surgeon Todd saves South American president Herbert Lom on the operating table but then gets mixed up in an assassination plot against the oily brute

Nowhere to Go (Ealing) d.Seth Holt: Maggie Smith, George Nader. Bleak melodrama in which socialite Smith gets tangled up with man on the run Nader

Gideon's Day (Columbia) d.John Ford: Jack Hawkins. An unlikely assignment for Ford charts a busy 24 hours in the life of police inspector Hawkins, including a maniac killer on the rampage, a hit-and-run killing, bribery, robbery with violence and three murders!

Innocent Sinners (Rank) d.Philip Leacock: June Brooks, Flora Robson. Lonely spinster Robson helps a slum child to realize her dream of turning a London bombsite into a garden

The Scapegoat (MGM) d.Robert Hamer: Bette Davis, Alec Guinness. Baroque tale in which mild-mannered Englishman Guinness, holidaying in France, is tricked into assuming the identity of an aristocratic lookalike. Among his newly acquired family is crazy old Bette Davis

Sea Fury (Rank) d.Cy Endfield: Victor McLaglen, Luciana Paluzzi. Seadogs McLaglen and Stanley Baker get tough with each other over who should splice Paluzzi's mainbrace in Spanish-set actioner with hurricane-force climax

Dunkirk (Ealing) d.Leslie Norman: Sean Barrett, Bernard Lee, John Mills. 'What a shambles we've made of this whole rotten business.' Listless account of the evacuation of the British Army from France in 1940. Concentrates on the muddle and complacency which led to disaster rather than hymning a national myth

The Square Peg (Rank) d.John Paddy Carstairs: Edward Chapman, Norman Wisdom. Gormless paratrooper Wisdom impersonates a German general in slapstick addition to hugely popular series

Nor the Moon by Night (Rank) d.Ken Annakin: Patrick McGoohan, Anna Gaylor. Four-cornered romantic drama in which Belinda Lee, Michael Craig, McGoohan and Gaylor sort out their problems amid the marauding wildlife of the African bush

A Night to Remember (Rank) d.Roy Baker: Frank Lawton, Laurence Naismith. Meticulously produced but inert anatomy of the sinking of *The Titanic*, based on the best-seller by Walter Lord

The Lady is a Square (ABPC) d.Herbert Wilcox: Frankie Vaughan, Janette Scott. Pop and classical music form an uneasy alliance as rock star Frankie romances Scott, the daughter of snooty aristocrat Anna Neagle

Bachelor of Hearts (Rank) d.Wolf Rilla: Hardy Kruger, Barbara Steele. German exchange student Kruger endures some of the more fatuous rituals of Cambridge University before winning the hand of Sylvia Sims. Steele will be more familiar to fans of the horror film

The Wind Cannot Read (Rank) d.Ralph Thomas: Yoko Tani, Dirk Bogarde. Sensitively handled weepie in which British airman Bogarde falls in love with Japanese teacher Tani in wartime India before becoming a POW in Burma

Law and Disorder (British Lion) d.Charles Crichton: Joan Hickson, Michael Redgrave. Ealing-style comedy in which con-man Redgrave decides to retire when his son – who thinks he's a priest – becomes a court official. Then Dad gets mixed up with a smuggling ring

Rockets Galore (Ealing) d.Michael Relph: Duncan Macrae, Ronnie Corbett. Anodyne sequel to the wonderful *Whisky Galore* (1949) in which the Hebridean islanders of Todday sabotage government plans to build a rocket base

Carry on Sergeant (ABPC) d.Gerald Thomas: William Hartnell, Kenneth Connor. Hartnell, the ramrod-straight Sergeant Grimshawe, is presented with a chaoticaly incompetent squad of recruits on the eve of his retirement. First of a hugely popular, and hugely vulgar series

The Horse's Mouth (UA) d.Ronald Neame: Michael Gough, Alec Guinness. Watered-down version of Joyce Carey's black comedy celebrating the Bohemian progress of artist Gulley Jimson. Guinness does his best to convey undisciplined genius but is betrayed by John Bratby's frightful paintings

The Hound of the Baskervilles (Hammer) d.Terence Fisher: André Morell, Peter Cushing. Disappointing version of the Conan Doyle classic, but Cushing hops around the Great Grimpen Mire in feverish form as the greatest of all detectives. Morell too stodgy by half as the admirable Watson

The Duke Wore Jeans (Anglo-Amalgamated) d.Gerald Thomas: Tommy Steele. But still managed to bore the pants off everybody. Vehicle for pop star Steele in dual role as wimpish aristocrat and chirpy Cockney sparrow lookalike

Count Five and Die (Fox) d.Victor Vicas: Nigel Patrick, Jefferey Hunter. Stylish World War II thriller in which intelligence chief Patrick suspects that his second-in-command Hunter's girlfriend is an enemy agent

Son of Robin Hood (Fox) d.George Sherman: June Laverick, George Woodbridge. Well, daughter actually. The ageing outlaws of Sherwood Forest enlist the aid of leggy Laverick to thwart the evil designs of David Farrar's Black Duke

A Tale of Two Cities (Rank) d.Ralph Thomas: Dirk Bogarde. Listless adaptation of Dickens tale of the French Revolution, with wastrel Bogarde going to the guillotine for love of Dorothy Tutin. Not a patch on the 1935 Hollywood version with Ronald Colman

Shake Hands with the Devil (UA) d.Michael
Anderson: Cyril Cusack, Don Murray, James
Cagney. Caricature of the Irish Troubles in which
Cagney plays an academic whose activities as
an IRA kidnapper reveal an addiction to violence
which goes beyond the bounds of idealism

North West Frontier (Rank) d.J Lee Thompson:
Kenneth More. Rattling good yarn in which British
officer More drives an ancient locomotive, and a
mixed bag of passengers, through 300 miles of
rugged terrain swarming with rebellious
Moslems

Orders to Kill (British Lion) d.Anthony Asquith:
James Robertson Justice, Paul Massie. Pointed
morality tale set in World War II. British agent
Massie is sent to France to kill a suspected traitor,
only to discover that he has assassinated a
innocent man

The Two-Headed Spy (Columbia) d.André de
Toth: Erik Schuman, Alexander Knox, Jack
Hawkins. Patchy version of a true story in which
Hawkins plays an English 'sleeper', infiltrating
the German officer corps in World War II

Ice Cold in Alex (ABPC) d.J Lee Thompson:
John Mills, Sylvia Sims, Anthony Quayle. Splendid
war drama, reeking of the period, in which
alcoholic officer Mills, grizzled sergeant Harry
Andrews, delectable nurse Sylvia Sims and
suspected German spy Quayle navigate a battered
ambulance across the desert after the fall of
Tobruk

Blood of the Vampire (Hammer) d.Vernon
Sewell: Barbara Shelley, Donald Wolfit. Ripe
performance from Wolfit as a vampire in charge
of a lunatic asylum, seeking sustenance from his
demented charges' blood. Victor Maddern
effective as his hunchback accomplice

I Was Monty's Double (ABPC) d.John
Guillermin: M E Clifton-James, John Mills. Wry
account of one of the war's most remarkable
intelligence operations in which an obscure actor
bearing a striking resemblance to Field Marshal
Montgomery was used in a brilliant deception
plan before D-Day. Clifton-James, the actor in
question, plays himself with disarming modesty

The Revenge of Frankenstein (Hammer)
d.Terence Fisher: Francis Matthews, Peter
Cushing. The Baron escapes from his persecutors
to assemble a new monster. Once again it goes
on the rampage. When will he ever learn?

Corridors of Blood (MGM) d.Robert Day:
Christopher Lee. Variation on the Jekyll and Hyde
theme in which drug-dependent doctor Boris
Karloff falls into the clutches of body snatchers
Resurrection Joe (Lee) and Black Ben (Francis
de Wolff)

The Strange World of Planet X (Eros) d.Gilbert Gunn: Gaby André. Spin-off from a TV serial in which bothersome scientist Forrest Tucker's experiments upset cosmic rays which blast a hole in the Earth's ionosphere. For no accountable reason this produces lots of big insects. Friendly alien Martin Benson sets things straight

The Trollenberg Terror (Eros) d.Quentin Lawrence: Forrest Tucker. Tentacled, Cyclops-like aliens settle on a Swiss mountain top, decapitate a few mountaineers, but find their plans for world conquest thwarted by blustering man of science Tucker

First Man into Space (Anglo-Amalgamated) d.Robert Day: Marshall Thompson. Astronaut Bill Edwards returns from a spell in space with a distressing skin condition. Scientist brother Thompson's shock treatment turns out to be terminal

Dracula (Hammer) d.Terence Fisher: Christopher Lee, Valerie Gaunt. Lee creates a strikingly elegant, forceful and very British vampire in assured re-interpretation of Bram Stoker's classic chiller

En Cas de Malheur (France) d.Claude Autant-Lara: Brigitte Bardot, Jean Gabin. The one in which Bardot startlingly signalled her sexual candor by lifting her skirts to show Gabin that she was most definitely not wearing knickers

Les Amants (France) d.Louis Malle: Jeanne Moreau, Jean-Marc Bory. Bored society woman Moreau submits to a swiftly consummated passion for chance acquaintance Bory. Lots of Brahms and wistfully sensuous photography

Les Bijoutiers du Clair de Lune (France) d.Roger Vadim: Stephen Boyd, Brigitte Bardot. Steamy Spain-set revenge melodrama in which Bardot – fresh from a convent school (!) – gets in lather over smoldering Boyd, who's out to kill her aristocratic uncle

Le Beau Serge (France) d.Claude Chabrol: Jean-Claude Brialy, Bernadette Lafont. Chabrol's first in which a young city dweller returns to the country village where he spent his childhood to find an old friend living in spiritual degradation

Les Tricheurs (France) d.Marcel Carné: Jean-Paul Belmondo. Wealthy young student Jacques Charrier throws in his lot with a band of Parisian beatniks in the faraway days when St Germain des Prés was where it was at

Mon Oncle (France) d.Jacques Tati: Jacques Tati. Monsieur Hulot's endearing attempts to be part of everything around him lead to brilliantly choreographed chaos. Winner of the Special Jury prize at Cannes

Enjo (Japan) d.Kon Ichikawa: Tamao Nakamura, Raizo Ichikawa. The story of a tormented acolyte who sets fire to the Golden Pavilion in the Shokaku temple to prevent its despoliation by the greed of modern times

Popiol i Diament (Poland) d.Andrzej Wajda: Zbigniew Cybulski. Stunning performance from Cybulski – a kind of Eastern bloc James Dean – as the right-wing resistance fighter ordered to murder a Communist district secretary on the first day of peace

Ercole e la Regina di Lidia (Italy) d.Pietro Francisci: Sylvia Lopez. Musclebound Steve Reeves tangles with a kinky queen who kills her lovers and then stuffs and mounts them (if you get our drift). In Steve's case, can one tell the difference?

Letyat Zhuravli (Russia) d.Mikhail Kalatozov. Internationally acclaimed mini-saga about a girl who marries another man while her fiancé is away at the front, but cannot shake off her guilt even after she learns of his death. Stylishly emotional

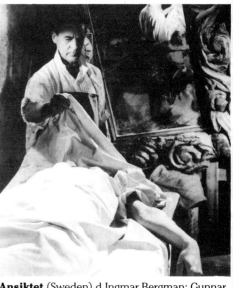

Ansiktet (Sweden) d.Ingmar Bergman: Gunnar Bjornstrand. The arrival of Dr Vogler (Max von Sydow) and his traveling 'health theater' at the middle-class home of Erland Josephson triggers a series of sinister events

Nazarin (Mexico) d.Luis Buñuel: Francisco Rabal (r). Bitter parable in which Rabal plays a priest whose attempts to lead a Christ-like life among sinners exposes the hypocrisy all around him

Der Tiger von Eschnapur (Germany/France/Italy) d.Fritz Lang: Walter Reyer. The first segment of an extraordinary Lang two-parter (Das Indische Grabmal was Part Two) marking a return to his rococo fantasies of the early 1920s. A European architect, hired to build a new city in India, falls in love with a Maharajah's concubine. From a story Lang wrote with Thea von Harbou in 1920

1959

MGM-Loew's, the last of the majors to hold out against the US government's anti-trust laws, finally split itself into two unconnected companies – Loew's Theaters and Metro-Goldwyn-Mayer. In September, MGM announced a profit of $7.7 million, its highest since 1951. Universal, facing heavy losses, was acquired by the MCA (Music Corporation of America) talent agency, which was eager to use the ailing studio's empty sound stages for TV production.

Once again, a single film dominated the year, William Wyler's *Ben Hur*, a colossal gamble for MGM filmed at Cinecittà studios in Rome for $15 million. As a young man Wyler had worked in B Reeves Eason's second unit handling the breathtaking chariot race in MGM's original 1927 version of *Ben Hur*. This time around Wyler entrusted the crucial sequence to Andrew Marton and Yakima Canutt, who responded with a slice of action cinema at its most thrilling. However, the rest of the film has an air of listlessness about it in spite of, or perhaps because of, its massive budget. Nevertheless, Charlton Heston was resolutely handsome and dignified as Judah Ben Hur; and Stephen Boyd – flaring his nostrils as savagely as his team of black steeds – was a worthy successor to Francis X Bushman as the snarling Messala. *Ben Hur* won the Best Picture Oscar and Wyler was voted Best Director. Heston picked up the Best Actor Award, a prize for stamina if nothing else, and Hugh Griffith won the Best Supporting Actor Award for his performance as Sheikh Ilderim – ham at its most succulent. Just as in 1927, *Ben Hur* was a make-or-break venture for MGM which paid off hugely at the box-office.

Alfred Hitchcock turned from the romantic obsession of *Vertigo* (1958) to a blithely implausible chase thriller, *North by Northwest*, in which Cary Grant was pursued across the prairie by a crop duster and Eva Marie Saint dangled from the stone lip of Mount Rushmore's George Washington. Cary Grant came in for a wicked impersonation by Tony Curtis in Billy Wilder's *Some Like It Hot* during a hilarious *seductio ad absurdum* of Marilyn Monroe on the beach and aboard Joe E Brown's luxury yacht. Doris Day, who had revealed a flair for romantic comedy in *The Tunnel of Love* (1958) and *Teacher's Pet* (1958), was teamed with Rock Hudson in *Pillow Talk* in which she breezily survived Ross Hunter's mildly salacious innuendo. Sandra Dee emerged from *Gidget* as every teen American boy's fantasy date. Orson Welles dominated *Compulsion*, playing Clarence Darrow and declaiming the need for mercy with all the bogus authority of Charles Foster Kane's Declaration of Principles. James Stewart was no less effective in Otto Preminger's *Anatomy of a Murder*, comfortably fraudulent as a deceptively easygoing country lawyer, a performance which won him the New York Critics Best Actor Award.

George Stevens' *The Diary of Anne Frank*, buried under a mountain of over-preparation and high seriousness, was in part salvaged by Shelley Winters as the slatternly, nervous neighbor Mrs Van Daan, a superb character study which won her the Best Supporting Actress Oscar. The Academy also awarded Buster Keaton an honorary Oscar for his contribution to the art of cinema, a classic case of Hollywood humbug and too little too late.

Death took Cecil B DeMille, exhausted by the strain of making *the Ten Commandments* (1956), during which he had suffered a heart attack; Preston Sturges, a sadly burnt out case after his triumphs of the 1940s; Edmund Goulding, polished manipulator of romantic melodrama and director of the superb *Nightmare Alley* (1947), Tyrone Power's finest hour; and Charles Vidor, director of *Gilda* (1946) and one of the more spectacular casualties of Harry Cohn's hard-driving regime at Columbia. Mario Lanza finally lost the battle with his waistline. Victor McLaglen, Hollywood's Beloved Brute, died of a heart attack, as did burly Paul Douglas. Others who died included portly Pickwickian British character actor Edmund Gwenn, purveyor of excruciating benevolence, who had played the real Santa Claus in *Miracle on 34th Street* (1947) and the professor who tried to talk to the monster ants in *Them!* (1954); delicious British comedienne Kay Kendall, tragically struck down by leukemia; cheerful action star Wayne Morris; and Ethel Barrymore, who had latterly specialized in female versions of the prickly characters played by her brother Lionel in the 1940s. Errol Flynn died at the age of 50, raddled with drink and drugs, his body that of a tired old man.

Simone Signoret won the year's Best Actress Oscar for her performance as Laurence Harvey's mistress in the British *Room at the Top*, directed by Jack Clayton. The film also picked up an Oscar for Neil Paterson's screenplay and nudged British cinema towards the greater realism of the early 1960s.

Swimming resolutely against the 'realist' tide – just as he had defied the documentary school in World War II – was Michael Powell, whose *Peeping Tom* – a complex, many-layered horror film – caused a critical furore and virtually ended his career in Britain.

In France there were two notable debuts; Jean-Luc Godard with *A Bout de Souffle*, dedicated to Monogram Pictures and Jean-Paul Belmondo's ticket to international stardom; and Francois Truffaut, with his semi-autobiographical *Les Quatre Cents Coups*. Truffaut charmed a movingly spontaneous performance from Jean-Pierre Léaud as his adolescent alter ego Antoine Doinel, ending on a famously frozen frame which anticipated the autobiographical link between actor and director in a number of subsequent films in which Léaud/Doinel literally grew up on celluloid before our eyes.

ACTION

Never So Few (MGM) d.John Sturges: Steve McQueen. Undistinguished war film in which McQueen was a last-minute replacement for Sammy Davis Jr. His solid performance secured him the key role in Sturges' *The Magnificent Seven* (1960) and a ticket to stardom

The Scarface Mob (Warner) d.Phil Karlson: Robert Stack. Rasping racket-busting thriller, based on the TV smash *The Untouchables*, with Stack as the incorruptible G-Man Eliot Ness and Neville Brand as Al Capone

The House of the Seven Hawks (MGM) d.Richard Thorpe: Linda Christian, Robert Taylor. Seadog Taylor is mixed up in shipboard murder and a scramble for long-lost Nazi treasure

Pork Chop Hill (UA) d.Lewis Milestone: Woody Strode, Gregory Peck. Edgy Korean War story, from which much of Milestone's best footage was reportedly cut at the insistence of Peck's wife, because it didn't feature her husband

North by Northwest (MGM) d.Alfred Hitchcock: Cary Grant. Ironic masterpiece casts Grant as a glibly feckless advertising man stopped dead in his tracks when he becomes the object of a cross-country spy hunt. Packed with classic set-pieces and embellished with a smolderingly sexy performance from Eva Marie Saint and James Mason's silky villainy

Up Periscope (Warner) d.Gordon Douglas: James Garner. Routine conflict between humorless submarine commander Edmond O'Brien and demolitions expert Garner, assigned the job of capturing a vital Japanese code on a Pacific atoll

Five Gates to Hell (Fox) d.James Clavell: Gerry Gaylor, Dolores Michaels. Raw drama, set in contemporary Vietnam, in which Communist Neville Brand kidnaps two doctors and seven nurses from a French hospital. In their subsequent ordeals the women prove more resourceful than the men

Odds Against Tomorrow (UA) d.Robert Wise: Robert Ryan, Gloria Grahame. Taut robbery drama in which racialist Ryan plans a heist with Harry Belafonte and ex-cop Ed Begley. It falls apart at the seams. Independently produced by Belafonte

Edge of Eternity (Columbia) d.Don Siegel: Mickey Shaughnessy, Cornel Wilde. Deputy Sheriff Wilde corners a killer in the Grand Canyon in cliff-hanging climactic shoot-out

The Wreck of the Mary Deare (MGM) d.Michael Anderson: Charlton Heston, Gary Cooper. Sea captain Cooper loses his ship but is cleared of negligence by Heston's bad-tempered salvage expert. Excellent special effects

ADVENTURE AND FANTASY

The Big Fisherman (Disney) d.Frank Borzage: Susan Kohner, Howard Keel. Lackluster epic, based on a Lloyd C Douglas blockbuster, in which Keel plays Saint Peter. The supporting cast – Herbert Lom, Martha Hyer, John Saxon – is redolent of the period

Solomon and Sheba (UA) d.King Vidor: Gina Lollobrigida, Yul Brynner. Vidor's last originally cast Tyrone Power as Solomon, but he died in Spain during filming. Brynner replaced him in gaudy Super Technirama tale of two of the Old Testament's most memorable monarchs. A bit like a big-budget western in drag

Hannibal (Warner) d.Edgar G Ulmer: Victor Mature. Italian-shot epic casts Big Vic as the great Carthaginian general, leading his elephants over the Alps and generally giving the Roman legions hell

John Paul Jones (Warner) d.John Farrow: Frank Latimer, Robert Stack. Samuel Bronston production with Stack as the American naval hero and Bette Davis flitting through as Catherine the Great

Ben Hur (MGM) d.William Wyler: Charlton Heston. Oscar-garlanded spectacular provided Heston with the ultimate test of his stamina as an epic actor. His chariot race against Stephen Boyd's Messala remains an action classic

Island of Lost Women (Warner) d.Frank Tuttle: Venetia Stevenson, Jeff Richards, John Smith, June Blair. Slab of hokum set on a remote island where crashed aviators Richards and Smith pay an unscheduled visit

Journey to the Center of the Earth (Fox) d.Henry Levin: Pat Boone, James Mason. Witty science fiction, adapted from a Jules Verne novel by Walter Reisch and Charles Brackett, with geologist Mason leading a team into the bowels of the earth. Excellent special effects

The Little Savage (Fox) d.Byron Haskin: Robert Palmer, Christiane Martel. Rambling Treasure Island-style yarn which kicks off when a shipwrecked boy discovers a pirate (Pedro Armendariz) left for dead by his shipmates after burying their loot

Third Man on the Mountain (Disney) d.Ken Annakin: James MacArthur, Norah Swinburne, James Donald. Energetic account of MacArthur's obsession with climbing the Matterhorn (called the Citadel in the movie). His mother, Helen Hayes, turns up in a cameo role

The Killer Shrews (Hollywood Pictures) d.Ray Kellogg: James Best. Paranoia at the cocktail cabinet as scientist Baruch Lumet's serum transforms lovable, furry little mammals into wolf-sized flesh eaters. Undoubtedly the best Killer Shrew movie

The Atomic Submarine (Allied Artists) d.Spencer Gordon Bennet: Arthur Franz, Paul Dubov, Dick Foran. Primitive, entertaining low-budgeter, directed by a master of the serials, in which Franz's atom sub discovers a Cyclops-like monster in a submersible flying saucer skulking beneath the North Pole

Invisible Invaders (Premium) d.Edward L Cahn. Evidently produced on an equally invisible budget. Martian invaders, under the leadership of John Carradine, take over the bodies of human corpses and lurch around looking disagreeable in dry run for George A Romero's *Night of the Living Dead* (1968)

The Tingler (Columbia) d.William Castle. Vincent Price returns to warn audiences that materialized thought, in the form of a clutching crab, is scuttling about in the auditorium. At which point specially wired seats gave lucky customers a mild electric shock!

The World, the Flesh and the Devil (MGM) d.Ranald MacDougall: Harry Belafonte. Wordy post-nuclear holocaust drama in which three survivors in a deserted New York – Belafonte, bigoted Mel Ferrer and Inger Stevens – represent the human condition

Bucket of Blood (AIP) d.Roger Corman: Dick Miller. Glorious spoof of horror conventions and the beatnik era in which wimpish busboy Miller impresses the jive-talking coffee bar sophisticates with a novel way of creating lifelike sculptures

Beyond the Time Barrier (Clarke) d.Edgar G Ulmer: Darlene Tompkins. Intriguing fatalistic Z-movie catapults jet pilot Robert Clarke into the future, where he finds subterranean Earthlings ravaged by the 'cosmic nuclear plague of 1971'

The Alligator People (Fox) d.Roy Del Ruth: Richard Crane, Beverly Garland. Poverty-stricken creature feature in which George Macready's new serum – intended to help amputees grow new limbs – turns Crane into an alligator. The last film of Hollywood veterans Del Ruth and cameraman Charles Rosher, who in their heyday were used to better things

On the Beach (UA) d.Stanley Kramer: Fred Astaire, Gregory Peck, Ava Gardner. Australia awaits the arrival of the nuclear fall-out which has already destroyed the rest of the world after an all-out war. A big theme which dissolves into a series of personal melodramas

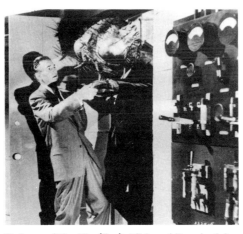

Return of the Fly (Fox) d.Edward Bernds: John Sutton. Hilarious sequel to *The Fly* (1958) in which Brett Halsey re-assembles his father's matter transference equipment only to run into the same bothersome technical hitches. Vincent Price comes to the rescue

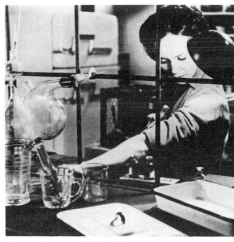

Wasp Woman (AIP) d.Roger Corman: Susan Cabot. Susan is the cosmetics queen experimenting with wasp enzymes in a search for eternal youth. She loses her wrinkles but keeps on turning into an insect at night

MELODRAMA

Vice Raid (UA) d.Edward L Cahn: Mamie Van Doren. A phony model agency is exposed as a B-girl headquarters in sleazy exploiter. Strictly for Mamie fans

The Story on Page One (Fox) d.Clifford Odets: Anthony Franciosa, Rita Hayworth. Tense courtroom drama in which Franciosa defends lovers Gig Young and Hayworth on a charge of murdering the latter's brutish husband

The Big Operator (MGM) d.Charles Haas: Steve Cochran, Mickey Rooney. Remake of *Joe Smith, American* (1942) with labor union racketeer Rooney going on the rampage when the Senate Rackets Investigation Committee starts rummaging around in his murky affairs

Al Capone (Allied Artists) d.Richard Wilson: Rod Steiger. Rough-edged gangster biopic with Steiger in bravura form as the king of the mobsters. Emphasizes just how closely this gifted actor needs the control of a strong director

The Young Philadelphians (Warner) d.Vincent Sherman: Paul Newman, Robert Vaughn. Slick soaper with Newman as a lawyer with a suspect past clawing his way to the top, Vaughn an alcoholic rich boy on a murder rap

Anatomy of a Murder (Columbia) d.Otto Preminger: Ben Gazzara, James Stewart. Gazzara is tried for the murder of the man who tried to rape his wife Lee Remick. Stewart a deceptively easygoing country lawyer, a kind of grown-up Mr Smith. In its day considered risqué in its theme and use of language

Platinum High School (MGM) d.Charles Haas:
Elisha Cook Jr, Richard Jaeckel, Mickey Rooney.
Little Mickey goes ape when he discovers that
his son's death at school was not accidental

A Woman Obsessed (Fox) d.Henry Hathaway:
Barbara Nichols, Susan Hayward. Canadian
farmer Hayward is afflicted with blizzards, rains,
forest fires, a miscarriage and surly husband
Stephen Boyd. As ever, she pulls through

Blue Denim (Fox) d.Philip Dunne: Brandon de
Wilde, Carol Lynley. Generation gap drama in
which pregnant Lynley and boyfriend de Wilde
agonize over a backstreet abortion

Jet Over the Atlantic (Columbia) d.Byron
Haskin: Virginia Mayo, Guy Madison. Ex-air force
pilot Madison saves an airliner with engine
trouble in between bouts of ogling Mayo in
capable programmer co-starring George Raft and
Ilona Massey

The Fugitive Kind (UA) d.Sidney Lumet: Anna
Magnani, Marlon Brando. Tennessee Williams
tale in which love-starved store-keeper Magnani
picks up and keeps exotic drifter Brando, who
plays hell with the women in her small Southern
town

Man in the Net (UA) d.Michael Curtiz: Alan Ladd,
Diane Brewster. Ladd is accused of murdering
his wife, fights to clear his name

The Last Angry Man (Columbia) d.Daniel Mann:
Paul Muni, Joby Baker. Muni's last film is an
appropriately sentimental story of an elderly
Brooklyn slum doctor whose life is to be the
subject of a TV program

A Summer Place (Warner) d.Delmer Daves:
Sandra Dee, Troy Donahue. Lush soaper of
adultery (Richard Egan, Dorothy McGuire) and
teen angst (Donahue, Dee) set in a Frank Lloyd
Wright-designed resort house on the Maine
Coast

This Earth Is Mine (Universal) d.Henry King:
Jean Simmons, Rock Hudson. Sagging saga of a
family of Napa Valley vintners during Prohibition
in which Rock romances British cousin
Simmons, clashes with grandfather Claude
Rains

The Crimson Kimono (Columbia) d.Sam Fuller: Victoria Shaw, James Shigeta. Characteristically offbeat Fuller outing in which two LA detectives investigate the murder of a stripper, Sugar Torch, in the city's Skid Row and Japanese sections

Beloved Infidel (Fox) d.Henry King: Linda Hutchings, Gregory Peck, Deborah Kerr. Peck is wildly miscast as F Scott Fitzgerald, and Kerr is equally unhappy as his English mistress Sheila Graham, in glossy account of the writer's last alcoholic years

Stranger in My Arms (Universal) d.Hal Kanter: June Allyson, Jeff Chandler. Mary Astor outstanding as the possessive mother determined to secure her dead son a Medal of Honor. Jeff is the man who knows the real truth

The Bramble Bush (Warner) d.Daniel Petrie: Angie Dickinson, Richard Burton. Doctor Burton's mercy killing of an old friend leads to a murder trial complicated by his love for the man's wife (Martha Hyer) and the infatuation of nurse Dickinson

The Beat Generation (MGM) d.Charles Haas: Ray Danton, Mamie Van Doren. Detective Steve Cochran tracks down a homicidal sex maniac in lurid exploitation movie lumbered with a laughable script

The Diary of Anne Frank (Fox) d.George Stevens: Millie Perkins, Joseph Schildkraut. A Jewish family hide in an attic for two years during the German occupation of Amsterdam. Stevens' meticulous approach only serves to emphasize the atrophy of his talent

The Best of Everything (Fox) d.Jean Negulesco: Suzy Parker, Joan Crawford. Typical late-period Crawford vehicle in which she plays a successful magazine tycoon taking out her frustrations on her attractive female employees

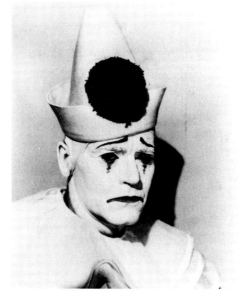

The Man Who Understood Women (Fox) d.Nunnally Johnson: Henry Fonda. Would-be critique of Hollywood in which Fonda plays an ageing boy-wonder film-maker making life a misery for wife Leslie Caron

The Blue Angel (Fox) d.Edward Dmytryk: Curt Jurgens, May Britt. Oh dear, an absolutely dire remake of the 1930 von Sternberg classic with Britt the palest imitation of Dietrich's divine slut Lola Lola and the otherwise admirable Jurgens eclipsed by the ponderous shadow of Emil Jannings

The Big Circus (Allied Artists) d.Joseph M Newman: Red Buttons, Peter Lorre, Gilbert Roland, Adele Mara, Tommy Gordon. Victor Mature battles to save his circus from floods, bankruptcy and the homicidal attentions of assorted rivals. Lorre the regulation clown with a broken heart

A Hole in the Head (UA) d.Frank Capra: Frank Sinatra, Eleanor Parker, Edward G Robinson, Thelma Ritter. Sinatra excellent as a slippery widower with romantic and business problems in underrated adaptation of a Broadway comedy-drama in which he also sings 'High Hopes'

COMEDY

A Private's Affair (Fox) d.Raoul Walsh: Gary Crosby, Sal Mineo. GI Barry Coe accidentally finds himself married to Jessie Royce Landis, who's Assistant Secretary of the Army. Gary and Sal sort things out

Visit to a Small Planet (Paramount) d.Norman Taurog: Jerry Lewis. Adaptation of Gore Vidal's 1957 Broadway satire in which Lewis' rational alien confronts emotional Earthlings. Too constricted a vehicle for Jerry's immensely individualistic humor

Who Was That Lady? (Columbia) d.George Sidney: Barbara Nichols, Janet Leigh, Joi Lansing. Lively Norman Krasna-scripted effort in which Tony Curtis and Dean Martin masquerade as a couple of spies to confuse Tony's jealous wife Leigh

Some Like it Hot (UA) d.Billy Wilder: Tony Curtis, Jack Lemmon, Marilyn Monroe. Jazzmen Jack and Tony witness the St Valentine's Day Massacre and seek refuge in all-girl band. Monroe deliciously provocative as the curvacious Sugar Kane, Curtis gives his celebrated impression of Cary Grant, a gag he unwisely repeated in a number of later films

Happy Anniversary (UA) d.David Miller: David Niven, Patty Duke. Misfiring comedy in which Niven's daughter Duke takes to TV to tell the nation about her father's youthful misdemeanors

The 30 Foot Bride of Candy Rock (Columbia) d.Sidney Miller: Lou Costello, Dorothy Provine. In his only film without Bud Abbott, handyman Lou discovers his girlfriend Provine turning into a giantess and is then despatched into the past in Jimmy Conlin's time displacer. He died shortly afterwards

Alias Jesse James (UA) d.Norman Z McLeod: Rhonda Fleming. Diverting Bob Hope vehicle in which he plays an insurance salesman mistaken for the legendary gunman. Wendell Corey very droll as the deadpan Jesse James

Count Your Blessings (MGM) d.Jean Negulesco: Deborah Kerr, Rossano Brazzi. Stately Debo makes the mistake of marrying philandering French playboy Brazzi. But a hideously winsome child brings them together again

It Happened to Jane (Columbia) d.Richard Quine: Jack Lemmon, Doris Day. Feathery, Capraesque comedy in which Main lobstery boss Day and her lawyer Lemmon tangle with over-the-top villain Ernie Kovacs

Have Rocket Will Travel (Columbia) d.David Lowell Rich: Moe Howard, Joe de Rita, Larry Fine. Slapstick cheapie in which the Three Stooges accidentally launch themselves into space. A surprise box-office hit

Ask Any Girl (MGM) d.Charles Walters: Gig Young, Shirley MacLaine. Bubbly comedy in which naive, husband-hunting MacLaine hits New York to find that most men's plans do not extend to matrimony

Don't Give Up the Ship (Paramount) d.Norman Taurog: Diana Spencer, Jerry Lewis, Robert Middleton. One of the more likeable Lewis movies casts him as a wartime naval officer who contrives to lose a battleship. Mickey Shaughnessy is the chum who helps him locate the missing man-of-war

It Started With a Kiss (MGM) d.George Marshall: Debbie Reynolds, Fred Clark. Breezy comedy, set in Spain, about zany night club dancer Reynolds and her army officer husband Glenn Ford trying to make a go of an unlikely marriage

The Gazebo (MGM) d.George Marshall: Carl Reiner, Glenn Ford, Debbie Reynolds. Mechanical black comedy in which television writer Ford decides to murder a blackmailer in possession of nude pictures of his famous actress wife Reynolds

Holiday for Lovers (Fox) d.Henry Levin: Jane Wyman, Clifton Webb, Carol Lynley, Gary Crosby. Boston psychiatrist Webb and wife Wyman take a trip to South America where their work is cut out protecting their daughters Lynley and Jill St John from predatory males

The Shaggy Dog (Disney) d.Charles Barton: Fred MacMurray. Disney's first slapstick comedy was a box-office smash in which an ancient spell turns a boy into a sheepdog. The start of MacMurray's extremely profitable association with Disney

MUSICALS

Never Steal Anything Small (Universal) d.Charles Lederer: James Cagney, Virginia Vincent. Cagney's last stab at a musical in which he plays a waterfront hoodlum hell bent on becoming a union boss. Best number, 'I'm Sorry, I Want a Ferrari'

Hound Dog Man (Fox) d.Don Siegel: Fabian, Stuart Whitman, Dennis Holmes. Fabian's screen debut in easygoing rural drama set in 1912 with Carol Lynley providing the love interest

The Gene Krupa Story (Columbia) d.Don Weis: Susan Kohner, James Darren, Sal Mineo. Sal is somewhat less than convincing as the wholesome lad who trained for the priesthood and then became a drug-powered drum maestro. Krupa dubbed the sound track

Porgy and Bess (Columbia) d.Otto Preminger: Dorothy Dandridge, Sammy Davis Jr. Sam Goldwyn's last film is ambitious version of the George and Ira Gershwin folk opera with Harry Belafonte as the crippled beggar Porgy and Dandridge the slum girl he loves. Davis superb as the dandified Sporting Life with excellent support from Brock Peters, Pearl Bailey, Diahann Carroll

Rock, Rock, Rock! (Columbia) d.Will Price: Teddy Randazzo, Tuesday Weld. Alan Freed teen exploiter in which 13-year-old Weld whips herself into a lather of pubescent agony over what effect arch-rival Gloria's blue strapless evening dress will have on the gormless Randazzo at the High School prom. Frankie Lymon sings 'I'm Not a Juvenile Delinquent'

Say One for Me (Fox) d.Frank Tashlin: Debbie Reynolds, Bing Crosby. Bing slips comfortably back into the role of a priest, Father Conroy, whose off-Broadway church provides a haven for show people

The Five Pennies (Paramount) d.Melville Shavelson: Louis Armstrong, Danny Kaye. Danny plays 1920s cornet player Red Nichols in overly schmaltzy biopic. Armstrong brings the house down with 'When the Saints Go Marching In'

For the First Time (MGM) d.Rudolph Maté: Kurt Kasznar, Mario Lanza. A slim-line Lanza warbles his way through a tear-jerking romance with deaf girl Johanna von Koszian. Low point comes when he tests her restored hearing with a rendition of Ave Maria

Born Reckless (Warner) d.Howard W Koch: Jeff Richards, Mamie Van Doren. Mamie wiggles around outrageously as a trick rider teaming up with down-on-his-luck cowpoke Richards and grizzled partner Arthur Hunnicutt. A kind of low-rent *Bus Stop* (1956)

WESTERNS

They Came to Cordura (Columbia) d.Robert Rossen: Richard Conte, Gary Cooper. Masochistic performance from Cooper as a disgraced officer despatched to find five men worthy of the Medal of Honor in 1916 Mexico. Exotic support from Rita Hayworth

Thunder in the Sun (Paramount) d.Russell Rouse: Jeff Chandler (1). Wagon train scout Jeff vies with immigrant leader Jacques Bergerac over gutsy Susan Hayward as they rumble westward to California

The Wonderful Country (UA) d.Robert Parrish: Robert Mitchum, Julie London. Bob runs guns along the Mexico-Texas line, romances London in brooding Robert Ardrey-scripted oater

Ride Lonesome (Columbia) d.Budd Boetticher: Karen Steele, James Best, Randolph Scott. Superbly crafted Western in which Randolph Scott uses a wanted outlaw as bait to flush out his murdering brother, only to find his ploy producing unforseen complications. Also James Coburn's screen debut

The Hanging Tree (Warner) d.Delmer Daves: Ben Piazza, Gary Cooper. Cooper is a frontier doctor with a past, nursing blind girl Maria Schell in literate, low-key Western set in the Montana Gold Rush days

The Horse Soldiers (UA) d.John Ford: John Wayne. Handsome Civil War actioner in which Colonel Wayne leads a sabotage raid deep into Confederate territory. William Holden plays his (in) subordinate

The Wild and the Innocent (Universal) d.Jack Sher: Joanne Dru, Audie Murphy. Tongue-in-cheek Murphy adventure in which naive Audie briefly dallies with dance hall hostess Dru before settling down with Sandra Dee. Gilbert Roland swaggers around as the local Mr Big

The Oregon Trail (Fox) d.Gene Fowler Jr: Gloria Talbott, Fred MacMurray. New York reporter MacMurray is sent West in 1846 to cover the opening of Oregon territory, winds up with Indian bride Talbott

Money, Women and Guns (Universal) d.Richard Bartlett: Jock Mahoney. Great title for a feeble movie. An old prospector's will causes problems for detective Mahoney in combination of Western and thriller

Hell Bent for Leather (Universal) d.George Sherman: Felicia Farr, Audie Murphy. Mistaken identity drama in which Audie finds himself the innocent victim of circumstances

Day of the Outlaw (UA) d.André de Toth: Venetia Stevenson, Tina Louise, Robert Ryan. Typically sardonic de Toth melodrama in which a town is taken over by Burl Ives and his murderous gang. Animated by the director's flair for the psychology of violence and treachery

Guns of the Timberland (Warner) d.Robert D Webb: Alan Ladd, Lyle Bettger. Timber men Ladd and Gilbert Roland fall out over horse trader Jeanne Crain and are soon trading lead in a forest fire climax

Yellowstone Kelly (Warner) d.Gordon Douglas: Andrea Martin, Clint Walker. Hulking fur-trapper Clint falls foul of the Indians and the US cavalry but proves indestructible

Face of a Fugitive (Columbia) d.Paul Wendkos: James Coburn. Early appearance from Coburn in a programmer starring Fred MacMurray as a man vainly trying to escape his past. Exciting climactic shoot-out in a dust-shrouded ghost town

Comanche Station (Columbia) d.Budd Boetticher: Randolph Scott. Another superb Boetticher-Burt Kennedy collaboration with Scott leading a group through Indian territory, hoping to find his kidnapped wife

The Hangman (Paramount) d.Michael Curtiz: Robert Taylor, Tina Louise. Efficient programmer in which surly lawman Taylor takes on a whole town to bring a wanted man to trial

The Unforgiven (UA) d.John Huston: Lillian Gish, Burt Lancaster, Audrey Hepburn. Tale of Texas in the 1850s with Hepburn struggling to come to terms with her Indian blood and providing the focus for conflict between two settler families and the redskins, who claim her as their own

ROMANCE

But Not For Me (Paramount) d.Walter Lang: Carroll Baker. Glossy remake of *Accent on Youth* (1935) in which middle-aged theater producer Clark Gable is pursued by young secretary Baker but sensibly settles for Lilli Palmer

Pillow Talk (Universal) d.Michael Gordon: Doris Day, Rock Hudson. A party line leads to romance between interior designer Day and songsmith Rock. Sleek as a brand-new Cadillac, with a superb cast including Tony Randall and Thelma Ritter

Cash McCall (Warner) d.Joseph Pevney: Natalie Wood, James Garner. Finagling financier Garner's business ventures almost destroy his affair with Wood. First-class support from Dean Jagger, E G Marshall and Nina Foch

AMERICANA

The FBI Story (Warner) d.Mervyn LeRoy: Gerry Gaylor, Scott Peters, Jean Willes, James Stewart. Strident tribute to the FBI in which Stewart plays an uxorious agent battling with a mobster's Hall of Fame, including Baby Face Nelson, John Dillinger and Pretty Boy Floyd, with Nazi spy rings and the Klan thrown in for good measure

Gidget (Columbia) d.Paul Wendkos: Sandra Dee, James Darren. Quintessential teen romance of the period in which virginal Dee vacillates between surfer Darren and beach bum Cliff Robertson. Numerous sequels followed

The Sound and the Fury (Fox) d.Martin Ritt: Joanne Woodward, Stuart Whitman. Murky Faulkner tale in which Yul Brynner's Mississippi family's misfortunes include alcoholism, nymphomania and idiocy, a quality in which the movie is by no means lacking

Suddenly Last Summer (Columbia) d.Joseph L Mankiewicz: Montgomery Clift, Elizabeth Taylor. Tennessee Williams play, adapted by Gore Vidal, in which Clift is cast as supposedly mad Taylor's understanding doctor. Katharine Hepburn, as her domineering aunt, wipes the floor with the rest of the cast

L'il Abner (Paramount) d.Melvin Frank: Bern Hoffman, Peter Palmer. Second attempt to transfer Al Capp's Dogpatch characters to the screen, based on a Johnny Mercer musical. Stubby Kaye in good form as Marryin' Sam

Compulsion (Fox) d.Richard Fleischer: Bradford Dillman, Dean Stockwell, Orson Welles. Court-room drama, based on the Leopold-Loeb case in which two sadistic upper-class boys commit the 'perfect' murder. Welles in barnstorming form as their lawyer

BRITISH AND FOREIGN

The Angry Silence (Allied Film Makers) d.Guy Green: Michael Craig, Richard Attenborough. Factory hand Attenborough is ostracized after he decides to work through a strike. Portentous drama featuring Oliver Reed in a small role as picket line thug

Look Back in Anger (ABPC) d.Tony Richardson: Mary Ure, Richard Burton, Claire Bloom. Screen version of John Osborne's landmark play with Burton glowering away as Jimmy Porter, archetypal Angry Young Man of the late '50s lashing out at all around him in a dull Midlands town

Blind Date (Rank) d.Joseph Losey: John Van Eyssen, Stanley Baker, Hardy Kruger. Kafkaesque thriller in which artist Kruger is framed for his girlfriend's murder but whose underlying theme is a cover-up by the hypocritical British Establishment. As true then as it is now

Room at the Top (British Lion) d.Jack Clayton: Simone Signoret, Laurence Harvey. Upwardly mobile slum boy Harvey scales the social ladder in a film which marked the first tentative British steps towards the 'realism' of the early 1960s

The 39 Steps (Rank) d.Ralph Thomas: Kenneth More. Remake of the 1935 Hitchcock classic with More stepping into Robert Donat's shoes as a breezily uncomplicated Richard Hannay. Craftsmanlike and enjoyable

Passport to Shame (British Lion) d.Alvin Rackoff: Odile Versois, Diana Dors. Feverish piece of hokum in which taxi driver Eddie Constantine saves Odile Versois from the clutches of nasty Herbert Lom's vice ring

Serious Charge (Eros) d.Terence Young: Anthony Quayle, Andrew Ray. Overheated drama in which frustrated spinster Sarah Churchill confirms teenage tearaway Ray's accusation that muscular man of the cloth Quayle has made a pass at him. A fascinating compendium of British social attitudes of the period

Whirlpool (Rank) d.Lewis Allen: William Sylvester, Juliette Greco. As this still hints, a complete turkey in which Greco takes a river trip down the Rhine with her murderous lover Sylvester

SOS Pacific (Rank) d.Guy Green: Eddie Constantine, Richard Attenborough. Engagingly hamfisted thriller in which alcoholic pilot John Gregson's 'plane deposits its passengers on an uninhabited Pacific island where the count down is about to begin for an H-bomb test. Constantine saves the day in a climax worthy of Flash Gordon

Ferry to Hong Kong (Rank) d.Lewis Gilbert: Sylvia Sims, Curt Jurgens. Down-at-heel British drifter Jurgens finds himself a permanent passenger on Orson Welles' Far Eastern ferry boat, which he saves from a typhoon and pirates

Libel (MGM) d.Anthony Asquith: Olivia de Havilland, Robert Morley, Dirk Bogarde. Stiff court-room drama in which wealthy English aristocrat Bogarde is accused by a former fellow inmate of a wartime POW camp of being an imposter

Killers of Kilimanjaro (Columbia) d.Richard Thorpe: Anthony Newley, Robert Taylor. Dim actioner set in the pioneering days of East Africa

Tiger Bay (Rank) d.J Lee Thompson: Hayley Mills, John Mills. Twelve-year-old Mills is kidnapped by seaman Horst Bucholz after she sees him murdering his unfaithful girlfriend. Filmed in Cardiff's famous Tiger Bay docklands, now sadly disappeared

The League of Gentlemen (Rank) d.Basil Dearden: Jack Hawkins. Hawkins assembles a seedy gang of ex-officers for a bank robbery to be conducted like a military operation. An interesting parody of war films of the period infused with the materialistic cynicism of the late 1950s

Hell is a City (Hammer) d.Val Guest: Donald Pleasance, Stanley Baker. Ruthless jewel thief John Crawford breaks out of jail and leaves a trail of violence behind him before police inspector Baker pulls him in. The forerunner of many a British cops-and-robbers TV series of the 1960s

The Siege of Pinchgut (Ealing) d.Harry Watt: Victor Maddern, Alan Tilvern. The last Ealing film is a competent Australian-set thriller in which four escaped convicts led by Aldo Ray hole up on a small island in Sydney harbor

Sapphire (Rank) d.Basil Dearden: Harry Baird, Michael Craig. Manhunt drama follows the search for the killer of a colored girl who passed for white. Thought controversial in its day but now seems patronizing and stilted

Tarzan's Greatest Adventure (MGM) d.John Guillermin: Anthony Quayle, Scilla Gabel. Standard Tarzan adventure with Gordon Scott flexing his muscles as Edgar Rice Burroughs' jungle king

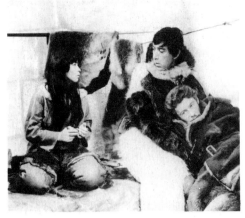

The Savage Innocents (Rank) d.Nicholas Ray: Yoko Tani, Anthony Quinn, Peter O'Toole. One of Quinn's best performances as an Eskimo coming into conflict with modern ways. Of all the 'noble savages' in which he specialized, this is the only one who possesses a genuine honesty and simplicity

The Stranglers of Bombay (Hammer) d.Terence Fisher: Guy Rolfe, Marie Devereux. India in 1826, and a fanatical cult of stranglers is on the rampage. Ramrod-straight army officer Rolfe undergoes several kinds of torture before restoring law and order

The Mummy (Hammer) d.Terence Fisher: Christopher Lee, George Pastell. Hammer drives a deep shaft into the traditional horror seam, coming up with a strikingly lit version of the ancient curse of the Big Bandaged One

The Horrors of the Black Museum (Anglo-Amalgamated) d.Arthur Crabtree. Crippled crime writer Michel Gough masterminds a one-man crime wave to fill his column. Lurid melodrama which slavers over a series of grotesque murders, in one of which a prostitute is guillotined in her own bed

The Man Who Could Cheat Death (Hammer) d.Terence Fisher: Anton Diffring. The finest hour of a much-loved character actor, usually confined to playing Nazi heavies. Here he is a 104-year-old man whose youth has been preserved by a grisly series of gland operations. Remake of B classic *The Man in Half Moon Street* (1944)

The Two Faces of Dr Jekyll (Hammer) d.Terence Fisher: Paul Massie, Christopher Lee. Interesting approach to the Robert Louis Stevenson novel in which Massie's Hyde is a clean-shaven debonair, coolly sadistic figure rather than the hirsute villain of earlier films

Peeping Tom (Anglo-Amalgamated) d.Michael Powell: Anna Massey, Carl Boehm. Powell's preoccupation with the nature of cinema and the romantic conflict between Life and Art are wrapped up in remarkably intricate horror film. Reviled at the time, it is now justly regarded as one of the masterpieces of British cinema

The Bridal Path (British Lion) d.Frank Launder: Alex Mackenzie, Bill Travers. Cheerfully innocent comedy in which Hebridean crofter Travers' search for a wife on the mainland pitches him into a series of scrapes

The Day They Robbed the Bank of England (MGM) d.John Guillermin: Miles Malleson, Peter O'Toole. Turn of the century Irish patriots enlist the help of American soldier of fortune Aldo Ray in bid to relieve the Old Lady of Threadneedle Street of her gold deposits

A Touch of Larceny (Paramount) d.Guy Hamilton: James Mason, George Sanders. Naval officer Mason devises a sophisticated scheme to steal money-minded Vera Miles from rival Sanders

Idle on Parade (Warwick) d.John Gilling: Anthony Newley, William Kendall, Anne Aubrey. Rock star Newley – as tediously ingratiating as ever – undergoes the rigors of National Service, inevitably falls for the CO's daughter

The Devil's Disciple (UA) d.Guy Hamilton: Laurence Olivier, Kirk Douglas. Star-studded adaptation of Shaw play in which Douglas plays the American colonist Dick Dudgeon mistaken for rebellious Parson Anderson (Burt Lancaster) and sentenced by the British to hang

Darby O'Gill and the Little People (Disney) d.Robert Stevenson: Jimmy O'Dea, Albert Sharpe. Ripe slice of Irish blarney in which Sharpe falls down a well and meets the King of the Leprechauns. Notable for an early appearance by Sean Connery as one of the juvenile leads

Once More with Feeling (Columbia) d.Stanley Donen: Kay Kendall, Yul Brynner. Tragically, the lovely Kendall's last film role, playing conductor Brynner's discontented wife in soggy sex comedy

The Angry Hills (MGM) d.Robert Aldrich: Marius Goring, Jackie Lane. Idiotic war story in which American journalist Robert Mitchum crashes around Greece with a bundle of vital codes and Gestapo chief Stanley Baker in hot pursuit

Our Man in Havana (Columbia) d.Carol Reed: Noel Coward, Alec Guinness. Reed's final collaboration with Graham Greene is wry Cold War fable in which Guinness' mild vacuum cleaner salesman becomes a British spy master in the Cuban capital. Coward a cosmically incompetent intelligence man, Ernie Kovacs a jovially sinister chief of police

Expresso Bongo (British Lion) d.Val Guest: Yolande Donlan, Laurence Harvey, Cliff Richard. Lively satire on the pop business with sulky rock idol Richard being given the runaround by old-style Tin Pan Alley wheeler-dealer Harvey

Carlton-Browne of the FO (British Lion) d.Jeffrey Dell, Roy Boulting: Peter Sellers, Terry-Thomas, Thorley Walters. Chinless wonder TT is despatched by the Foreign Office to sort out a spot of bother in a forgotten island colony and tumbles into an international crisis engineered by Sellers' oily Prime Minister Amphibulos

I'm All Right Jack (British Lion) d.John Boulting: Ian Carmichael, Peter Sellers. Another in the Boultings' cheerful sideswipes at the British malaise, capturing them on the cusp of affluence when trade unions and management were equally pigheaded and venal. Masterly performance from Sellers as the touchingly blinkered shop steward Fred Kite

The Danger Within (British Lion) d.Don Chaffey: Donald Houston, William Franklyn, Richard Todd. Stylish drama, set in an Italian POW camp during the long hot summer of 1943, where there is a traitor at work among the tunnelers

Yesterday's Enemy (Hammer) d.Val Guest: Philip Ahn, Stanley Baker. A British patrol in Burma shoots hostages for information and later finds itself in the same position at the hands of the Japanese. Uncompromisingly stark and unheroic

L'Avventura (Italy) d.Michelangelo Antonioni: Monica Vitti, Gabriele Ferzetti. During a yacht cruise a girl disappears on a lonely island. Her girlfriend and her lover search for her and strike up an uneasy relationship. Antonioni has called the movie, 'a detective story back to front'

La Dolce Vita (Italy) d.Federico Fellini: Marcello Mastroianni, Anita Ekberg. Marcello is Federico's alter ego, the flip gossip columnist maneuvering his snappy sports car around the fleshpots of decadent Roman society on a journey which turns from chic cynicism to despair and disillusion. Lex Barker excellent as a washed-up Hollywood star

Orfeu Negro (France/Italy) d.Marcel Camus: Breno Mello. Drama set against the kaleidoscopic backcloth of the Brazilian carnival with a haunting score by Antonio Carlos Jobim and Luis Bonfar, one of the finest ever written for a film

Jungfrukällan (Sweden) d.Ingmar Bergman: Max von Sydow. Stark fable of the rape and murder of a young girl and its supernatural consequences. Very loosely remade in 1972 by Wes Craven as *The Last House on the Left*

Nobi (Japan) d.Kon Ichikawa: Blistering indictment of war following the desperate, terrified odyssey of a starving Japanese soldier, who finally resorts to cannibalism

Les Liaisons Dangereuses (France) d.Roger Vadim: Jeanne Moreau. Modernization of an 18th-century epistolary novel of sexual betrayal tricked out with a score by Thelonius Monk

En Plein Soleil (France) d.René Clement: Alain Delon. Delon is a homicidal playboy in superbly photographed adaptation of Patricia Highsmith's 'The Talented Mr Ripley'

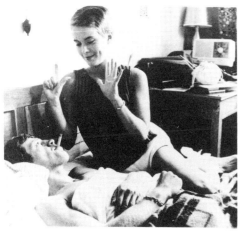

A Bout de Souffle (France) d.Jean-Luc Godard: Jean-Paul Belmondo, Jean Seberg. Belmondo's ticket to stardom as the Parisian hood facing death with a shrug like his hero 'Bogie', Jean Seberg credibly degulgasse as his American girlfriend. Dedicated by Godard to Monogram Pictures, remade in 1983 by Jim McBride

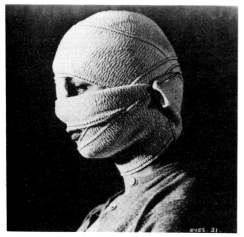

Les Yeux Sans Visage (France) d.Georges Franju: Edith Scob. Bleakly poetic masterpiece in which doctor Pierre Brasseur steals the faces of young women and tries to graft them on to his daughter's features, hideously scarred by an accident for which he was responsible. A stock horror theme given an unforgettably eerie edge

Le Testament d'Orphée (France) d.Jean Cocteau: Jean Cocteau. Narcissistic conceit marked Cocteau's farewell to the cinema, recalling George Steiner's remark in the *New Yorker* that 'in Cocteau homosexuality breeds ingenious tinsel'

Les Quatre Cents Coups (France) d.Francois Truffaut: Jean-Pierre Léaud. Moving auto-biographical study of a troubled childhood, dedicated to the great cinéaste Andre Bazin, who baled Truffaut out of reform school at the age of 14. Ends on a famously frozen frame

Babette s'en va-t-en Guerre (France) d.Christian-Jacque: Brigitte Bardot. Cheerful romp in which BB plays a British agent helping the Resistance

Les Cousins (France) d.Claude Chabrol: Gerard Blain, Jean-Claude Brialy. Blain arrives from the country to stay with relative Brialy, who is leading a decadent life in the city. Something of a companion piece to *Le Beau Serge* (1958)

Les Mains dans les Poches (France) d.Robert Bresson: Marika Green, Martin Lassalle. Absorbing, elliptical study of the interior life of a petty thief

Le Dejeuner sur l'Herbe (France) d.Jean Renoir: Paul Meurisse, Catherine Rouvel. An attempt to evoke the spirit of the early Impressionists filmed by Renoir with five simultaneous cameras and in chronological order in 24 days, using his father's home

Hiroshima Mon Amour (France) d.Alain Resnais: Emanuelle Riva, Eiji Okada. A sensual love affair between a French actress and a Japanese architect in the town of the title – five years after the dropping of the A-bomb – evokes bizarre memories of the past and visions of the future

ALTERNATIVE TITLES

The titles listed in the main body of the book are original titles. The list below
is organized alphabetically by year to show the alternative titles of some British
and foreign films released in the United States.

Original Title	US Title	Original Title	US Title

1950

Elusive Pimpernel, The	Fighting Pimpernel, The
Gone to Earth	Wild Heart, The
Into the Blue	Man in the Dinghy, The
Journal d'un Curée de Campagne, Le	Diary of a Country Priest
Luci del Varieta	Lights of Variety
Miracolo a Milano	Miracle in Milan
Morning Departure	Operation Disaster
My Daughter Joy	Operation X

1953

Acte d'Amour, Un	Act of Love
Carrosse d'Or, Le	Golden Coach, The
Destinées	Daughters of Destiny
Gycklarnas Afton	Sawdust and Tinsel
Maestro di Don Giovanni, Il	Crossed Swords
Million Pound Note, The	Man With a Million
Net, The	Project M7
Red Beret, The	Paratrooper
Saikaku Ichidai Onna	Life of O'Haru, The
Salaire de la Peur, Le	Wages of Fear, The
Weak and the Wicked, The	Young and Willing

1951

Appointment With Venus	Island Rescue
Gift Horse, The	Story at Sea
Hunted	Stranger in Between, The
Jeux Interdits, Les	Forbidden Games
Sceicco Biancho, Lo	White Sheik, The
Scrooge	Christmas Carol, A
Vacánces de Monsieur Holot, Les	Mr Hulot's Holiday
Woman With No Name	Her Paneled Door

1954

Beautiful Stranger	Twist of Fate
Du Rififi Chez les Hommes	Rififi
Diaboliques, Les	Fiends, The
Father Brown	Detective, The
Knave of Hearts	Lovers, Happy Lovers
Lilacs in the Spring	Let's Make Up
Maggie, The	High and Dry
Pokoleni	Generation, A
Seagulls Over Sorrento	Crest of the Wave
Seekers, The	Seven Samurai
Shichinin No Samurai	Land of Fury
Ulisse	Ulysses

1952

Card, The	Promoter, The
Cosh Boy	Slasher, The
Derby Day	Four Against Fate
Ikiru	Living
Imbarco a Mezzanotte	Stranger on the Prowl
Man Who Watched Trains Go By, The	Paris Express
Mandy	Crash of Silence
Mother Riley Meets the Vampire	Vampire Over London
Planter's Wife, The	Outpost in Malaya
Sound Barrier, The	Breaking the Sound Barrier
Stazione Termini	Indiscretion of an American Wife
Time Bomb	Terror on a Train
Top Secret	Mr Potts Goes to Moscow
24 Hours of a Woman's Life	Affair in Monte Carlo
Where No Vultures Fly	Ivory Hunter

1955

Albert RN	Break to Freedom
Attila Flagello di Dio	Attoia Hun
Bidone, Il	Swindlers, The
Carnets du Major Thompson, Les	French They Are a Funny Race, The
Carrington VC	Court-Martial
Dark Avenger, The	Warriors, The
Elena et les Hommes	Paris Does Strange Things
Feminine Touch, The	Gentle Touch, The
Happy Ever After	Tonight's the Night
Mio Figlio Nerone	Nero's Mistress
Quatermass Xperiment, The	Creeping Unknown, The
Ship That Died of Shame, The	PT Raiders
Sommarnattens Leende	Smiles of a Summer Night
Timeslip	Atomic Man, The

Original Title	US Title	Original Title	US Title

1956

Abdullah the Great	Abdullah's Harem
Battle of the River Plate, The	Pursuit of the Graf Spee
Biruma No Tategoto	Burmese Harp, The
Condamné à Mort s'Est Echappé, Un	Man Escaped, A
Et Dieu Créa la Femme	And God Created Woman
Hill in Korea, A	Hell in Korea
Ill Met by Moonlight	Night Ambush
Intimate Stranger	Finger of Guilt
Kanal	They Loved Life
Long Arm, The	Third Key, The
Notti di Cabiria, Le	Nights of Cabiria
Seven Waves Away	Abandon Ship!
Town Like Alice, A	Rape of Malaya, The
Yangtse Incident	Battle Hell
Yield to the Night	Blonde Sinner

1957

Admirable Crichton, The	Paradise Lagoon
Barnacle Bill	All at Sea
Donzoko	Lower Depths, The
Fatichi di Ercole, Le	Hercules
Fortune is a Woman	She Played With Fire
Grip of the Strangler, The	Haunted Strangler, The
Interpol	Pickup Alley
Kumonosu-Jo	Throne of Blood
Man in the Sky	Decision Against Time
Manuela	Stowaway
Naked Truth, The	Your Past is Showing
Night of the Demon	Curse of the Demon
Quatermass II	Enemy from Space
Seven Thunders	Beast of Marseilles, The
Sjunde Inseglet, Det	Wild Strawberries
Smultronstället	Seventh Seal, The

1958

Ansiktet	Face, The
Bijoutiers du Clair de Lune, Les	Heaven Fell That Night
En Cas de Malheur	Love is My Profession
Enjo	Conflagration
Dracula	Horror of Dracula, The
Ercole e la Regina di Lidia	Hercules Unchained
Gideon's Day	Gideon of Scotland Yard
Ice Cold in Alex	Desert Attack
Letyat Zhuravli	Cranes Are Flying, The
Mon Oncle	My Uncle
Nor the Moon by Night	Elephant Gun
Popiol i Diament	Ashes and Diamonds
Tiger von Eschnapur, Der	(Cut and combined with Das Indische
Trollenberg Terror, The	Grabmal and released in the US as
	Journey to the Lost City)
	Crawling Eye, The

1959

A Bout de Souffle	Breathless
Babette s'en va-t-en Guerre	Babette Goes to War
Carlton-Browne of the FO	Man in a Cocked Hat
Danger Within, The	Breakout
En Plein Soleil	Purple Noon (later retitled Lust for Evil)
Idle on Parade	Idol on Parade
Jungfrukällan	Virgin Spring, The
Mains dans les Poches, Les	Pickpocket
Nobi	Fires on the Plain
Passport to Shame	400 Blows, The
Quatre Cent Coups, Les	Room 43
Serious Charge	Touch of Hell, A
Siege of Pinchgut, The	Four Desperate Men
Two Faces of Dr Jekyll, The	House of Fright
Yeux Sans Visage, Les	Eyes Without a Face

INDEX